The
Remote
Borderland

SUNY series in National Identities
Thomas M. Wilson, editor

The Remote Borderland

Transylvania in the
Hungarian Imagination

László Kürti

State University of New York Press

Published by
State University of New York Press, Albany

© 2001 State University of New York

For information, address State University of New York Press,
90 State Street, Suite 700, Albany, NY 12207

Production by Michael Haggett
Marketing by Patrick Durocher

Library of Congress Cataloging-in-Publication Data

Kürti, László.
    The remote borderland : Transylvania in the Hungarian imagination / László Kürti.
        p. cm. — (SUNY series in national identities)
    Includes bibliographical references and index.
    ISBN 0-7914-5023-6 (alk. paper) — ISBN 0-7914-5024-4 (pbk. : alk. paper)
        1. Hungarians—Romania—Transylvania—Ethnic identity. 2.
    Ethnicity—Romania—Transylvania. 3. Hungary—Relations—Romania—Transylvania. 4.
    Transylvania (Romania)—Relations—Hungary. I. Title. II. Series.

    DR279.92.H8 K87 2001
    949'.0049511—dc21

                                                                        2001020751

10 9 8 7 6 5 4 3 2 1

Contents

Preface

This book is an exploration into the creation of a national unity not only in Hungary but in Transylvania, where Hungarians can be found. The discussion of the contested and negotiated nature of the Hungarian nation-state is intended to reveal the cultural assumptions so profoundly mortgaged to twentieth-century notions of home, nation, state, and people. The starting point is to achieve an understanding of the process by which intellectuals, politicians, and artists locate their nation's territory, embody it with meaning, and reassert its importance at various historical ruptures. I want to demonstrate the value of emphasizing territoriality in the creation of the nation. By focusing on a specific territory, Transylvania, instead of on a particular village or group of people, the emphasis has been shifted to a realization that nationalism and territories are both fundamental in the creation of national identity: for both the state and for the nation it is the homeland that is of utmost importance, but not in any mechanical, unidirectional, or contradictory sense. It is not only important to recognize that nations are imagined but how and where they are imagined, which must be studied if we truly want to understand the transformation of twentieth-century European societies.

The perspective taken in this book is anthropological: comparative, historical, and critical. The idea is not to look at Hungarian nationalism and dismiss it as an obstructive and a conservative force of history; rather, this book prompts a critical reevaluation about the links between nationalism, state formation, and territory. By viewing the contests between the Hungarian and Romanian states over Transylvania, we come to the recognition that both states and nations have been territorial animals. They expanded and grew, but they decreased as well; in fact, the principality of Transylvania, a largely independent polity for hundreds of years, ceased to function as soon as historical forces changed its fate. This case study of the Hungarian imagination of Transylvania illustrates that, at times, states and nations need each other, yet at other times, they exhibit vicious hostility to each other. Thus the primary aim here is to reveal those political, social, and cultural movements through which both the state and the nation realize their dream through territoriality. It is through these intersections that we gain important insights into how regions receive their function and meaning as border cultures and archaic ancestral terrains and, in return, provide important accoutrements to state and national mythologies.

The history of Hungarian national identity as it relates to Transylvania is too large a subject for one scholar and one book, for it touches virtually every aspect of the interactions between the Hungarian and Romanian states and nations since at least the early stages of feudalism. I have therefore confined myself to a more modest argument in the edifice of national identity. Central to this argument is the notion of reification: the tendency to imagine Transylvania as a concrete territorial entity engulfing the very essence of the Hungarian national identity. This subject is treated in an anthropological way by utilizing historical and sociopolitical definitions of territory and their place and significance in the remaking of national identities. By using Transylvania as an example, various political and cultural debates and negotiations between Hungarian and Romanian elites are elucidated in order to reveal the underlying assumptions about the intersections of regional thinking in the politics of nation making.

This study is an effort to describe and analyze the development and impact of this thinking on the internal and international politics of the Hungarian nation-state from an anthropological perspective. A basic assumption of this study is that the Transylvanian regionalist movement was not a significant force among Hungarian intellectuals prior to World War I. Without question, many insights could be gained regarding the roots of nationalism extending into the cloudy and controversial feudalist period. However, such an exploration is beyond the scope of this book and is left to competent historians. The growth of Transylvania as a politically sensitive regional issue has to be traced back to the disastrous end of that war and the incompetence of several key players. Included among them are Western politicians assisting at various "peace settlements," extremist nationalist leaders in Hungary and Romania, and educated middle classes feeding on the ideologies of irredentism, secessionism, and territoriality in their eagerness to contest and negotiate the great national state of their dreams. With regard to Transylvania, several such contestations are analyzed through a discussion of: (1) the demagoguery and scholarly manipulation of Transylvanian history by showing how the past serves as a justification of present political aims; (2) how state socialist ideology, despite the common Marxist–Leninist foundation, attempted to homogenize the nation-state of Romania and, in turn, assisted in the rise of fundamentalist Hungarianism, regionalism, and transnational identity; (3) a particular nationalist process, populism, by revealing how this ideology shifted the emphasis away from the centrality of peasants to Hungarian populations in Transylvania; (4) a newly awakened generational politics—the dance-house movement, a folkloristic turn of politics that managed to subvert communist state ideology; and (5) how, after the collapse of socialism, and despite the foundation of democracy, a renewed sense of Transylvanianism has been maintained as a core doctrine of nationalist controversy between Hungary and Romania.

There is much that connects regions and nation-states. Besides the fact that both are cultural constructions politicized out of proportions, they also are vehemently contested and negotiated at various intervals by neighboring groups. Transylvania—similar in many ways to other contested terrains elsewhere, such as Northern Ireland, the Basque lands, Corsica, Cyprus, Silesia, Kosovo and Macedonia—is analyzed here as a prime example of twentieth-century national struggles in the heart of Europe. The importance of this study is manyfold: it points to how a particular territory becomes paramount in nationalist thinking; it reveals how elites have imagined this region for the purpose of fashioning powerful images and ideas to remake the national self and the neighboring other; and it points to the ways in which a region is clothed with specific characteristics, meaning, and symbols that in turn serve the center in its argumentation for entitlement for that land. The Transylvanian case illustrates how Transylvania has acquired the meaning of a faraway border culture in the Hungarian mentality and how in return it has helped the nation's elites to produce an enduring, powerful message about its importance for the nation.

Numerous individuals and institutions helped me during the decade-long process of researching and writing this book. The International Research and Exchanges Board funded the years 1985–1986 and then 1991–1992 so that I could research national identity in Hungary and Romania. From the period 1995–1996, a Fulbright grant allowed me to remain in Hungary to continue my research on national identity. The Research Support Scheme of the Open Society Fund in Prague awarded me a research grant to compare Hungarian and Romanian national identity, first in the period 1993–1995 and then again in 1998 to continue my fieldwork in Transylvanian communities. In the period 1997–1999, funding from the Harry Frank Guggenheim Foundation in New York permitted me to undertake research on nationalist conflicts in both Hungary and Romania. In 1999 and 2000, the Hungarian higher education and research program (FKFP) provided me with a research grant to continue my research on this topic. The members of these agencies did everything possible to assist me, thus to these institutions I am greatly indebted.

In Romania and Hungary several colleagues and friends offered helpful insights and critiques of my work throughout the years. At the Babes–Bolyai University, Professor Ion Aluas, an institution in Cluj, was instrumental in assisting me in gathering sources on Transylvanian history and multiethnic relations. At the Department of Sociology at Cluj, Ágnes Neményi and Elemér Mezei offered invaluable aid; the latter colleague was especially helpful in designing a computerized questionnaire. Tiberiu Graur at the Ethnographic Museum in Cluj was an important influence in that I was forced to abandon many of my "ethnocentric" ideas about Hungarians and Romanians in Transylvania. Professor Aluas also assisted me with necessary permits, while the latter provided me with possibilities to travel in Cluj county in Transylvania in the museum's jeep.

I also thank Helene Loow and Charles Westin, both at the Center for Migration and Ethnic Studies, Stockholm, Sweden, for inviting me to present some of my initial findings and for sharpening my ideas in the series of conferences and seminars organized by them. Steven Sampson also was instrumental in providing me with useful ideas about both Romania and Hungary, as well as for inviting me to Bergen, Norway, to the Nordic Anthropological Conference in 1997. Him and Katherine Verdery, who also was a keynote speaker at that conference, offered many suggestions on contemporary Romania as well as supportive critiques of my ideas concerning research in both countries. I am indebted, moreover, to the Dean's Office at the University of Miskolc, especially to Viktor Kovács and Lóránt Kabdebó, and the University's Pro Rector, Aladár Nagy, who supported me throughout the past years while teaching at the university.

It is, of course, not possible to give proper credit to all members of the communities in Hungary and Romania, in particular those of Csepel and Budapest in Hungary, Cluj, Bucharest, and Jebuc in Transylvania. There are a few individuals, however, on whom I repeatedly called over the course of the years, whose help demands commensurate notice. The assistance of Anna-Mária Bíró at the Hungarian Democratic Union's main office in Bucharest was crucial in obtaining several documents and information on Hungarians in Romania, especially the Hungarian party's programs. Finally, I would like to thank my colleagues in Cluj, Ferenc Pozsony, János Péntek, and Éva Borbély for all their help and support. In Csepel, two people I often called upon for assistance and connections to community members were D. Bolla and I. Kis. In the Hungarian community of Jebuc in Transylvania, Mr. and Mrs. J. Molnár, I. Biró, and E. Szalai Ruzsa were crucial to the success of my project. I would like to acknowledge as well the invaluable assistance of Michael Haggett at the State University of New York Press for his keen editorial skills. For the errors that remain, I alone am responsible. Finally, I am grateful to State University of New York Press series editor Tom Wilson for his invitation to contribute to this series on "National Identity." He guided me in the right direction through his solid anthropological ideas and editorial comments as well as his personal help during much of the period while writing this work. Without his help and enthusiasm, this book would not have been completed. Transylvania will never be the same, Tom!

Chapter 1

Introduction:
Regions, Identities,
and Remote Borderlands

*I went up to him and took his hand telling him to come with me
for I wanted to ask something important. Friendly, he followed
me almost dancing. After a few steps I placed my hand on his
shoulder, looked deeply in his eyes and said, "Your soul is very
pure now, tell me: why are we on this earth?" The black man's face
froze for a moment, then he began to laugh. He said, "Strange,
strange, very strange." Again he froze, stared at me and replied,
"We are on this earth so we will be at home somewhere."*

—Á. Tamási, *Ábel Amerikában*, 638

Territorial disputes, border skirmishes, and increasing local ethnonational violence have been with us ever since the Berlin Wall was chiseled
away. Since 1989, contested terrains have become key elements in
redesigning the new Central and Eastern Europe. After the collapse of the
Soviet Bloc, as scholars have increasingly noted, contemporary Europe is
"characterized by the emergence of new forms of nationalism and regionalism."[1] This is in fact the primary aim in this study: to locate the origin
and forms of contestation and representation of territoriality in the
processes of national identity formation and the recreation of national
consciousness among Hungarians. The negotiation of national identities,
however, is not a recent nor a specific East European form of nationalism.
Such contestations began in Western Europe in the 1970s, and their
forms and results are discussed in many excellent studies.[2]

In the East Bloc, it took more than forty years after World War II for the procrustean vulgar variety of Marxism–Leninism to accept the fact that ethnicity is alive and well and that nationality groups must be allowed to thrive if the state is to survive. As usual, this revelation came too late for the totalitarian regimes that tried to solve minority issues by expulsion, forced assimilation, and terror. The Leviathan communist state tried in vain to abolish pre–World War II institutions, such as ethnic churches, parties, and printing, when in their places they re-erected similar institutions to promote state ideology. The problem was not in the institutions themselves but in what the institutions represented. In Bulgaria, Yugoslavia, and Romania, the dormant ethnic rivalry between Turks and Bulgars, Serbs, Croats and Albanians, Hungarians, Germans, and Romanians facilitated the collapse of the much-hated regimes. With these regimes gone, hostilities escalated in Kosovo, Transylvania, Armenia, Georgia, the Baltic Republics, and Central Asia and in a matter of days made headlines in local as well as international newspapers. The year 1989 signaled an unprecedented resurgence of national movements, the creation of new nation-states, and the revitalization of territorial conflicts. While some nations were recreated anew (Czechs, Slovaks, Slovenes, Croats, Serbs), others also redefined themselves (Poles, Hungarians, Romanians). Many ethnic groups found their newly invented, reinvigorated sense of identities (Gypsies, Lippovans, Jews), while new nation-states were also born on the ashes of the burned-out Soviet Empire, as illustrated by the Macedonian, the Moldova and the Sakha-Yakutia. As we learned from the gruesome images—among others the Baltic, Balkan, Chechen–Ingus, and Nagorno–Karabakh conflicts—these new forms of polities were not created in a peaceful fashion such as the German unification, the Czech–Slovak separation, or the creation of Slovenia. The dispute over the region (as well as its name and cultural heritage) of Macedonia between the states of Bulgaria, Greece, and the current Republic of Macedonia is one of the most sensationalized international cases.[3]

Such conflicts illustrate that many regions are continually contested and that their borders remain problematic as "Europe is currently undergoing a virtual orgy of self-construction."[4] One of the reasons for this is the centrality of territoriality, borders, and boundaries in theories of national identity. To know this, and especially to understand its nuances and cultural variations as well as its significance to various national conflicts, is more important today than ever before, as both the European Union (EU) and the North Atlantic Treaty Organization (NATO) are embarking upon expansion into Eastern Europe.

The concept of national space and territory has been central to national consciousness and the creation of nation-states in this part of

Europe. That this is becoming more and more of an agenda in the transnational European policies of the European Union, European Parliament, and Council of Europe has been clear for some time. This has especially been the case since the Vienna Declaration in 1993 and the meeting in Fribourg in 1995, where a new language policy for the European Union was promulgated based on regionality and transborder cooperation among European states. In particular, in the European Union itself, a shift could be detected in using "regions," "territorial" and "non-territorial minorities," "cultural identity," and "cultural community" as the new buzzwords instead of the familiar concepts of ethnicity, minority, and nationality.[5] This changeover has, it must be argued, been made not because of the goodwill of Western leaders and politicians but, more importantly, because of necessity. The 1989 collapse of the bipolar world resulted in enormous population movements from east to west. In particular, refugees from poverty-stricken parts of Eastern Europe and warn-torn Balkan regions made their way to the west. They were not, however, greeted with cheers. On the contrary, they were the victims of racism, prejudice, interethnic violence, and distorted multicultural policies.[6]

What facilitated these movements, and what were the preconditions that led to regional and border conflicts and national hostilities? As anthropological studies have shown, an acknowledgment of the political nature of regional identities, especially the significance of border regions and cultures, is more important now than ever before in answering these questions. In this sense, sound analyses and anthropologically informed data of how groups and regions are coping with the economic and political transformations of states and nations may add to our understanding of local-level conflicts. For not only in history but the present-day realities of those contesting their identities from the borders and peripheries must be investigated if we want to fully understand the intricacies of how individuals and groups cope with the major transformations of Europe.[7]

In this context, to analyze the contests over Transylvania—the land beyond the forest, for this is what the Latin "Trans-Sylvania" entails—is of paramount importance. This is especially true for both anthropologists and East European specialists, for it provides a way to understand how national movements in their East and Central European settings have privileged the question of national and state borders, and moreover how such national identity movements have affected European and global national movements and politics. The contested region known as Transylvania (Siebenbürgen in German, Ardeal in Romanian, Erdély in Hungarian), in the northern part of the Republic of Romania, has seen far more subdued hostilities recently, in comparison to its bloodier past.

This discussion on Transylvania highlights the ways in which small states dispute borders and question the territorial integrity of their neighbors. This study is an anthropological analysis describing Transylvania as a politically sensitized region and the way in which two nations and states contest its meaning, belonging, and history. Hungarian and Romanian intellectual perspectives in the twentieth century are analyzed for the effect that they have had on the negotiation and contestation of Transylvania. This region is viewed here as a political frontier land, shaping twentieth-century national identities in the construction of both Hungarian and Romanian national identities. Specific political and cultural movements are analyzed that have influenced Transylvania—its history, its boundaries, and populations living on its territory.

Drawing upon recently completed research involving Hungarian communities in Transylvania and among elites in Hungary, I trace the fluid, much-contested boundaries by which ethnic and national identities have been both internally generated and externally manipulated and contested. Transylvania often has been referred to in nationalist discourse as a faraway, remote territory functioning as a national frontier. In particular, it has been viewed by both nations as a quintessential cultural zone in the politics of their national geographies. Thus, in this book, my primary objective is to raise questions and stimulate discussion about nation-state formation and the way in which territorial disputes take shape in the political contestations of national identities.

SPATIAL BOUNDARIES

Twentieth-century borders were always problematical to East European states. To legitimate the state borders following World War II, and to uphold the agreements of Potsdam and Yalta, Joseph Stalin defined "nation" as a historically formed stable community possessing not only a common language, economic life, and shared culture, but the right to self-determination and a common territory.[8] East European borders were decided after 1918 and then again in 1945, a date that sanctioned them by both Moscow and the Western powers. Some politicians as well as scholars took them for granted; others were more skeptical. In fact, in the 1960s and 1970s, most ethnographic and anthropological literature in East and Central Europe focused on the question of the symbolic boundaries to national language and culture as specific and left border questions untouched.

In retrospect, it is easy to argue that native scholars were slow in realizing that the Stalinist nationality and territoriality project had been flawed since its inception. Nations are far from being stable communities, and their right to self-determination was impeached constantly during state socialism. Viewing the adulatory creation of the common Soviet, Yugoslav, and Czechoslovak nations, it can be stated with certainty that Marxist-Leninist theories did not work in practice either.[9] As Ronaldo Munck has pointed out, in Marxist scholarship, it was Nicos Poulantzas who warned that the territory and the national question are one and the same. In his words: "The modern nations, the national state, and the bourgeoisie are all constituted on, and have their mutual relations determined by, one and the same terrain."[10] Poulantzas' reminder notwithstanding, the territorial issue has remained a nonentity for state planners and for many anthropologists—both native and Western—working in East and Central Europe.

In contrast to the Stalinist foundations of the "existing state socialist" societies, Western scholars celebrated Frederik Barth's *Ethnic Groups and Boundaries* as a central concept for ethnicity. This has been a rather odd development, for even though Barth couched his study within the notion of "boundary," his study is not about boundary or border conflicts in the political sense. To be fair to Barth, however, it must be stressed that ideas of space and in specific boundaries are implicitly embedded in the Barthian notion of cultural boundary, but not the cultural organization of space into borders or border zones that serve as politically sensitive arenas, both undermining and reinforcing identities. Barth, in fact, argues that "The boundaries to which we must give our attention are of course social boundaries, though they may have territorial counterparts." He continues, "Ethnic groups are not merely or necessarily based on the occupation of exclusive territories."[11] Yet there is only a fine line separating Barth's view from Anthony Smith's, the latter arguing for the juxtaposition of ethnicity and nationality by recalling the inherent territorial problems of both.[12]

For better or for worse, however, the Barthian framework of ethnicity was certainly a less political and sensitive way to deal with the problems of ethnic and minority groups and majority state-supported nationalism. This was at least the case during state socialism in the Soviet Bloc, especially in those countries in which scholars, while trying to refine the Stalinist model, increasingly began to rely on the Barthian framework.[13] Similarly, by the early 1980s, several contradictory ideas emerged to counter such symbolized boundary maintenance theory, emphasizing a new vista for theories of nation and nationality: the community's will to become a nation. Connected to the name of Benedict Anderson, this is the much-celebrated notion that nations are imagined communities, a theory that I do not want to rekindle here. Rather, it should be emphasized that as the national elites imagine their nation, they also are at work to create a system of representation for the geographical and spatial location of both culture and nation.

Of course the argument that the state and the nation—two historical systems that, when successfully united, make up the nation-state of desired leaders—are in an incessant and a dialectical relationship over territory, both real and symbolic, is not a twentieth-century idea. For as Max Weber argued long ago, the state is a compulsory organization with a territorial basis. Ethnic communities, precursors of nations, as Anthony Smith informs us, also are territorial, both in the sense of the imagined and the real national space. For Smith, "Territory is relevant to ethnicity, therefore, not because it is actually possessed, nor even for its 'objective' characteristics of climate, terrain, and location, though they influence ethnic conceptions, but because of an alleged and felt symbiosis between a certain piece of earth and 'its' community."[14] Smith ventures into suggesting that, for ethnic communities, their (real or imaginary) homelands are based on three special aspects: "sacred centers, commemorative association, and external recognition."[15] Through excellent analyses, anthropologists have shown that, indeed, sacred sites, commemorations, and legitimation make up much of the nationalistic fervor throughout the world.[16]

Similarly to Weber and Smith, others have argued that "traditional" borders are such because they fulfill "both functions of dividing and connecting."[17] The nation-state encloses a virtual and self-contained space, which being sovereign it should not, but in reality it is always transcended. As the historian Heesterman suggests, "The modern boundary is by far more risky and explosive" than historical ones.[18] Or, as the anthropologist Renato Rosaldo argues, the modern nation-state boundary is "always in motion, not frozen for inspection."[19] Thus the question of territory is even more explosive when this nation-state is a small European one. A small state by definition is based largely on the lack of economic self-sufficiency, internal markets, and economic and cultural developmental momentum.[20] But as Eisenstadt remarks, the problem of small states exists not only in strictly economic but, equally important, in the cultural sphere as well. In his words:

> In the educational sphere, small countries are under cross-pressures which may endanger their self-identity and make it necessary for them to emphasize their own tradition, history and internal problems, as opposed to sharing the more universal traditions of the large societies. In the cultural sphere, one of the problems of small countries is how to absorb cul-

tural "floods" (in terms of quantity) from prestigious international culture and still maintain their own identity and obtain
international recognition.[21]

These small European states—Eisenstadt names among them Hol-
land, Switzerland, Belgium, Finland, Czechoslovakia, and Austria as well
as Hungary and Romania and the small states created after the breakup of
Yugoslavia—must also fight a center-periphery relationship with the more
advanced, larger states. During the time of state socialism, the countries of
the former East Bloc also were in this dependent relationship with the
Soviet Union. Yet Eisenstadt's argument is important here for other reasons
as well. One is that, besides the question of state boundary, nationality in
East-Central Europe had special aspects of territorialism (i.e., the making
of sacrosanct, rigid national territories). Moreover, these states have had to
fight their bracketing "as a small state" with the continual onslaught of foreign ideas, consumer goods, and military or economic exploitation. All of
these things, as Eisenstadt suggests, have had enormous repercussions on
the country's elites and their cultural mentality that determined the way in
which identity was pursued relentlessly. Nationalistic ideas did not suddenly then spring up in the minds of the native elites but always had particular historical preconditions within which they were triggered.

BORDERS AND BORDERLANDS

Paralleling the ideas of Eisenstadt, Smith, and Heesterman, John
Coakley argues cogently that based on *jus sanguinis* and *jus soli,* states
always try to operate within clear-cut definitions of the physical reality of
state boundaries and nationality.[22] However, ethnic and national communities ingeniously may devise and accommodate ideas allowing for the
possibility of crisscrossing, transcending, and subverting state borders.
"People and land," writes Coakley, "[are the] two primary stimuli of patriotism and nationalism in that they act as powerful foci of group loyalty."
Moreover, "Ethnic communities feel a strong association with a particular, so-called 'national' territory and use historical, pseudo-historical, or
even mythical arguments to press their claims to it."[23] When such a
national territory or region lies outside of the nation-state, or might be
inhabited by other groups, a powerful association with that land may be
even more fundamental to national leaders. The Basque region, Northern
Ireland, or the Danish Slesvig-Holstein, Kashmir, and East Timor may be
considered special regions where territories and borders have been contested and arguments over them have persisted for some time now.[24]

Coakley's argument highlights another important anthropological insight: that as states unite national groups into a legal framework of citizenry, they have at their disposal legitimate force over boundaries or traditional regions considered special by the groups holding titles to them. Therefore, ethnic and national groups may feel rather uneasy, if not outright injured, when their space is intruded upon by states or neighboring groups. A group may make territorial demands on the state, depending on its size and spatial distribution. In return, the state may react to territorial demands by either gerrymandering ethnonational boundaries or dispersing the group outside of its homeland. With regard to the troubled twentieth-century Transylvanian history, as subsequent chapters will reveal, both responses have been recorded.

What will become clear from this analysis of the Transylvanian case is that the more the state impinges upon or exploits certain territories, local groups may feel, and justifiably so, that their sovereign right has been infringed upon and their homeland raped. Another dimension of this territorial conflict is the violent actions and reactions triggered by contending groups in defense of their national homelands. These locales often are mapped with the help of historical sites (or sacred centers, as Anthony Smith has suggested), buildings, and monuments. They receive extreme importance when the "indigenous group" feels that "newcomers" occupy them. Needless to say, nations and states often receive legitimation from such territories that are themselves legitimated by state privileges. Similar to Transylvania, Ayodha, Jerusalem, Northern Ireland, and the Kuryle Islands off the coast of Japan are all sensitive territories so imbued with special meaning and disproportionate mythical status that states and nations rely upon them for their legitimation.

National homelands and territories often are bounded spaces surrounded by dangerous or highly explosive frontiers and borders. France, for instance, gave us the modernist European political symbolism concerning the state-bordered national space. France possesses borders which, according to the 1872 Larousse's Grand Dictionaire du XIXe Siecle, are "all the frontiers that God's hand traced for her, those of her Celtic and Roman past, which she reconquered at the time of her revolutionary regeneration and which should at any rate include the battlefield of Tolbiac and the Tomb of Charlemagne."[25] This illustrates the idea of how territoriality and historical borders, no matter how much they change with time, become sacred and divine to states and nations living within their confinements. Perhaps Peter Sahlins' study concerning the borders between France and Spain illuminates best the contested nature of European boundaries in history.[26] Sahlins points to the key position of local identities and borderlands in making the state and the nation: "the shape and significance of the boundary line was constructed out of local social relations in the border-land" [for] "it was the dialectic of local and national interests which produced the boundaries of national territory."[27] But Sahlins goes one step further when he argues that in the making of French and Spanish national identities, the periphery played an initial key role only later appropriated by the center. States define their borders, issue regulations allowing border crossings, and utilize documents (in the form of passports and transborder permits) to sanction cross-border traffic and cooperation. Yet the more these regulations are issued, the more attempts there are to counter them. The phrases "illegal aliens," "guest workers," "asylum seekers," and "refugees" used in European Union countries represent the problems of maintaining the borders of both nation-states and supranational polities.

As Sahlins argues, borders and border regions are becoming essential as nation-states are invented in the modern European world system. According to Benedict Anderson's theory, "Communities are to be distinguished not by their falsity/genuineness, but by the style in which they are imagined."[28] While this may be true to a certain extent, admittedly such imagination must take place in a specified geographical locale with defined dimensions both in time and space. For nationalists this locale is contained within some specific borders that often rely on historic frontiers. For nationalists, Transylvania is one such locale that had a different history, different from the rest of Hungary (i.e., the Balkans and the former Soviet Empire to the east). In fact, this difference is transposed on the whole area enclosed by borders.

This book examines the very process in which Transylvania has been politically constructed as well as contested as a remote borderland in which different populations had been brought together by different forces of history. It illustrates the cultural manifestations of the geographical imagination by locating myths of national identity through contests between Hungarian and Romanian elites. As mentioned above, Coates correctly suggests that a bordered space is viewed by nationalist leaders and elites as strictly belonging to them, and that neighboring populations also view it with a like-mindedness. But as sociologist Florian Znaniecki argued earlier in the last century, territorial "claims are not merely economic, but moral and often religious; they are superimposed upon whatever rights of economic ownership to portions of this land may be granted to smaller groups or individual members."[29] He added later that, "Thus, 'our land,' the 'land of our ancestors,' becomes for the masses of people the spatial receptacle of most, if not all, of their important values."[30] This is indeed the notion that recalls the classic ideas of the German romanticists, most notably Herder and Johann Fichte, who equated a nation with its language and territory. As Kedourie quotes Fichte:

> The first, original, and truly national boundaries of a state are beyond doubt the internal boundaries. Those who speak the same language are joined to each other by a magnitude of invisible bonds by nature herself . . . they belong together and are by nature one and inseparable whole. From this internal boundary . . . the making of the external boundary by dwelling place results as a consequence; and in the natural view of things it is not because men dwell between certain mountains and rivers that they are a people, but, on the contrary, men dwell together . . . because they were a people already by a law of nature which is much higher.[31]

For Fichte and other idealists, and not only those of the Romantic period, each nation is endowed with "natural frontiers" given to them by law, God, and nature. But as we know, there are no "natural" boundaries or frontiers per se. For Kedurie, for instance, "Natural frontiers do not exist, neither in the topographical sense . . . nor in the linguistic. . . . Frontiers are established by power, and maintained by the constant known readiness to defend them by arms."[32] Mayall argues similarly: "It is quite obvious that while some frontiers—for example, mountain ranges, deserts, lakes, the sea surrounding islands, and so—may seem more plausible than others, particularly if they have persisted for a long time, none is natural: they are political and cultural, usually established by conquest and maintained by occupation."[33]

With these in mind, I propose here that in order to understand the conflict over Transylvania between two neighboring states, we should understand how elite perceptions of the homeland are formed, contested, and negotiated in an international political arena. How topographical features and interpretations of the past serve nationalist elites—"professors of linguistics and collectors of folklore," as Kedourie puts it[34]—to legitimize claims for a certain terrain with clearly marked borders will be analyzed with specific reference to Transylvania. Despite the fact that historic borders are sometimes difficult to prove, nationalists initiate gruesome geopolitics, which then may turn to brutal state policies deciding territorial questions. Territorial nationalism of this kind is extremely dangerous, for it "is internally unifying and externally divisive over space."[35]

Systematic nationalistic drives for a region may take irredentist and secessionist forms but other attempts also are known. Mass population exchanges and the expulsion of groups, the dreaded word of "ethnic cleansing," which still rings very close from the war in former Yugoslavia, and the troubled relationship between twentieth-century Hungary and Romania provide ample examples for these, a topic discussed in detail in later chapters. Aside from these, the other extremist nationalist "solutions" include genocide and the economic subordination of a people by relegating them to the periphery of the labor market and denying them basic civil and political rights.[36]

EUROPEAN BORDERLANDS AND IDENTITIES

In order to grasp the full meaning of nationalist contestations over Transylvania, the notion of borders and border areas must be problematized accordingly. Borders, as Ken Coates remarks in his study of border differences between Canada and the United States, are true "political artifacts" with "considerable historical and contemporary impact."[37] The study of border cultures then is of utmost importance for the social sciences:

> It should reveal, first and foremost, the risk of assuming the inevitability of national boundaries and the dangers of rooting one's studies in national settings, rather than in the evolving historical/geographical contexts out of which modern societies evolved. Further, such examination illustrates the importance of considering the manner in which the modern state created, imposed, maintained, and empowered boundaries, not just by establishing border crossings and implementing custom duties but also in creating and sustaining a sense of national distinctiveness. . . . It is in the borderlands, where country rubs against country, where citizens have regular contact with a different way of governing and living, that one finds the true test of nationalism and nationhood. The study of borderland cultures, both in their historical development and contemporary manifestations, demonstrates that nations do matter and will, in all likelihood, continue to matter well into the future.[38]

Similar to Coates, anthropologists have shown that European nationalistic movements often have involved disputes over territories, populations, and the realignments of borders, as well as the creation of new border cultures.[39] Loring Danforth, for instance, reveals the ways in which the making of Macedonian identity has had significant transnational connections to Macedonian diasporas in Western Europe, Australia, and Canada.[40] From these multicultural metropolitan diaspora communities have sprung strong identity mechanisms influencing the eventual outcome of the Balkan-Macedonian nation-state, its identity, structure and meaning.[41] What the Transylvanian case study demonstrates is how complex the borders have been in Eastern Europe. This region has, throughout the past centuries, been viewed—as well as invented ethnocentrically through both political geography and cultural cartography, as Larry Wolf puts it[42]—as the easternmost border of "Western civilization." As such, it has been designated as a border terrain between Europe and Asia, sensitized and contested by both scholars and politicians. A recent definition states, for instance, the external boundaries of Eastern Europe as ". . . the lands between the linguistic frontier of the German- and Italian-speaking peoples on the west and the political boundaries of the former Soviet Union on the east. The north-south parameters are the Baltic and Mediterranean seas."[43] Such definite topographical closures have been constructed in ways similar to their histories as a whole through political negotiation, often with the assistance of literary fabulous facts, mythopoetic themes, and barbarian tribes. When viewed from the historical-political angle, the borders of Eastern, or East-Central Europe, have been redesigned by wars, economic boom-and-bust cycles, interethnic violence, literary fiction, and shifting international power relations. It is not without justification then that many earlier scholars referred to this region as exhibiting an extraordinary number of upheavals, wars, and, in general, "un-European" qualities. For the British H. G. Wanklyn, writing at the turn of the twentieth century, this region was "the eastern marchland (borderland) between Russia and Germany."[44] Following World War I, Viscount Rothermere—aide to the British prime minister at the Paris Peace Conference in 1919—uttered that it was "Europe's powder magazine."[45] When analyzing the first half of the twentieth century, a Hungarian historian called it "a crisis zone."[46] Anthropologist John Cole, discussing the economic development and ethnic processes of the region, referred to it as "an ethnic shatter zone."[47]

These definitions have as their precursor the geopolitical notion that the eastern part of the former Holy Roman Empire and then the Austro-Hungarian Monarchy were relegated to the periphery and referred to as a border region between the more developed West and the technologically less advanced East. This idea was firmly embedded in the humanities and social sciences, where Eastern Europe's regions received privileged geopolitical connotations of a Latinized, Westernized, and developed part and the epithet Central Europe, in contrast to the backward, orthodox Muslim East.[48] In this scholarly and political contestation, both history and economic development processes have been powerfully connected to the creation of Eastern Europe as a remote, peripheral region. Dudley Seers has put this rather bluntly:

> As within the Western European system, broadly, the further a country is from Germany, the worse the social conditions of an East European country. . . . Hungary and Poland can be considered intermediate between core and periphery. . . . Bul-

garia and Romania are more clearly peripheral in economic structure, income levels, and social conditions, as well as more dependent on imported technology.[49]

Hungarian historian Jenő Szűcs, relying considerably on his perceptions of similar economic history and uneven technological development, concurs, insisting that between the democratic, Catholic/Protestant, and economically advanced West and the backward, orthodox, and feudal East lies a central region of Europe that was always behind and (in vain) has attempted to catch up with the West. Keeping in line with nationalist historiography, for Szűcs this central region exhibits features that identify it with its easternmost neighbors. The intelligentsia of the region's various countries have continually tried to modernize and liberalize, but in their eagerness, they were perennially caught between outside forces midway through their halfhearted attempts and were thrown even further back into stagnation and nationalist intrigues. One of the most important features of this backwardness was, as the argument goes, the absence of a strong middle class, such as in Germany or Austria.[50] In Szűcs' writings, the major characteristics of this backwardness also included an economy marginalized in the global market, an authoritarian state with a huge bureaucratic machinery, and increasing social atomism of the population at large. Religious and ethnic conflicts were two additional factors that contributed to the backwardness region theory. On the one hand, Catholicism and Protestantism in opposition to orthodoxy and the use of a Latin and not a Cyrillic alphabet were seen as important dividing lines between East and Central Europe. On the other hand, an all-important ethnonational politics—helping the establishment of nineteenth-century nation-states—had been the hallmark of the specific Eastern Europeanness.[51]

Whether these labels befit a region in which millions were dislocated and borders rearranged several times in the past hundred years and in which ethnic conflicts and nationality tensions continue to mount needs to be addressed on an individual basis with specific reference to each nationality conflict. In this book, my aim is to discuss the development of the contestable mechanisms and ideology of making Transylvania a special backward and faraway region, a process in which these labels occur quite often by all sides concerned.

HISTORICAL TRANSYLVANIA AS BORDERLAND

As we have seen above, Transylvania as a faraway locale has had its share in its own Orientalizing project. To be sure, this region occupied the imagination of writers, statesmen, and generals since at least the early Middle Ages, when tribal kings, religious leaders, and local warlords tried to master it. While historical facts often have been obfuscated or relegated to national mythologies, it is easy to see why this multiethnic mountainous terrain invited various historical populations. Since Roman times, the provinces of Pannonia and Dacia "remained border regions to the end, known as the least civilized provinces."[52] While most of the early populations disappeared, the notion that this part of Eastern Europe was a border zone was imprinted in the collective national memory. When Hungarians settled the Carpathian Basin (a geographical reference discussed later) in the tenth century, they had a considerable military superiority and advantage. This worked well against emerging state powers whose empires bordered this region, most notably the Kievan Rus to the north and east and the Byzantine Empire to the south.[53]

Obviously then the reasons the Carpathian or Danube Basin region was looked at as a border region were numerous, but two stand out. One had to do with geography, the other with the competing states as well as their national elites, who were keen in defining its extent. British historian Carlyle MacCartney, when writing about the early medieval history or the region (in a sense providing support for the later theory of Anthony Smith), suggested that the Middle Danube Basin forms a "natural unity" and "one harmonious whole."[54] Viewing the political history of this region, it becomes obvious that two powerful empires exerted considerable pressures on the state and border formations within this region: the Austrian House of Habsburgs and the Turkish Ottoman Empire. Thus Transylvania experienced a form of special vassalage by its different associations with often hostile polities. After a considerably long attachment to the Hungarian kingdom, the Ottoman intrusion into the East European region carved out separate states and redivided the whole area. As a consequence, Transylvanian nobles, described as the Union of Three Nations (Magyars, Szeklers, and Saxons), tried to hold on to their privileged positions within their estates, but they managed to do so with considerable infighting and intrigues.

After defeating the Ottoman Empire at the Battle of Buda in 1686, Transylvania was encircled by what was known for two centuries as the Austrian military frontier. To maintain control over this large swath of terrain—the southern areas of the former Hungarian kingdom, Croatia, Slavonia, and Banat, and the southern part of Transylvania to the north to Bukovina—Austria established military frontier districts to defend its borders. This special border zone existed in the Austro-Hungarian Empire until the mid-nineteenth century, when the military districts were abolished. Following World War I and the collapse of the Austro-Hungarian

Monarchy, the region Transylvania was incorporated into the newly formed Romanian state, and aside from the brief period between 1940 and 1944, it has remained there.

However, Transylvania for the Hungarian intellectuals, is not simply an empty historical space but a "cradle of Hungarian civilization." By virtue of its distance from the center, this cultural zone has been viewed as an ancestral terrain encircling the historic national space. To them, this terrain stopped something and began something else; its regions and topographical features have been identified with national history, the extent of speech communities, specific folklore complexes, and a "nationally" recognizable way of life. In East-Central European national myth makings, the faraway region as the birthplace, or at least the cauldron, of national culture is a common view of national elites. In the Slovak nationalist culturology, the image of the Highland Tatra Mountain shepherd is such a quintessential trope, as Slovak ethnographer Krekovicova argues cogently.[55] Similarly, for Polish nationalist history, the region known as the Kresy, a huge historic region now partly in Lithuania, Belarus, and the Ukraine, is "the cradle of civilization in Poland."[56]

In Hungarian nationalist discussion, this type of reasoning is linked to the notion that Transylvania has been and continues to be the real eastern border of Hungarian culture. Somewhat comparable to the American Wild West frontier, in the minds of nationalist intellectuals, the real borders between Hungary and Romania are not the present state borders between these two states but, on the contrary, lie at the farthest reaches of the physical (and often imaginary) Transylvania. Actually, regions bordering Transylvania on the east—Moldavia, the Ukraine, and Oltenia—are viewed by Hungarian intellectuals as separating and ultimately connecting Hungary to the orthodox, Slavic, and Balkan lands. In opposition to these borders, the central and western parts of Hungary—mainly the Austrian Burgerland on the Leitha River zone—have been far less important culturally and politically for Hungarian history. Similarly, the northern province—parts of present-day Slovakia—while slightly different, is closer to Transylvania, but not as significant and not as sensitive for Hungarian national consciousness.

Transylvania, the epicenter of the frontier land—ironically both for Romanians and Hungarians with its melting pot of cultures and slightly sadistic, if exotic, history—has managed throughout the past to reinvigorate the intellectuals (often living in the centers) in their superiority but successfully resist homogenizing influences and pressures. Stuart Hall makes the point that the recovery of the past constitutes an essential "resources of resistance" for all groups that have been marginalized and misrepresented by the dominant regimes.[57] Similarly, as Michael Taussig observes with reference to the mixing of the Third and First World divides, "The border has dissolved and expanded to cover the lands it once separated such that all the land is borderland."[58] This borderland then is the frame of reference within which Transylvania has received its qualities as a quintessential, remote area in nationalist cartography. Even when Hungarian intellectuals and politicians discuss the possibility of joining the European Union, the borders of Hungary refer to those of the Hungarian nation, a concept that includes, in their minds, rightfully, Hungarians living in Romania and thus Transylvania as a whole.

THE REMOTE REGION

As we have seen so far, intellectuals and politicians have always theorized about the borders of the nation, often in contradistinction with those of state borders. In Europe in general and Transylvania in particular, such discourse has privileged the periphery, described often as a borderland or a border zone, but still as a faraway locale. In fact, Transylvania has been described by many travelers as Europe's Shangri-la. It is viewed not only as a self-contained border culture but is elevated to a special terrain that could best be understood by the phrase suggested by Edwin Ardener, as a "remote area."[59] This notion has much to offer scholars of contemporary national identity and borderland cultures. In a sense, Ardener may be considered a predecessor of those in anthropology who study state and national borders or who conduct regional studies. His idea allows us to reinvigorate discussions about regionality and national conflicts over terrains and offers a chance to situate Transylvania, the remote region, at the center of Hungarian nationalist discourse.[60] It is instructive to reveal how Hungarian nationalist imagination carved up geography according to a hierarchy of regional dialects. As opposed to the Great Plains of Hungary—which itself also has the image of the national prairie (the *puszta*)—the eastern part of the former Hungarian kingdom is Transylvania, a region that equally belongs to that well-nigh border zone of access to difference. This region exists far from the center, where most of the nationalist politics takes form and shape—in our case, either Budapest or Bucharest—and in the minds of nationalists is a pure and true national geospace.

Ardener discusses the problem of identity, both majority and minority, and social space as they interact through the notion of remote areas. For him, "Distance lends enhancement, if not enchantment, to the anthropological vision."[61] Certainly in the case of contested Transylvania, this enchantment has been true for scholars and politicians alike, a point that will become obvious in subsequent chapters. Ardener, however, departs from the familiar center/periphery discussion and devises a scheme in which remoteness involves both "imaginary" and "real" localities. At the same time, "The actual geography is not the overriding feature—it is obviously necessary that 'remoteness' has a position in topographical space, but it is defined within a topological space whose features are expressed in a cultural vocabulary."[62] Ardener identifies several paradoxical features of such areas: the presence of strangers; the generation of innovations and novelties; the presence of the ruins of the past and rubbish; constant contacts with the outside world; the influence of incomers; and labor market segmentation and microeconomic pluralism. Thus Ardener seems to be right on target when he writes that, "Remoteness is a specification, and a perception, from elsewhere, from an outside standpoint; but from inside the people have their own perceptions . . . a counterspecification of the dominant, or defining space, working in the opposite direction."[63] In contrast to the center, this double specification of remote areas also creates an "event—richness." However brief and cursory this interpretation, Ardener's idea of the remote area ingeniously juxtaposes the political and scholarly impulses concerning regionality, identity, and the contestation over faraway border zones.

In order to celebrate one's past as unique or to reject it as outright alien, history has been manipulated and contested by nationalist elites to justify territorial integrity and gains. In this history the involved parties needed a place to locate events and characters within, and nothing served this better than the remote border zone. For the nationalist minds, this place is even imbued with a heightened sense of symbolism, for it is connected to the formation of the nation and the turning points of that history, for as Ardener suggests, "Remote areas are full of ruins of the past." In this "archaic" locale, nationalists need a population or groups of coalescing ethnics whose mission is to carry on a culture deemed sacred by the elite. The past then is inextricably interwoven with everyday life there than outside of its boundaries. If these boundaries seem elusive and at times roughly drawn and shifting, for the nationalist, this is a point where he or she can find justification in utilizing historically sore points. This suits a nationalist well, for a ". . . nationalist is not strictly confined by any particular ethnic criteria. He is concerned about establishing his nation's credentials, not about formulating universally valid principles for the legitimization of a nation."[64] Writing at the end of World War II, George Orwell correctly suggested that, "In nationalist thought there are facts which are both true and untrue, known and unknown."[65] All this, naturally, leads to Orwell's unique notion that three characteristics define nationalist thought: obsession, instability, and indifference to reality.[66] To create a nation, one has to imagine its national land, thus all three characteristics may be required in order to be successful in establishing a nation's credentials to claiming a certain territory. In fact, we may see all of these elements, not only in the Transylvanian dispute but in the post–1990 former Soviet Bloc, a region experiencing border disputes and contestations of territory.[67]

The center of national territory prides itself on being the sole defender of this locale it helped refashion, but the faraway frontier region must suffer all of the privations and mistreatment for its privileged role as a culture carrier and history maker. This romantic geopolitics is stipulated on the following contradictions: (1) The center must reassure its leading position renewed from time to time over the frontier; (2) The peripheral zone, in contrast, must remain as such, a remote frontier in a state of suspension, like a spider limited by its ability to weave its net, by its fragility, minuteness, and disadvantageousness. National historiographies, as well as nationalized sciences of folklore, ethnography, and linguistics, the subject of later chapters, may be suspected for their roles in ideologizing as well as idolizing the image of the faraway border area. As it is textualized in nationalist controversies, life in this region is fraught with immense cultural and political upheavals; crises ebb and flow across it, affecting various inhabitants. The regions' populations face challenges adapting to the pressures of friendly and hostile groups. As a direct result, they need to manage their daily affairs in close proximity to foreigners, guests, or tourists. As Ardener sees it, those in remote areas must constantly be in contact with strangers and incomers. For example, this may be one of the reasons such regions, at one time or another, exhibit violent and extreme behavior against both intruders and their own populations. At the same time, peaceful existence is also required by the inhabitants for their survival. Yet in nationalist historiography, the center always feels that the national borderland is under attack by invading foreigners. When the center is attacked, the margins are appointed as the carriers—in fact, the saviors—of the tradition by preserving it for future generations.

Nationalist history notwithstanding, all populations living in Transylvania have been midwives to its growth, culture, and history, and even their native tongues are littered with foreign expressions. Their cuisine, music, clothing, dance, and buildings, almost by law, also exhibit this nearness, assimilation, and borrowings. For populations in the remote region, this coexistence, whether wanted or not, is an everyday reality. Transplanted to the intellectual world of the center, such cultural eccentricities are framed by scholars, ethnographers, and historians as exoticism into the national ideology and identity aimed at preserving the archaic, remote nature of the faraway territory. For national scholars, as Marc

Augé points out, this is "not tied to geographic distance or even to ethnic belonging: ethnologists studying Europe at first took for objects surviving customs, traditions, and human milieux (peasants, artisans) that were imbued for them with a kind of internal exoticism."[68]

As we have seen above, the center glorifies such remoteness and backwardness, for unlike the center, the remote area is imagined as representing "lawlessness." With that, as Edwin Ardener suggests, such regions are in a state of constant event richness. In fact, there exists a different sort of legality: its polychrome, ethnic makeup has bred "noble savages" in the portrayal of sunburned peasants such as the Kalotaszeg or the Csángós for the Hungarians or the Maramures villagers for Romanians, as we will see later. But people living in remote regions should not be thought of as only hybrids, or of having no definite sense of nationality, or even that they are helpless denizens of faraway settlements. On the contrary, what Donna Flynn describes for the multicultural Nigerian borderland is true for Transylvania as well. Residents of such border regions "recognize that it is precisely because they belong to separate nations that they can manipulate and negotiate the border to their mutual advantage. . . . Being the 'border' implies separation as well as unification, exclusion as well as inclusion, independence as well as interdependence."[69] This is just one of the contradictions that characterizes border cultures. Perhaps another important one is the question concerning ethnonational identity, emanating from the country's ruling elite, which may or may not find friendly reception at the margins. There the question of belonging is never simple or unidirectional but multiple and contradictory at the same time, oscillating between allegiance to the state, region, nation, and ethnicity:

> The center celebrates the region's remoteness to and oneness with its superior position: when the cultures of the periphery celebrate, they mostly cry out their "nearness" to and distinction with each other . . . the spirit of life at the borders is predicated upon interaction and true cross-culturality; sharing, borrowing and assimilating are not quite adequate words to describe this cultural amalgam. This cross-pollenization, in fact, may just be the postmodernist nightmare.[70]

Border regions are not simply imagined by national elites but are created and recreated as the border region itself grows and contracts under the weight of political forces, a notion that owes much to the analysis of French–Spanish borderlands by Peter Sahlins, mentioned earlier. The real Transylvania has given rise to many Transylvanias. They have been manufactured out of native experiences, stories, and a variety of representations.

It seems true, as Aldous Huxley wrote sometime ago—which should be remembered when Benedict Anderson is hailed—that, Nations are to a very large extent invented by their poets and novelists. For Hungarians and Romanians alike, Transylvania has been invented many times over by various writers, artists, politicians, and scholars.

As indicated by ethnographers, folklorists, linguists, and writers, Transylvania's regional eccentric culture patterns function as markers or warning posts that something else is different there. Remote regions not only close in and keep out—as we have seen above—they produce their own logic of their own sense of "being there." Such regions are not really empty, dark, or impenetrable, characteristics that are at times exacerbated by the writers' fancy at the center. To paraphrase Edwin Ardener, remote areas are full of ruins of the past and "pots," and maybe these facilitate their constant contact with the outside world. It will suffice to recall how Transylvania was catapulted to international fame with its folk art or the Dracula myth of the British Bram Stoker, so familiar to Westerners.[71] In fact, border regions are full of (inter)actions, entanglements, and ambivalence, as they represent thresholds of cultures that never end but lead to newer forms of life. As viewed by the contending sides, borders are necessary in fashioning national traditions, for they reveal that dichotomies and hard core facts are rarely justified. To paraphrase Aldous Huxley, who put it in another context, and one that well characterizes one's entrance into such regions, to travel is to realize that everyone was wrong. But more than that, to cross into the frontier is to realize how much we have wronged. How much we have to transcend our own boundaries. That is why the number of travelers, often anthropologists, and strangers are lurking in these regions.[72]

How is this remote region best described? Transylvania in the nationalist imagination is sullen, neat, and uncontaminated, the *true* nature where people live more natural lives than those living outside of it. This wholeness is seen to be the characteristic pattern of life there, distinguishing it from the cosmopolitan, isolated, individualistic, and commercialized existence in the center. As it will become obvious in subsequent chapters, for most writers Transylvania conjures up images of animals, forests, mountains, and fields of grassland where herds of sheep, cows, goats, and buffaloes make their harmonious peace with humans.[73] Transylvania exhibits wilderness, quasirationality, and preponderant folk beliefs where the daily round of life has been defined by nature, the seasons, and the animals. As Ardener argues, "Remote areas offer images of unbridled pessimism or utopian optimism, of change and decay, in their memorial."

How is Transylvania connected to the center? Transylvania, to be sure, is remote as imagined by nationalist elites, but not always so as experienced by visitors and local citizens alike. There are, of course, natural things—bridges and roads through which one can enter the real zone. For Transylvania, this Western transition is the Parts (Partium in the nineteenth century) and the Királyhágó Pass, the latter being a military post in former times. More importantly, however, there are living links of family relations (as said by Hungarians, every third family in Hungary counts relatives in Transylvania). This may be an overgeneralization, even though the past seventy years experienced a massive population influx from Romania into Hungary, yet what this statement really points to is the powerful emotional tie with which Hungarians continue to view Transylvania, and its Hungarian population living there. Romanian elites have been equally vocal about the location of their ancestral land: "The territory on which Romanian people was born lies within two fundamental coordinates: the Carpathians and the Danube. The Carpathian Mountains traverse the Romanian territory building inside it the Transylvanian stronghold, the central region of the country, its nucleus."[74] More recently, another Romanian historian connected territory to nationality: "It has been too easily overlooked, also, that today's Transylvania is not an ethnical mosaic as some people think, that the Union of 1918 was a legitimate act, and that Romanians now represent about 75 percent of the population. . . . Why should Transylvania belong to Romania? The answer is simple: Transylvania belongs to Romania because the Romanians represent the absolute majority of the population and they expressed collectively their wish to live in Romania."[75]

However, for such nationalist intellectuals living in the center, whether in Bucharest or Budapest, their ancestral land is under construction and continually receding: by the 1950s and 1960s it became more industrialized and cosmopolitan than agrarian and rural. The nationalist elites have expressed concern over the past decades about the region being overrun by modernization and urbanization, about the socialist reorganization model, and about their fear that Transylvania has become the overtly exploited garden! For writers of the center, the frontier of Transylvania represents true archaic lore and skills, not a wasteland but an unconquerable, unassimilable region inhabited by survivors resisting progress and forced reforms. In Canaan, heroes can be—and will be—killed but never conquered or forgotten. It is visualized often in the character of a sturdy peasant who loves its contradictions, vicissitudes, and hardships. His universal skepticism—both toward other populations and the state— is displayed by the main character Ábel in Áron Tamási's trilogy.[76] Ábel, a disembodied voice, plays a trickster, but he is in reality a true trickster who has to cross many borders. Interestingly, as the motto of this chapter indicates, Ábel receives the true message: "We are on this earth so we will be at home somewhere" (strangely, not from a fellow émigré Hungarian but from an African American, himself also an outcast)—that he has to return home. What this really means is obvious:

> It is true: I have to go home at once, so I can be at home some-
> where on this world. You are right: there is no other purpose
> in life than to know everything possible, as much it is possi-
> ble. To know all the colors and corners, to people we should
> forgive, the groups fighting with each other; and after we
> achieved all that, we return where we can be at home.[77]

To Ábel, as to Tamási, that home was the Hargita Mountains, the east-ernmost border of Transylvania.

Similar Transylvanian-Hungarian experiences have been recapitulated colorfully in literary narratives that connect the nation with its home ter-ritory. Other classic Transylvanian novelists (Nyirő, Tamási, Horváth, Katona Szabó, and Berde, earlier in this century, or Sütő, Kányádi, and Lászlóffy recently)[78] imagine Transylvania not only out of sheer nostalgia and fantasy, have experienced it firsthand. Their books are not only about the search for the self, they are, at the same time, also about the clash of cultures. Their literary contestation foregrounds Hungarian Transylvania as a territory in which actors, events, and actions reveal the significance of birthplace as Tamási's culture hero, Ábel, aptly remarks. Clearly, in the lit-erary imagination, Transylvania is a remote place of many cultures and ethnic and religious groups, but for the writers and their heroes, is first and foremost a region very close to the heart, the birthplace of Hungar-ian culture. Just how this imagination is created, contested, and negoti-ated will be the topic of the following chapters.

ORGANIZATION OF THE BOOK

This book is based on a theoretical and an ethnographical under-standing of the interconnectedness of nationality processes and territori-ality. By providing such a theoretical backdrop for remaking East-Central European ethnic and national identities, it attempts to steer the discus-sion from nonterritorial models of nationality and identity studies. The Transylvanian case illustrates that territories and border cultures, often perceived by national elites as remote peripheries, have much to offer to anthropological analyses of states, nations, and identities. It reveals the fundamental ways in which nations and states engage in contesting, redefining, and negotiating their identities and by so doing influences others' as well. What follows then are chapters detailing specific instances and means by which two states and nations have battled over a region common to both for much of the history of their statehood. By looking at the scholarly and political entanglements, we witness the emergence of various issues, debates, and arguments that have shaped different understandings of the contested region under discussion.

In Chapter 2, Transylvania's history is discussed with specific reference to nationalistic drives to gain scholarly supremacy over this terrain. Historical Transylvania serves as a backdrop to analyze how statesmen, national leaders, cultural workers, and groups living there as well as outside of it have been influenced by these forces and how they have reshaped the region in return. From conflicts, often with bloody results, to scholarly quagmires, from international intrigues to border transfers, Transylvania has been placed in the center of national and global political maneuvers.

In Chapter 3, my personal fieldwork experiences are added by highlighting important insights to the remaking of Hungarian national consciousness since the mid-1980s. Through a comparison of Hungarian communities in Hungary and in the Transylvanian part of Romania, I discuss my anthropological understandings of studying nationalist processes and how an ethnographic imagination of Transylvania has been centrally located in this nationalist discourse.

Chapter 4 shifts its perspective by focusing on an important contestable mechanism provided to the Hungarian elites: populism. It suggests ways in which, despite neighborly relations, Hungarian elites were able to produce and utilize ethnographic and literary images to create a population (that of Hungarians in Transylvania) as the trustees of Hungarian culture and identity. Eventually this literary and political populism served the country's elites in subverting the communist state's agenda to create communist men and women and instead reawaken Hungarian national identity.

Chapter 5 demonstrates how Transylvanian ethnic and minority issues became a central theme in both Hungary's and Romania's attempts to create their communist selves after World War II. Relying on the fashionable socialist and internationalist slogans of the time, various Transylvanian populations were appropriated by both Hungarians and Romanians as they strove to prove their supremacy over that terrain. Such a communist nation making notwithstanding, however, transnational forces also were evoked; the Hungarian diaspora in North America assisted in creating an image of the Hungarian nation living in the Carpathian Basis, and at the same time, it refashioned the Romanian state known for its brutal suppression of minorities and anti-Hungarian policies.

As Chapter 6 demonstrates, a specific youth subculture emerged which had an enormous impact on the way in which Hungarian identity resurfaced during state socialism in the 1970s and 1980s. Yet despite state repression, the region and its peoples survived, providing ample food for thought for scholars and politicians to ponder regarding their (mis) understanding of terrains, identities, and conflicts. In this chapter, the troubled relationship between the Hungarian and Romanian states is described, with specific reference to the question of Hungarians in Transylvania and the Hungarian elite in Hungary. This analysis is especially important, for it reveals how both managed to refashion their noncommunist identities and democratic image in the wake of the death agony of the two state's regimes.

However, it soon became clear that "a return to Europe" (to which many statesmen, among them, Vaclav Havel, have referred), following the period 1989–1990, cannot be achieved overnight, a topic treated in detail in Chapter 7. Such a contestation of ethnonational identities has brought the territorial and border issues into the forefront of transnational and global politics. With the dismantling of the communist borders—following the collapse of the Warsaw Pact and the Soviet Bloc—new, and heretofore unknown, borders were created both internally and externally. As states collapsed (Czechoslovakia, the Soviet Union, and Yugoslavia), and the European Union expanded, new borders were erected as the result of the Maastricht and Schengen treaties. In Chapter 8, I conclude by suggesting that the creation of new states and nations and the redefinition of borders are fundamentally interconnected. This chapter reveals an anthropological understanding of how Transylvania has managed to carve out its central role in creating new Hungarian and Romanian identities, and moreover that such analyses will facilitate a better comprehension for the importance of contested regionality and nationality in the New Europe in the beginning of the third millennium.

Chapter 2

Contesting the Past:
The Historical Dimension
of the Transylvanian Conflict

In Chapter 1, I outlined the theoretical basis for viewing territories as border zones and remote regions, and I argued that this shift was essential in understanding nationalist controversies concerning border conflicts and territorial divisions in East-Central Europe. This chapter analyzes first the nineteenth- and twentieth-century developments between the two states and then highlights how these affected the controversies between Romanians and Hungarians concerning Transylvania as a historic border culture. Viewed as a highly charged national landscape, in fact, as an archaic ancestral remote area for both Hungarians and Romanians, the Transylvanian controversy prompts us to consider how this contestation has taken place, not only in the international political arena but, equally important, in the scholarly pursuit of the nations involved. The reemerging nationalism and sensitive ethnic issues currently plaguing post–communist East European states alert us to the importance of utilizing such historical controversies.[1] The question of how anthropologists shall attempt a critical inquiry and assess the significance of the development of scholarly tension is a problem of tremendous significance, akin to the opening of an anthropological can of worms.[2] First it involves critical reassessments of the broadly defined anthropological discipline, its history and politically committed nature. It also asks us to reconsider the uses of sciences, both in nationalist ideologies and state interests. Clearly, these are at the heart of any discipline that takes itself seriously and relies on critical insights to advance and push its boundaries to their limits and beyond. Therefore, this chapter is about both the evolution of history concerning Hungarian nationalism and the scholarship of the evolution of Transylvania as a national terrain at the interstices of Hungarian and Romanian national identities. In order to proceed, a short historical introduction will illustrate Transylvania's sensitive place between two nation-states and an analysis will follow regarding the form and content of the scholarly negotiations, both in their national space and outside of it.

HISTORY, DEBATES, AND TRANSYLVANIA

At this point I touch upon those areas that figured most prominently in influencing twentieth-century Hungarian–Romanian controversy, eventually leading up to the rise of the state socialist contestable mechanism. Hungarian and Romanian nationalist historiograpy since the turn of the twentieth century has been a complex and much debated phenomenon. So distorted has its meaning become that even at the dawn of the third millennium, a bipartisan discussion on the matter between scholars and politicians of the two countries is a chimera. Katherine Verdery has nicely summarized this problem as follows: "Thus, in relations between Romania and Hungary, questions of territory and of political and economic reform became thoroughly knotted together with questions of history. Historiography was in effect the basic ground upon which those international relations were reproduced."[3] For this reason, it is of utmost importance to consider briefly the social, political, and economic conditions that helped create and further the Transylvanian conflict, to follow its rise and intensification and to examine its image and legacy.

As described in the previous chapter, scholars have debated at considerable length about how much Transylvania, similar to other eastern and southern parts of the Habsburg Empire, existed on the periphery of Europe.[4] Development and exploitation worked side by side: on the one hand, the influx of foreign capital helped create agro-industrialized states out of both Hungary and Romania; on the other hand, surplus and local goods were all taken away rather than allowing the buildup of advanced local conditions in Transylvania. During the period 1880–1920, industrial complexes started to draw agricultural laborers in great numbers who were searching for wage labor from the villages to the urban centers. With industrial expansion came the growth of an aggravated urban proletariat, an ethnically heterogeneous mixture with little or no power but with a growing awareness of its being. At times when economic production and consumption were on the upswing, workers and peasants were faced with higher prices and fluctuation in the labor force; when times were bad,

during economic crisis, widespread unemployment, a slump in agricultural prices, and growing social discontent inevitably followed. Such conditions led, in large measure, to agrarian and industrial unrest, for
instance, the 1904 peasant rebellion in the Transylvanian city of Alesd,
the 1907 peasant uprising in Bukovina and Moldavia, the "Storm Corner" peasant uprisings in the southern part of Hungary, and the workers'
strikes in the Jiu Valley in 1916 in Romania.[5]

The economic marginalization and its resulting climate, characteristic of the turn of the century in much of Eastern Europe, did little to help
Hungary and Romania solve their own problems and their relations to
each other.[6] Industrialization and the Habsburg political movement to
attain hegemony over the entire area of the empire were paralleled by
other factors as well. Cultural awakening, the discovering of the peasantry
by the intellectuals as the "only class" capable of retaining cultural patterns from the past, and the search for new artistic modes of expressions
were unmistakably heralding a new era in which Hungarians and Romanians were once again face-to-face as adversaries.[7] With the trembling of
the Austro-Hungarian Monarchy, nationalists tried to institute sociopolitical changes to promote one nationality group at the expense of the
other, for example, Hungarians rejoicing in the 1867 *Ausgleich* (The
Compromise), which allowed the unification of Transylvania and Austro-
Hungary, and instituted sweeping changes in the Transylvanian judiciary,
administrative, and educational system. Hungarianization was in full
swing.

This was the time when the aging Lajos Kossuth, leader of the
1848–1849 revolution and war, who was then living in Turkey, developed
his idea of the "Danube Confederacy." This was to be a system of unified
but independent confederations among the peoples of the Habsburg
Monarchy. His program, however, fell on deaf ears, both in Austro-Hungary and Romania. The awakening Romanian national intelligentsia were
not willing to compromise, either with the Kossuthian program or the
Hungarian aristocracy's forced assimilation attempts. In 1881, the newly
reorganized Romanian National Party of Transylvania united Romanians
on a common political platform in order to fight the Magyarization
process and regain Transylvania's autonomy from the Austro-Hungarian
dual monarchy. In 1882, associations such as *Carpati* in Bucharest and
Astra in Transylvania were formed to aid Transylvanian Romanians in
their liberation struggle. And, in 1891, perhaps the most important organization was founded, the *Liga Culturala* (The Culture League), with an
overt political propaganda, which included creating a new Romanian
state, one that would encompass Transylvania as well as Moldavia and
Wallachia.[8]

However, there were some exceptions to the rising nationalistic spirit, especially in progressive radical circles. Among the most noteworthy successes were the creation of the artistic, literary, and political movements of Transylvanism, chiefly among Hungarians, Ginderism among Romanians, and populist political parties for both nations, which added a new momentum and flavor to the existing nationalism and helped recreate new images of Hungarianness and Romanianness in a waning era filled with contradictory tensions and political conflict. The emerging artistic and populist movements of Transylvanism, *Erdélyi Fiatalok* (Transylvanian Youth) and *Tizenegyek* (The Eleven), were alike in that they attempted to form a new common consciousness along ethnic lines.[9] For example, their form of liberal populism, known as Transylvanism, was largely based on the slogan *közös múlt-közös sors* (common heritage—common fate), a phrase treating the past of both Romanians and Hungarians as unavoidable and common to both nations. Its strong intellectual current united Hungarian, Romanian, and Saxon scholars, artists, and writers in promoting a balanced relationship among the nationalities of Romania. These sympathetic views, unfortunately for the peoples of Transylvania, remained primarily outside of the actual controversy between Hungarian and Romanian politicians and nationalist leaders, who were more under the influence of extreme populist ideology and political territorial integrity. No doubt due to its intellectual scope and obstacles, Transylvanism as an innovative cultural and political agenda could not fully develop into a viable, interethnic program.

It should be emphasized that not all attempts to resolve these conflicts were hostile, homogeneous, and wholly without the understanding of the other's point of view. Some Romanians in Transylvania (i.e., the Hungarianized, upwardly mobile ones) were not in agreement with the Romanian nationalist political movement emanating from Bucharest. G. Moldován, a Romanian from Transylvania, declared: "I am a Transylvanian and a Romanian, a citizen of the Hungarian state and do not identify with the so-called youth of Bucharest."[10] He pointed out some of the differences in the cultural background and political aspirations of Romanians living in Transylvania and those of the Old Kingdom, citing a variety of regional and historical Romanian identities existing among groups he called "Vlach," "Kutsu-Vlach," "Arumun," Tsintari," "Moti," "Lippovan," and others. Other Transylvanian Romanian intellectuals, notably I. Nadejde, M. Gaster, and E. Huzmuzaki, also rejected the emerging popular notion of Daco-Roman theory, originally advanced by a few autodidactic Hungarians in the eighteenth century.[11]

Hungarian liberal circles also were aware of the rising form of populist nationalism (a topic treated in detail in subsequent chapters) and the burning problems of nationalities in the Dual Monarchy. Following the 1869 law on education, the Hungarian government began to support Hungarian language education, not only in Transylvania but in Bukovina as well, a step that outraged Romanian national leaders. In a questionable move, even the Hungarian government was even convinced that Hungarians in Bukovina—under constant attacks by the Romanian majority and facing overt hostilities—could only be saved by resettlement. In 1883, 4,000 Szeklers from Bukovia were transported closer to home, one of the first peacetime population transfers known to both countries.

Clearly, then, this was the period when population and territory were connected in the minds of both national elites. One of the most prominent Hungarian politicians at the turn of the century who fought for the rights of nationalities raising their voices against similar Magyarization attempts was Lajos Mocsáry. He exclaimed in 1888: "The only way Hungary can become a sovereign state is by creating a political consolidation based on a healthy relationship between the various nationality groups."[12] In harmony with Mocsáry's view were the Romanian Andrieu Sagune, fighting for the Transylvanian Romanians' rights and the Hungarian Oszkár Jászi's unique but Kossuthist vision of a Danube Confederacy, fashioned on the Swiss model by recognizing minority rights and cultural differences. Jászi advocated territorial autonomy for ethnic minorities and the termination of forced Magyarization and Magyar nationalism.[13]

Despite such attempts, twentieth-century relations between the two neighboring countries were fraught with similar suspicion, mistrust, and hostility. Therefore, it is even more ironic that at times the Hungarian and Romanian states were political allies. World War I was a turning point for both. The Paris Peace Settlements following World War I, when the Romanian kingdom received Transylvania and the Partium (roughly the present regions of Crisana, Maramures, and Salaj), are seen by Hungarians as the root of all current problems.[14] The "Tragedy of Trianon," as it is referred to by Hungarian patriots, continues to be misunderstood by both sides. To be sure, it was not an act of aggression by Romanians but more a mismanaged international decision by the Allied Powers, with no referendum about the wishes of the local populations.[15] Yet Romanian nationalists did manage to make the most of it: they achieved the unity of Great Romania.

The process of unification of these "Romanian ethnic" areas was long in the making. During World War I, as early as September 1914, Romania and Russia managed to sign a secret document. What concerns us here is the way in which territory and population became playing cards on the international tables. In that secret treaty, "Russia pledges to guarantee and defend the territorial integrity of Romania and recognizes Romania's right to the territories of Austria-Hungary inhabited by Romanians, in exchange for Romania's benevolent neutrality."[16] Two years later, a similar treaty of alliance was signed between Romania and France, Britain, Russia, and Italy. Here, "one of the conditions of Romania's entry into the war on the side of the Entente is the fulfillment of the desire for union with Romania of the territories of Austria-Hungary inhabited by Romanians."[17] In the month following the signing of the treaty, Romania declared war on Austro-Hungary, and in August 1916, Romanian royal troops entered Transylvania.

Romanian actions ensued in rapid succession. In the spring of 1917, a Romanian delegation arrived in Washington, informing the public and the government about Romania's claims for the "Romanian territories" of the Hungarian monarchy. In November 1918, more than 100,000 Romanians held a grand national assembly in the Transylvanian city Alba Iulia, where they unanimously declared the union of Transylvania with Romania. Surprising Hungarian politicians even more, in November 1918, at the Belgrade armistice between the Allies and Hungary, an arbitrary line of demarcation was fixed between Hungary and Transylvania. This act was of international significance, for it acknowledged the presence of the royalist Romanian army in Transylvania and the legal incorporation of Transylvania into the unified (Greater) Romania. When the Peace Treaty of Trianon was signed, on June 4, 1920, Romania—already a full-fledged, founding member of the League of Nations—was granted the legal cessation of Transylvania and the Partium, despite the Hungarian state's adamant efforts to stop the signing of the peace treaty.

The success of Romanian politicians at Trianon, a watershed event separating Hungary and the Hungarians from Transylvania, also was achieved partially because of the events that occurred in Hungary in 1918, the Bolshevik revolution and the Council of Soviet Republic, set up by Béla Kun and his followers, which took Hungary and the world by surprise. Neither the Allies nor the East European monarchist states were ready for another Bolshevik state in the heart of Europe.[18] Even though the leftist Hungarian regime of Béla Kun did not aim at reincorporating Transylvania into Hungary, the Bolshevik Hungarian state did not have a chance. Thus these transnational forces were tightly interrelated with the future status of Transylvania and the interrelationship between the Hungarian and Romanian states.

There is a tendency among Hungarian nationalists to interpret the Romanian intervention in suppressing the Bolshevik government in Hungary as an act of extreme nationalist aggression. Such interpretation neglects two key points: first, the support for the leftist regime in Hungary, albeit minimal, from the Romanian left,[19] and second, the determination of the fate of the revolutionary council by the extreme rightist Hungarian aristocracy, notably the politicians I. Bethlen, Gy. Károlyi, and Gy. Andrássy, who formed the Anti–Bolshevik Committee, requesting that Western powers speed up military actions against Bolshevik Hungary. Noteworthy is the fact, as Roger Brubaker reminds us, that the Transylvanian reactionary nobles assisted in the White Terror and suppression of Hungarian socialist attempts. For instance, Prince Bethlen, a member of one of the oldest aristocratic families in Transylvania, instigated the Romanian Royal Army's intervention in suppressing the Bolshevik Hungarian regime. This was a clear instance of class alignment prevailing over nationality or ethnic interests. Moreover, the German-speaking Schwabians of the Banat region and the Saxons of Transylvania also were not willing to sacrifice their secure and privileged economic dispositions granted in the Romanian kingdom. They did not, as a natural consequence, support Hungarian reunification with Transylvania, especially the uncertainty of their status in the newly formed proletarian dictatorship.[20]

FASCISM, IDENTITY, AND TERRITORIAL CONFLICTS

The end of the Great War brought the collapse of the Tsarist, Habsburg, and Ottoman empires and the creation of nation-states in East-Central Europe. These came together with military realignments of the borders. These moves, however, did not solve the problems of nationality conflicts and the congruent economic backwardness in much of the "successor states." As Henry Roberts, in his classic book *Rumania—Political Problems of an Agrarian State*, demonstrates, Romania, despite its gain of mineral-rich Transylvania, remained a poor agricultural state.[21] The agrarian reforms could not change the dismal situation of the peasants in Romania. As Roberts puts it, "Statistics on housing, disease, medical service, education, and illiteracy confirm the impression that the Rumanian peasant had one of the lowest standards of living in Europe."[22] Despite industrialization and increasing national productivity, as well as the influx of Western capital, Romania remained a predominantly agrarian country until the end of World War II. As we learn from the prolific Hungarian economic historians Ivan Berend and György Ránki, the situation in Hungary was only slightly better, but because of the territorial losses that Hungary incurred, progress had a different outlook and effect on the county and its population.[23] Industrial and technological progress supported Western capitalistic interests, especially in Nazi Germany, while the country as a whole felt the pressure of the world market in crisis. As a natural consequence, agricultural production suffered the greatest losses.

The conditions of workers and peasants had scarcely improved since the turn of the century. Wages were still beneath the level of increasing consumer prices. Inflation, stagnation, and the proletarianization of large masses of workers were inevitable. Strikes, demonstrations, and clashes with the police were everyday occurrences in both countries.[24]

With such economic marginalization and backwardness, nationalist and religious hostilities were common matters. With the consolidation of power by the ruling monarchist aristocracy, post–Trianon Hungary and Romania were once again nominal political allies. This, however, did nothing to lessen the hostilities with which the two regarded each other. Both states turned more nationalistic than ever before, and both looked toward the international power players, most notably the League of Nations—to the former, to the eventual return of the "lost" homeland, and to the latter, to continual justification to keep Great Romania undivided by thwarting off Hungarian separatist and irredentist sentiments. In their eagerness to live up to the expected level of nationalist dreams, both slowly progressed toward the ideal presented by Nazi Germany in the 1930s. In fact, an unprecedented exodus of Hungarians from Romania to Hungary followed: between 1918 and 1940, about 360,000 were repatriated to Hungary.[25] Among them were destitute agricultural laborers, disheartened aristocrats, disillusioned intellectuals, and workers and their families fleeing Romania in search of better opportunities in Hungary or, in some instances, overseas.

Increasing manyfold by the influx of Transylvanian refugees, the Hungarian aristocracy supported the nationalistic ideology of the Horthy regime. This ideology can be best summed up by quoting the popular irredentist slogan of the interwar period: *Nem nem soha* (No, no, never), meaning we shall never accept Transylvania to remain in Romanian hands. This nationalistic propaganda tried to divert attention from the social malaise plaguing Hungarian society at that time, and it openly championed the idea of Great Hungary. This move was no doubt facilitated by extreme Romanian state nationalism; in fact, it meant complete denationalization attempts of the Romanian government to create a homogeneous Greater Romanian nation-state. As hope for a peaceful solution waned, Hungarian nationalists became increasingly hostile and violent toward the successor states of Czechoslovakia, Yugoslavia, and Romania. Writers, historians, sociologists, and artists resorted to the most "noble cause" of convincing the society at large, as well as the international public, of the "injustice" and "suffering" meted out by Trianon on the Hungarian nation.

In order to gain more international recognition for this "just" cause, it is important to note that some Hungarian publications insisted that the turn-of-the-century interethnic situation in Transylvania under Hungarian rule was not as dire as Romanian works suggested. They cited as evidence, for instance, the number of Romanian religious institutions (1,525 Greek-Catholic and 2,571 Orthodox parishes), cultural activities (more than 113 singing societies), and economic security (150 banks and financial institutions) provided by the Hungarian state.[26] A Hungarian writer, Miklós Móricz, in citing the nationality statistics for 1910, argued that Romanians were not so helpless and exploited under the Austro-Hungarian Monarchy.[27] Implicit in his argument is of course the Hungarian nationalist ideology that Transylvania and all of its people would be better off under Hungarian rule than under the regimes of the Romanian kings Carol and Mihai. Even a village-level interethnic situation at that time, as Pál Binder has argued, was less hostile as Hungarian, Romanian, German, and Slavic speakers lived in relative harmony and peace in several multiethnic communities. To them, high-power politics was played out not only in Bucharest and Budapest but elsewhere in Vienna, London, and Paris.[28] The developing Transylvanian proletariat, a curious mixture of foreign migrant workers, also demonstrated that revisionist and irredentist ideology was not an inherent feature of its consciousness, demonstrating that class interests can, at times, take precedence over ethnic and religious conflict.[29] For this very reason, nationalists hoped that support was forthcoming, mostly from the peasantry. To them, this class experienced firsthand the crises of the world economy of the 1930s and the mistreatment by the semifeudalistic landed aristocracy, both in Romania and Hungary. They felt that when the time is right the peasantry will support popular resistance or even uprising in winning back Transylvania.

During the interwar period, however, peasant, or populist, politics was not allowed to be liberal or progressive. In this, the contestation over Transylvania took yet another dangerous turn. Despite their common fascist ideologies in the late 1930s and early 1940s, Romanian General Antonescu and the Hungarian leaders of Gömbös and Szálasi were in no closer agreement with regard to the fate of Transylvania.[30] At the beginning of World War II, when realignments were questioned and a tighter squeeze forced closer cooperation among the fascist allies, the partition of Transylvania was the top priority for both governments. From 1940 to 1944 (commonly referred to by older Hungarians in Transylvania as the "Magyar times"), borders were realigned as Hungary was awarded the northern part of Transylvania, while Romania kept the smaller, southern part. That fateful Second Vienna Award was signed on August 30, 1940, under the watchful eyes of Nazi Germany, and (if we can believe history) the Romanian minister of foreign affairs, Mihail Manoilescu, who led the Romanian delegation, fainted on the spot when he heard the decision

FIGURE 2.1   Following the Second Vienna Award, the Hungarian army entered Transylvania. Hungarian soldiers and denizens in the village of Jebuc, Romania on September 15, 1940. (Author's collection.)

announced.[31] This border shift placed over 2.5 million under Hungarian rule (of whom 1 million were Romanian), while about a half-million Hungarians remained in Romanian sectors.[32] Obviously this radical solution of the "contested terrain" did not end but furthered the problem of ethnic conflict and nationalist controversy over borders in the area. Right after Trianon, new population transfers occurred: about 200,000 Romanians left Hungarian Transylvania and took refuge in Romania, and about the same number of Hungarians left Romanian Transylvania and moved to the Hungarian sector.[33]

The four years of Hungarian rule in Transylvania and the era that followed may be counted among the most dismal in the two states' twentieth-century history. Throughout Transylvania, while Hungarians celebrated the unity of their country and nation, Romanians took to the streets demanding possession of the lost territories. To save his throne, King Carol II of Romania appointed General Antonescu as prime minister, a move that resulted in his abdication on September 6, 1940. With that political change over, Romania was handed to the Iron Guard and became Germany's solid and willing satellite. Well-documented cases and eyewitness accounts demonstrate the unjust treatment committed by both sides in these years.[34] The Hungarian army and especially the notorious gendarmerie (csendőrség), driven by the zeal and official propaganda of the extremist Imrédy, Lakatos, and Szálasi governments, were far from sympathetic to Romanians, treating them quite cruelly.[35] Some Romanian historians tried to turn these unfortunate events into a genocidal Hungarian master plan. "The aim stubbornly pursued all the time through assault, torture, and maltreatment was to annihilate Romanians and drive them out of Transylvania," wrote one Romanian historian.[36] For their part, Hungarians continuously condemn the actions of the Iron Guard of the late 1930s and 1940s, the anti-Hungarian policy of the Antonescu regime, and especially the actions of the Maniu commandos who killed thousands of Hungarians, shipped them to prisons, and tortured many.[37] In this tense historical controversy, both blame the others for the extermination of Jewish populations in Transylvania.[38] Few historical periods have been so gravely misunderstood as that of fascism in Hungary and Romania, specifically the military maneuvers during the period 1940–1944 in Transylvania. Regrettably, the overideologized historical climate and mismanaged political milieu contribute little to the development of a more neutral historical research required to assess this complex issue in the fashion that it deserves.[39]

In 1944, Transylvania became a hotly contested border region in another way, as the Soviet army advanced into the region, treating it as a form of payment for both the Hungarian and Romanian regimes to be "awarded" in return for military assistance. Further, it is noteworthy that in his secret discussions with the Soviets concerning Hungary's fate after the war, Admiral Miklós Horthy was reassured that if Hungary were to break with Nazi Germany, it would be granted Transylvania. It is the irony of history that this promise was of course also the "gift" the Nazis promised Horthy if Germany won the war. However, on August 23, 1944, Romania changed sides and became an ally of the Soviet Union, while Hungary remained fascist until the last moment. This turn of events finally sealed Transylvania's fate.

At the subsequent peace settlements at Potsdam and Yalta, and later at Helsinki, the inviolability of European borders was reiterated and the issue of noninterference into internal matters was legalized. Romanian communist leader Petru Groza emphatically stressed that as far as Transylvania was concerned "the border question is a secondary matter to be settled between the two nations; the real goal is to strengthen democracy for the peaceful coexistence of the Danubian states."[40] This act alone guaranteed continuous Romanian rule over Transylvania, officially sanctioned by Moscow and ratified at the Peace Treaty of Paris in January

1947. With the Bukovinian Szeklers settled in Hungary and given the land and houses of ethnic Germans who were expatriated to Germany, and with the Peace Treaty documents signed, the border question between Hungary and Romania was settled. With these (mostly forceful) population exchanges and coerced territorial settlements, a new era opened in the relations of the two neighboring states, but with that, new problems surfaced.[41]

STATE SOCIALISM AND THE TRANSYLVANIAN CONFLICT

It soon became obvious, however, that the nationalistic controversy over Transylvania and the situation of the coinhabiting minorities—a new phrase invented by the socialist regime—could not be solved overnight and that the contest over this terrain would continue. The coming of age of socialism in Eastern Europe resulted yet again in the realignment of Hungary with Romania and another overcharged territorial dispute. Nevertheless, it grew gradually clear that the original promise of Marxism–Leninism—namely the cessation of antagonism between nations and the replacement of nationalism with international-ism—was not in the offing.[42] These longtime adversaries agreed, under Soviet rule, to adopt Marxist–Leninist principles, to join the Council for Mutual Economic and Cooperation (COMECON) and the Warsaw Pact, and to sign agreements for mutual assistance, fraternal love, and peaceful coexistence among the friendly socialist states. However, Transylvania and the question of ethnic Hungarian and German minorities in Romania still remained a sensitive issue for the governments involved. Though obviously uneasy, the relationship between Hungary and the first Romanian government, whose leader was the populist Petru Groza and whose government was composed of Moscow-trained communists of different ethnic backgrounds, was relatively amicable.

The period 1945–1948 of communist rule in Romania saw considerable improvement in the treatment of ethnic minorities in exchange for the settling of state and national borders. The young socialist Romanian state was quite aware of the fact that by far the most serious and perhaps the most troubling problem remained the question of Transylvanian Hungarians. For the time being, and in comparison to the realities of the German and Hungarian minorities of Czechoslovakia, both facing forced evacuations and mistreatment by the regimes in power, the Hungarians in Romania were relatively well off.[43] "Equal" treatment of ethnic groups was legally guaranteed by the Romanian socialist constitution in which minority education and native language publication was respected. The overall political atmosphere of rebuilding warn-torn Romania also fostered a healthy milieu among Hungarians, Romanians, and other ethnic populations.

Yet the governments of Petru Groza, Gheorge Gheorgiu-Dej, and Nicolae Ceauşescu, had apparently done little in thirty years to ease interethnic tension and resolve the uneasy situation of the minority in Romania. During the late 1940s, the only legally recognized Hungarian organization, the Hungarian People's Federation, was relegated to a puppet organization of the Communist Party, as its leaders were jailed on trumped-up charges. The 1952 administrative law reorganized the country into eighteen territorial units (*judet*, county) and perhaps to keep interethnic tensions from surfacing created an Autonomous Magyar Region (AMR) by uniting the formerly Szekler-dominated pre-war counties. Geographer Ronald A. Henlin viewed this geopolitical situation in the following way:

> Modeled closely along the lines of the autonomous oblasts in the USSR, this Autonomous Magyar Region (AMR) became both a symbol of Rumanian [*sic*] faith in the relevance of Stalinist nationality and a vehicle for placating the traditional hostility of Transylvania's Magyars toward rule from Bucuresti and toward Rumanians in general. Communist ideologists may have hoped, also, that it would help convince the outside world that Rumania's minorities were implementing socialism of their own free will.[44]

Even though Magyar could be used as a second language in local administrative matters, this was not a democratic regionalist solution for Romania's troubled relationship with the Hungarians in Transylvania. In 1960, the Autonomous Magyar Region had already received new boundaries and a political-territorial redefinition, with two important consequences: "(1) it divided administratively the largest node or compact Magyar settlement in Transylvania; and (2) it reduced from 77 to 62 percent the Magyar majority in the Region's population."[45] The fact that it was renamed with a Romanian prefix, as the "Mures-Magyar Autonomous Region," and now with less of a percentage of Hungarian minority inhabitants, clearly indicates that Romania's reorganization and political economic restructuring were dictated more and more by nationalistic concerns. Even though this showpiece of cultural autonomy was hailed as a victory of socialist nationality policy, in other regions the regime slowly embarked upon its course of full-scale Romanianization. In 1959, the fusing of the Bolyai University in Cluj (and renaming it as Babes-Bolyai University, thereby taking away its original autonomy and Hungarian character) was a fatal blow to Hungarian identity and fuel for the growing Hungarian minority nationalism. Teachers were jailed, and many found a way out by committing suicide in the 1950s. After the 1956 revolution of Hungary, thousands of Hungarian leaders and cultural workers in Romania were jailed and harassed by the Romanian secret police. At the same time, the Romanian Communist Party agreed to the Soviet plan to secretly jail members of the revolutionary government of Imre Nagy, who found temporary refuge in Romania in 1957. It is clear that Nagy and his comrades believed in the "goodwill" of the Romanians and returned—after much pressure from both governments—to Hungary, a fatal mistake costing him his life.[46] This faithful Muscovite stance of the Romanian government had stabilized Hungarian–Romanian relations until 1968, when Ceauşescu began to create his own distorted policies concerning national identity and majority-minority relations.

In the Ceauşescu Era ("Epoca Ceauşescu"), the Romanian regime had attempted to view all of those living in Romania as citizens. According to official pronouncements, all, regardless of nationality, religious background, or language, were "united" in the goal of building the future communist state of Romania. Slogans such as "Ceauşescu Eroism, Romania Communism" (Ceauşescu heroism, Romania communism) and "Ceauşescu şi poporul, Patria şi Tricolorul" (Ceauşescu and the people, Romania tricolored) abounded in Romania, echoing the regime's wish to create a Romanian nation out of the country's millions of minorities. In *Nations and States*, Hugh Seton-Watson raised the important point that in the nineteenth century, nation-states legitimized themselves through the policy of "official nationalism," often with the assistance of invented national traditions.[47] This was the course that the Ceauşescu regime inherited from its pre-World War II predecessors: full-scale Romanianization, lack of democratic principles, and a complete denial of the territorial question with regard to Hungarian minority autonomy.

Ceauşescu's views regarding the role of ethnic groups were clear from the beginning. In his words, "All of us—Romanians, Magyars, Germans, and people of other nationalities—have the same destiny, the same aspirations—the building of communism in our homeland, and we are determined in full unity to ensure the implementation of this ideal."[48] These smug words notwithstanding, the situation of Romania and its ethnic groups continued to worsen considerably; their status had changed from "minority" and "nationality" to "Romanians of [a] different mother tongue." That the gap between the Hungarians and the regime was never as wide as it was in those years was clear from the popular retitling of Romania as "Ceauswitz."

In fact, reality bore little resemblance to official propaganda. In spite of the extremely difficult socioeconomic conditions and dogmatic political rhetoric facing the peoples of Romania, an increasing moral and social resistance to governmental pressures developed in the early 1980s. Among Hungarians in Transylvania, this resistance and this ethnic revivalism were reflected in various forms of political acts—from underground publications (called *samizdat*) to defections—but they were manifested most clearly in the notion of what Ardener called the "counterspecification," or the awakening, of a new, contestable minority national identity. German-speaking minorities, for example, left Romania in search of a better life in their motherland (in German the *Heimat*), specifically, West Germany, Austria, and to a lesser extent, the then-functioning German Democratic Republic. Many took advantage of the family reunification programs and the West German state's policy of "buying them out," and they left Romania in great numbers.[49] Hungarians were either trying to do likewise, or managed to remain indifferent to the goals of the Romanian regime. For Hungarians, always looking toward the "mother country" of Hungary was the only hope, since Romanian citizenship was meaningless. Their cultural awareness and measure of ethnic identity were strongly influenced by the nationalistic sentiments emanating from Hungary and western Hungarian émigré circles, a situation discussed later in more detail.

In 1968, the year of abolition of the "Mures-Magyar Autonomous Region" and replacement of Hungarian grade schools with Romanian ones was a major blow to Hungarians. All of these anti-minority actions fell on deaf ears in Western circles, for Romania was increasingly considered a "maverick" among the East European states until the early 1980s. The basis for this privileged status came because of its policies of rapid industrialization and the development of an eccentric and at times even anti-Soviet stand. However, it was clear that by the late 1970s, Romania's situation had deteriorated considerably.[50] The program of *sistematizare* (systematization),[51] the socioeconomic reorganization of the country by creating urban centers and huge agro-industrial complexes, which, as was planned, would result in the rapid growth of the standard of living of all Romanians, backfired. Although the forced developmental policies helped reduce Romania's foreign debt, they created unrealistic target plans, inflation, food and energy shortages, rising consumer prices, a dislocation of huge masses of laborers, questionable social and pronatalist policies, and unforeseen consequences in the situation and political mobilization of the country's minorities.[52] Trying to combat these, the Romanian state became even more nationalistic and antagonistic toward minorities. It managed to establish de facto policies of forced assimilation and the Romanianization of Hungarian and other minorities, while at the

same time it allowed the German-speaking minority to emigrate in growing numbers. The condition was that the Federal Republic of German
was willing to pay for them, a policy similar to solving the Jewish emigration to Israel.[53]

At the same time, Hungarian ethnic institutions, publishers,
churches, schools, and ethnic broadcasters were all subjected to the same
pressure of forced assimilation policies since Ceauşescu stepped up his
Romanianization policies.[54] As the Romanian state became more and
more serious in its attempt at creating a homogeneous Romanian nation,
it abolished, for example, the Hungarian television station in 1985, and
the number of Hungarian language publications was decreased at an
alarmingly rapid pace. Some of the most obvious cases were made public
by writers, human rights organizations, and Western newspapers.[55] The
fact was that for Hungarians in Romania, as well as those living in Hungary and in the West, the trauma of forced Romanianization was becoming increasingly unbearable.[56] That the tensions were mounting was easy
to see then, but from the way the interethnic situation was worsening, no
one could tell just how far the Ceauşescu regime would go to force Hungarians to give up their identity and culture.

Scholarly Debates over Transylvania

Ceauşescu's rule was indeed the time when a debate also ensued
among anthropologists in the United States. Prompted by the writings of
Hungarian ethnographers and Transylvanian refugees in Hungary, the
émigré anthropologist Michael Sozan offered a damning critique about
the Romanianization efforts of the Ceauşescu regime in the journal *Current Anthropology.* A polemic ensued immediately by American anthropologists who, unlike Sozan, conducted fieldwork in Romania.[57] The
specifics of this debate do not concern us here, for the impact on the
Transylvanian issue as it affected that region was minimal. However, the
disputes between Hungarian and Romanian scholars of the time are especially relevant.

Unlike the *Current Anthropology* debate, the historical aspects of the
political and scholarly confrontation over the terrain of Transylvania
between Hungarians and Romanians during socialism touched upon several important sets of problems.[58] One of the historical controversies
ignited, and an attempt made by Romanian protagonists to justify the
incorporation of Transylvania into the Romanian nation-state, was by
proving that present-day Romanians are descendants of the historical
Dacians, Geto-Romans, and Romans. The second concerns Hungarian

attempts to justify the Hungarian presence in Transylvania. Hungarian scholars aim to prove that at the time the various Hungarian tribes entered the Carpathian Basin—referred to as the period of Conquest, roughly between 800–1000 A.D.—no Daco-Roman or Romanian populations in Transylvania were found, thus Hungarians justly occupied an empty territory. Since bones, stirrups, and ruins cannot speak for themselves, Romanian and Hungarian linguists, archaeologists, folklorists, ethnographers, intellectuals, and politicians have spoken for them. In this way, they reproduce a nationalist mission that, in the words of historian John Campbell, amounts to nothing but a "barren historical controversy,"[59] with no real solutions to current problems and issues of ethnic tension.

The hallmark of most scholarly negotiated nationalism, and in this case the Hungarian and Romanian contestation is no exception, is historical determinism and essentialism. During state socialism, notions of the Daco-Roman continuity on the Romanian side and Hungarian ethnogenesis on the Hungarian side were "supported" by incessantly fabricating new sets of "scientific" data. No wonder that these were supported by Marxist–Leninist interpretations of historical, linguistic, and archaeological "facts," all amounting to Romanian and Hungarian claims of "rights" and "cultural heritage." According to the Romanian official version, Transylvania, known to the ancient Romans as Dacia, was the original homeland of the Romanian people for more than 2,000 years. Some specialists even went so far to suggest that this state "myth" of Daco-Roman continuity is indeed a central aspect of the Romanian national ideology,[60] thus reinforcing the unity and territorial rights of the Romanian state over Transylvania.[61]

One of the most crystalized versions of the Romanian view was published by scientists in *The History of the Rumanian People*. All authors accepted the ethnogenesis of the Romanians from the time of the Dacian tribes, a claim documented by referring to the heroic deeds of the historical figure of Burebista, the Dacian king.[62] Burebista and his descendants are taken by Romanian nationalists to be the true progenitors of the Romanian nation. Similarly, authors of *Relations between the Autochtonous Populations* argue that some Romanians following in Burebista's footsteps simply migrated back and forth between Wallachia and their other original homeland of Transylvania, accounting for the preponderance of historical records of Wallachians in medieval sources.[63] Such an imaginary history became political claim when it was endorsed officially by no less of a source than General Ilie Ceauşescu, brother of President Ceauşescu.[64] In 1984, this military officer even published a treatise, pointing out that, "The archeological evidence conclusively shows the uninterrupted ethnic, political, and military continuity of the Romanians."[65] That the country's president and his brother, the first military leader of Romania, endorsed the official history of the nation is telling regarding the extent to which the Romanian regime endorsed and reinforced a specific nationalist view of historical scholarship and elevated this myth in legitimating official state policies. Stephen Fisher-Galati correctly pointed this out when he wrote, "The reinforcement of these myths through the refining and redefining of the character of Romanian nationalism merely adds chapters to Romanian historical mythology."[66]

To counter Hungarian critics, Romanian scholars invented their version for the Magyar intrusion into the Carpathian Basin in the tenth century as no more than a "barbarian" and "ruthless invasion" against the Daco-Roman indigenous tribes inhabiting Transylvania at that time. They have even ascribed the dates of the Magyar "conquest" and its subsequent population of Transylvania in 896 A.D. and the following centuries. This attribution was substantiated by the presence of royal chronicles describing the administration of land to faithful vassals and borderguards (the Szeklers) as fiefs.[67]

Romanian historians, as pointed out by adversary Hungarian historians, have continually used the Hungarian *Gesta* of the thirteenth century uncritically as their primary source to reflect back on what happened a few hundred years earlier.[68] In short, this historical stance on the first settlement of Transylvania by Daco-Romans, and its uninterrupted habitation, has continually served the Romanian regimes in their attempts to legitimize their nationalistic propaganda aimed at justifying Romania's historic rights to possess Transylvania. French historian Rene Ristelhueber, for instance, frames this controversy as follows:

> The Roman province established on the ruins of the kingdom of Decebal included mountainous Transylvania. This explains and possibly justifies Rumanian claims to a region also contested by the Hungarians. . . . This is the origin of an interminable dispute in which ethnic arguments conceal political claims.[69]

Not only was the French historian correct on this point, interestingly enough Hungarian protagonists have been adopting a remarkably similar line of reasoning. It is not coincidental, however, that they too rely on equally nationalistic historical determinism. For a long time, the "Turanian" or Central Asiatic origin myth served as a legitimate state ideology in Hungary. This myth is an equally blurred concept, a curious mixture of dubious facts and concocted fiction to prove that the Hungarian tribes of the period of Conquest are descendants of the Scythian and Hunnish warrior tribes, actually predating 896 A.D.[70] What an essential part of this argument relates is the myth of Transylvania as a remote, historical Hungarian border region, which assumes that the Szeklers, settling in the mountainous part of eastern Transylvania, possess various myths about their ethnogenesis that tell stories about the Hunn incursion into the Carpathian Basin, predating the Magyar conquest of the ninth century. While the "Turanian" hypothesis does not figure prominently in current Hungarian historiography (except among extreme nationalistic and right-wing circles), the Hungarian conquest of Transylvania and its settlement by Hungarian tribes are central issues, with the added touch that the various Szekler populations settled Transylvania before that conquest. This way, not only the Szeklers receive a special place in Hungarian nationalist mythology but Transylvania as an ancestral terrain is also connected to Hungarian ethnogenesis. Thus, Transylvania and Hungarian ethnicity is fundamentally interconnected in the Hungarian scholarly and popular consciousness. What Gail Kligman observes with regard to the significance of the Transylvanian region of Maramures to Romanian national identity is equally true for the Hungarian official view—that the particularities of geographic location, its "archaic" and "ancient" traditions, serve "the interests of the state in its claims for political and territorial legitimacy."[71]

This scholarly controversy over gaining supremacy over Transylvania's mythical past acquired a new momentum when the Hungarian Academy of Sciences commissioned the writing of the three-volume *History of Transylvania* (*Erdély Története*).[72] Published in 1986, this book was an instant success, thanks, no doubt, to the official air surrounding its publicity. It also received the blessing from the Hungarian regime and its highest official body, the Academy of Sciences. Because the bookstore shelves were rapidly emptied, despite the exorbitant price at that time, the set was republished in 1987. This ambitious undertaking took more than ten years to complete—its origin actually dates back to the 1960s, after the four-volume *History of Romania* was published by the Romanian establishment—and has been hailed by many historians as a milestone in East-Central European historiography. Yet no one was ready for the ensuing controversy, for this publication ignited entirely new debates, resulting in a renewed transnational scholarly quarrel of intensified proportions from both sides of the question.

Romanian scholars lost no time in attacking the publication, raising their voices against the "unscientific" and "nationalistic" claims of the Hungarian writers. A one-page advertisement appeared in the *London Times*, on April 7, 1987—just two months after Ceauşescu gave his tirade against these forgeries—by C. Marino from Athens. It called the *History of Transylvania* a "conscious forgery under the aegis of the Hungarian Academy of Sciences." In the same month, articles appeared in various journals in Romania, followed by an English version in the *Romanian Review* under the same title and signed by three Romanian historians.[73] It is likely that the London *Times* article was commissioned by official circles in Romania, for the tone and content of both are very close to each other. Nevertheless, to my knowledge, this was the first such public stand on the debate in a Western newspaper by Romanians. This move might well have been learned from the example of the Hungarian émigré group, the Committee for Human Rights in Rumania, which published an advertisement in the *New York Times* a decade earlier, condemning the mistreatment of ethnic Hungarians in Romania, a topic that will be dealt with later in more detail.[74]

HISTORIES AND MYTHS
OF THE NATIONAL HOMELAND

The Hungarian position on the Romanian Daco-Roman continuity and Magyar conquest is straight from the pages of the *History of Transylvania* and the subsequent "explanatory" volume, *Studies in the History of Transylvania.*[75] For centuries, Hungarians also have argued that Transylvania is their own having arrived there first. As their claim goes, Romanians are latecomers to Transylvania, since they migrated from their original homeland in Wallachia (the *Regat*) and the Southern Balkans only in the thirteenth century and afterward. Just as Romanian archaeologists interpreted artifacts of the historic Dridu culture in the region of Maramures as being Romanian (Daco-Roman) in origin,[76] so too have Hungarians seen specific elements of Hungarian culture in the archaeological assemblages dating from the period of Conquest in Transylvania.[77]

Based on historical interpretations of medieval sources, archaeological analyses, and linguistic and geographical-etymological studies, authors of the *History of Transylvania* dismiss the theory of Daco-Roman longevity and continuity. Briefly, the Hungarian argument proceeds as follows: The Roman general, Aurelianus (270–275 A.D.), withdrew all Roman legions from Dacia, and the settlers were repatriated to Moesia, leaving historic Transylvania empty. What proves this beyond a shadow of a doubt is that all Dacian cemeteries used until the end of the third century A.D. were abandoned and showed no signs of later burial practices. The sole exception to this was the Romula-Malva settlement in Dacia

Inferior, along the rivers Danube and Olt. As far as the presence of Dacians, Hungarian historians adamantly argue that no early medieval written sources mention an original Dacian population inhabiting Transylvania after 270 A.D. They use etymologial research to point out that no original Roman or Dacian geographical names remained in Transylvania—those used since the 1920s were fabrications and additions by the Romanian state. Instead, between the fourth and seventh centuries, the Gepidea, Goths, Huns, Avars, and Slavs populated the area, a migration indicated by the availability of archaeological assemblages. During the fourth to eighth century A.D. period, the Avars and Slavs lived side by side, as shown in such places named the river Küküllő (of Avar-Turkic origin, still used by the Hungarians), whose Slavic name is Tirnava (still used by Romanians). Finally, in the ninth century, Magyar tribes arrived and populated the Carpathian basin, including Transylvania, with Saxon migrants arriving in the twelfth century. Following this, a large-scale mass migration of Romanians occurred in the thirteenth century into Transylvania, as a direct result of the Tatar invasion, from their original homeland in Wallachia (terra Olacorum, Silva Blacorum) and the Balkan Peninsula.

No doubt, these attempts to debunk the Daco-Roman myth of the Ceauşescu-manipulated Romanian nationalism were anchored in the concept of Hungarian primacy over historic Transylvania. This region was, to be sure, remote in both time and space but extremely close to the hearts of Hungarians, and at the same time it claimed historical justification for subsequent events on the Hungarian side.

Interpretations of later centuries of Transylvanian history also have been clouded by similar emotional reactions on both sides. During the height of Ceauşescu's official nationalism, Romanian historians continued to view the *Supplex Libellus Valachorum* of 1791 as a popular call in claiming their original land. This manifesto of awakening Romanian national consciousness claimed equal rights with the three privileged *nationes* of the Saxons, Magyar nobles, and Szeklers.[78] Taken with the existence of the unified areas of Wallachia, Moldavia, and Transylvania in the summer of 1600 by Michael the Brave (Mihai Viteazul), these historic events are highlights of Romanian historiography.[79] Surely the dismal feudal conditions that characterized Transylvania and much of East-Central Europe in the eighteenth and nineteenth centuries gave plenty of reasons for peasant rebellion and social turmoil among the lower classes, especially Romanian serfs.[80] The Horia, Closca, and Crisan peasant rebellion in 1784 is just another illustrious example for the appropriation of history for nationalistic gains. Originally triggered by the imperial decree allowing Romanian serfs to become border guards but later turning into universal peasant demands of abolishing serfdom and allocating land to disenchanted Romanian peasants, this uprising has been magnified out of proportion in current Romanian politics in Transylvania. Sculptures of these peasant heroes were erected in the early 1990s by eager Romanian politicians. While Hungarian historians see this rebellion in class terms (i.e., as a genuine peasant revolt against the feudal aristocracy), Romanian historians interpret it in terms of interethnic conflict per se, in fact, as a victorious uprising against Hungarian nationalist landlords.[81]

Nationalistic sentiments in Ceauşescu's Romania and in Kádár's Hungary forced Hungarian and Romanian scholars to take extreme sides over the 1848–1849 War of Independence. Originally hailed by both Marx and Engels as the "Springtime of the Peoples," this event was slowly transformed by the two sides from a genuine expression of revolutionary spirit to a nationalistic warfare. However, as we know, both Marx and Engels were wrong: the Magyars were not set free to have a "bloody revenge on the Slav barbarians," and the reactionary classes while dynasties disappeared from the face of the earth.[82] Romanians joined the Hungarian revolutionaries only for a short time in 1848. As historian J. H. Jensen has argued:

> In fact the whole thrust of Romanian propaganda was towards its acceptance as one of the "received nations" of Transylvania, so that Uniate Romanians (and specifically the elite among them) could share in the privileges enjoyed by the other good subjects of the conservative bureaucratic Habsburg state.[83]

It was soon clear that the demands presented by the rebellious youths to the Habsburg house had meaning only to the Hungarians fostering a nationalistic spirit, which left large masses of ethnic groups outside of the political arena. As a natural consequence, the Hungarian army found itself fighting against Czech, Slovak, Serb, Croatian, Romanian, tsarist, and Austrian forces in no time. With such an insurmountable army, the Hungarian revolution was bound to fail.[84]

Hungarian nationalists, both then and now, understand these as actions of awakening anti-Hungarian nationalism among ethnic minorities living within the borders of the Habsburg Empire. It is a strange twist of irony that while the period 1848–1849 represented the "Springtime of the Peoples" for the Germans, Poles, and Hungarians— the revolutionary standard-bearers of progress in Engels' mind—for the smaller nationalities of the Habsburg Empire, the "Springtime of the Peoples" was yet to come. Interestingly enough, for both Hungarians and Romanians, the independence and unification of their national territories were primary components in their emerging national consciousness. Both groups attempted to realize these dreams during the period 1848–1849, which had seen the bloodiest confrontations between Hungarians and Romania in Transylvania. Many national heroes were immortalized from these clashes—Pál Vasvári, József Bem, and Gábor Áron for the Hungarians, and Avram Iancu and Nicolae Bălcescu for the Romanians. The horrors committed by both the regular army units and peasant insurrectionists also were elevated into nationalist myths through the media, literature, and especially the nationalist school curricula.[85]

The beginning of the twentieth century saw the creation of modern nation-states in East-Central Europe for all of these nationalities, but not without some major sacrifices.[86] The history of the Hungarian and Romanian controversy contesting the terrain of Transylvania as it developed in the twentieth century, and highly ideologized during state socialism, is instructive for many reasons. For one, it highlights the fact that border regions may become highly politically charged zones of nationalistic controversies. The actual realignment of state borders went hand in hand with the nationalistic drives of both the Romanian and Hungarian elites. The situation of Transylvania, either as part of Romania after 1918 or Hungary during the period 1940–1944, reveals that when military confrontations subsume and states resume diplomatic relations, territorial controversies do not wither away but assume newer forms. One such form, as shown above, has been played out not in direct political confrontation but in intellectual and academic contexts between scholars and statesmen. This contestation, moreover, illustrates the ways in which states and contending elites relate to one another through political hegemony and cultural ideology. This ideology calls attention to the fact that despite the implementation of a common political system and rhetoric— as was the case during fascism and socialism—nationalist controversies and territorial and interethnic confrontations create their own momentum. At times they may take on a life of their own and may not necessarily follow central state directives but may sometime override them. It would be too easy and incorrect to dismiss this historical controversy as resulting from the overt Marxist–Leninist ideological disposition of state socialist regimes. It is clear that these controversies have been ongoing, not only in state socialism but, equally viciously, both before and after as well. As Stephen Fischer-Galati has argued for Moscow, the controversy over Transylvania was more of a blessing than a curse. For it "has been instrumental in the attainment of the Russian goal, as laid down by tsars and restated by the Comintern and the Kremlin, of securing hegemony in

Eastern Europe."[87] This historical and scholarly debate points to another important issue: that contending national elites work, as most elites do, not in isolation—though nationalist ideology is rather introverted in many respects—but within a much larger political climate, transgressing state and national borders. What this really entails is the notion that there are powerful nationalist forces operating outside of the immediate confinement of nation-state politics, exerting considerable pressures on the scholarly community, a theme that will be investigated thoroughly later. Just how this really works may easily be witnessed by the scholarly treaties published outside of Hungary and Romania *after* the collapse of state socialism.[88]

Finally, this chapter has dealt with a specific historical aspect of territorial conflict between Hungary and Romania. What we have to understand now is how national elites become socialized and united in a common ideological framework to contribute to such nationalistic controversies. In other words, in the following chapters, important social undercurrents will be described that favored the rejuvenation of negotiation and contest over Transylvania, its cultures, and its peoples. Specifically, the development of Hungarian populist ideology, and its content and heritage will be examined in subsequent chapters as an important aspect of nationalistic mythologizing. Moreover, I also will analyze the way in which various ethnographers, folklorists, and other scholars have contributed to the fashioning of Transylvania as a remote border culture and how this terrain has contributed to the making of Hungarian national identity. In order to proceed, however, the next chapter will first detail personal fieldwork experiences in Hungarian communities, both in Hungary and Romania.

Chapter 3

Fieldwork on Nationalism: Transylvania in the Ethnographic Imagination

This chapter will provide a retrospective analysis of anthropological fieldwork in Hungarian communities in Hungary and Romania. In the retrospective aspect, I deal with my fieldwork experiences and analyze how possibilities have changed in these two countries. My concluding discussion will suggest some of the important research and theoretical questions facing former communist (East Bloc) cultures to which we, as anthropologists and field-workers, should pay closer attention as we embark upon constructing them both in reality and into texts.[1] By establishing the similarities and differences of conducting fieldwork in nationalist movements in socialist and post–socialist Hungarian communities, I argue that the sociocultural context of the transition in East-Central Europe needs to be problematized differently than in previous times. More open systems now call for renewed ethnographic concerns than before. Earlier theories and fieldwork methods under state socialism may no longer be adequate for studying the post–socialist period of the 1990s,

This chapter is a revised and an expanded version of a paper originally prepared for a seminar entitled "The Anthropology of Post–Communism" at the Nordic Anthropology Conference, Department of Social Anthropology, University of Bergen, Norway, and also presented on September 13, 1997, at the ERCOMER Barcelona Summer School in May 1998. I would like to thank the organizers for inviting me, as well as the participants, and for their courteous hospitality and challenging discussion, from which I have benefited a great deal. An earlier and a slightly different version was published in "Cameras and Other Gadgets: Reflections on Fieldwork Experiences in Socialist and Post-Socialist Hungarian Communities," *Social Anthropology* 7, no. 2 (1999): 169–87.

a notion that emerges in many of the anthropological studies published since the mid-1990s.[2] One of the most serious questions to answer is whether earlier anthropological practices can now be accepted without serious critical revision of their foundations and backdrops. In order to clarify this, I provide—from a particular "native anthropologist" perspective—a comparative retrospective analysis of my own fieldwork before and after socialism in Hungary, and in Transylvanian Hungarian communities in Romania.

Anthropologists learn much about the need for fieldwork from classic studies by E. E. Evans-Pritchard and P. Rabinow regarding nature and structure and the way in which data gained from firsthand experiences must coexist with theoretical concerns.[3] What Evans-Pritchard noted in his short essay on fieldwork in the Sudan in the 1920s is still paramount today. For him it was essential "that we record what were the material, physical circumstances in which the fieldworker of the past conducted his research, because these circumstances surely have to be taken into account in evaluating its results and assessing their significance."[4] In fact, what Edmund Leach has suggested concerning fieldwork is even more true regarding the realities of anthropological circumstances under communism. Leach writes, "The essential core of social anthropology is fieldwork—the understanding of the way of life of a single particular people." He then goes on to emphasize that, "This fieldwork is an extremely personal traumatic kind of experience and the personal involvement of the anthropologist in his work is reflected in what he produces."[5] This "traumatic experience is even more punctuated when we take into consideration what Kirsten Hastrup has pointed out so correctly, that "Fieldwork is situated between autobiography and anthropology. It connects an important personal experience with a general field of knowledge."[6] Fieldwork is about crossing both borders and boundaries. One, however, looks in vain for the disclosure of these experiences in the anthropology of Eastern Europe, a reason I wish to stress this in this chapter with regard to the nationalist ideology concerning Hungarianness and the Hungarian nation, specifically the Transylvanian issue.

Theory and fieldwork practice are oxymoronic terms, especially when discussed in relation to personal experiences in the former Soviet Bloc countries. Little has been published concerning the fieldwork experiences of Western anthropologists in the East, especially on the border crossings.[7] Therefore, the personal experiences of anthropologists who have conducted fieldwork in the Soviet Bloc and its successor states—the faraway field "Out There," as Raymond Williams has suggested,[8] and one that closely relates to Ardener's remote regions model—sadly demonstrate the truth in the premonitions. While research conducted on Eastern Europe has had the potential to offer excellent glimpses into states, both planned and unplanned, these studies are far from being widely known to anthropologists. Such experiences, when written and elaborated upon adequately, may provide anthropological accounts that replicate neither those written about Third or Fourth World backgrounds, nor those describing Western states.[9] For the accounts of what went on in existing socialist countries, how they have been transformed, and how anthropologists have been able to record and analyze them belong to the very core of the discipline's epistemological makeup. For one example, anthropologists studying the socialist societies were placed, whether they wished so or not, at the center of anthropology's leftist legacy. This mission, either to support or critically rethink the role of Marxism in anthropology, however, has not, we must sadly admit, been fulfilled. Thus, the anthropology of Eastern Europe—or to use Chris Hann's term, the anthropology of socialism—has been unable to contribute to the debate that has raged through anthropology between the Marxist/materialists (political economy) and the symbolic/structuralists or the later postmodernist debates. Another reason for this is that the anthropology of Europe in general and the anthropology of Eastern Europe in specific, despite some brave and recent attempts, have remained marginal in mainstream anthropological debates and discussion.[10]

One may wonder then why this has been the case, but my conviction is that both the theory of fieldwork and fieldwork practice in Eastern Europe were at odds with ruling—colonialist, Western, and capitalist—the anthropological paradigms of the 1970s and 1980s. The anthropology of East Europe was quite parochial and specific at worst and rather eccentric at best. It wished to study the details of the otherness of the East, yet most monographs of the time seemed to agree with state ideology in general, carefully avoiding the problems of the communist experiences on the local level. This topic was especially acute with nationalism and minority issues.[11] To conduct research in Hungary, one had to demystify "window" or "goulash socialism." In Romania, as Gail Kligman writes, one "had to go 'beyond Dracula' and demystify the mythical Transylvania."[12] Yet how Hungary became the former and how Romania became the latter has not been elicited by anthropologists.

With regard to minority issues and national identity, anthropologists in the East were rather nonconfrontational in contrast to anthropologists conducting research in Third and Fourth World cultures. The latter have been the champions of human and minority rights and ecological and local developmental dilemmas and, by so doing, they have provided their expertise through various possibilities by acting as go-betweens for their communities and for state or international organizations. Such attempts have been largely unknown in the anthropology of "socialist" Eastern Europe. This odd situation may have been created in part because some anthropologists who had (latent or manifest) leftist leanings were intent upon studying the socialist experiments and simply were not critical enough of the states, governments, and institutions of their studies. By the late 1970s, human and minority rights were all over the media and in the *samizdat* (the unofficial publications relegated to the annals of history nowadays) publications of the East. Western anthropologists, however, were either accepting the bafflement of the East European bureaucrats concerning such problems or, since they took the Marxist-Leninist project for granted (Remember: "The working-men have no country," etc.), they could not indulge themselves in studying "non-legitimate" subject matters such as interethnic conflict and national reawakening.[13]

Clearly, then, the nature of fieldwork practice and a possible ideological divide are surely what may be at the heart of separating the "foreign anthropologist" from the "native scholar," concepts that have been questioned recently by various scholars.[14] In his early article, "Anthropologists and native ethnographers in Central European villages," a Hungarian ethnographer proposes, perhaps too naively, sharp differences in personality, interests, and specialization between North American anthropologists and European "native" ethnographers.[15] Opposing such a traditionalist point of view, and writing in another context while reflecting back on his own fieldwork, Renato Rosaldo has queried the anthropological category "native point of view." He writes: "Surprisingly, discussions of the 'native point of view' tend not to consider that so-called natives are more than reference points for cultural conceptions. They often disagree, talk back, assert themselves politically, and generally say things 'we' might rather not hear."[16] This conflict, which was missed by both "native" ethnographers and Western counterparts, must be addressed before progressing any further.

I too had to learn that the fact that I was born Hungarian did not automatically provide me with carte blanche to know local communities, especially with regard to questions such as national identity, minority rights, and Hungarians outside of Hungary. These distinctions—the kinds of questions asked, the tools and methods utilized, and the areas of knowledge emphasized—presuppose genuine interest in, and thorough identification and engagement with, the "others" who are purported subjects of study, even if they are supposed to be one's fellow citizens. Moreover, my Hungarian background sometimes provided me with unusual access to individuals' ideas and aspirations, a topic that I will elaborate upon in detail below.

In a sense, this duality between the "native" ethnographer (although in Anglo-American anthropological practice, "indigenous anthropology" is preferred) and the "foreign anthropologist" may mean several things. First, since the anthropologist feels that she or he has a "real home" as opposed to the faraway fieldwork site—the dialogic anathema of Williams's "Here" as opposed to "Out There"—she or he may choose various identities or degrees of engagement with those studied. Second, the anthropologist might claim a degree of detachment from them in accordance with the current direction of theoretical concerns. Thus the anthropologist acquires and even assumes the "liberty" (or power) to decide just how "native" she or he wishes to be. Moreover, she or he holds a powerful and advantageous position to select informants and topics at will. Yet such a positioning of the anthropologist may be extremely problematical, if not outright Eurocentric, classist, and egocentric. As Lévi-Strauss aptly pointed out in *Tristes Tropiques*, "Never can [the anthropologist] feel himself 'at home' anywhere: he will always be, psychologically speaking, an amputated man."[17] Even if such an "amputated" anthropologist has the freedom to "go native," what measure of freedom has the native-born ethnographer who, having departed, returns to that native community in the guise of a foreign anthropologist to question his or her informants' national identity?[18]

To answer this dilemma and to provide the backdrop for the above reflections, I utilize my multiple fieldwork experiences in Hungarian communities over the past two decades.[19] By so doing, I hope to share my ideas, neither as an amputated or as a "halfie,"[20] but simply as a professional anthropologist traversing various boundaries, the "third time-space," as Lavie and Swedenburg would call it.[21] Lavie and Swedenburg combine the notion of "third space"—as suggested by Homi Bhaba as a possible detour of anti-modernist theoretical exploration and Trin Minh-ha's "third space/time grid" to suggest the politicization of location in the examination of the everydayness.[22]

FIELDWORK AND NATION IN "SOCIALIST" CSEPEL

"Social anthropology is packed with frustrations," Edmund Leach notes, and surely no research can take place without frustrations, trial-and-error procedures, and grave mistakes.[23] This is a proper motto for the anthropology of Hungary, a subfield that is a minuscule part of the anthropology of Eastern Europe. Eastern Europe itself often has been described as a border region or a marginal zone sandwiched between the prestigious anthropology of the Mediterranean and Western Europe.[24] Since its inception, anthropological fieldwork in Hungary has been centered on the study of villagers, a topic itself marginalized in mainstream anthropological discussion. In fact, most practitioners conducted field-work in small-scale peasant worker communities in Hungary.[25] Their 1970s' and 1980s' research locations and focus of anthropological inter-ests emphasized collectivization, the peasant worker, and other aspects of life that differentiated Hungarian socialist peasants either from other peasants or from their predecessors in Hungary. In this endeavor, many attempted to replicate Third World peasant studies or, better, they searched for the cultural specificity of socialist experiments in Eastern Europe. Studies either argued either for the peasants' collective, anti-state activities, or their support in undermining stalest hegemony. But we find inadequate explanations in the works of the 1970s and 1980s, whether the state socialist societies' differences "Out There" came from just that (i.e., the fact of being under the ideological strains of Marxism or Lenin-ism) or from the theoretical/ideological disposition of the anthropolo-gist/fieldworker.[26]

Mentioning the words nation and ideology elicited smiles among Hungary's intellectuals when I arrived in Hungary in 1985. With the aid of an International Research and Exchanges Board (IREX) doctoral dis-sertation grant, I felt modestly self-assured, although slightly intimidated by most of the political-science-influenced anthropological literature on the "cold" realities of the Soviet Bloc and the native scholars' traditional ethnographic-folkloristic models. Equally frustrating were the complaints of Hungarian sociologists and political scientists about the current eco-nomic situation in Hungary, the impossibility of conducting surveys, and the presumably valueless effort of carrying out participant observation among Hungarians, especially on subjects of national identity or inter-ethnic relations between Hungarians and Romanians.

One sure sign of being placed into the border or "third timespace zone" had to do with official seals of approval, permitting me to cross into the field. Many anthropologists who conducted fieldwork in the former Soviet Bloc knew all too well that official permissions and ministerial and collegial approvals were of primary importance. One could not do much without them, even if they were absurd. Once I had to obtain permission to enter the "Closed Section" [*Zárt Osztály*] at the National Library in Budapest. The stamped letter simply stated that I was a researcher who needed to look at historical records. With that paper, all doors opened up for me. If things could always have been that simple![27]

For a number of reasons, the native ethnographers did little to improve my outlook. Most were willing, however, to offer sympathetic letters of support legitimating my presence in Hungary and at various institutions. Ensconced in museum offices among dusty, nineteenth-cen-tury objects or seated at desks in the ethnographic institute atop Buda

Hill, surrounded by Western tourists and relentless traffic, most remained insulated from my concerns. Few studied minority communities in Hungary. Studying Gypsies (Roma) was even more "illegitimate" as a subject of serious fieldwork. The study of Hungarians in Transylvania was off limits, and the subject of nationalism did not meet the approval of Hungarian colleagues. For many, studying peasant communities was important, but only from the historical or traditional ethnographic perspective. To them, urban and working-class culture, translated through the "dreaded" words of "workers' culture" and "workers' folklore" (*munkáskultúra* or *munkásfolklór*), was inherited from the Stalinist 1950s. It seemed that these were meaningful as subjects only if they were grounded in nineteenth-century traditions and related to the hallmark of their science, the chimerical Hungarian "proper peasants."

When I discussed my plan to conduct fieldwork in the Csepel district, with specific reference to the level of national consciousness of the workers at the Csepel Works, a few were noncommittal, some supported my idea, and others found ways to discourage me. They argued, for example, that the industrial site was too large, ill suited for an in-depth study, and no longer a functioning community. Too many workers were either committed socialists or were simply disgruntled and found satisfaction in illegal work and nonstate occupations.

Despite such discouragement, I adhered to my original idea and secured permission to enter the Csepel Works, an industrial park of some military significance. As Budapest's largest industrial district, Csepel has attracted the fascination of writers and travelers beyond the borders of Hungary. To evoke its impact, two sources, both Western, bear testimony to Csepel's contradictory but enduring power, at once both real and symbolic. German writer Hans Magnus Enzensberger describes it as follows in *Europe, Europe*:

> Today the ironworks of Csepel is one of the dinosaurs of the socialist planned economy. Red Csepel is also a symbolic place for the economic reformers. For them this state-owned concern is not the engine of the economy but a brake block, an unprofitable, immovable relic of Stalinism. The machinery still dates, in part, from the forties; the fittings and infrastructure are obsolete. In truth, Hungary's crisis can be read quite literally from the dust in the passageways, from the resignation in the faces, from the rust in the factory halls.[28]

Seeing the Csepel Works for the first time in the mid-1980s, I too was struck by its behemoth size, ear-splitting din, and lively atmosphere and the contradictory (socialist/nonsocialist) images it projected. People moved in and out of the factory and at the gates, through which only those with identification badges could pass. Banners, signs, and packed stores signaled a strong life force. Outside of the main gate, single-family workers' houses were erected with small vegetable gardens, which reminded visitors of the remnants of the interwar working-class culture. The main square, with its central location for a Catholic Church, police station, city hall, the Hungarian Socialist Workers' Party (MSZMP), Communist Youth Association (KISZ), trade union, stores, and bus stations, exuded a sense of importance and centralized power. Farther away, huge, ten-story apartment complexes dominated the city's landscape, results of the "glorious victory" of Stalinism and state socialism over bourgeois capitalistic individualism. These terms were freely mentioned, even during the mid-1980s.

The town's contradictory identity was obvious from the start: information was readily available, especially concerning the struggle of the communist underground in the interwar Horthy era, from the parents of my informants, some of whom found their way into my studies.[29] The workers of Csepel offered an excellent laboratory in which to study the clash of local-level, state-level, and national-level socialist ideologies. Workers in general provided a fascinating glimpse into the way in which local populations might counter the pressures of state domination of their lives.[30] In Csepel, the socialist ideology clashed with the local and national ones in important ways.

Informants in Csepel have all been proud of their radical and socialist working-class backgrounds. At the same time, next to the ideal socialist town there has always existed another, equally important but anticommunist religious and ethnically heterogeneous town. To bridge the gap between these two populations, I had to become, in the words of Rosaldo, the "positioned" and constantly "repositioned subject."[31]

To approach workers at the socialist firm, a hierarchical progression, from the top down, had to be followed. In fact, the first informants were company managers, party and communist youth organization secretaries, and trade union stewards who were genuinely eager to learn what "this American" wanted to do in Csepel and also willing to tell me just how socialism worked. With more and more interviews behind me, I learned that many of my initial hypotheses concerning the socialist personae, work ethic, and national identity were outdated, if not simply wrong. Fieldwork does, and should for that matter, challenge prevailing notions of theories. The contradiction between the state ideology of socialism and the locals' sense of their national identity was becoming increasingly obvious. Feeling like a heretic, I became increasingly convinced that state socialist and Marxist-Leninist urtexts presented a world found less and less in workers' everyday culture. The more time I spent in Hungary, this seemed true for both Csepel and Hungary as a whole.

The world of labor and the continuum between the socialist cum national identity were equally fascinating and in a sense almost chaotic. In fact, the absurd images of Ridley Scott's *Bladerunner* seemed to be superimposed on the world of George Orwell's *1984*. A single, descriptive local ethnography seemed more and more impossible, for the industrial complex was composed of many factories, vast and complex organisms requiring many different vital connections to maintain themselves. Socialist identity seemed to be confined within the walls of the industrial plant. From socialist brigades to factory rituals, from vocational training to club events, these connections among the various "body parts" revealed the workers' sense of socialist factory-dominated existence as well as the hidden dimension of their non-factory, national identity.[32] Especially for the younger generations, it was as though the world of socialist labor was nonexistent. They expressed different ideas and values and behaved differently than what was expected of them at the workplace. Most young workers frequented discos (not punk concerts) and smoked and drank incessantly (not French cognac or wine but beer and *pálinka*, home-brewed plum brandy), and some visited churches (not museums). Many of my informants read science fiction (not Gogol), attended soccer games (not classical concerts), and watched crime movies as well as the evening bedtime folktales on television.

These elements of their everyday culture were certainly not the ideal socialist culture espoused by the state ideologues. The denizens of Csepel had a different sense of identity from the socialist men and women categories offered to them by the state. The town was constantly described as a famed stronghold of socialism: all Soviet leaders from Leonid Brezhnev to Mikhail Gorbachev visited Csepel as a symbolic gesture to the victory of socialist ideology. Contrary to this facade, the workers' way of life was much more contradictory and filled with elements undermining state ideology. For one, despite the strong state indoctrination and political socialization, workers have adhered to a religious ideology. As many informants vividly recalled, the jailing, intimidation, and fines of religious believers were not unknown, even in the 1970s. In the Csepel district alone, there are six churches belonging to Catholic, Protestant, Baptist, Evangelist, and Orthodox denominations. The Jewish community was decimated during World War II and did not manage to revitalize itself in the district during state socialism. Visiting these was a private matter during the 1970s and 1980s, and even though regular church membership had declined from its pre-war level, weddings, baptismal feasts, and funerals were all religious affairs observed by most families.

It became evident that workers were not a homogeneous mass, regardless of their ethnic and regional backgrounds, as state planners extolled. Originally Csepel's eighteenth-century inhabitants came from German and South Slavic backgrounds, an ethnic composition that was revitalized in the 1990s, with much success. Adding to this interethnic makeup, the Csepel Protestant Church was built in 1920 by Transylvanian refugees (about 150 families in all) who left Romania after the Peace Treaty in Trianon. Most were lured by the steel mill, which provided ample opportunities for jobs. Thus the radical "Red Csepel" (as it has been known since the 1920s, when workers' strikes made Csepel a household name in Hungary) received a good dosage of national spirituality with the influx of Transylvanian Hungarians. While this population added fuel to the nationalist state's irredentist and chauvinistic ideology during the interwar period and became a source of suppressed knowledge during much of state socialism, by the mid-1980s, Csepel's Protestant Church managed to revitalize itself. It found several Hungarian communities in Romania with which it has managed to keep close relationships. Many of these were based on former family contacts; others were created by church authorities supporting minority churches struggling during Ceauşescu's rule. Thus religiosity and nationality have coalesced in Csepel, a strange, popular force in a place hailed as a communist workers' town by Hungary's ideologues. The rising nationalist ideology and the disinterested nature of workers toward the state ideology were the main causes for the collapse of the state socialist system during the time of the Velvet Revolution in 1988 and 1989, a topic discussed in detail in later chapters.

POST–SOCIALIST EXPERIENCES IN CSEPEL

Between the period 1992–1995, I was able to continue my comparative anthropological analysis of the changes that had taken place since 1989, in particular, what had happened to my informants in Csepel. Because of the events of 1989 and 1990—the "Springtime of the Peoples," as many Western observers referred to it—much had changed in Hungary, like elsewhere in the former Soviet Bloc countries. Most countries became free from Soviet domination as the Soviet Union itself collapsed, and single-party rule was abandoned in favor of multiparty representation. Hungary had its first free elections in more than forty years; it elected a president, and with the aid of a new constitution, it legitimized a parliamentary representative system. In 1990, a new law went into effect that made illegal the presence of political parties in workplaces and allowed the dismantling of former state enterprises. This had fundamentally affected all state factories, including the industrial giant, the Csepel Works.

To my surprise, Csepel suddenly became a nonsocialist city: in 1990, the Socialist Workers' Party was voted out of office, and mostly non-communist leaders filled the seats of the district's council and mayoral office. Many signs of the old system had been demolished and removed, both inside and outside of the factory's gates. An observer/traveler in the early 1990s, when the state enterprise was slowly being dismantled as the result of the 1989–1990 transformation, saw the non-communist nation being reborn as follows:

> According to a 1990 map, the short little 'Grass-street' in Csepel ends at a square where the statue of V. I. Lenin stands. However, one looks in vain for Vladimir Ilich Lenin: instead we find a few, beaten up containers, dog droppings, and patches of grass here and there. The bronze statue of the leader of the revolution was removed in March 1990. Where? No one knows. One thing is sure: it is gone now. To rework the past is not what people think of these days. The market economy is at the doorstep of the country requiring the full energy of all; clearly new times are coming to Csepel.[33]

One informant admitted that it was not the anti-communists who took it down but, contrary to popular opinion, members of the Communist Party and its youth brigade. These two organizations had decided that, rather than wait for a large-scale riot, which would have been embarrassing to them, it would be better to take it down themselves. Similarly, street names also had been changed, a practice that was central to post–socialist politics not only in Hungary but elsewhere in the former Soviet Bloc. This time, too, the Communist Party and the communist youth association were the "culprits." These communist statues, plaques, and signs may now be seen in the local historical society's little museum, a similar move described by Catherine Wanner for post–Soviet Ukrainian nationalism.[34]

These changes were facilitated by the intellectual ferment between a small but vocal political opposition, known as the "democratic opposition" and the social undercurrents from below. The two camps also were described as "populists" and "urbanites." Although both populists and urbanites concerned themselves with questions of "democracy" and a liberalized economic structure, the urbanists' emphasis clearly focused on these issues rather than on notions of "Hungarianness" (*magyarság*) or

"Hungarian culture" (*magyar kultúra*) as elements for political unity and power. However, by mid-1988, when Hungary was experiencing an influx of Hungarian refugees from neighboring Romania, Hungarian popular attention turned favorably toward the oppositional "Democratic Forum," a group espousing the plight of ethnic Hungarians outside of Hungary. The language of this newly emerging political discourse was anti-state and overtly populist, and it openly addressed what it considered the devastating impact of thirty-five years of communist rule of Hungarian citizens.

At the 1987 historic Democratic Forum summit, at Lakitelek, critical issues emerged: ecological disasters, poverty, police brutality, illegally stationed Soviet troops, lack of funding for health and education, and especially the plight of the Hungarian diaspora in neighboring states. These issues were wholly avoided at that time by the state and its arm, the Socialist Workers' Party, and its youthful alter ego, the Communist Youth League. Communist slogans were debunked. "Eight hours work" and "Forward to building a socialist internationalism" incantations often heard at May Day parades were ridiculed in light of grave human rights violations in Romania and Czechoslovakia. This intellectual movement became an accepted political force by 1988, when one of the first (and largest) peaceful demonstrations took place in Budapest on June 27, 1988. By organizing this solidarity march, it condemned Nicoale Ceauşescu's genocidal plan for the destruction of thousands of Saxon, Hungarian, and Romanian villages in the Transylvanian region of Romania. This march was tantamount to a victory procession for the opposition and, at the same time, a funeral dirge for communism.

At first, workers were rather nonchalant about these largely "intellectual" pursuits. The residents of Budapest, just as others throughout the country, were soon introduced to this new "Hungarian consciousness" (*magyarságtudat*) when their workers' hostel was targeted as a site to provide affordable housing to Hungarian refugees from Romania. "The responsibility," proclaimed an editorial in the local paper, "for the fate of Hungarians in Transylvania is ours; and the way in which the refugees will assimilate here will depend on every one of us."[35] Although not the first wave of Transylvanian refugees, to the generation of the late 1980s it nonetheless posed a reinvigorated sense of their already-shaken class identification as the refugee issue was soon taken up as a nationwide concern.

In the months following the more relaxed political atmosphere of the short-lived Grósz government after Kádár's dismissal, churches addressed the welfare issue of Transylvanian refugees. In the words of a local Protestant church leader, this issue was a "radical anti-state force capable of uniting all Hungarians along these lines." Catholic and Protestant, and Evangelical and Baptist churches in Hungary thereby spoke with one voice to reradicalize grassroots religious communities that were marginalized during much of the preceding decades. The idea of national unity between Hungarians in Hungary and those in Transylvania was then facilitated by the revitalized religious communities in Hungary. This reawakening certainly lends credence to Mart Bax's observation concerning the significance of religion in modern nation-state formation. For the newly emerging Hungarian nationalist state (non-communist and religious) relied heavily on the symbols and power derived from Catholic and Protestant icons and ideology, a transformation that was abundantly evident by the official visits of John Paul II to Poland and Hungary.[36] In the former Red town of Csepel, the Evangelical parish, for example, adopted the Romanian town of Sacale (Bácsfalu, with a sizable Hungarian minority) as its sister city in November 1988, a gesture that soon encouraged other cities to follow suit. Immediately after the first free elections in 1990, visits back and forth between such settlements became commonplace occurrences, dealing a death blow to the socialist image of a town whose residents' identity had been bound to official communism, industrialization, and a unified working-class tradition.

After the spring elections of 1990, this new nationalistic spirit continued unabated, more open now than previously, with the exception of the interwar period mentioned above. As a result of the growing hostility between the Hungarian and Romanian states, in March 1990, the local Democratic Forum (MDF) organized a Transylvanian photographic exhibit, a cultural event that subsequently was to exert far-reaching political influence in a climate overheated by propaganda from the forthcoming local election. This Transylvanian-centered agenda of the ruling MDF, as many observers noted, substantially facilitated its popular support in the workers' town. The now-official "Transylvanian connection" continued during the summer of 1991, when the local government sponsored the summer vacations of thirty-five Hungarian children from Romania, a gesture with historical antecedents in Hungary. In a nearby settlement, the Transylvanian Federation in Szigethalom, for example, sponsored a dinner dance on April 24, 1991, to foster community connections with ethnic Hungarians in Transylvania. Nevertheless, the emphasis on such nationalistic ideology proved detrimental to MDF politics in Csepel, for as we shall see, the MDF and its allies sustained significant losses in the elections when the engine of unchecked nationalistic spirit had already been set in motion. As a result, the 1990s witnessed the remaking of most of Hungary's national holidays, which became historically, nationalistically (March 15, October 23), or religiously determined (August 20). Consequently, virtually all former communist or working-class celebrations (May Day, March 21, and November 7) were relegated to the annals of history.[37]

Such a nationalistic revival of ethnic consciousness, however, also has worked to "resuscitate" minority identities and minority rights issues throughout the region. However, as Katherine Verdery states:

> Contrary to the view widespread in America, the resuscitation of those ethnic conflicts is not simply a revival of "traditional" enmities from the interwar years—as if the intervening half-century were inconsequential. To begin with, ethnic ideologies were reinforced rather than diminished by socialism's "shortage economies," which favored any social device that reduced competition for unavailable goods. Ethnic ideas, with their drawing of clear boundaries between "in" and "out," are . . . one such device. Second, with the end of government repression, eth-nonational resentments flare up in an environment extremely unpropitious to managing them: an environment devoid of any intermediate institutions for settling disagreements peaceably.[38]

As a result, then, and to counter such overtly state-sponsored nationalistic behavior, other smaller ethnic groups and associations surfaced in the vacuum, not only in the workers' town, but in Hungary at large. Between 1990 and 1994, the center-right governments of Antall and Boross certainly supported such developments at the local level. Csepel also witnessed an ethnic renaissance: the two most controversial nationality organizations to take the stage were the local Gypsy group (*Rom*) and the Schwabian–German Cultural Association. Because of the general anti-Gypsy attitude in Hungary, the former was reluctantly accepted by workers, and then only as a minor political party known as Brotherhood (*Phralipe*), the latter simply as a "cultural" organization and not a political party. The ambiguousness of these ethnic organizations was openly elaborated on by residents of the district. The Gypsy community, while fairly sizable (estimates in the mid-1990s ranged about 10,000), was regarded as a newcomer to Csepel and hence not of working-class origin. Although specific to the district, these objections nevertheless adumbrate commonly held ethnocentric ideas of Hungarians concerning Gypsies in their country.[39] In this connection, it must be mentioned that the political visibility of Hungary's half-million Gypsy minority provided Hungary's nationalist majority with a base to rekindle anti-Gypsy sentiments, a feeling of superiority among the Magyar populations that one could detect nearly ubiquitously in Hungary. Chalked graffiti proclaiming neighborhoods "Gypsy-free zones" have been common in Hungary ever since this neo-nazi slogan was first introduced by Hungary's infamous punk rock band "Smile" (*Mos-oi*) in the early 1980s.[40]

The reemergence of the Schwabian (*Sváb*) nationality, a group deci-mated in Csepel after 1948, also may be seen as a response to insecurities created by rising unemployment, relaxed state policies, and the rising national idea of "Hungarianness." Curiously enough, despite the sub-stantial number of Schwabian communities on the Csepel Island and around Budapest that survived anti-German expatriation and prejudice after World War II, a coherent political agenda has not yet emerged among them. This may be explained in large part by the uneasiness with which the German nationality is viewed by many in Hungary, primarily because of its wartime alliance with Nazi Germany. Resulting perhaps from the state's iron-hand policy concerning folkloristic programs—sub-sidizing a token number of South Slavic, German, Slovak, and Gypsy communities—a viable German ethnopolitical agenda remains to be forged. The creation of an ethnic party during the 1998 election cam-paign resulted only in a meager 22,000 votes throughout the country.

Nevertheless, in other ways as well, the district was not spared the new, severe nationalistic political propaganda that emanated from downtown Budapest in the wake of dissolving socialism. As the new Budapest govern-ment canceled the World's Fair scheduled for 1996, it became clear that not Csepel but the South Buda section of the capital was to receive the funding required to expand its budget. Csepel was originally targeted for large-scale real estate development and the construction of hotels, roads, and busi-nesses in a vision of a "Hungarian Manhattan." It was at that point that a decision was made to delay the World's Fair and to offer the opportunity of naturalization to residents of Hong Kong who wished to settle in Hungary in order to bring business into the country. As far-fetched as these schemes may appear, Csepel citizens actually argued in favor of subsidies for such developments. During an interview in the early 1990s, I could not help but wonder (along with Csepelers themselves) how a town whose conservative value system had succeeded in maintaining the marginalization of non-Magyar groups would be able to sustain the influx of hundreds of Chinese families from Hong Kong. Despite this crypto-capitalist fantasy of sky-scrapers, resorts, and a multiethnic mélange, Csepel's history was to prevent it from becoming Hungary's Manhattan, and the World's Fair brouhaha was finally settled in favor of a more culturally oriented event for 1996.

In line with what Katherine Verdery suggests above, it is easy to dis-cern why alienated workers reached to embrace religiosity and nationality during the last years of state socialism in a social vacuum left by the party and its supporting institutions, and why they opted for voting the social-ist out of office in 1990 by overwhelmingly supporting the center-right government, a regime in office between 1990 and 1994. However, during this time, some of Csepel's residents often complained to me about the positive discrimination of Transylvanian refugees settled in Hungary, in general, the favorable treatment with which the Hungarian government treated the Hungarian minorities in Romania. In the national media, not only anti-Transylvanian but anti-Gypsy and anti-foreign rhetoric was printed. This strange twist of events was undoubtedly facilitated by the rising unemployment following the large-scale privatization of former state companies, the rising inflation rate, and the growing insecurities resulting from Hungary's incorporation into the world economy.

These feelings also were needed to elevate extreme politics into the national political discourse. The emergence of Hungary's extreme right parties also was a key element in the rise of radical nationalism. Two parties in specific must be mentioned: the "Hungarian Justice and Life Party" (MIÉP), an offshoot of the ruling Democratic Forum and a legitimate parliamentary force after the 1998 elections, and the marginal but vocal neo-fascist "Hungarian Welfare Association (MNSZ). Both state-supported nationalist ideology and the overwhelming governmental right-wing ideology contributed to the socialist government's victory in the 1994 election. However, between the period 1994–1998, during the socialist-led government of Gyula Horn, the national project did not show any sign of diminishing. As it will be detailed in the following chapters, Hungary's relationship with Romania, especially the situation of the Hungarian minority in Transylvania, has continued to remain strained, despite the governmental changes in the late 1990s. A contributing factor, no doubt, has been the strong and powerful local-level national adherence to the nation-state ideology in Hungary and the overwhelming support for the political attempts of the Hungarian political party in Romania in facing Romanian majority and state nationalism.

Post–socialist Experiences: Hungarians in Transylvania

By the time I started to conduct my fieldwork in Hungary in the mid-1980s, Transylvanian Hungarians had already made headlines in Western as well as anthropological circles. As mentioned in the previous chapter, this controversy started as a special anthropological debate published in *Current Anthropology*.[41] With that debate, Transylvania entered into the Western anthropological discourse as a contested terrain for native and foreign anthropologists alike.

Aside from these developments, Csepel's hidden Transylvanian past and family connections to Transylvania led me to investigate the situation in Romania with specific reference to the Hungarian cause. Although I was able to visit Romania several times while residing in Budapest in the period 1985–1986, I entered Romania on a tourist visa, paying all of the exorbitant fees and charges that every other Westerner was forced to do at that time.[42] Crossing the border between these two countries, one immediately realized the ever-watchful eyes of the state. Regulations made it illegal for foreigners to stay overnight with families in towns as well as villages. One was forced to play a kind of hide-and-seek game with the authorities—sleeping in barns and haystacks, running ahead of the Romanian police, and lying to the border guards when leaving the country about where one stayed and what one carried. This kind of "lawlessness" and "remoteness" in the Ardnerian sense had its own feeling of romanticism.[43] Gail Kligman correctly noted that in the mid-1980s, for anthropologists "Research has become increasingly more difficult; at present, [it] is virtually impossible."[44] Although not able to stay in Romania as an "official anthropologist" at that time, the Transylvanian controversy in *Current Anthropology*, as well as the Hungarian scholars' stories, forced me to be relentless in my search for the truth about Transylvania and the Hungarian minority there. Eventually these experiences made their way into publications, even though I felt uneasy that until I had conducted funded (i.e., legitimate) fieldwork, I would not be able to express these experiences in an open forum.[45] Yet these clandestine semi-fieldwork trips assisted me in developing an ethnically based, nationally reliable network. Hungarian priests, teachers, students, and writers, as well as ordinary villagers, all came to my aid—just like all "good" informants are supposed to do—to provide data and connections to more isolated Hungarian settlements, contacts that proved invaluable in subsequent years.

Aside from the Szekler regions, Cluj and its vicinities have been the center of Hungarian ethnographic attention. As will be discussed in detail in subsequent chapters, two regions in particular received the most attention: the Mezőség (Lowlands) and the Kalotaszeg, both for their archaic Hungarian population adhering to its national traditions. Cluj, however, also had its own share in this nationalist attention. For Hungarians, it has been the capital of Transylvania, with its churches, archives, buildings, and schools all extolling a sense of a unique Hungarian past.[46] Throughout the centuries its epithet has been the "town of a treasure-trove" (*kincses város*). Yet since the late 1960s, it has seen a systematic destruction of its interethnic past, a situation inherited at least since the reorganization of Transylvania following the post–World War I treatises. Most Cluj Hungarians have been extremely keen in pointing out their town's historical uniqueness and volatility. Irina Livezeanu aptly summarizes the contested nature of Transylvanian cities, including that of Cluj, after that problematical peace treaty: "Transylvania's town and cities constituted a stronghold of Magyarism against the Romanian populace, a citadel which the Romanians naturally wished to conquer after 1918. The protracted battle for the urban areas exacerbated the Romanians' sense of inferiority, even though the state was on their side."[47]

Hungarians were keen in assuming that Cluj was a town singled out by Ceauşescu for a complete de-Hungarianization policy. All signs of its Hungarian (and previously German!) character underwent a systematic Romanianization. A young American anthropologist saw this in the mid-1970s as follows:

> To dissociate herself symbolically from Hungarian ties, the name of the city of Cluj was recently "latinized" so that its identity might not be mistaken despite the dense Hungarian population living in and around it. Today, Cluj-Napoca is the proper place-name of this Transylvanian capital that in 1974 was still recognized as Cluj on the official physical administrative map of Romania. It often surprises visitors to encounter the famous statue of the "suckling wolves" in the center of the city. The she-wolf, symbol of Rome commonly found in Italy, was a gift from the municipality of Rome in 1924—a testimony to Romania's Latin ties.[48]

Hungarians too were quite frank about the consequences of the forced Romanianization policies of the Ceaşuescu government. They asserted that Hungarians were laid off from their jobs and only Romanians from the Wallachia and Moldavia were hired as replacements.[49] Moreover, women were forced to give birth to many children or otherwise had to pay a fine. In defiance of that inhuman 1966 law—illegalizing abortion and other birth control methods—Hungarian families opted for even less children.[50] Informants also argued that Hungarian pupils in state schools faced extreme forms of discrimination from Romanian teachers and peers alike.[51] Hungarian young men and women often lamented that in the Romanian army, they were harassed by their officers and cruelly punished for speaking Hungarian. Such stories and the beatings, jailing, and silencing of Hungarian leaders were on the lips of everyone. As Hungary's populist writer Sándor Csoóri wrote "Such stories cannot even be ascertained as to their truth because they are beyond any comprehension. . . . I would believe them to be true, and only the figment of imagination, newly made myths, but such cruel myths cannot exist anywhere except in a country where such hair-raising accidents have both historical and psychological chances to exist."[52]

The mid-1980s' craze concerning the demolishment of Transylvanian villages—an event that prompted members of the American Anthropological Association to present a resolution[53]— added considerably to the already growing hostilities and insecurities of living in Transylvania for both Hungarians and Romanians. It seemed that an ethnography of the growing nationalistic tension and the antagonistic relationship between the two nations, and countries, could have been written from the plethora of rumors, evasions, accusations, and lies one heard from Hungarians, both in Transylvania and Hungary.[54]

These local experiences in Hungarian communities in Transylvania as well as the 1990 transformation allowed for a much more anthropological formulation of interethnic conflict and national identity. I applied for a grant, eventually receiving "official recognition" as an anthropologist studying nationality conflicts at the present. Earlier, the exacerbation of the conflict between Hungary and Romania was seen largely as historical, in part because of the failure of state socialism. Specifically, most studies offered evidence that Kádárism and Ceauşescuism failed to cope with the problems of ethnicity and majority-minority relations. After 1990, anthropologists increasingly came to the conclusion that these conflicts were not simply the survival of old, historic debates, although history has been constantly manipulated and contested by all of the sides, but that they reflect the current state of controversies over Transylvania.

During my many meetings with scholars and cultural workers in both Hungary and Romania, I realized that the 1990s provided a different setting from the 1970s and 1980s for rekindling nationalist arguments. Most of these earlier decades were almost free from nationalistic hatred and tension, or so it seemed from the major publications available. In the 1980s, the Hungarian government did not want to openly confront the Romanian government. Officials and scholars were cautious about offering specific advice about Hungarians in Transylvania, especially about how to approach Hungarian leaders and institutions in Romania. Information and statistics were not available officially, though many bureaucrats were aware of the real conditions plaguing Hungarian communities under the last years of Ceauşescu's rule. This changed instantaneously after 1990, when the Hungarian center-right government of Prime Minister József Antall opened a special state department for Hungarian minorities abroad (*Határon Túli Magyarok Hivatala*, or HTMH). Before embarking upon fieldwork in Romania, this office—actually a clearinghouse or an information service agency—was able to provide important information: names, addresses, phone numbers, dates of gatherings, political rallies, and contacts of Hungarian minority leaders in Transylvania. Compared to the clandestine contacts and personal networks provided by the ethnographers and family members during the mid-1980s, this was a real revelation and an added advantage to the demystification of Transylvanian remoteness.

With this kind of assistance and theoretical accoutrements, I arrived in Cluj in January 1993. My official contact was with the local Romanian Academy of Sciences office, an outpost of the Bucharest headquarters. Being a "foreign scholar" (they did not grasp what anthropology really was all about and certainly did not care to get involved with the serious issues of nationalism and national identity), I constantly struggled to make my point and to get along with them. A much more friendly, collegial relationship developed with the head of the Sociology Department, the late Professor Ion Aluas, at Babes-Bolyai University. He was a key person in obtaining for me a letter that gave me all kinds of freedom.[55] This affiliation proved extremely valuable for meeting both Hungarians and Romanians, as I was able to show this letter whenever I had to deal with the local bureaucracy.[56] Interestingly, the passage of years notwithstanding, what was strikingly similar between my Csepel and Transylvanian research was the need to obtain an official permit—even if it was in the guise of a collegial endorsement—so that a foreign anthropologist could conduct research.

Mobility and the exchange of information with Romanian and Hungarian colleagues in Cluj were not without its difficulties and funny moments, despite the democratic changes occurring in the country. For example, bureaucrats at the Romanian Academy of Sciences office wanted to know my movements and contacts. I nevertheless pleaded with them and tried to cite what I believed to be the profession's Fifth Amendment right: that I have the right to remain silent about certain informants, their names, and the subjects discussed. In return, my official hosts cited their own rights and responsibilities. If I wanted to be paid for my travels, I had to tell them exactly where I went. If I wanted to be paid for the rent I paid to my village host, I had to tell them where I stayed, with whom, and for how many days, thus openness in fieldwork started to be more and more uncomfortable, and I did not feel that I had the upper hand. Yet anthropologists must be willing to compromise and find other ways to handle such sensitive, embarrassing issues. So I willingly complied with the wishes of my official hosts and revealed all of the names and addresses of the locals who gave me permission to do so (there were not many). Other names were never mentioned (this was the majority). However, my village hosts smiled when I told them about this verbal hide-and-seek game, and said that the Romanian secret police know everything anyway. One thing is certain: fears die hard in the field, and "secrecy," whether the anthropologist's or informants', is one of the most neglected issues in the debates concerning the fieldwork and the entire anthropological enterprise.[57]

During the early 1990s, the county seat Cluj was experiencing renewed, curious conflicts between members of the Hungarian minority and the Romanian majority. By focusing on various cultural and political institutions as well as on elements of everyday culture—such as the politics of native language education—it was easy to realize that the conflict between Hungarians and Romanians was open and vicious. While most Hungarians saw this as the character of Romanians, it became obvious that the national rivalry had other causes. One had to do with the mismanaged minority policies of the Iliescu government, the other, the transnationalist ideology emanating from neighboring Hungary. As Hungarians in Transylvania eagerly explained that Budapest can be credited with giving them a sense of Hungarian identity, they often remarked that by far the most important has been the state-sponsored Duna Television, a program created solely for Hungarians outside of the Hungarian nation-state.

True, in daily life, cooperation between the two groups was not easy to discern, even though the Hungarians are now able to rely on the leadership of their own ethnic party, the Democratic Alliance of Hungarians in Romania, or RMDSZ. What came as a surprise was that while aggression and hatred were minimal and mostly avoided in the open, this was not because of democratic thinking on the part of the population at large but because of the insistence on separate spheres of existence by the two groups. In the city of Cluj, in cultural, political, and religious life, for instance, Hungarians and Romanians continue to live in two separate "realities." In everyday culture, Hungarians visit their own cultural institutions (theaters, clubs) but less so their cinemas, which play only Romanian and Western films, either synchronized or subtitled. Hungarians, to give another example, frequent the Hungarian theatre but rarely the Romanian National Theatre. Also, at the market square in Cluj, Hungarians often select those sellers who commute from nearby villages and are themselves of a Hungarian ethnic background. Yet this too seemed to be the case with Romanian city-dwellers. After a little chat, closeness is established between sellers and buyers, and trust develops, allowing the transaction to take place. Needless to say, some of the producers are bilingual, and city residents are easily fooled.

These urban markets were extremely lively locations for observing the interaction of the various nationalities and the way in which national stereotypes are played out. For example, Gypsies utilize their language skills to communicate fluently with Hungarians and Romanians alike, and some are extremely skillful as beggars. The city of Cluj also is an excellent place for testing the level of liberalization and democracy in Romania as well as the Romanian government's minority policy in action.

Street signs and Hungarian nameplates—put up during the enthusiastic first years of the 1990s—have practically disappeared. Some were smeared with paint, while others were simply knocked down. Cluj, just like the Budapest district of Csepel, experienced a similar transformation in shedding its communist heritage, with one important difference: a nationalistic stance by the xenophobic mayor to completely eradicate the city's Hungarian past. When I wanted to film an old street sign in Hungarian, Romanian passersby cursed at me. Similarly, when I took pictures of the Romanian statue of the peasant leader Hora at the main square in Cluj, Hungarians made racist remarks. Cameras and videos, just like in the 1980s, were still looked at with distrust and trepidation. Tourists and foreigners often are asked to stop filming and to put away their cameras. Clearly the past decades of totalitarian terror and state indoctrination were so successful that Transylvanians still feel uneasy about being photographed or filmed.[58] Yet members of both national communities eagerly express the proper subject to record visually.

The logistics of such actions, both by the state and by citizens, have for a long time been that recording anything the state and the police deemed sensitive, including the nationality situation in Romania, was out of the question. By the mid-1990s, however, it seemed rather odd that there would be such misgivings about using a recording device. Yet, as it was, even in 1996—after the signing of the bilateral treaty between the Hungarian and Romanian governments in September 1996—issues relating to the situation of the Hungarian minority were still too sensitive to be recorded, especially by a "foreigner." Adding to the already sensitive, somewhat strained neighborly relations, a foreigner in Romania is even more suspicious if he or she comes from Hungary and drives a car with Hungarian license plates. These visitors are doubly burdened by (stereotypical) identities. Clearly, monuments and nationally significant landmarks are endowed with their own spatial markers and borders. Crossing such borders, one must deal with several ascribed and assumed identities, for these are genuine representations of the actual border zone or third timespace, mentioned earlier.

Such fieldwork conflicts aside, it became clear that along with religion, language has been used as the most important cultural marker of Hungarian national identity in Transylvania. Both Romanian state nationalism and Hungarian minority nationalism are trying to control and contest this. The Romanian Constitution, passed on December 8, 1991, recognizes the freedom of expression of ethnic, cultural, linguistic, and religious identities and proposes that Romanian education "has an open character guaranteeing the access of every citizen to all grades and forms of education," including minority language education. At the same time, however, it reinforces a one-sided Romanian nation-state ideology. It asserts that Romania is a "unitary national State . . . [and a] common and indivisible homeland of all its citizens," that "all-grade education is provided in Romanian." Moreover, the constitution states that "Romania's history and geography shall be taught in Romanian," and that "Romanian language and literature is a compulsory test at the school-leaving examination."[59] It also codifies that "faithfulness towards the country is sacred."[60] With this in mind, it is easy to argue, with Sabrina Ramet, why "the political configuration of Eastern Europe in the 1990s appears in some ways to replicate patterns of the 1920s."[61]

Aside from landmarks and street signs, literature, newspapers, and schoolbooks are all language-based, highly politicized, and contested national institutions separating the Romanian majority and the Hungarian minority. In the main square in Cluj—similar to other cities—are separate newspaper stands that cater strictly to Romanians and do not carry any Hungarian language newspapers. In the same way, there are few Hungarian sellers who sell only their "own" publications, both actions because of the recent politicization of national identities discernible in the wake of the resurgence of transnational and diaspora identities in Hungary and Romania, as well as elsewhere in Europe,[62] and because of a continuing tradition of separateness and distance between these groups. Hungarians, villagers and urbanites alike, often voiced stories that they could hear only from their parents concerning the period they conveniently termed the "Hungarian world/time," a topic mentioned in the previous chapter. In Hungarian, these ideas are expressed by one word (*világ*). To them, it was natural to recall that during the time of the Hungarian occupation of Transylvania, between 1941 and 1944, their whole world was transformed. Hungarians in Transylvania continue to view history from a liberationist perspective: they see the Hungarian occupation of Transylvania as liberation from the two decades of Romanian state oppression. Equally true was the follow-up period, when the Romanian Communist Party did everything in its power to diminish ethnic and national identities other than the majority Romanian. As informants claimed, books, maps, money, and passports—Transylvanian Hungarians received citizenship from the Budapest government between the period 1940–1944—were hidden or burned when Romanian socialism was established in 1945.

Such nationalist narratives and memories aptly demonstrate that everyday actions or inactions, when it came to the lack of correspondence between the two groups, are rationalized by the real or perceived facts of what it was to be a member of a minority group. Living under extreme conditions and suffering from the side effects of state-supported nationalism created powerful emotional togetherness between both groups. At various occasions, voicing these remembrances has provided powerful images of "us" and "them" rationalizing their cautious if not outright xenophobic behavior toward one another.

Such thinking pervades daily life not only in Hungarian urban enclaves but, equally important, in rural communities as well.[63] In addition to my fieldwork in Cluj, I resided for several months in a Hungarian village (Zsobok in Hungarian, Jebuc in Romania), about 35 kilometers from that city, where I learned about local-level differences as well as similarities in Hungarian nationalistic perceptions. Compared to the city of Cluj, the village commune of Zsobok felt like a "remote place" where "real" anthropological fieldwork could be conducted with face-to-face interaction between the anthropologist and informants. In this setting, with about 150 families living fairly isolated from the hub of city traffic, nationalistic stereotypes and images have appeared in striking ways. Traditional "participant observation"—a phase that has been referred to by Vincent Crapanzano as "meaningless" but one that brought locals' ideas very close to me[64]—resulted in personal discoveries not encountered in the ethnographic literature on Hungarians in Transylvania previously. Following the 1989 December revolution in Zsobok the event everyone talked about was the restitution of Hungarian property. Unlike Romanian communities in Transylvania, Hungarians not only viewed the collective farms with the usual hatred against the former communist state, they saw their national identity attached to the collectivized land. By reclaiming their landed properties, they also repossessed their identity forcefully taken away by the Romanian state in the late 1950s. In less than a few months, Hungarian villagers dismantled the state farm, demolished the walls, ripped out the cables, and redistributed the animals there to individual families. By early 1991, all families in Zsobok had returned to farming on their own land.[65] These were happy times for many, although some families quarreled seriously about the exact amount of land that they should receive.

Adding to my previous, and rather naive, understanding of Hungarian nationalistic behavior, villagers' perceptions revealed how implications of ethnic stereotyping and nationalistic, ethnocentric rhetoric were embedded in the popular consciousness. In questions about stereotyping Romanians, Hungarian villagers expressed their disdain and wish to remain separate from them, arguing that it was best to carve out a separate ethnic space for both groups. Most Hungarians expressed their overt desires that they did not want to live with Romanians, adding that in the past, such closeness always resulted in "trouble." Specifically, when asked about their acceptance of the Romanians' proximity to Hungarians ("Would you mind if Romanians buy land in your village?"), about 50 percent of Hungarian adults in the settlements answered a resounding "no" (more men answered in the affirmative, though). However, when asked whether they had misgivings about Romanians moving in and buying a house next to them, most of the Hungarians (95 percent) replied that they did not wish this to happen. But such intolerance was even more of an accepted local rationalization when interethnic coexistence concerned Gypsy settlers. Although Hungarians accept Gypsies as musicians at their weddings or as itinerant traders, they are reluctant to accept them as close residents of their village. Balancing such a nationalist distancing mechanism between Hungarians and Romanians has existed as a reality. In Transylvania, marriages between the two groups are common occurrences. Several rural families had such arrangements. Marriages between Gypsies and Hungarians are rarely, if ever, sanctioned, however.

Even after the democratic changes in Romania, Transylvanian Hungarian urban and village institutions were designed quite obviously to maintain separateness between the majority and minority groups. A few artistic (mostly elite) circles do exist, but even at the Babes-Bolyai University in Cluj, Hungarian students form their separate cultural, political, and artistic clubs and circles, and there are few institutions that transgress national group boundaries. This has been an even more acute problem since from the beginning of 1997 the separation of the university into a Romanian and Hungarian university was voiced by many Hungarians. The RMDSZ, with the leadership of Béla Markó and Bishop László Tőkés, has been intent on pressuring the Romanian government to make concessions, specifically asking for the full return of confiscated Hungarian property, but also the reinstatement of the Hungarian university in Cluj.[66]

These ideas, which to the Romanian leadership are tantamount to full-scale separatism and autonomy, even after the thaw resulting from the new government in office since 1997, have been expressed by many Hungarians, the educated and the villagers alike. Obviously the elites use the language of Europeanness, European stability and democracy, and they refer to the various international treaties and documents that highlight the contradictory nature of the Romanian constitution.[67] Villagers and urbanites translate these words into everyday parlance as simply acts of cultural preservation, maintenance of heritage, belonging to the Hungarian nation, and even frictionless coexistence with the majority Romanians. Both villagers and urbanites harbor a deep-seated resentment of each other. Often this is based on memories of border realignments, past injustices, and bloody conflicts during the interwar period and the heyday of Stalinism. Mistreatment at the hands of Romanian bosses is a frequent grievance. A story of an elderly lady in the village where I lived for six months illustratives how national conflict may be generated locally with transnational consequences. While this account concerns her solely, it also is extremely important, for it reveals the continuation of the hidden tensions between the two nationality groups and, moreover, how members of the Hungarian diasporas in Transylvania are connected to Hungary. In the community of Zsobok, there is only one general physician who visits the settlement occasionally. When this elderly woman needed serious medical care, she was sent to the local county hospital for treatment. Here a young Romanian doctor inquired about her condition, and she tried to explain, to the best of her knowledge, what she felt. Not finding adequate words in Romanian to describe her condition, she resorted to Hungarian. The doctor replied sarcastically that she should learn Romanian well enough to communicate with doctors, since it is the state language and that, lacking an adequate description, she might not be treated by (Romanian) doctors.

The elderly in Zsobok, just like elsewhere in European rural communities, are marginalized. However, their marginalization is especially acute here, since the majority of youth moved to nearby towns and only visit their native village on weekends, leaving the elderly to fend for themselves. This story (of which various versions exist in folklorized forms among Hungarians in Transylvania) indicates why Hungarian villagers prefer to travel forty or fifty miles to another town, or in special cases, even to neighboring Hungary, where they feel that they can rely on the care of Hungarian doctors, avoiding the Romanian county hospitals at all costs.[68] Since the Hungarian state set aside special funds for treating Hungarians from neighboring states—a case similar to students wishing to study in Hungary—the antagonism between Hungarian minority patients and Romanian majority doctors is more easily understood.

Such stories also illustrate the sense of belonging to a minority group and how these new times force Hungarians and Romanians to cope with their everyday realities and shape their conceptions accordingly. Naturally, the 1990s also forced Hungarians in Transylvania to redefine and contest the repoliticization of their identities and relations with other nationalities. This was a period during which Transylvanian Hungarians saw the birth of their political party as well as the creation of one of the most xenophobic, anti-Hungarian Romanian organizations, the Great Romania Party. This party was even too chauvinistic for the ruling coalition, hence it was banned from it in 1995. Unfortunately, the tension and distance between the two populations in Romania have been growing ever since. Despite governmental changes in 1997, and in the beginning in 2001, both villagers' and urbanites' statements about the different spheres of existence are sadly but truly reinforcing this cleavage in present-day Romania.

Conclusions:
A New Anthropology of the New East?

In this chapter, the main concern has been the personal experiences of fieldwork in the 1980s and 1990s, with a focus on how the state and nation were specifically constructed and contested in Hungary and Transylvania. Through such an anthropological lens we are provided with fascinating glimpses of the ways in which the Hungarian and Romanian states have experienced the collapse of state socialism and have negotiated the creation of their new polities and national selves. Why this case is specific may be pointed out by stressing that the emergence of non-communist Hungary and Romania was neither similar to the remaking of German identity nor the peaceful separation of Czechoslovakia into Czech and Slovak nation-states. Hungary and Romania, moreover, experienced the period 1989–1990 wholly unlike the breakup of Yugoslavia and the creation of independent nation-states of the war-torn Balkan peninsula.[69] Specifically, the remaking of two Hungarian communities has been juxtaposed to reveal how the 1990s transformed the notions of state, nation, and community in Hungary and Romania. What were these new developments that warranted serious, in-depth anthropological attention? For one, ethnicity and nationality have both been politicized, a phenomena widely attributed to the reshaping of European identities since the 1980s. Another important factor has been the presence of multi-party democracy and liberalized and (mostly) privatized economy that is fully dependent now on the market forces monitored by the European Union and transnational corporations.

The anthropological fieldwork in socialist Csepel turned out to be quite an ethnographic can of worms. The socialist town was found to be a largely nonsocialist, atheistic community that exhibited lively signs of religious adherence. The homogenous socialist working-class community was in reality a heterogeneous one: regional, gender, class, and ethnic backgrounds divided local residents. Adding to their already heightened sense of Hungarian identity, both urbanites and villagers realized that they have been situated at the center of the remaking of the post–socialist Hungarian nation. When in 1990, after his inauguration as prime minister, József Antall uttered the historic words that in spirit he considered himself the prime minister of not 10 million but 15 million Hungarians, referring to those Hungarians outside of Hungary, leaders of the neighboring states were shocked. Yet his words were followed by actions: the Duna television station and a special department of Hungarians outside of Hungary (HTMH) were set up to reconnect the Hungarian state with the Hungarian diaspora, regardless of citizenship and locality. In 1995, after the socialist government took office, a new economic policy foundation ("New Handshake") was initiated to develop financially solid trade and business enterprises between Hungarian and Romanian companies in Transylvania. These acts have fundamentally altered the way in which Hungarians in Transylvania have started to view Hungary, the Romanian society at large, and themselves. This new collective selfhood was a constructed and negotiated creation out of common perceptions and interests mediated by the new nationalist power elites, both in Hungary and Romania. Finally, by reflecting upon fieldwork experiences in Zsobok and Csepel, we are provided with an important insight into how research practices form and shape the way in which anthropologists gain firsthand knowledge of how local issues are nationalized and how transnational concerns shape local events.

Chapter 4

Literary Contests: Populism, Transylvania, and National Identity

As we have witnessed before, nationalistic representations and contestation have been entangled with forms of historiographical and political representations of a Hungarian "nation." Yet for the past 200 years, a particular ideology known as populism—and its nature and imminence in national consciousness—has preoccupied Eastern European scholars and statesmen alike. Questions such as "What is a Hungarian?" "Who is a Hungarian?" "Why is it important to ask such questions?" have haunted writers, poets, politicians, and historians. For Hungarian intellectuals, especially scholars and writers, answering these questions may even be said to be an obsessive pastime. For it is in the historical and literary narratives where we find the most crystalized form of definition for nationhood, identity, and boundary. What Homi Bhabha calls the "locality of national culture" is where the center of the literary nationalist polemic lies concerning Transylvania, Hungarianness, and its related Hungarian–Romanian dispute.[1]

This chapter analyzes the populist ideological fiction by which Hungarian peasants—"proper peasants" of the classic ethnographic tradition in Hungary—were turned into "proper Magyars."[2] The phrase "proper Magyar" is used here to explain the common nationalistic assumption suggesting that, by defining the "proper," "real," or "true" subjects of a nation (i.e., the "true Magyar"), one can identify those who belong to the nation, and hence exclude those who do not.[3] This exclusive boundedness implies, wrongly to my mind, a set of common assumptions as to what constitutes a nation and those who live in it. Especially true in this thinking is the implied notion that those who are the "real" or "proper" subjects of this nation have certain responsibilities and rights that others do not. This concept of national belonging, as shown in the previous chapters, has then a justified territoriality at its core. This notion easily conceives of border realignments and the exclusion (or expulsion) of others often described as aliens and strangers within the indigenous nation-state. What this chapter attempts is to ascertain how the scholarly and geopolitical contestation of Transylvania has been based on several, but interrelated, definitions. Central to them are: what constitutes a nation, who belongs to it, and, moreover, the location of the national space, homeland, or territory as it has related to that terrain and its various populations.

Populism

When anthropologists discuss questions of "race," "physical purity," or "blood," they do not subscribe to these as valid scientific criteria, particularly as a basis for establishing eligibility to membership in a nation or an ethnic group.[4] However, these concepts constitute the core of long and enduring debates, not only in anthropology but in related disciplines as well. Today's anthropologists take it as a given that no one is endowed with genes or blood cells that prompt him or her to weep or curse when a national anthem is played. But since in nationalistic ideology the connections between nationality, blood, and origins are valid assumptions, both of the terms "proper" and "Magyar" are therefore problematic. Even more problematic furthermore is their relationship to each other, and it is precisely this troubled intersection that needs to be deconstructed here (therefore, the concept "proper Magyar" has to be deconstructed). I take this concept to be an ideologically motivated cultural construct, aiming at influencing the outcome of both national and international politics as they relate to the status of Hungarians in Hungary as well as in Transylvania.

Despite scholarly claims to the contrary, Hungarian nationalism, and its cultural offshoot, populism, has been envisioned by elites as a homogeneous, unified concept, a loosely structured mosaic of values, historical representations, and political claims defining ethnonational criteria for membership in the Hungarian nation. Populism as a political ideology is a rural reform movement that uses the government as an instrument to promote the advancement of lower social strata against industrial capitalism, urbanization, and unemployment. Populists favor a strong government to fight inequality, disorder, and large businesses by extolling the benefits of agrarian life.[5] Since the mid-1800s, populism in its original East European form—of which the Russian *narod-*

nikism was one of the earliest and most well-known examples—was an elite-led liberal and socialist rural-based movement. This ideology was loosely connected to the French utopian socialist tradition of Saint-Simon, Proudhon, and Fourier.[6] The connection between populism and nationalism was easily made in the Eastern European mind. As Anthony Smith suggests, "When some intellectuals began to identify the small man with the 'people' and the people with the 'nation', urging a return to rural and small-town simplicities, the ensuing populist nationalism found a mass following."[7] From the beginning, however, Hungarian populism differed from other East European populist movements, in four important ways. First, following World War I, Hungary did not initiate and execute large-scale agrarian reforms directed primarily against minority ethnic groups, as was the case in Czechoslovakia, Romania and Yugoslavia.[8] Second, Hungarian populism was slowly transformed from a strictly agrarian-based popular revolt into an elite-supported literary and political movement, a move facilitated by the interwar Hungarian government's shift to the extreme right. Third, since the 1920s, populist elites transformed their strong anti-capitalist stance into a more moderate and liberal one—favoring a middle-road solution between socialism and capitalism and realizing that Soviet agrarian policies did not manage to bring about desired alternatives for the peasantry. Finally, populism of the Hungarian kind has privileged the peasantry, specifically, the Transylvanian rural Hungarian populations, as the makers and carriers of "real," "archaic," and "authentic" Hungarian culture. Moreover, in their mind, this population's heritage and survival had to be protected at any cost.

What Hungarian populism really entails then may be best summed up with the whimsical, thought-provoking "potato principle" phrase of Ernest Gellner. Gellner has suggested that this principle overvalues peasants at the expense of industrial or urban populations. For Hungarian populists, and East European nationalist scholars in general, Theodor Shanin's maxim seems to support Gellner's ironic wisdom that "peasants are a mystification."[9] What both Gellner and Shanin have in mind is very close to the ways in which populist nationalism has been homogenizing populations in its attempt to fashion a unified national identity. Gellner has stated poignantly: "Nationalism usually conquers in the name of a putative folk culture. Its symbolism is drawn from the healthy, pristine, vigorous life of the peasants, of the *Volk*, the *narod* . . . it revives, or invents, a local high culture of its own, though admittedly one which will have some links with the earlier local folk styles and dialects."[10] In order to reveal how this reification and homogenizing attempt has worked with Transylvanian culture, I describe here the elevation of the folk culture into high literary mystification, which entails an unprecedented essentializing tendency of Hungarian nationalists with peasants, Transylvania, and national unity.

From Nobles to the Proper Subjects

As known from historical studies, the long period of feudalism was an extremely rigid, hierarchical society with the King, the Emperor of the Habsburgs, at the top, the nobles below, and the rest of the population, an interethnically mixed one, beneath them. The Hungarian Empire of the Habsburgs was indeed an amalgam of culturally diverse populations. On the eve of World War I, only 51 to 53 percent were Magyars; the rest were Slovaks, Ukrainians, Romanians, Serbs, Croats, Slovenes, German-speaking groups (Schwabs, Saxons), Armenians, Czechs, Jews, and Gypsies. These populations, albeit loyal subjects of the Empire for the time being, did not, however, belong to the historical "political nation" but were simply referred to as the *misera plebs contribuens*, the "wretched, tax-paying people." On the contrary, the concept of nation (*natio*) was not used in the sense that we understand it today but was used since the thirteenth century as a privileged, class-based religious category.[11] The conservative political economic system known as the "second serfdom" facilitated a class ideology based on exclusion. In this, only noblemen were considered the politically capable force of forming a "nation." This privileged status was slightly reformulated during the eighteenth and nineteenth centuries when the two homelands (*haza*)—Hungary proper and the Transylvanian Principality—were united. Now the *nobilitas* included the Hungarian nobles, the *Szeklers*, a privileged Hungarian group in eastern Transylvania, based on their military organization on the frontier regions, and the Saxons, a German-speaking population.

The privileged nobility advocated for itself historical descent from the first Hungarian royal dynasty, the Árpád House (ruled until 1301). In some cases, a fictive memory of an even earlier Asiatic (Scythian or Hunnish) origin also was invented. This archaic origin of the Hungarians, especially the Transylvanian Szekler population, becomes extremely important for fashioning exotic indigenous Hungarian populations in Transylvania. Medieval chronicles are replete with genealogical records listing the royal lineage's relation to the ancient tribes dating back to the period of the Conquest in the tenth century. We must bear in mind, however, that many of these noble families, such as the Csák, Hunyadi, Zrinyi, and Czillei, were invited from elsewhere and came from non-Magyar ethnic backgrounds.[12] Nevertheless, they claimed legitimacy for possessing a historic right (*ősi jog*) to many of their privileges, including, of course, land. For instance, in the fascinating memoir of Arthur Patterson, an English traveler of the 1860s, we can read a passage from a proud Hungarian patriot: "The memory of our barbarian past causes even the wealthy magnate, who walks about with a quizzing-glass stuck in his eye, and who does not even know how to speak Hungarian, to be proud of the name of Magyar."[13]

This suggests that the historical and political nation meant, above all, a noble status, land ownership, and exclusiveness limiting the rights of millions of rural inhabitants in spite of language, religion, or ethnicity. Thus the question of who is the proper Hungarian or Magyar was embedded in the status quo of the nobility, its historic and legal rights, and its values and lifestyles. This was, however, an uneasy marriage, for many privileges of the *nobilitas* depended upon inheritance and/or rights granted by the Emperor. For the House of Habsburg, the reward of aristocratic titles entailed the creation of an unprecedented group of loyal supporters. While many of these noble families boasted of their "native Magyarness," beginning in the nineteenth century and especially after the *Ausgleich* (The Compromise) in 1867, they came more and more from German, Romanian, Slovak, and Jewish ethnic backgrounds.[14] Since Latin and then German were the *lingua franca* of the Empire, knowledge of the Magyar language was not a decisive element, that is, not until the early decades of the beginning of the nineteenth century, when the first breeze of official nationalism swept through Hungary.

In fact, the intellectuals of this period, György Bessenyei (1747–1811) and Ábrahám Barcsay (1742–1806), both cavalry officers in the Empress Maria Theresa's Hungarian Guards, began to criticize their contemporaries who did not speak Magyar. It was not without the influence of the emerging German and French literary nationalism—especially Herder's concept of *Volkgeist* (spirit of the people, the folk)—that these writers propagated the knowledge of Magyar as the country's language, its distinct culture, and its "heroic Asiatic" past. Bessenyei, for instance, believed that the "common people were the *trustees* of Hungarian culture . . . and while the serfs speak in Hungarian their overlords cannot dismiss that language."[15]

Despite this, nineteenth-century noble families disregarded the language question: both Baron József Eötvös (whose name is connected to organizing Hungary's educational system and its minority laws) and Count István Széchenyi (often called, in nationalist historiography, the "Greatest Hungarian," *a legnagyobb magyar*) learned German as their mother tongue. They did not speak Magyar fluently until well into their middle-age years, thus language and religious preference were not in contention as long as they fit into the ideology of the imperial divide-and-rule ideology. While in 1792 the government required every official to show competence in the Magyar language, it was proposed to be the Kingdom's official language only in 1836, and not until 1848 did it become compulsory in public schools. From this point on, we can speak of a special form of ethnonationalism, when language became one of the foundations for identification with the dominant group, the Magyars.

Even after the outbreak of the 1848–1849 War of Independence, when Lajos Kossuth first considered the idea of a nationality law, the name of the country was changed from the Latin "Hungaria" to "Magyarország." This shift in perception espoused the view that the country belonged to the Magyar "nation" and that all other non-Magyars were its "nationalities." It will suffice to recall that the word "Magyar" was used in legal terms in its Latinized version of "Hungarus," while the nationalities were referred to as "Hungarus nativus." Among them were Slovaks, Romanians, and Croats, who were considered "the natives of Hungary." It is safe to say that until the implementation of the Magyar language in state, legal, and educational matters, the lower classes were on somewhat safer ground with their group identification. Their status was that of the "peasants" (*parasztok*) or, more archaically, "poor people" (*pórnép*)—the "wretched tax-paying people" mentioned earlier—without an identification based on nationality and the mother tongue.

PEASANTS, THE NOBLE SAVAGES

Michael Herzfeld suggests that "local archaism within the modern nation-state belongs to a long, Eurocentric tradition."[16] This Eurocentric thinking first received a great boost during the making of the Hungarian nation-state in the 1840s, a period of intense social and cultural upheaval known as the "Springtime of the Nations," which was signaled by emerging nationalistic conflicts, hatred, and border questions. Belatedly joining the French revolutionary spirit, the elites in Central and Eastern Europe were engaged in a discovery of their nation by attempting to create a new political entity: the non-Habsburg independent nation-state. The revolutions of 1848 were not isolated events but part of a general domino effect, causing monarchs to flee, governments to disband, and thousands of heads to roll. What led to the 1848 revolution in Budapest is a complex historical process which, I would argue, could not have happened without a new nationalist spirit. But this also was a cultural spirit, a cultural renaissance in which nationality and the concept of the archaic "folk" coalesced into a political agenda to separate Hungary from Habsburg rule.

Some historians have called this new literary representation not populism per se but popularist (hence the writers' names popularizers *népies*) as an attempt to elevate the peasantry first into the literary and then into the political arena. As Hungarian literary historian Lóránt Czigány asserts:

> It was called *népnemzeti* because it was thought that slowly and gradually the best features of *népies* literature were coming to assume wider implications: their validity was extended to national traditions (hence: *nemzeti*)—or rather, to use political terminology, "the people" and the "nation" were successfully amalgamated in a unity of national literature which was supposed to express the cultural aspirations of *all* Hungarians.[17]

How it happened that writers and poets quintessentialized the peasants and mystified territories, namely the Alföld (the Lowlands, or the Great Hungarian Plain) and Transylvania, is important to understand, for it provides the key to the essentialization of Transylvania and its populations by the literary elites. It was the literary imagination that provided, first in the Hungarian national consciousness, a terrain with a characteristic, rustic quality, local dishes, customs, landscape, and color. From the sixteenth century on, we can witness Transylvania's privileged position in Hungarian literary narratives. As mentioned before, this is the time when Transylvania enjoyed a somewhat separate and semiindependent status from the Kingdom of Hungary, even though a large part of it was under direct Ottoman control. The writings of Count Zrinyi (1620–1664), of Croatian background, are telling in this respect. Along with other nobles, Zrinyi saw Transylvania as the last bastion of Christianity, a phrase that was used interchangeably at the time for the Italians by Dante, Petrarch, and Mazzini, for the Germans by Herder, Fichte, and Wagner, and for the Poles by Adam Miczkiewicz.[18] In several of his letters, Zrinyi addresses the governing prince of Transylvania, Rákóczy György II, as follows: "What is the reason for us to defend Transylvania, if her Governor does not give us hope and courage. . . . But the Transylvanian Governor should feel secure that I will be supportive of all his actions."[19] And later: "God help us that through you, Hungarians could rise again. And let us not complain, Hungary's and in fact Christianity's shield, although separated from Pannonia, is still capable of defending itself."[20]

Similar to Zrinyi's concerns, the letters of Transylvanian Kelemen Mikes (1690–1761), written from exile in Turkey to his aunt, similarly praise Transylvania. In particular, Mikes adores the Szekler landscape, a region where he was born. In one letter he compares the waves of the Mediterranean Sea to the "mighty mountains of Transylvania"; in another letter he calls Transylvania his "beloved fairyland."[21] From the eighteenth century on, the epitaphs for Transylvania as a "fairyland" and a "treasure trove" (of Hungarian history and culture) have become standard tropes in populist thinking.

The land and its archaic peasant populations were voiced in the eighteenth century in literary fiction. One of the most notable voices was József Gvadányi's (1725–1801), a retired cavalry general of Italian extraction. In his travelogue epic "A Village Notary's Journey to Buda" (*Egy falusi nótárius budai utazása*), we meet a diverse group of happy, pristine, and hospitable country folk, described not unlike Chaucer's pilgrims. As it was, in Gvadányi's literary recollection, all Magyar speakers were the peasants, but on the contrary the town of Buda represented their antithesis: it was filled with aristocrats who, while priding themselves on their Hungarianness, spoke German and followed the latest fashions of the West. Conversely, the "real" Hungarian peasant was presented as being proud of his or her heritage, tradition, and fancy folk attire.[22]

Perhaps the most eloquent nineteenth-century testimony comes from poet Sándor Petőfi (1823–1849), who is claimed in the national literary pantheon as one of the "great national poets" whose Slavic ethnic origin is largely ignored in the process of nation formation. His poem *The Great Plains* (*Az Alföld*) beautifies it while comparing it to the mountain range of the Carpathians:

> *What are you to me, land of the grim Carpathians,*
> *For all your romantic wild-pine forest?*
> *I may admire you, but I could not love you,*
> *For in your hills and valleys my imagination cannot rest.*
>
> *My home and my world are there,*
> *In the Alföld, flat as the sea,*
> *From its prison my soul soars like an eagle,*
> *When the infinity of the plains I see.*
>
> *How beautiful you are to me, Alföld*
> *Land of my birth where my cradle was rocked,*
> *It is here that the shroud should cover my body*
> *And my grave rise up over me.*[23]

[Author's translation]

Written in February 1847, in "I am a Magyar" (*Magyar vagyok*), Petőfi expands the horizons of the Alföld to embrace the entire country. In a patriotic voice that characterizes the poetry of his contemporaries (the Ukrainian T. Shevckenko, the Russian Pushkin, or the Polish A. Mickievicz), Petőfi declares: "I am a Magyar, my country is the loveliest land in the great expanse of the five continents." Hearing such literary utterances this is perhaps why another English traveler of the nineteenth century, John Paget, wrote:

> The Magyar peasant has a strong feeling of self-respect, at times bordering perhaps on foolish pride. . . . The Magyar has a passionate love of country, united to a conviction that no one is so happy and prosperous as himself. . . . Not a mother wails more bitterly over her lost child than the wine-softened Magyar over the fallen glories of the Hunia.[24]

Following (perhaps unconsciously) in the literary tradition founded by the illustrious names of Bocaccio, Cervantes, Chaucer, and Fielding, the rural intellectuals of Hungary exerted an influence upon common perceptions concerning the lives and plight of the peasantry. Writers such as Csokonai (1773–1805), the Kisfaludy brothers, Sándor (1772–1844) and Károly (1788–1830), and Mihály Fazekas (1766–1828) are well known for this. For instance, Fazekas's comic narrative poem in hexameter, *Ludas Matyi* (*Matthew, the Goose-herd*), idealizes the peasant hero who, after suffering enormous physical and emotional hardship, rises up to outsmart and finally eliminate the wicked landlord. It was, however, Mihály Vörösmarty (1800–1855) who recorded perhaps more than anyone before the conditions of the poor by inventing the trickster-like figure of Balga in his epic play *Csongor and Tünde* (1831). But Vörösmarty's play goes deeper still, beyond irony, stereotyping, and mythologizing. The name of Balga is a form of doublespeak, for it can be rendered both as "Lefty" (from *bal* "left") and "stupid" or "foolish." His first appearance before the play's hero, Csongor, reveals his true social status: Balga has fallen from the branch of a tree, a clever play on words, for in Hungarian the poorest of the poor is referred to as *ágrólszakadt* (literally "fallen off a branch"). Balga's position in society, like that of millions of his fellow peasants in the Habsburg Empire, is epitomized in Vörösmarty's poetic lines as the "tailor of the barren earth" who "clothes it with ears of corn."

But more than the story of the parodic representation of peasants—which lasts well into the 1930s and 1940s, when the Hungarian film industry recreated this image more vividly by placing servants, cooks, farmhands, and cotters at the mercy of middle-class mockery—Vörösmarty offers even more examples. In his *The Poor Woman's Book* (*A szegény asszony könyve* , 1847) a pathetic, elderly, poverty-ridden woman is portrayed, an image unequaled well into the twentieth century.[25]

Aside from poverty, the free-spirited herdsmen of the *puszta* (prairie) has been created to ennoble the countryside with true peasants. Not unlike the American free-spirited cowboys of the nineteenth century, the roaming outlaw horsemen of the Hungarian prairies, the *betyár* had become the number one representative figure of Hungary's national literature.[26] From novels to theater plays, from folk songs to fine arts and films, the outlaw figure has been at the center of the most quintessential, Orientalized Hungarian popular culture genre welding nation and territory.[27]

In the literary imagination, aristocrat Baron József Eötvös (1813–1871) stands virtually alone in essentializing and fictionalizing Hungarian peasant themes by transplanting his thinking into public education as well, for he was Minister of Education. In his sympathetic yet realistic portrayal of the lower classes, Eötvös not only invented the archaic, but suffering, peasant, he found ways to personalize this class. In this way, he managed to make it more acceptable for public and popular use. From Eötvös' on, the Hungarian village scenery was nothing like before. For example, his long novel *The Village Notary* (*A falu jegyzője*), published in 1845, is even more formidable in its literary and stylistic invention in light of Eötvös's age. He was thirty-two at the time and not fully a native Hungarian speaker (he received poor marks in Hungarian language and literature in school). Yet his description of the lives of petty aristocrats and civil servants is well situated within subplots that serve as a mirror to criticize the appalling rural conditions of the nineteenth century. Although Eötvös never deserted his class—he was a member of the Diet, a leading politician, and Minister of Education and Religion in the 1848 Kossuth government—his literary images are truly populist. His warm, down-to-earth characterization of the peasants of his time positions him ahead of later romantics (such as János Arany [1817–1882] and Miklós Jósika [1794–1865]), whose folkloristic brush painted a tapestry of peasant culture without much critical edge. On the contrary, Eötvös' writings, especially his short stories, such as *A Slovak Girl in the Lowlands* (*Egy tót leány az Alföldön*, 1854), *The Miller's Daughter* (*A molnárleány*, 1854), and the *Winter Market* (*Téli vásár*, 1859), perceptively and uncompromisingly reveal the condition of peasants and minorities.[28]

How literature and ethnicity coalesced in his writing can be seen in his novels. In the first, we witness the adoption by a Hungarian peasant of a little Slovak girl facing the prospect of becoming an orphan. Eötvös moves beyond the conventional to draw minority group issues into popular discourse. This story could only have been written by an insider who knew intimately the antagonisms between the two ethnic groups. Eötvös might well have felt obliged to counter the terrible injustices suffered by peasants living in northern Hungary under his father's tyranny. Eötvös' later political career was statesmanlike in his handling of the Kingdom's minority and nationality problems, a formidable foregrounding of liberalist thinking on ethnicity, further developed by Oszkár Jászi.

But a description of the peasantry alone—emerging now as the new literary class (the "folk" or the "people")—would not differ greatly from a depiction known in the works of Slovak, Ukrainian, Polish, and Romanian equivalents. What is unique to these pioneers of the mid to late nineteenth century is that they shifted from romanticizing to openly criticizing the Hungarian aristocracy and its poorer mirror image, the gentry. This century's literary minds were directed toward politics and questions of national independence as well as the social malaise plaguing the Habsburg Monarchy. What they saw was unarguably the connection between the leisurely lifestyles of the nobility, with its conspicuous consumption, and the wretchedness of its class counterpart. No longer mildly ironic, as in Gvadányi's self-criticism of his own class, these writers were seriously committed political, patriotic, and—for lack of a better term—critical thinkers, all essentializing peasant culture.

Vörösmarty's satirical allegory *Fate and the Hungarian Man* (*A sors és a magyar ember*, 1846), describes the idle, pipe-smoking, "rusty-knight" who "goes to vote at the sound of the drum" and lives like a tyrant in his country estate. No doubt this leads Vörösmarty to close the last stanza of *Mankind* (*Az emberek*), written in the same year, with the pessimistic: "There is no hope! There is no hope." Vörösmarty's contemporary, Petőfi, however, had a much greater dislike for the Hungarian nobles (*magyar nemes*), a group undergoing an internal crisis that tried to maintain its status as an aristocracy carrying the burden of the "political nation"—and with it all of the privileges assigned to it—even in the battlefields. In his unbridled criticism, Petőfi was a spokesman for the peasants of the Alföld and more unconsciously than not, those of the Croat, Romanian, Jewish, and Slovak dispossessed minorities whom his Magyarized Petőfi–Petrovich family also represented.[29]

Clearly, these writers witnessed that the social abyss between the haves and the have-nots was intensifying as the end of the nineteenth century drew near. This also can be illustrated by the neurotic obsession with which the déclassé nobility and gentry attempted to maintain their symbolic status in the upper echelons of social structure as the trustees of national culture and identity. Although Baron Eötvös' attempt to emancipate other nationalities living inside of the Dual Monarchy gained the sympathy of the court by the period 1867–1868, it took the last decades of the century to achieve legal status for them. This was evident not only in the educational laws but also in the status of the religions of the "others," the non-Magyar populations. Hungarian law distinguished between *religiones receptae* (accepted religions) and *religiones toleratae* (tolerated religions). The first category grouped those denominations (Catholics, Calvinists-Protestants, Evangelists-Lutherans, and Unitarians) that possessed certain rights and privileges granted by the state. The tolerated ones were, among others, the Eastern Greek Orthodox and Jews. It was due to the perseverance of Eötvös and his colleagues that the status of the latter groups was finally changed to the more advantageous privileged *religio recepta* in 1895, following years of intense debates in the Parliament.

To further complicate the issue of class hierarchy and the reemergence of the problematic issue of Magyarness, there was the creation of the nouveau riche after the turn of this century, mainly by the ennoblement of foreign, mostly Jewish, German, and Slavic well-to-do bankers, landowners, and industrialists. Contrary to the practice of the previous centuries, to become a new noble meant not only a respectable deed for the country, admitted and required by the highest authority, but full Magyarization as well. According to statistics, Hungary boasted as many as 5 percent of the country's population in the class of nobles. This was, in fact, the highest anywhere in Europe, save Poland. For example, among them there were altogether 346 Jewish families—again, the highest anywhere in Europe—of which 220 acquired their noble rank during the period 1900–1918.[30]

There were nonetheless limited possibilities for advancement for the country's many nationalities, especially the poorer classes. While education and industry were reserved for the well-to-do, the Habsburg Royal and Imperial Army (*K. u. K.*) was a more democratic, "ethnic-blind" institution.[31] As rendered so beautifully in the novels of the Viennese Joseph Roth, *Radetzky March*, and the Czech Jaroslav Hasek, *The Good Soldier Schweik*, Jews, Slovaks, Serbs, Croats, Germans, Romanians, Rusyns, Czechs, and Magyars, as well as other minorities—excluding Gypsies—tried to distinguish themselves and prove their loyalty and patriotism to the Emperor and Monarchy by enlisting in the army.[32] This facilitated a great degree of homogeneity of the institution through diversity but did nothing to counter the Great Magyar nationalism and rampant anti-minority sentiments.

It is clear that this new ideology paralleled the Dual Monarchy's push toward modernization and Westernization, forming a political economic system that fostered class antagonism as well as interethnic conflict. In a sense, the nationalistic fervor of the turn of the century also upheld a conception of racial and cultural superiority of the Magyars, compared to neighboring populations. Thus they too believed that the Magyars were not unlike the "chosen people," the "selected nation" found also in other nationalistic ideologies.[33]

In making the populist agenda, symbols and values were created by the elites that were both arbitrary and dangerous for the coexistence of nationality groups but that reinforced, through literary representations, notions of nation and territory as being one and inseparable. For example, national colors and holidays were invented. March 15, 1848, was singled out as the primary symbol of Magyarness and Magyar national independence. This date has been vividly inscribed in the memory of every schoolchild, marking the outbreak of the "lawful revolution," to use the phrase of historian István Deák. The year-long war against the Habsburg Empire had resulted in tremendous losses (some more symbolic than real), but it also epitomized the positive aspects of "denationalization" that ended the long term of feudal rule and the aristocratic "nation."[34] The new Magyardom—the "thousand-year-old-empire of Saint Stephen" as nationalists refer to the unity of the Hungarian nation in East-Central Europe—was envisioned as an independent nation-state with its large territory. In this picture the colorful, proud, and archaic Hungarians of Transylvania and the freedom-loving herdsmen of the Plains were fitting reminders that the nation of Hungary transcended state borders, an idea well illustrated in school textbooks at the turn of the century.[35]

Since there were millions living as the plain "folks," it was natural for the country's intelligentsia to turn to them both for sources of inspiration and help, especially since they adamantly believed Herder, Fichte, Goethe, and earlier Romantic writers, that these people alone were capable of preserving the nation's past and culture. A love for the country folk, the peasant way of life, had haunted writers of the early twentieth century as well, especially those from a rural background. Those who came from the Transylvanian provinces were still more attuned to the call of the native soil and its peoples. In the case of Endre Ady (1877–1919), a poet from the Szilágyság region in Transylvania, this was less a call than a pull, in his phrase "gravity." Ady saw the gentry as doomed to extinction, its agony dependent upon the maintenance of the "Great Hungarian fallowland" (*a magyar ugar*, as he called his Hungary). For him, Hungarians were like a cast stone, always falling back to the ground. Hungary was to remain a ferry-land (*komp-ország*), a bridge between East and West, as some of his contemporaries—in particular László Németh, who used the same ideas extensively in developing populist ideology in the 1930s[36]— also wished.

Yet the pull of the land in Ady's images was not simply a reproduction of the romantic illusion of the racist German idea "Blut und Boden." For it meant, at the same time, economic backwardness, illiteracy, poverty, exploitation of the masses, parochial attitudes, mismanagement of state funds, and bureaucracy. For Ady, and his populist friends, the

combination of social plagues was just too numerous to permit Hungary
to measure up to twentieth-century standards. His disillusionment with
the gentry found consolation only in his love poetry and depiction of his
native Transylvania, a land symbolizing the Hungarian hopelessness and
marginalization in Europe. Ady's literary vision is a dynamic, if dark and
morbid, oscillation between the feminine and the patria. Writing in 1914,
at the outbreak of World War I, in *On the Bank of the Kalota River* (*A
Kalota partján*), he mythologizes out of proportion the Transylvanian
peasant of the Kalotaszeg region.

> Pompous Magyars . . .
> Security, summer, beauty and serenity.[37]

Ady was by all accounts a dreamer, not a rabid nationalist, who
befriended Octavian Goga, the Romanian poet—but in any case, not free
from the populist sentiments of the time. When Transylvania was already
celebrated by Romanian nationalists as an organic part of the Romanian
nation-state, Ady could not help his Hungarocentrism from surfacing.
Though he flatly rejected criticism of nationalistic sentiments in his
poetry, in a scathing statement he summarized his credo in his essay
"What If Romanians Take Transylvania?"

> I would give it to them . . . but wouldn't it cause Romania's
> death? . . . Transylvania you are Hungary, and if the world
> needs Hungary, you will remain with us. . . . We can survive
> the Romanian ghost . . . but the Romanians will destroy them-
> selves if they try to live in our cultured cities. . . . But luckily
> they will not find that out for we want our Transylvania, and
> we will keep it as such.[38]

THE DREAMERS

Such literary discourse shaping the conflict between Hungarian and
Romanian elites over Transylvania has remained focused in the twentieth
century on this region as a contested terrain. As argued earlier, the territorial nature of the conflict and struggle over the historical right to Transylvania have been the two foremost issues. What has figured preemi-
nently in this contestation was the notion of Transylvania as the
repository of archaic cultural forms possessed by its indigenous populations. In opposition to the herdsmen of the Great Plains, who were eradicated by the industrial developments of the twentieth century, the Tran-

sylvanian Hungarian minority was entrusted with solely preserving Hungarianness. It was the philologist Pál Magda who legitimized first the notion of Transylvania as a remote border region. By arguing for the Transylvanian's primacy in preserving the nation's past, culture, and language, he wrote: "Pure Magyar may be found only among those who live far away from Hungary's borders and away from foreign enclaves. Hence the Magyar tongue should draw, as much as possible, on this source for its standards."[39] Obviously, for the elites, this populist ideology legitimized the connection between territoriality and national unity for the Transylvanian Hungarian population, whose mission is to carry out and preserve the archaic national traditions. As Terry Eagleton puts it: "The metaphysics of nationalism speak of the entry into full self-realization of a unitary subject known as the people."[40] With him, as with Gellner, we may emphasize that the "folk" was the peasantry inherited from the literary predecessors and continually recreated by the writers' imagination at the beginning of the twentieth century. This literary imagination forged the notion that Magyarness and its ways were represented by the essence of Transylvanian peasantness. It was as though the very color of that life bore testimony to its force and gravity, which coincided with the influence of self-congratulatory state celebrations around 1896, when the Hungarian government spent huge sums of the state treasury on the thousandth anniversary of the founding of St. Stephen's Crown's Land.

Turn-of-the-century popular culture was, to say the least, anything but modest. Both Hungarians and Romanian engaged in heated debates concerning the authenticity of their peasant cultures and tried to discover the "most" beautiful and archaic folk songs, dances, folk dress, ballads, and remnants of material culture.[41] The Millennial celebrations in 1896, as it was called then, saw the first open-air museum (The Millennial Village). Here, Transylvania received a central place with the assistance of eager ethnographers, among them János Jankó and Ottó Herman.[42] In the City Park of Budapest, an exact replica of the Transylvanian castle of Vajdahunyad (Romanian Hunedoara) was built to honor the fifteenth-century Hunyadi family of nationalist pride, this very family itself claimed by both Hungarian and Romanian historiography.[43] Lavish celebrations, operettas, officers' duels, horse races, pompous state funerals, fashion shows, and cabarets characterized much of nationalizing Hungary at that time. The ladies and gentlemen of Vienna, Prague, and Budapest elevated folk motifs into haute couture; the "fancy Hungarian" dress (*díszmagyar*) and the anti-Habsburg red, white, and green costumes came into being. In painting and sculpture, enormous landscapes represented Hungary's glorious mystical terrain. Battles of the past preserved Magyardom in the face of Habsburg colonialization. It is enough to mention the monumental paintings of Mihály Munkácsy and Árpád Feszty to recall the colors (not only the red, white, and green) of the nation, its past and heroic tastes. The former, for instance, embarked on an expedition looking for true Hungarian faces for his paintings. One of his most famous paintings, *Conquest* (*Honfoglalás*), today housed in the hall of the Parliament, has a story attached to it that reinforces the intersection of literary and visual representation concerning nationalist history and the supremacy of Transylvania in the Hungarian imagination. The region between the town of Cluj and Jebuc (Zsobok), a place of my fieldwork, mentioned previously, was discovered by the Hungarian elites. Not far from Jebuc, in Jegenye (Leghia in Romanian), a health resort catered to the Budapest elites: writers, composers, ethnographers (both János Jankó and Otto Herman spent considerable time there), painters and architects, and all visited Kalotaszeg. Accordingly, Munkácsy traveled this special Transylvanian countryside in 1891 to search for models of the "true Hungarian types."[44] In this region the elites from Budapest found plenty of signs of "true" Hungarianness. With such an illustrious beginning—and later through the literature of Mrs. Zs. Gyarmathy, K. Kós, Szeffedin Szefket bey,[45] and, later, I. Katona Szabó—the myth of Kalotaszeg was created as one of the most quintessential Hungarian regions in Transylvania.

With such idyllic representations of Transylvania, as historian McCagg observes, from the beginning of the twentieth century, nationalism of the "old" type (the nobility equaled the Magyar) slowly gave way to a newer type, the "gentry equaling Magyarness," hence the term *gentry nationalism*.[46] This shift in perception entailed an unprecedented confusion about who was noble and who was not—especially since landholding, industry, and wealth became coterminous as Hungary experienced an alteration of its economy after the collapse of the Dual Monarchy. To be a "Magyar," one needed a certain occupation, élan, and lifestyle. In short, one had to live like a real gentry (*dzsentri*). This meant belonging to a casino, gambling, playing the horses, keeping mistresses, playing card games, regularly attending coffee house parties, and listening to gypsy music and all-night serenades, all this, however, without regard to ethnic and religious origin, anti-Semitism, chauvinism, and xenophobia. As one contemporary observed:

> Eating, drinking . . . cards; an exclusively animal life, with a few external adaptations which they have aped from the high society. No education, thus no future. I prefer the company of the very last Jewish writer or journalist who has had an education to the company of a member of the Danube Basin landed gentry for whom life consists of hunting, drinking, and I. O. Us.[47]

Populism not only discovered the true location of the national culture in Transylvania, and its peasants, it also developed an extreme answer to social problems. Some populist writers saw a way out of this chaotic situation by resorting to racist and eugenist ideology. Extreme nationalist ideology—for example, that expressed by the Rákosi brothers, originally of ethnic German background—proclaimed the building of a Great Magyar Nation of 30 million souls by population increase and the forced Magyarization of ethnic minorities.[48] But even more than the social Darwinist Rákosi brothers, it was—once again—literary discourse and imagination that refocused and revitalized the issue of "proper Magyarness" and nationhood. In particular, it was Zsigmond Justh (1863–1894), a nobleman of a substantial family estate, whose views on politics and culture were interfused with a self-analysis of his class. In his patriotic dreams, he had imagined saving the Magyar nation through the intermarriage of the nobility with the peasantry.[49] Justh was an educated, well-traveled man. He was, as most of his contemporaries were, knowledgeable about Germany, Switzerland, and Paris, and he believed that earlier views of saving the "Hungarian nation" from extinction were inadequate for changing times. Nineteenth-century thinkers such as Barons Zsigmond Kemény (1814–1875), Eötvös, and Count István Széchenyi (1791–1860) espoused the future of the country, led by the nobility, as a bridge between East and West, but with the understanding that it must modernize and develop in order to "catch-up with the West."

Justh, on the contrary, argued that in order to develop Hungarian identity for the future, it had to turn inward: the way to save Hungary from the "decadent," "neurological," "suicidal," and "incestual" bourgeois spirit was by a cultural and literal blood transfusion. In his writings, Justh espoused the view that the West and its values could not save the country, as it had not saved the gentry, and that only by the addition of "real" Magyar peasant blood and traditional Magyar peasant culture could it be revitalized. "We aristocrats," wrote Justh, "must protect the soil on which our country was built and which through centuries has supported out homeland and its two strongest elements, the nobleman and the peasant."[50] In his novels, the depiction of love relations between aristocrats and peasants provides a key to his utopian nationalistic vocation as a writer. He offers provocative material for psychoanalytic explorations of the turn-of-the-century mentality. There is only a fine line dividing Justh's love of the archaic peasantry from its somewhat romantic lifestyle and later racist ideology. Justh's robust stall boys falling in love with rich proprietors or servant girls providing heirs for infertile wealthy couples recall to some extent the novels of the American South. While Justh remained

a loner, similar ideas emerged in combination with the reactionary, chauvinistic *Turanian* ideology of the 1920s and 1930s.[51] This is, in fact, what
separated the dreamers from the extremists.

TURANIA: BLOOD AND DEATH OF A NATION

As argued before, the peace treaties after World War I were neither
successful in creating peaceful existence among the contending nationalities, nor were they able to settle age-old grievances. As old empires collapsed and new nation-states emerged, national industries were forced to
readjust in the wake of economic reorganization. Post–war East-Central
Europe was not only the terrain of new nation-state but an intellectual
enigma as well. Truncated in size, Hungary became both a republic and a
kingdom without a king; Romania, enlarged by Transylvania, a monarchy
ruled by a foreign dynasty; Czechoslovakia, invented by avid patriots in
America; Yugoslavia, the result of feverish Pan-Slavism; and Poland,
which reemerged after 150 years of a virtual shadow existence.

The social ills pertinent to the new Hungarian nation-state were
blamed on the nobility and its middle-class (gentry) counterpart. Liberal,
Western-educated critics of the system, such as Oszkár Jászi, tried to facilitate the creation of the class-conscious bourgeois. Their task was to rid
Hungary of these "robber-barons" and further its course toward progress
and technological development by solving economic and nationality
problems at once. While the gentry class—which, we must remember,
was the heterogeneous, aspiring but poorer middle class—lived as civil
servants and wholly entertained nationalistic sentiments, many in the
more prosperous middle and upper classes turned away from such indul-
gences, traveled widely, and enjoyed university education, primarily in the
West. This explains the bifurcation of the "urbanist liberalist" tradition
(i.e., highly educated, liberal, left) looking toward Western values and
technology on the one hand, and on the other hand, the "populist" cultural vision of a marginalized, often lesser-educated intelligentsia turning
inward to search for Hungary's solution in an oscillation between a peas-
ant-oriented tradition and an extreme reactionary nationalism. This van-
guard bourgeois, however, was so fragmented by the end of World War I
that any hope of a common liberal bourgeois tradition in Hungary after
the establishment of the Horthy regime was merely a chimera.

The gentry, high-clergy, and, in some instances, the nobility reacted
by feverishly organizing political parties and voicing their dissatisfaction
with the new conditions under which Hungary "suffered." Questions of
"Magyarness" and the fate of the truncated "nation" intertwined, to be

exploited in propaganda speeches, educational curricula, and a media reactionary revolution. The notion that post–Trianon Hungary—a reference to the place where the peace treaty was signed—would disappear from the face of the earth, no matter how absurd it may sound today, was taken seriously during the interwar period.

Concepts such as death of the nation (*nemzethalál*) and the revitalization of Magna Hungaria made fascinating if somewhat utopistic discursive practices. But as Donald Horowitz points out, such a fear has been a common trope of extremist national ideologies.[52] The new but suffering "nation"—expressed in elite parlance as the "thousand year-old curse—— was no longer the archaic and aristocratic "political nation" of the feudalistic period. Instead it encompassed two nation-states separated by the Hungarian and Romanian state borders: the smaller one referred to literally as the "truncated Hungary" (*csonka Magyarország*), and the other endowed with the illusionary title "Great Hungary" (*nagy-Magyarország*). In the eyes of nationalistic leaders, Trianon was seen as a cause for all ills, and its damaging effects—especially the loss of Transylvania, the southern and northern provinces—were voiced in international forums. Special educational propaganda was created to carry on the regime's propaganda. Hungarian students organized into the Union of Hungarian Students and the Hungarian Foreign Society, both aimed at disseminating Hungarian revisionist attempts to restore Hungary to its former borders.[53]

Others also saw that the new borders of the Hungarian nation-state were not only a Bolshevik deed but, equally important, a Pan-Germanic and Pan-Slavic geopolitical machination against the Hungarian nation as well. Transylvanian aristocrat and politician István Bethlen was one of the intellectual engines of the Transylvanian irredentist movement. He was an avid advocate of the "revisionist" political school and argued that Hungary was forcefully wedged between Slavonic and Romanian aggressive nations and therefore must fight for its very survival.

Clearly, this type of propaganda served well to mobilize tens of thousands under the banner of nationalistic interwar politics. But this itself was a sign of a cancer metastasizing throughout Hungarian society. Political lobby groups and parties of the nationalistic persuasion mushroomed with names such as the Home Defense Party (*Honvédelmi Párt*), the National Unity Party (*Nemzeti Egység Párt*, NEP), the Hungarian Race Defense Party (*Fajvédő Párt*), the Hungarian National Defense League (MOVE), and the Association of Awakening Hungarians (ÉME). Between 1920 and 1940, these were among the more extreme organizations allowed and even encouraged by the Christian, center-right Horthy regime.[54] While Hungary's territory was reduced by two-thirds and its population fell below 9 million, the country's size became more manageable—if smaller—and the

nation-state ethnically more homogeneous. To the revisionists and irredentists, however, the loss of former territories was tantamount to the
death of the nation. Their new ideology was epitomized in the three most
commonly uttered slogans of the era: *nem nem soha* (No, no, never—will
we submit to the Trianon decision) and *Emlékezzetek és Emlékeztessetek!*
(Remember and see to it, that no one forgets Trianon). The third was a
rhymed couplet that schoolchildren were required to memorize and recite
when needed: *Csonka Magyarország nem ország, Nagy Magyarország men-
nyország* (Truncated Hungary is not Hungary; Great Hungary is Heav-
enly). The exhortation to memory and remembering—just as in the previous century, when the nobility insisted that its subjects "remember" their
Asiatic and Árpádian heritage—became the quintessential underlying
agenda of all literary, cultural, and political endeavors. As Leo Pasvolsky
observed in the 1930s, "Of the five heirs of the Austro-Hungarian Monarchy . . . the treaties of peace left three contented and two discontented
nations . . . Czechoslovakia, Rumania, and Yugoslavia belong to the first
group; the defeated and dismembered Austria and Hungary belong to the
second."[55]

Feeling such an injustice, the ideologues of populism, now with far
greater force and dynamism, refabricated their movement as a radical and
critical literary and cultural direction. As I mentioned earlier, while the
gentry served as a potential source of ridicule, in post–Trianon Hungary,
the nations of the successor states (Romania, Yugoslavia, and Czechoslovakia) and the Jewish middle class were seen as the enemy within. In a bitter contestation between the political factions for the "true" representation of Magyardom, a new generation of popularizing writers came to the
scene. Among them were such illustrious figures as Zsigmond Móricz
(1879–1942), Kálmán Mikszáth (1847–1910), and István Tömörkény
(1866–1917), all continuing in the footsteps of their predecessors Petőfi,
Vörösmarty, and Pál Gyulai. In their often-romantic peasant themes,
however, they were less inclined to criticize the Horthy regime, for that
task was reserved for another group of intellectuals, the populists (*népi
írók*), who had the true zeal to uplift the peasants, both literally and
socially. They also were more agile, numerous as well as radical and
formed a more or less unified political platform to promote claims to
property, social benefits, health issues, and basic human rights on behalf
of Hungary's millions. Their radical political agenda had, however, as its
basis the idea that the peasants, the peoples, should have the right to self-
realization and a better future. Moreover, they desired that the Hungarian
peasants in Romania also should have the right to the land they worked
on and once owned. Thus nationality and territory were combined in the
radical populist agenda unknown before in Hungarian history.[56]

Many of these popularizing authors found solace in and were infatu-
ated by the mythical themes of the Central Asian (*Turánian*) origin of the
Hungarians, the "ancestral power" (*őserő*) of the peasants, and the
Romantic *Volksgeist* presumed to emanate from the culture of rural life in
Transylvania.[57] While *Turanism* was a powerful political and artistic force
supporting the status quo of the rightist and Christian government, by
claiming a Central Asiatic "difference" for the Magyars it degenerated into
an aimless mysticism akin to Richard Wagner's Aryan mythologizing.
Turanist ethnographers and folklorists privileged the peasants' cultural
"uniqueness," locating a cultural essence of Magyarness in everything
from fishing hooks and methods of animals husbandry to ritual folk
songs, archaic, "individualistic" dances, spicy dishes, and superstitions.[58]
They also were assisting in the fabrication of archaic regionalism as they
published numerous monographs on the ethnographic uniqueness of
Hungarians living in Transylvania.[59]

What is fascinating about the interwar research on Transylvania is
that various regions and settlements were suddenly discovered for their
archaic, extremely beautiful folk songs, instrumental music, embroidery,
wood carving, storytelling, dances, and house styles. The Kalotaszeg,
Szekler, and Csángó regions were identified as the most archaic populations living in Transylvania, the latter two occupying as they were the
slopes of the easternmost Carpathian Mountains.[60] In a strange fashion,
while Hungarian nationalists tried in vain to gain the sympathy of the
West to regain their territorial losses, Transylvania had already conquered
the center stage of Western mythology. This happened with the help of
Bram Stoker's bloodthirsty Count Dracula, played by Béla Lugosi, a Hungarian émigré actor in Hollywood. The two myths, the contested Transylvania and its Hollywood counterpart, had little in common, but the
popular fictional representation became known throughout the Western
world as the only Transylvania.[61] Yet connecting the two may only be possible with the narration of Transylvania, a fictional, scholarly, or nationalist contestation, that then "has the function of confirming expectancies
and therefore reinforcing the commonplace."[62] In a strange coincidence,
Hollywood celebrated Dracula (Béla Lugosi) sucking the blood of unsuspecting victims—through such classics of the horror genre as *Black Fri-
day* (1940), *The Devil Bat* (1941), *Night Monster* (1942), and *Return of
the Vampire* (1943). At the same time, Hungarian scholars were conducting blood tests on Hungarian villagers in Transylvania reconquered after
the Vienna decision in 1940.[63] The racist ideology of Turanism worked
well for the Hungarian regime in justifying its military occupation of
Transylvania. Serological and other "scholarly tests" were supposed to
prove that some Hungarian villagers possessed traits similar to those of

the Crimean Tatars. More importantly, they were eager to show that Hungarians and Romanians in Transylvania differed considerably from each other, not only in folk culture but in their genetic and bodily traits.[64]

Both the natural and social sciences were nationalized in this endeavor. In order to cater to the insatiable desires of the nationalist elites, a special form of narration also was developed during the 1930s. Inaugurated by launching the journal *Hungarian Studies* in 1935, the discipline itself "Hungarian Studies," or Hungarology, as it has been called, was initiated in 1939. Researching Hungary and Hungarians from a special interdisciplinary aspect has become a separate field of inquiry itself and has signaled the way in which humanities and social sciences can be put into the service of the national.[65] In so doing, however, this form of nationalistic endeavor not only separated the Magyar peasant from "others" of the same class in Slovakia, Romania, Poland, and Yugoslavia but, more importantly, it endowed its creation with an heir of an ancestral/Asiatic quality unique unto itself. While Turanism as a mythology was a figment of the imagination of writers and politicians—such as Gyula Pekáry (1867–1937), a state secretary, first to combat Pan-Germanism—it soon backfired. By focusing on exclusivity, on difference, it rejected the similarities and interrelationships of Eastern European peasant cultures. In turn, this fostered competition for literary and political primacy. Questions such as who was "there" first, who remained more faithful to the most ancient culture, and who was the giver and the receiver all translated into political claims and controversies over populations and territories. In a way, this form of transnational Magyarness thus not only fostered the making of the truly unbounded Hungarian nation but at the same time the emergence of Pan-Slavism and Great Romanianism.

THE POPULIST AGENDA AND TERRITORY

The populism that emerged in the 1930s was not, however, only a reactionary and conservative idea but was coupled with a good dosage of liberalism and radicalism defending Hungarian peasantry in the successor states,[66] for the populists' concerns were couched in the exploitation of small peasants by landlords, injustices of the court system, economic deprivation, emigration, and the illness rampant among peasant children. A significant difference between the new populists and the "popularizing" writers was the mixture of social backgrounds of those who boasted about their lower-class origin.[67]

The new populist writers rejected the existing order by a consolation in leftist radicalism. Turning away from the Horthy government and its supporting social strata—the gentry, reactionary clergy, and aristocratic circles—they sought to learn how peasants really lived. Many took ethnographic trips to the poorest regions to see firsthand the "secrets of the *terra incognita*."[68] It was, for them, the real "Discovery of Hungary" (*Magyarország felfedezése*), a phrase initiating a series of books with similar themes. The result of these "village explorers" (*falukutatók*) was a plethora of publications in drama, poetry, fiction, and "sociography," a blend of narrative between "sociology" and "ethnography," extolling as well as criticizing the peasant way of life.[69]

The "discovery of the new Hungary" meant, among other things, new information about parts of Hungarian rural life that had been previously unknown and the plight of the Hungarian minorities in Romania, Czechoslovakia, and Yugoslavia. To be sure, it was not always a pretty picture. Suicide, alcoholism, illness, brutal work conditions, loneliness, violence, family feuds, and poverty combined with stories of charm, warmth, and beauty. But there was self-proselytizing and indignation as well. For many populist writers it became clear that there was no "ancestral force" (*őserő*) in peasant culture, but rather a class force. But in Horthy's Hungary, this was dangerous subject matter to write about; many writers were indeed indicted or fined for a crime described as "slandering the nation" (*nemzetgyalázás*).[70]

Finally, what characterized the populist writers of the 1930s and 1940s was their unmitigated denial of the old order and their hope for the reconfiguration of a new future system. The question of survival of the Magyar nation had reached a level of obsession. The idea of the "nations' death" (*nemzethalál*) followed the populists until the end of World War II, when both the so-called "third road," or "separate Hungarian road" followers emerged from these considerations. These rather escapist philosophies argued that the nation's survival depended on its own resources and on the separation from either East (Soviet Union) or West (Nazi Germany). In the struggle for national survival, Hungary's strength was in its peasantness. Dramatist László Németh, for example, advocated a vision of populist "garden Hungary" (*kert Magyarország*), a reference to Hungary's agricultural potential in small farming in saving Hungary.[71] It is at this point that the radical populist paradigm fragmented, losing its activist, democratic, and humanist edge.

Gyula Illyés, perhaps unknowingly, summarized this dynamic in his autobiography *People of the Puszta*: "Every nation has a splendid image of itself; I took this image for reality and pursued it ferociously, having to discard more and more living Hungarians in the process."[72] This Magyarness, this characteristic resourcefulness, meant that minorities and nationalities had no real role to play in the creation of a new, properly

Magyar nation. In fact, Zoltán Szabó's writings—celebrated out of proportion during the 1930s—are replete with rejection of German and Jewish minorities and their contributions to Hungarian culture.[73]

In tandem with the government's revisionist aims, intellectuals relied on the populist message often with the help of their publishing house, "The Hungarian Life" (*Magyar Élet*). Their main concern was to keep alive the plight of Transylvanian Hungarians now under Romanian control. No other book was as successful in raising popular consciousness about this issue than György Bözödi's *The Szekler Chronicle*, which provided all of the important populist agenda, among others, the suffering under foreign control, the injustices and wounds of the past not healed, and the decreasing number of Hungarians.[74]

The (re)discovery of the peasantry as possessing "real" cultural values and being carriers of "real" and "true" Magyar traditions was appropriated by those who did not necessarily share the views of the extremists. One such development was the Pearly Bouquet (*Gyöngyösbokréta*), a folkloristic revival movement started in 1931. In this national fervor, villagers from all over the country were brought to Budapest to perform their native dances, to sing songs, to restage local customs, and to parade in their Sunday best in front of thousands of Hungarians as well as Western tourists.[75] This is how the movement's founder, Béla Paulini, wrote about its beginning:

FIGURE 4.1   Ethnographic populism 1: Hungarian cowboys in the Hortobágy region as captured in propaganda postcards of the 1930s. (Author's collection.)

The groups of peasants, in their original peasant costumes, sang their ancient songs, danced their ancient dances and exhibited their ancient customs, and these primitive but manifold manifestations of the folk psyche turned out to be an event of the most arresting beauty. Even in the Hungary of Trianon, which has been so sorely mutilated, there is still an infinite variety of Hungarian peasant art. The Hungarian Bouquet movement is a fairy tale come true. The gorgeous pomp of the East amidst the perfect culture of the West.[76]

After 1940, following the reconquering of regions lost to Slovakia, Romania, and Yugoslavia by the Trianon Treaty, the Hungarian regime tried to organize a cult to forget the terrors committed.[77] State pageantries and lavish celebrations were organized, and the populist celebration of peasantness received a new boost by the Pearly Bouquet. Village groups also were invited to participate in the processions of Saint Stephen's Day, on August 20, in the Castle district of the nation's capital. Authentication of these village performing ensembles went far enough to convince the (mostly Western) audience that what they saw was real. On occasion, tourists were taken to some of the villages for a special fair. Antedating present-day ethnotourism, villagers paraded in their best, most colorful clothes and staged miniature wedding celebrations.[78]

What Shanin calls the "mystification of the peasants" had begun in earnest in a public arena: now tourists were invited not only to Budapest but to regional centers to observe and enjoy "typical" peasant weddings, grape harvests, and the "hospitality of the Hungarian peasant." As the movement developed, the original ten villages grew to over 220 village groups, and the intellectuals devised the movement's own newspaper. Since the industrial working class did not possess anything as colorful, richly embroidered, and distinct, it fell naturally upon the few selected peasant communities to carry the burden to play the "natives" in the nationwide reservation. This museum-theater backfired in certain instances: folk costumes became more colorful and showy, losing their authenticity in the process. Moreover, where dances were not "fiery" or "earthy" enough, steps, formations, and songs were added to impress the Western audiences. In some instances, ethnographers were eager to "authenticate" these invented stage productions. Their efforts, however, were met with resentment, both on the part of the organizers and in some cases the local village elites, who did not wish to be left out of the glory of state festivities and perhaps shake the hand of Hungary's governor, Miklós Horthy.

FIGURE 4.2   Ethnographic populism 2: A Hungarian Pearly Bouquet village group performing a wedding ritual from Lunca de Jos, Romania in 1941. (Author's collection.)

The areas of the Great Plain region—such as the Palóc, Matyó, Hortobágy, and Sárköz—and those of Transylvania (the Szeklers, Csángó, Kalotaszeg, and the Mezőség) became important "ethnographical centers." The national and international attention singled them out as potential sources of hard-currency earnings. At the same time, many of these regions were especially hard hit by the irregularities of the climatic conditions, the world recession, and the encroaching industrialization. As indicated by one of the most remarkable books on the Matyó villages, the poorer the villagers grew economically, the fancier their costumes became. Their indulgence contributed to a certain extent to the economic disempowerment of many peasant families, as all of their meager earnings were spent on colored ribbons, pearls, and silk, wool, and cotton fabrics, most of which came from the West. The Pearly Bouquet movement invented for the stage the true and colorful "peasantness" and, strange as it may seem, associated it with proper Magyarness.

THE POPULIST ELITE REBELLION

As I indicated in the previous chapters, the borders were realigned several times between Hungary and Romania during and after World War

II. In 1945, the reconquered Trianon territories were reawarded to the successor states, and Hungary, along with her neighbors, embarked upon building fraternal socialist states. This was the course that Czech writer Milan Simecka referred to as the building of *moribund utopias.* The peasantry, as in decades earlier, was the first group to feel the immediate results of this change. Following the establishment of Stalinism, massive and rapid collectivization deprived them of their land, farm equipment, animals, and, subsequently, even their consciousness. They were peasants no more. They became, in the eyes of the Stalinist state, retrograde, backward, and an unrevolutionary force. The "idiocy of the countryside" that Marx envisioned for the peasants was translated by the ideologues as actions. In order to create the revolutionary working class, the peasantry had to be eliminated and elevated into the conscious, politically correct class, such as "socialist, collectivist workers."

This was in fact one of the few "successes" of the Stalinist and later the Kádárist state in Hungary. This also occurred in Romania under the rule of Petru Groza, Gheorgiu-Dej, and later Ceauşescu. Forced collectivization, intimidation, and jail sentences achieved their aims: by 1960, all land was incorporated as collective and state farms, and tens of thousands of rural youth found new occupations in the mines and steel mills. In a sense, it might be argued that "proper Magyarness" within the socialist state was predicated upon one's working-class status and membership in the Communist Party. While the creation of the much-needed socialist "man" and "woman" failed, the ideology of proletarian internationalism and communist brotherhood managed to refashion the now "outdated" and "backward bourgeois" image of Magyarness, however, it was not based on peasantness or archaic cultural values but on working-class alliance and proletarian consciousness.

During the 1950s and 1960s, themes of Magyarness and Transylvania were rarely found in artistic or literary works. As the peasant middle class was silenced or eliminated by the regime, its artistic death also was signaled for the time being. Some attempts were made by the country's literati to redress this dispossessed mass in the form of "socialist" literary and artistic works. Novels, plays, and cinema critiqued the former capitalist system and its mistreatment of peasant culture. One prime example of this production is the cinema of Miklós Jancsó. But Jancsó too dealt not with the plight of the peasantry during the time of Stalinism and the early years of the Kádárist era—subjects that obviously were taboo—but with "safer" themes, foregrounding his characters within historical periods but with acceptable socialist or class conflict themes.[79] Romanian cinema also portrayed peasants as heroes, engorged in the historical themes of the Dacians, Romanian historical heroes, and folkloristic outlaw heroes.[80] No films produced in the 1960 and 1970s, either in Hungary or Romania, dared to mention territorial questions or even the minority situation in Transylvania. These themes only surfaced a decade later under a new movement of neopopulism, a topic that I will discuss later in detail.

To create the socialist peasantry and values, the regimes disbanded most of the populist writers' circles. Many of its more talented writers, such as Imre Kovács and Zoltán Szabó, had opted to emigrate and live their remaining lives in oblivion. Others such as Gyula Illyés, István Sinka, Pál Szabó, László Németh, and József Erdélyi were either silenced by the regime or withdrew into a self-imposed exile. Many, such as Péter Veres, Ferenc Erdei, and József Darvas, originally were enthusiastic supporters of the socialist era and took up leading positions supporting the Stalinist regime. It was, however, only after the amnesties of the early 1960s when signs emerged on the horizon beckoning former populists to manifest themselves, even though movements similar to the radical literary populism of the 1930s or the Pearly Bouquet between 1931 and 1944 were not allowed to surface. Some, such as Illyés or Németh, helped pave the way for the establishment of their youthful alter ego, the neopopulists. The neopopulists, most notably Ferenc Juhász, László Nagy, István Ágh, and especially Sándor Csoóri, demanded attention by opening up a more relaxed political climate that encouraged mild criticism, experimentation, and diversion from the officially favored "urbanist" (bourgeois humanist) and "socialist" literary forms.[81] But with the emergence of this group, there was another equally if not more significant literary direction led by those writers whose family and regional backgrounds were located in the geopolitically sensitive region of Transylvania—Istvan Csurka, Ferenc Sánta, Zoltán Jékely, and Zoltán Zelk. These writers, along with the Grand Man of populism, Illyés, recreated populism in a newer, more acceptable form. In specific, they called for the readmission of the peasantry in literary and political life. In *Good Mother*, for instance, Gyula Illyés writes in a way that describes well this neopopulist agenda and the way in which Hungarian national consciousness slowly but surely gained admittance into the accepted socialist art in Hungary:

> *She takes me in her loving arms,*
> *Dispensing justice, giving warmth,*
> *As son she desires only me,*
> *I alone will then Hungarian be.*[82]

In László Nagy's *The Bliss of Sunday*, we find a much more settled voice in his celebration of his native countryside as he takes pleasure in citing local place-names:

My villages, yellow, white, watchers along the road-dust.
I see you tip your roof-caps to disaster.
To number your names is music: Vid, Nagyalasony, Doba,
Egeralja, Káld and Berzseny, Kispirit, Csögle, Boba.
A universe you were.[83]

Similar to the turn of the century, common themes were part of school textbooks and the popular press. By the late 1960s and early 1970s, however, Hungarian literature enjoyed a special position under the tutelage of socialist minister György Aczél. This acceptance, however, already signaled that new social undercurrents were taking place in literature and in the arts in general. Clearly, the influence of a renewed sense of national identity and consciousness was felt in the culture and politics of the time. It was Gyula Illyés—often referred to as the professional nationalist—who, being privileged as he was, raised his voice openly against the oppression of Hungarian minorities in Czechoslovakia and Romania. An eyewitness saw Illyés and his quest as follows:

Cursing the "rotten Czechs" and "those impossible barbarians— the Rumanians—who are tormenting our poor peoples in Transylvania," Illyés insisted that "a poet must have the courage to talk because the politicians can't. . . ." To him, the principal idea is that "when people can't express their ideas in a constitutional, legal way, they express them in literature. . . ." Illyés sees Hungarian poetry, from its very inception, as a literature of resistance.[84]

CONCLUSION

To conclude, in the beginning of this chapter, the term *proper Magyar* was introduced and analyzed as a cultural construct. This construction was the single most important element in Hungarian populism influencing the creation of the nation-state. As this chapter has demonstrated, two major nationalistic movements took place in the last two centuries of the second millennium. The first, best described as "denationalization," occurred when a new spirit of anti-Habsburg sentiment arose. Language use became of utmost importance, and the nobility, the "proper Magyar nation," was under direct attack by the aspiring Magyar (or Magyarized) intelligentsia. In order to undermine the hegemony of the aristocracy, Magyarness became identified as a political and cultural ideology. It drew its sources from the past as well as the literary images of the *peasantry*. It identified the nobility as its double: "*We* are the proper Magyars," and in turn it denounced the nobles and gentry as non-Magyars. Politically and legally until well into the mid-nineteenth century—and culturally well beyond that date—the nobility was perceived as the sole trustee of the nation. The equation between nobility and Magyarness was clear, unquestionable, *and* unproblematic. It meant, first, the unconditional acceptance of the Habsburg House's legitimation; second, the maintenance of the status quo of aristocratic positions; and, finally, the upholding of the Kingdom in order to guarantee and maintain the privileges of the nobility. However, it soon became clear to the country's elites that in contrast to the nobility, the peasantry was endowed with the burden of carrying archaic culture, maintaining ancient traditions, and preserving the nation's language.

The second period lasted well into the middle of the twentieth century and could be largely attributed to a process called "gentrification": the creation of another social stratum opposing development and progress. The process's hobby horse was Hungary's loss after World War I, but this also led to the emergence of populism, or more specifically, peasantism, which formed a radical new political force by the 1930s. The "Magyar Peasants" took over the role of "Magyar nobility" and were elevated to the trustees of "real" Magyar culture and identity. While this Magyarness identified the peasants, especially those in Transylvania, it also rejected its nonpeasant counterparts. It was inherent in populism that its creation also paralleled other, more extreme reactionary developments that rejected other minorities.

As we have seen, all of these cultural essentializing constructions, periods, and contestable movements had their own longevity and dynamism. Each is related to its predecessor in subtle ways, but neither politicians nor nationalist leaders could succumb to the frontiers imposed upon them by the Treaty of Trianon. British writer Cecil Street was quite correct when he suggested a close parallel between the Transylvanian dispute and the Sinn Fein irredentists' claim of Ulster.[85] In the minds of the nationalist elites, the borders between Hungary and Romania were only temporary, meaningless lines to be overlooked and transcended at all costs. For them, the national homeland, what in fact Homi Bhabha calls the locality of national culture, has always been Transylvania. In this chapter and in the previous one I described how Transylvania was contested by military, historiographical, literary, and scholarly means. The following chapters will bear eloquent testimonies that Cecil Street was correct on many points: he saw that territorial issues and the partition of homelands would continue until the end of the twentieth century. The Pearly Bouquet movement and literary neopopulism during state socialism created their own management of territorial conflicts for the people of Hungary and Transylvania in the 1970s through which Hungarian national identity came in quite a radical fashion.

Chapter 5

Transylvania between the Two Socialist States: Border and Diaspora Identities in the 1970s and 1980s

With all of the literary and scholarly controversies between the two socialist states, questions naturally arise: How did Hungarians in Transylvania cope with their situation in Romania at the height of Romanian state socialism? Were they capable of mobilizing their resources in combating popular majority nationalism? How did Hungarians in Hungary experience the rising tide of official state nationalism of the Romanian regime? And, finally, how was the notion of Transylvania as a remote region affected by the changing international political relations between the Hungarian and Romanian states and Western émigré communities? It would be impossible to sum up the whole array of Hungarian actions and reactions to the Romanian states' antipathy and xenophobia in a few pages. To begin with, it must be stated at the outset that since Nicolae Ceauşescu came to power in July 1965, Romania was slowly but surely transformed into one of Eastern Europe's, and perhaps one of the world's, most severe autocracies.[1] Despite all of the official propaganda to the contrary, the Romanian state had managed to embark upon a monstrous course of national communism: the creation of a unified and an ethnically homogeneous Romanian nation-state. As expressed by its main ideologue Ceauşescu himself: "Life, realities—the true judge—show that all these hardships could not prevent the making of the Romanian people, of the Romanian nation, of the unitary nation-state, could not hamper Romania's, our people's advance on the path of progress and civilization."[2] This nationalistic policy had fundamentally rearranged Hungarian and

Romanian relations; moreover, it affected Hungarian identity in both Transylvania and Hungary adversely. Just how this happened is the central theme of this chapter.

MOBILIZATION OF HUNGARIAN ETHNICITY

Whispered rumors, highly ethnocentric jokes, and ethnic slurs have been reproduced by the three cultures on a daily basis.[3] Even duing the 1990s, I was able to hear various ethnic slurs. The Romanian word *borgoz* ("homeless") has been frequently used for Hungarians. The Hungarian response is the Romanian phrase *cine mintye* ("don't forget"), reminding Romanians of Hungarian superiority and the suffering during Romanian occupation and the "Magyar times" of the 1940s.[4] Ethnic Germans are not immune to such verbal abuse. The word *bakszász* ("male Saxon") and the Saxon pejorative *Bloch* ("Vlach," used to describe Romanians as "lazy," "dirty," and "clumsy") have been uttered in many conversations in Transylvania. Yet as expressed by Hungarians in Cluj, Tirgu Mureş, and villages such as Jebuc, these ethnic images are very difficult to erase from the collective memory of these minorities, who are all reminded by the government of the past glories and injustices committed by one group over the other.

While dissent and opposition, so prominent in Hungary, Czechoslovakia, and Poland since the late 1970s, was not able to develop in Romania to the same extent, jokes and rumors provided the materials for the oppositional culture. Such cultural discursive battles also were developed by Romania's elites around the idea of the Romanian nation. As Verdery sees it: "The place of the Nation, and with it an ideology that was national, were reproduced not simply because the Party saw the Nation as a useful instrument but because discoursing on the Nation was how groups of intellectuals drew their boundaries and sought their advantages."[5] In that discursive battle, national communism worked extremely well: through political socialization, formal schooling, and stringent media control, the Romanian nation-state celebrated the unity of the Romanian people. In this official discourse, only the phrase "'Romanian minorities' with different mother tongues" was accepted. What Yorick Blumenfeld wrote on Romanian communist control of the media at that time was certainly true during the era of Ceauşescu: "Rumanian officials emphasize that their programming concentrates on education, information, and the general 'upgrading' of the admittedly low cultural level of the people."[6]

Aside from the general fear and workings of the secret police, this was certainly the cause for the clandestine emergence of a minority opposi-

tional publishing industry among Hungarian intellectuals in Transylvania. In the late 1970s and early 1980s, several Hungarian individuals in
the largely Hungarian cities of Oradea, Cluj, and Tîrgu Mureş published
important clandestine letters and pamphlets (*Ellenpontok, Transylvanian
News Agency,* etc). Many of these enumerated grave human rights violations and the deteriorating conditions of Hungarian ethnic institutions.
The small groups that formed around the *Ellenpontok* (Counterpoints)
clandestine publication between the period 1981–1983 was disbanded
successfully by the Romanian state. Hungarian intellectuals involved were
forced to emigrate to Hungary and the West.[7]

Aside from these noted examples of organized dissent and individual
actions, I was able to observe that the majority of Hungarians in Romania were fairly quiescent throughout the 1980s. Groups in Hungary and
the West did, however, take the lead in providing information to the
Western media and in raising the consciousness of Hungarians all over the
world about Transylvania. Since the Hungarian elite in Transylvania was
virtually decimated, most carved out their niche in Budapest. Illustrious
figures, such as those of Géza Szőcs, Attila Ara-Kovács, and Miklós Tamás
Gáspár, took up the issues of human and minority rights and managed to
foster alliances between Hungarian intellectuals for the just cause of Transylvania. After 1989, the first and last of these three intellectuals became
leading politicians—Szőcs, as we will see later on, in the Hungarian party
in Romania, and Tamás Gáspár in Budapest. One situation, however,
does deserve special mention: in the 1980s, Hungarian emigration from
Romania to Hungary increased to a phenomenal proportion, a situation
that was disquieting both to the Romanian and Hungarian governments.

The movement of Hungarians from Romania to Hungary, mostly
through marriage and family reunification programs, was not altogether
new. One popular saying in Hungary during that time was that "every
third family in Hungary has relatives in Romania." The increasing proportions of emigration, however, had no parallel in the history of Hungarian-Romanian interstate relations. As discussed previously, Hungary
received large groups of Transylvanian refugees at the end of World War I
and again at the end of World War II. Among them were the 17,000 repatriated Szeklers from Bukovina.[8] The Hungarian government settled these
refugees in southern Hungary, giving them houses and plots, mostly the
ones that belonged to German minorities. These so-called Schwabians left
Hungary with the withdrawing German army, or they were subsequently
expelled from Hungary in the period 1944–1945. In the 1950s and later,
the number of repatriated Hungarians was kept to a minimum, but strong
kinship ties remained between families in the two countries. As important
as these ties have been on the family level, the Hungarian government tried

to downplay their significance on the political sphere. There was not much that the two states could do, however, in order to stop the notion of the lost territory and the fate of the Hungarians in Transylvania from surfacing in local and national media from time to time. As time went by, individuals from such families managed to enter the job market as newspaper reporters, teachers, and artists, thus sooner or later their former homeland across the Romanian border was bound to surface. What made the difference though was that whether such Transylvanian themes remained within the confinement of a family or small intellectual enclave, they coalesced into a more political form of nationalist obsession.

This is indeed what took place in Hungary after the period 1950–1968. Most of the Transylvanian refugees from Romania quietly conformed to the way of life and politics in Hungary, though not fully assimilating as new citizens of Hungary. In contrast, Hungarian refugees leaving Romania in the 1980s resettled in Hungary during peacetime. They left not because of military evacuation or massive population transfer but largely because of a political cause. Plagued by material shortages as well as political and economic crises, Hungarians faced increasing hostility from the majority population. Many opted for illegal border crossings, and many simply asked for tourist visas to Hungary; once there, they simply applied for temporary residency. The following calculation shows the number of foreign citizens, for the two peak years, applying for permanent residency in Hungary in 1986 and 1987:

	1986	1987	Total
Total number of residency applications	4,952	9,068	14,020
Out of former Romanian citizens	3,284	6,499	9,783

Source: *Magyar Hirlap*, January 29, 1988.

According to this, 95 percent of former Romanian citizens who applied for permanent residency were ethnic Hungarians, and the remaining 5 percent were ethnic Romanians. The latter group was seeking political asylum in the West and only remained in Hungary temporarily. Most of the repatriated Hungarians remained in Hungary. Since there was no sound statistical data available at that time about the social background, professional qualifications, family situations, former economic status, and actual reasons for the repatriation of these "refugee Hungarians," it is very difficult to see clearly the internal momentum of the "Hungarian flight."[9] As I was able to observe during my fieldwork in Budapest in the mid-1980s, the following are some of the characteristic features: The majority of émigrés were from urban areas, many with rural ties. Most were skilled workers, professionals, and intellectuals. Nuclear families and single men and women in their twenties and thirties were the rule rather than the exception. Numbers notwithstanding, a good percentage of these repatriated Hungarians have been influential in Hungary's artistic and intellectual life since arriving in Hungary. The very presence of "Transylvanian Hungarians" gave an impetus to the public discourse on the problems of Hungarian minorities living in the neighboring successor states, especially in the fight for human rights in Czechoslovakia and Romania. A few who volunteered became spokespersons for human rights organizations and joined the intellectual opposition. Others have lived in oblivion, with little or no interest in the "struggle for Transylvania" between the two governments. Although there has not been a language barrier for Transylvanian Hungarians resettling in Hungary, some of these refugees have complained about the "cultural distance" existing between them and the "real" Hungarian citizens.[10]

IDENTITY, REGIONALISM, AND STEREOTYPES

Concomitant with the continuation of development of Hungarian-Romanian tensions, Hungarian national identity as a whole underwent a radical transformation during the 1980s. In fact, spurred by nationalistic sentiments and an increasing awareness of Western support by human rights groups, there was a new Hungarian consciousness in the making that was affecting Hungarians in the East as well as the West. The renaissance of the new Hungarian cultural awakening had, as its most profound characteristic, created a new political movement and image that united Hungarians across political borders. This new ethnopolitical process placed the Hungarians in Transylvania at the center of attention and projected a unified sense of Hungarian identity against the Romanian state. How were the various Hungarian groups in Romania affected by these developments with regard to their identity and ethnicity? In order to answer this question, we must confront the regional and class distinctions of Hungarians in Romania that I was able to detect.

All too often it is forgotten by protagonists of Hungarian nationalism, both in Hungary and in the West, that while Transylvania represents the largest concentration of Hungarians in Romania, it is nevertheless not the only region in Romania where ethnic problems have abounded. There are regions north and west of Romania (the counties of Timiş, Arad, Bihor, Sălaj, Satu Mare, and Maramureş) with a concentration of Hungarians. These "parts" were known as the Partium (*Részek*, or simply Parts) before World War I. By being outside of the historical and geographical entity of Transylvania, these areas also have been considered as playing a key role in the Transylvanian issue. True as it may be, these regionally diverse groups have exhibited a conscious Transylvanian identity. This identity has been based largely, though not wholly, on the opposition to the Romanian majority. Furthermore, their main concern was to support Transylvanianness per se, as well as the drudgery of living conditions and the fight against concomitant Romanian nationalism. Yet most of these people have been educated by Hungarian intellectuals to think of themselves as organic parts of the Transylvanian Hungarian population.

Another complementary element of the homogeneous Hungarian ethnic identity projected by nationalists is the existence of two populations with values quite different from the rest of the Transylvanian populations. As mentioned in Chapter 2, one is known as the "*Csángós*," the other the Szeklers. The origin and identity of the two have created another heated nationalistic controversy between Hungarians and Romanian.[11] The group known in Moldavia and Gyimes as "Csángós" is itself a contested community, for both nations claim it as their own. For the Romanian nationalists, the Csángós are an archaic Romanian ethnic group that converted to Catholicism during the forceful Magyarization process throughout the centuries. The Hungarian stance is equally spurious as well as dubious. All historical, linguistic, and ethnographic evidence to the contrary, Hungarian intellectuals continue to see the Csángós as distinctly but fundamentally Hungarian. In fact, they view the Csángós as a minority within a minority, and this in itself is an interesting nationalistic contradiction. While on the one hand Hungarian intellectuals believe that the Csángó diaspora is different in many ways from the surrounding populations, this difference actually reinforces their attachment to the Hungarian nation on the other hand. In the Hungarian argument, there are various Csángó groups in the regions of Ghimes (Gyimes), Moldavia, and around the industrial city of Brasov in southern Transylvania. The ethnic identity of these diaspora groups is not based on Transylvania, and less so on the use of the Magyar language, but on adherence to Catholicism and, in some instances, common historical and socioeconomic occupations. The problem of difference, or otherness, in the Csángó case is neutralized by the very argument that the Csángós are actually Szeklers who were forced to cross the Carpathian mountain borders and migrate further eastward hundreds of years ago. Their separation from the main group of Szeklers in fact justifies the Csángós' distinct culture patterns: they remained at an even more archaic level of civilization.[12]

In Hungarian nationalist mythmaking, the Transylvanian Hungarian population received their temporary and spatial location within the national culture. If the Szeklers are "remote," the Csángós are even more distant. To be sure, the fate of this diaspora is far more problematical, since they live in virtual isolation from Hungarians. They are surrounded by Romanian villages, with practically no connection to Hungarians either in Transylvania or, more decisively, Hungary. To the Csángós, the Hungarian "motherland" has been more distant and symbolic than to any other population in Transylvania. Hungarian intellectuals have, however, since the 1970s, capitalized on this distance. In Hungary, there has been a rising awareness among Hungarian intellectuals about the fate of the Csángós, and ties have been continually reinforced between the two groups, a point that will be dealt with in the next chapter with specific reference to their rediscovery by the 1980s' youth movement.

Similar to the Csángó question is the long-debated issue concerning the Hungarian group called Szekler (spelled *Székely* in Hungarian). As indicated earlier, the ethnogenesis of the Szeklers provided the interwar Hungarian government with a powerful myth of the "Turanian" or proto-Hungarian argument. In this way, Hungarians have attempted to counter the extreme Romanian view espousing a Greater Romania in which the Szeklers have been viewed as being of Romanian origin.[13] Here is how a Romanian scholar essentializes them:

> The Szeklers represent an island with a particular configuration on the Magyars' spiritual map. Mountain people inhabiting the counties of Trei Scaune, Ciuc, Odorhei, and part of Mures, surrounded by large Romanian areas, their nature, thinking-habits and language have acquired in the course of time a characteristic that makes them differ in many respects from the common Hungarian type.[14]

Such a nationalist view and the lack of a clear-cut unbiased analysis of the Szekler culture have provided the various Romanian regimes with yet another possibility of utilizing the divide-and-rule ideology by arguing that the Szeklers are not Hungarians per se. Neither archaeological or historical sources confirm this opinion, but nationalistic ideology continues to create enduring and powerful images to support the historical "remoteness" of this population. Here remoteness refers not only to spatial distance from the nationalist center but to actual ethnogenesis. There has been, to be sure, a separate and an important Szekler consciousness discernible in the counties of Harghita, Mureş, and Covasna in eastern Transylvania. This ethnic consciousness is based in part on the myth of Scythian and/or Hunnish origin (and not the Finno-Ugrian, as the Magyars thought). Moreover, Transylvanian Szeklers are proud of their former noble status and the privileges bestowed upon them by the Hungarians kings, especially by the Habsburgs for their services as border guards.

The number of Szeklers is considerable. In fact, it is the only Hungarian group in Romania with a slightly growing population in contrast to the rest of the Hungarian population.[15] Numbers aside, the Szeklers are known for their skills as craftsmen and traders, as well as for their extreme superiority complexes. Szeklers also are known to dislike Romanians. Several scholars have suggested recently that key elements of the Szekler culture should be viewed as essential constituents of its regional identity; among other things, in particular, the carved gates—referred to as the "Szekler-gate"—that have been idealized in Hungarian ethnographic works.[16]

These groups aside, a further complication of the question of Hungarian ethnic identity concerns other regional populations. These are smaller minorities, such as Czechs and Slovaks, Jews, Gypsies, Armenians, and German speakers who, for various reasons, were assimilated into the Hungarian ethnic groups or lost their separate ethnic identities. Moreover, there are various diaspora enclaves of Hungarians in the southern part of Romania and especially in the nation's capital, Bucharest. In the former case, people of diverse ethnic backgrounds are less likely to identify with Hungarian nationalistic sentiments at the expense of the ethnic groups that they might have come from. In the latter case, assimilation might be more voluntary than forced. All in all, these groups differ from the previously mentioned Szekler or Csángó groups, in that their relationship to Hungarian culture, language, and ethnopolitics has largely been affected by mostly Romanian surroundings. Also, interethnic marriages have been more common among these groups. As I was able to observe in Transylvania, children growing up in mixed families are more likely to lose their monolithic Hungarian identity and to possess flexible ethnonational identities.

Hungarian ethnographers have proudly boasted that the Szeklers and, in certain instances, regional market centers and villages specializing in small crafts in the Szekler region have exhibited a strong sense of local identity. This may, at times, be just as important to them as their overall Hungarian identity. This adds a considerable amount to the already ambiguous nature of Szekler identity. The prevailing tendency has been noted in several Szeklers areas. For example, several "pure" Hungarian settlements have been described, namely, Corund (Hungarian Korond), known for excellence in pottery making, Madéfalva, a settlement proud of its connection to the ill-fated battle in 1764, when hundreds of Szeklers were massacred by the Habsburg army,[17] Csikszentdomokos (Sindominic in Romanian), known for its village solidarity and adherence to local customs and fashion,[18] or Gyergyó, Kászon, and Ghimes, where local identity may far outweigh any other larger identities.[19]

Ethnographers and historians often have exuberantly acclaimed the majestic sense of entering into the Szekler region once crossing the geographical borders of the Lowlands of Transylvania (*Mezőség*). To these writers, various geographic features emphasize the uniqueness of this region as being the most important border markers for difference. For example, the Lake Saint Anne (*Szent Anna tó*) and Hargita Mountains—mythologized by the Ábel trilogy of Áron Tamási—are the two most important. These are imagined as a "specific mental map in which the snow-capped mountain and the lake at its foot compose a picture of the bathing fairies, the sleeping meadows and the tractors . . . [it] is like a mythical space uniting contrasting elements."[20] Since at least the famous travelogue of Balázs Orbán, "Description of Szeklerland"—a pioneering study utilized ever since by national ethnographies and historiographies as a model[21]—numerous historical landmarks add to the already mythical and remote sense of Szekler identity. From castles to ruinous manors, from village churches to cemeteries, this border territory is littered, to paraphrase Edwin Ardener, with things of the past. Although the Hungarian territories are now part of Romania, "their nineteenth-century history proves them to be ours," according to a Hungarian Transylvanian intellectual.[22] For Hungarians and Szeklers alike, there are hardly any landmarks, aside from those remnants of hundreds of years of Saxon history, recalling the Romanians' presence in this national terrain. For them, Roman or Dacian archaeological sites are suspicious, fake, or meaningless.

As far as the Hungarian national map is concerned, the two most important sites visited regularly are two cemeteries. One is the monument erected to the above-mentioned nobleman, Balázs Orbán, and the other is a small parish cemetery of Farkaslaka, a village where the author of the Ábel trilogy, Áron Tamási, is buried. Aside from Lake Saint Anne (where thousands of Hungarians gather every year for picnics), there are no other sites in Transylvania that summarize the Hungarian nostalgia for and presence in this region more dramatically then these two cemeteries.

To go to the picnic grounds around Lake Saint Anne was, and continues to be, an act of bravery and solidarity for Hungarians, thumbing their noses at the Romanian state as well as the Romanian majority. This was the area where one could hear Hungarian folk songs and of course the Hungarian or Szekler anthems sung at campfires. The Szekler anthem (banned during Romanian rule) is an anathema for Hungarians. Its winding melody and contrived and overdramatized stanzas would make this song a strong candidate for a melodramatic nineteenth-century opera. But the meaning and associations of the verses—recalling the heroic deed of the mythical king of Csaba, leading the victorious Szeklers to the battlefields—made a powerful, emotional anti-Romanian and anti-Ceauşescu statement. Thus Hungarians actually possess two anthems in Transylvania—the Hungarian and the Szekler. This is an interesting contradictory concept in itself, but more intriguing is the fact that these two national songs far outweigh any other claims for symbolic representation of a Hungarian and a related, but still separate, Szekler identity in Romania. After 1990, singing the Szekler anthem in Hungary is an everyday occurrence.

Nationalizing geography has been a continual favorite pastime of Hungarian nationalists, especially with reference to Szekler history. As seen above, the cemeteries and graves of historical figures are well-known landmarks for nationalist image making. The monuments of Orbán and Tamási are equally charged with nationalist as well as anti-Romanian sentiments. Both are true nationalist pilgrimage sites with their sacrosanct air. But like all national(ist) landmarks, these too are fraught with contradictions and difficult justifications. Referred to as "the greatest Szekler" (similar to Count Szechenyi, who is the "greatest Hungarian"), Balázs Orbán emerged as one of the most important cult figures reinforcing this idea. But Orbán came from the Szekler nobility and, in addition, his maternal grandmother was of German-Greek origin, thus he had little to do with either the traditions of the peasantry or with full-bloodedness, so dear to the hearts of populist and neopopulists alike. Although Orbán—who became a member of the Parliament—died in Budapest, he was buried on his family's estate in Transylvania. Having no descendants, Orbán left all of his worldly possessions, in his words, "to my family, the Hungarian people, they alone should be my chief inheritors as well. More than that, I want to assist my Szekler blood . . . my estate and landholding . . . should go to the Transylvanian Educational Association [Erdélyi Közművelődési Egylet], especially for its program to stop Szeklers' emigration from Transylvania."[23] Adding to this mythmaking of Szekler uniqueness is the fact that Balázs Orbán was reburied four times in the past 100 years by Hungarians concerned with preserving his remains "in a respectful and fitting manner."[24]

Equally ambiguous in Hungarian nationalist mytho-geography is the site where Áron Tamási, the famed writer of Szekler literature, is buried. This is a site of nationalist nostalgia as well as full contradictions. Tamási was born in Farkaslaka, and his whole life was tangled up with Romania's and the Szeklers' troubled twentieth-century history. His Ábel trilogy faithfully captures his travels from Romania to Hungary and then to America. After 1945, Tamási finally settled in Hungary, occasionally visiting his relatives in Transylvania. His monographic description of rural life often is compared to the Romanian writer Ioan Creangă's equally breathtaking peasantism.[25] Tamási died in 1968 in Budapest before he could see his elevation into the pantheon of neopopulism. His grave is situated in his home settlement in Transylvania, a village more Romanian today than Hungarian. While Hungarians from Hungary regularly visit his gravesite, the majority of the village residents are nonchalant about the grave of one of the "greatest Szeklers."

But sites of great men, no matter how removed they were in history, are rarely about "memento mori." They are, on the contrary, truly sites for a memento of the nation. In her book *The Political Lives of Dead Bodies*, Katherine Verdery observes nationalism as a "kind of ancestor worship, a system of patrilineal kinship,[26] in which national heroes occupy the place of clan elders in defining a nation as a noble lineage." In this sense, it is understandable why Hungarian youth and intellectuals decide to drive for days from Hungary to spend a quiet moment at the burial sites of the greatest Szeklers, who they perceive to be among the greatest Hungarians in the national genealogy. To these cultural pilgrims, it is this closeness, and not the actual mileage—and certainly not the state border—that counts: they are provided with an air of history, a sense of national unity, and the possibility for self-reflection.

These descriptions notwithstanding, the exact nature and extent of Hungarianness and ethnic identity among the various Hungarian populations in Romania is a task fraught with even more complexity, for regional and local identity is connected at times to powerful and diverse, even opposing, class and rural-urban differences that affect the way people view themselves as well as others. Despite the all-important national identity, class distinction, while viewed negatively and minimized by forty years of state socialism, nevertheless has existed among ethnic Hungarians. This was equally the case with other East Europeans experiencing the forced restructuring of class relations and the labor force in the last decades of the socialist period. Even if we were to agree with some aspects of Romanian official statistics concerning demographic changes in the Hungarian population, we must confront the fact that more than 900,000, or almost 50 percent, of Hungarians in Romania are urban dwellers, a trend continuing somewhat even today.[27] As my informants' lifestyles faithfully illustrated in Cluj and its vicinity, the forced and rapid industrialization and urbanization policies of the Romanian government achieved their aims. The disposition of a large workforce from the southern and eastern provinces of Romania into the growing Transylvanian areas was a characteristic and much criticized feature of Ceauşescu's Romanianization. These state policies have caused enormous shifts in the ways in which people earn their living, reproduce their social relations, and view the world.[28] To Hungarians, these changes were and are especially problematic. For them, the influx of a large number of Romanian migrant workers into formerly predominant Hungarian towns and areas

was not simply a step toward restructuring the labor market and achieving target plans but a conscious attempt to change the interethnic composition and ethnic character of Transylvania.[29]

Is there a discernible separate urban or class identity among Hungarians experiencing these socioeconomic transformations as waves of
Romanian nationalism? The answer is both yes and no. There is, without
a doubt, a rural-urban distinction that has pervaded Romanian-Hungarian society, but it alone does not equal that of neighboring Hungary. For
although Hungarians in major cities, such as Cluj, Tirgu Mureş, Tir-
naveni, Oradea, and Timişoara, have viewed Hungarian villagers as "peasants able to maintain their standard of living and fill their stomachs,"
their relationship was and is not antagonistic.[30] For example, as my fieldwork interviews in Cluj and Jebuc revealed strong kinship ties that connected tens of thousands in the rural-urban continuum, illustrated by the
longevity of the socio-occupational category known as peasant workers or
commuting workers during the period of state socialism.[31] Many families
in the two locations studied during my fieldwork exhibited a common
living arrangement where children left to study or work in the city, while
parents, as well as grandparents, lived in the village and worked in the
local farm or household economy. Most adult males in Jebuc and its
vicinity in Cluj county, for example, have occupied industrial, working-
class jobs, commuting to Aghires, Huedin, or Cluj, or they have worked
for the state railroad. Most females remain proletarianized agricultural
laborers who work in the local cooperative, a pattern solidified at the turn
of the century but aggravated by the forced industrial planning of the
socialist Romanian state.[32] In this manner, a regular flow of family members visiting each other is maintained. Another reason that rural-urban
distinction was less noticeable in Romania than, for instance, in Hungary,
was the harsh everyday realities with which Romanian citizens had to
cope, regardless of their residency and ethnicity.[33] During state socialism
long hours in line to obtain food rations, the struggle for proper medical
attention, and deprivation of heating, electricity, gas, water, and gasoline
made people less likely to think about prejudices and class disposition,
reinforcing rural-urban ties even more.[34]

Some groups, especially businessmen, black marketers, and people
with special connections, have benefited from this situation. As far as the
peasants were concerned, however, some regions were wholly exploited,
producing poverty and a generally unhealthy existence. In others, for
example the mountainous terrain in the Szekler provinces, where land was
not fully collectivized, some families fit the native description of "rich
peasants," even in the 1990s. The Hungarian intelligentsia in Romania
felt the repercussions of acute regional crises emerging since the late

1970s. Just as in the past, some of the committed (and sometimes bitter and disillusioned) individuals have been active agents in the resistance against the Romanian government's anti-Hungarian politics and in the ongoing proletarianization of the Hungarian ethnic minority. Few, however, have been committed to socialist ideals. To illustrate the complexity and sensitivity with which Hungarian intellectuals have approached the subject of being Romanian citizens, I quote a short passage from Pál Bodor at the March 13, 1978, plenary Meeting of the Council of the Working People of Magyar Nationality:

> The Hungarians in Romania love their homeland. The Hungarians in Romania are patriots of this country. We have never played truant or shirked responsibility either in history or in revolution—or in work either. The leadership of the party and country may rely on us; the Romanian nation may have full confidence in us; we are the militants of the homeland's territorial integrity, sovereignty, independence.[35]

That, of course, was written in 1978, and by the early 1980s, majority-minority relations worsened considerably in Romania. The writer of this passage, for instance, Pál Bodor, the former editor in chief at Romanian Radio and Television, moved to Hungary and has been classified by the Romanian government as a "traitor." Then again, the Ceauşescuism and Romanian nationalism of the 1980s was a fundamentally different concept than in the 1970s.

HUNGARY, ROMANIA, AND TRANSYLVANIAN IDENTITY IN THE 1980S

From the late 1970s, the relationship between Hungary and Romania may be characterized as quiet antagonism. Diplomatic relations had been scarce and superficial since Ceauşescu came into power. Aside from the brief visit of Kádár in Romania in 1958, Kádár and Ceauşescu met only in 1966, 1967, and 1968.[36] By the mid-1970s, it was clear that Ceauşescu prided himself in being the wizard of the East Bloc, capable of manipulating anyone from Moscow to Berlin and from China to Washington, D.C.[37] To a certain degree, this was true. While Ceauşescu enjoyed his globe-trotting fame—he received conspicuous medals and diplomas from the East and West alike[38]—cultural exchanges between the two countries were virtually nonexistent. While Hungary imported a large number of Romanian publications and newspapers, Romania imported only a fraction of the available language publications and newspapers from Hungary.

Although the two states signed agreements for cultural exchange and scientific and economic relations, first in the period 1947–1948, then in 1961, and again in 1972, they were not renewed, or reiterated. Scientific exchanges between Hungary and Romania were below the level that one would expect from two neighboring, "fraternal socialist countries." Crossing the border into Romania was becoming more and more difficult for Hungarians in and outside of Romania. Ceauşescu's anti-Hungarianist policies not only worked in favor of making Transylvania and Transylvanian Hungarians even more remote from Hungary but effectively provided more and more fuel for Hungarian nationalistic sentiments. Hungarian folklorists, ethnographers, linguists, musicologists, historians, and others wishing to do fieldwork and archival research in Romania were discouraged by the Romanian government and forced to carry out "pirate researches" anonymously as tourists. The Romanian regime, of course, viewed them as troublemakers and agitators. One cannot really blame the Romanians for their paranoia: travelers from Hungary—and émigrés from the West—were not innocent cultural tourists but were bringing food, medication, newspapers, and information from the outside into Hungarian communities. As I was able to witness several times myself, the long lines at the Hungarian-Romanian border crossings were zones of infamy and lawlessness. As an observer has written, "Hungarians and Germans could rely on some religious literature smuggled over the border until the clamp down of Hungarians."[39] In certain instances, the denial of entry, bodily searches, and the confiscation of goods may have been justified, but in most such acts were seen by Hungarians as acts of conscious intimidation, encouraged by the Romanian regime to stop the flow of Hungarians into Romania.[40] In this climate, inviting Hungarian theater groups, performing ensembles, exhibitors, artists, and musicians to Romania utterly ceased. This, however, cannot be said about Romanian artists and dance troupes who regularly visited Hungary during the 1980s. Since artists in Romania were pressured by the government to remain committed to artistic directions set by the state and were exhorted to produce works of "patriotic value" and "socialist merit," Hungarian artists interpreted this as an anti-Hungarian attitude of the Romanian regime, and not without justification.

During this heightened symbolic confrontation, few Hungarian artists and writers, save the privileged few who enjoyed international acclaim, were allowed to publish or exhibit in Hungary, or even to send their manuscript outside of the country. Transylvanian Hungarian playwright András Sütő, was virtually the sole dramatist whose work was presented in the repertoire of theaters in Hungary. In 1986, Sütő's play, "Advent on the Harghita" (again, those mysterious mountains!), had its premiere in Hungary after some difficulties. Two years later, his "Dream-Commando," a play describing a Nazi concentration camp, with obvious reference to Romanian conditions, was staged in Budapest. These theater productions added a considerable amount to the already tense relationship between the two countries as well as provided further support for rising Hungarian national identity by celebrating Transylvanians in Hungary in an open fashion. But others of lesser fame in Romania, whose names were not circulated in the Western media and in Hungarian émigré circles, were reduced to minimal importance. The regime of Ceauşescu also forced many Hungarian artists into menial jobs or to emigrate. Suicides and other manifestations of physical and mental breakdown were not unknown among Hungarian intellectuals. It is difficult to establish whether these were caused directly by the Romanian government's assimilation policies or were perhaps versions of Hungarian national fear. Some clearly were facilitated by social and psychological pressures, and many were based on rumors of beatings and the torture of Hungarian intellectuals who dared to speak out against the government.[41]

As a further instance of the antagonistic relationship between the two states, Hungarian cinema, enjoying its renaissance both in Hungary and in the West in the 1980s, was largely unknown to the Romanian public. Hungarian audiences were able to view Romanian films. Filmmakers from Hungary were discouraged from filming in Romanian locations, and historical settings depicting Transylvanian and Romanian scenes often were shot elsewhere.[42]

Transylvania was, in a sense, off limits and made very difficult to enter, which contributed to an officially fostered, reinforced sense of remoteness, a topic largely missed by Edwin Ardener in his discussion of remote areas as cultural concepts. For Ardener, the remote area is created mostly by the outside, in reality, from the epicenter of cultural ideology. In the 1980s, Transylvania became a true remote region viewed from Budapest. The Romanian regime, by implementing insidious visa requirements, travel restrictions, and the surveillance of foreigners entering the country, made Transylvania even more remote.

This removal was not only visible in cultural relations between the Romanian and Hungarian states but also was paralleled by their minuscule economic relations. In general, much of the period of the 1980s may be characterized by relative stagnation and a decrease in trade. Although Hungary's 1987 import and export trade balance still showed that over 60 percent of its budget was committed to COMECON (Council for Mutual Economic Assistance) trading, Romania's share was only about 10 percent annually. Romania played an insignificant role in Hungary's foreign trade, ranking around eleventh, after the United States, West Germany, Austria, Switzerland, and Italy. The quality of goods shipped from Romania to Hungary declined to the point where it was ridiculed publicly, perhaps accounting for the reduction of Romania's share of Hungary's foreign trade from 2.3 percent in 1976 to 1.9 percent in 1986.[43] Perhaps the most critical moment in the two countries' relations occurred between October 15 and November 25, 1985, when Budapest occupied the center of international attention by hosting the Cultural Forum of the Helsinki Agreement. Despite the substantial international participation and accompanying aura of positive interaction between delegates from the East and West, no closing agreement was achieved. Béla Köpeczi, minister of culture and editor of the controversial *History of Transylvania* (mentioned in Chapter 2), criticized Bucharest with the following comment:

> Our delegation has done its work in this spirit from the beginning to end, and it was not its fault that the Cultural Forum adopted no closing document. . . . The Hungarian delegation, after the first rejected draft, proposed a short closing document: this draft almost achieved consensus but the Romanian delegation disagreed, claiming that the document had nothing substantial to say.[44]

It is clear that both the scholarly community and the political hierarchy were in agreement on how to handle the issue of Transylvania, its Hungarian population, and Romania's isolation of Transylvania. In a speech to the nation, a member of the Hungarian Central Committee of the Socialist Workers' Party, István Horváth, openly declared the following concerning Romania:

> We believe that we cannot live together as good neighbors by continuously throwing at each other both valid and fabricated accusations about the distant and recent past. On the contrary, we must build our future together by respecting each other, by respecting the rights of our minorities on both sides of the border.[45]

Implicit in this speech was the fact that the Hungarian government proudly displayed its successful policies of treating Romanian minorities living in Hungary. By the time the follow-up session to the Helsinki Agreement occurred in Vienna, a leader of the Hungarian delegation remarked with a statement foregrounding the developments of the 1990s,

> The Hungarian government proceeds from the notion that the rights and interests of national minorities should be defended by the country and government where the members of such minorities live and of which they are citizens. This defense must be in accordance with the principles guiding interstate relations since the adoption of the Helsinki Final Act in 1975. Any kind of nationalism, especially one of its worse forms, forceful assimilation, as well as restrictive tutelage over the national minorities, must be forcefully rejected.[46]

The spirit of the 1980s, with reference to the Helsinki Human Rights Act, was clearly in the air, fundamentally altering Hungarianness and Hungarian identity, both in Hungary and Transylvania. By this time, Hungarian national consciousness managed to transcend all borders identifying the major issue of the decade: national unity of Hungarians regardless of citizenship and state borders. The adamant Hungarian government's efforts on behalf of Hungarian minorities' rights in Romania are further revealed in the following statement by a member of the Institute of Hungarology, an organization set up by the Hungarian government to specifically deal with the Hungarian diaspora in neighboring countries:

> The Hungarian state and society recognize the present status quo and the inviolability of the borders. At the same time they consider the Hungarians living beyond the country's borders as integral components of Hungarian national culture and naturally condemn efforts to prevent and break up the eleven-century-old bond of history by administrative, psychological, and other means.[47]

This statement aptly summarized the way Budapest elites have felt for a long time. The borders set by the Treaty of Trianon—though real and inviolable—were largely an artificial, meaningless demarcation between the two states but on the contrary helped the Hungarian nation to achieve unity rather than separateness. What was important was what went on beyond the borders, not what they represented. Despite this rhetoric, it was clear that the border issue had to be transcended and that the situation of the Hungarian culture in Romania had to be couched in terms of a human and minority rights agenda to make it more acceptable, both in the East and West.

This point of view clearly motivated the changes that occurred in 1988, when a group of Hungarian intellectuals protested against a government action that returned Transylvanian Hungarians, who were asking for temporary residence in Hungary, to Romania against their will. Surprisingly, however, it was not only the so-called "Democratic Opposition" that took responsibility for such public outcry but the Patriotic Peoples' Front—the only legitimate political body aside from the Hungarian Socialist Workers' Party. It charged the communist government with the forceful expulsion of Hungarians back to Romania as not only illegal and inhumane, but it considered it a crime against the Hungarian nation. United, these forces managed to revitalize the questions concerning both nationality and citizenship. Arguing as they were, nationalists had a sound claim: Hungarian refugees from Romania should not be repatriated, for they are rightfully staying in Hungary as Hungarians. This was an extremely important point, for it not only raised issues of the Treaty of Trianon and the socialist ideology of the inviolability of state borders but asked for a complete revision of Hungarian citizenship law. This law was rather clear: anyone who was born of Hungarian parents or in Hungary was considered a Hungarian citizen. Many of the Transylvanian Hungarians, receiving official recognition of their Hungarian citizenship after 1940, rightfully claimed Hungarian citizenship.

Although precise figures remain debatable, the opposition claimed the forceful removal of several hundred Hungarian refugees in January 1988, a charge later denied by Mátyás Szűrös, Secretary of the Central Committee of the Hungarian Socialist Workers' Party (HSWP), who responded that no Hungarians were expelled. However, this issue so galvanized the Hungarian opposition elite that by the beginning of 1988 it dared to speed up its open confrontational manner against both countries' regimes. Subsequent actions followed in swift succession: by March of the same year, a growing concern manifested itself in newspaper articles about the housing situation and work possibilities of repatriated Hungarians. To combat these mounting problems, various organizations, including church shelters, city councils for employment, and the Red Cross, asked for state assistance. On March 17, 1988, the National Assembly voted in favor of a bill allowing the Hungarian state to establish a fund of 300 million forints to aid the "former citizens" of Romania resettling in Hungary.

Despite the fury of the Romanian regime, the remaking of national identity and unity was slowly but surely achieved by the adamant efforts of Hungarian elites in Budapest, Transylvania, and, as it will be shown shortly, from the western diasporas. Public consciousness and concern about the fate of Hungarians in Transylvania was clearly mounting, and the growing intellectual dissident movement placed considerable pressure on the Hungarian government to take serious steps in defense of the Transylvanian Hungarian culture and human rights. There was no return. Facing a growing internal crisis and daily criticism from the nationalist elites, the Hungarian Foreign Ministry had to act. It went so far as to denounce the Ceauşescu government's plans to create large agro-industrial complexes, to consolidate Transylvanian villages, and "to erase the Hungarian heritage in areas of Transylvania that were severed from Hungary after World War I."[48]

The ghost of Trianon surfaced—as some Romanians claimed—but the language of discourse was surprisingly up-to-date to international standards. The uneasy situation between the two governments accelerated further in the wake of the May 1988 changes in the Hungarian leadership. With the Kádár government's replacement by the slightly more reform-oriented socialist Grósz government, and the new members in the Central Committee, the new regime had to start a different, more radical offensive. This move facilitated by the then-ongoing social undercurrent the Transylvanian folkloristic "dance house" movement, a theme I develop fully later. All things considered, it is safe to say that the Hungarian government's reactions had been gradually evolving from noninterference to accusations and overt political charges against the Ceauşescu regime's "bulldozer politics."[49] This evolution in Hungarian policy made the Romanian government cautious and suspicious, and not without justification. Protagonists of the Romanian political machinery saw the Hungarian actions as being analogous to the dismal events of the early years of this century, already mentioned. Claims of "reawakening Magyar chauvinism," "irredentism," "fascist revanchism," and the appearance of "the ghost of 1940," however, demonstrated on their side the extremes of Romanian distrust. At the June 28 plenary session of the Central Committee of the Romanian Communist Party, its leader, the nepotistic Nicolae Ceauşescu, announced:

> We understand that there are many difficult problems in Hungary today, and the Hungarian workers struggle. But we cannot understand the agenda of certain chauvinistic and nationalistic circles, who while trying to divert attention of the mounting problems and realities, try to fight with the old tactics even—and I can state this with full responsibility—by surpassing the Horthyst methods.[50]

As this message clearly indicates, by this time Romania and its leading nepotistic family not only celebrated its official course of national communism but was fully aware of the Hungarian process of national unification. Although few extremists in Hungary have been serious about revisionist claims, border realignments, or even secessionism, nationalistic fears were ingrained deeply in the attitudes of the Romanian majority and the state apparatus. So much so was this the case that at the same meeting the Council of Working People of Hungarian Nationality in Romania—the official body of the Hungarian minority—also declared, no doubt under the direct pressure of the Central Committee, that

> we must fight against dogmatic influences, nationalism, racism and other reactionary tendencies. Similarly, we will not allow any interference into our internal affair, and we will refuse any kind of attempts that aim at damaging the unity of our socialist society.[51]

While it would be foolish to deny that racism and reactionary tendencies were far removed from the Hungarian nationalists' agenda, it must be asserted that Romanian state nationalism was myopic and, as most totalitarian regimes, it tended to obfuscate the issue by reverting to old-style slogans. From these perspectives, it became quite obvious that the two regimes, despite the continuation of the common Marxist-Leninist agenda, could not foment a workable solution for the ongoing hostilities between the two national elites concerning the Transylvanian question. In a bold move, and obviously yielding to international as well as national pressure, on August 24, 1988, Romanian leader Nicolae Ceauşescu and Hungarian leader Károly Grósz met in the Romanian city of Arad. This was the first interstate meeting since the one between Ceauşescu and Kádár in 1976, in Debrecen and Oradea, respectively. More of a farce than a stately affair, the meeting ended without solutions or agreement about the viability of a friendly concession concerning the Romanian state's minority policy and the noninterference of the Hungarian state. What is more, this ironic but historic summit further reinforced the existing ethnic bias and nationalistic fervor of the two regimes. What was obvious from the above statements and from the halfhearted summit between Ceauşescu and Grósz was that the two regimes were not willing to settle current problems. They would not discuss the burning situation of interethnic conflicts and rising state nationalism in Romania and the concomitant rising national consciousness developing both in Hungary and among the Hungarian populations in Transylvania. Rather, by reverting to repetitions of Marxist-Leninist ideology, they continually reproduced hostile attitudes toward each other by evoking the past and throwing accusations to divert attention from the real issues of basic human rights and possibilities for a solution. However, by this time, the winds of change were blowing strongly and steadily. In the western Romanian town of Timisoara (Temesvár), a young Hungarian Protestant minister, László Tőkés, began preaching his symbolic but nevertheless antigovernmental "sermons of liberation."[52]

TRANSYLVANIANISM AND THE
OPPOSITION IN HUNGARY

What I have done so far is illustrate the developing sense of Hungarian national identity and unity throughout the last years of state socialism. The question I address now is: Why did the Hungarian government change so rapidly its earlier attitude of noninterference to interference regarding matters that the Romanian regime considered exclusively the prerogative of the Romanian state? Or, to put it another way, why this change and why in the mid-1980s? To me, the answer is provided on the one hand by the changing political economy of Eastern Europe, and, on the other hand, the emergence of the grassroots opposition movements, both in Hungary and in the West. This opposition had provided for the first time in the history of the East Bloc an institutionalized outlet for nationalist ideology that served as a critical political platform for these groups.

First let us see how the political economic situation altered attitudes of the Hungarian state planners. Since there has been a plethora of scholarly studies produced concerning the Hungarian economic performance and its societal results during the late 1970s and 1980s, here I only highlight some of the most important features that had direct bearing on this subject. Hungary's economy had deteriorated considerably since the late 1970s, a feature paralleling that of neighboring Romania to some extent. Radical transformations in terms of trade between consumer good and energy products, stagnation in world trade, and external economic shocks, first during the period 1973–1975 and again during the period 1978–1982, had adverse consequences and immediate reverberations for Hungary.[53] Productivity declined, consumer prices increased, inflation followed, and Hungarians felt, for the first time after the initial successes of the 1968 reforms of the New Economic Mechanism, the devaluation of their currency. At the same time, the level of Hungary's foreign debt jumped from $7.5 billion in 1978 to almost $18 billion by the end of 1988. From these economic changes a marked, more explicit social differentiation was inevitable. As several sociological works so prolifically explain, Hungarian social structure also was realigned. The processes of proletarianization of the industrial labor force and the embourgeoisement of certain segments of the agricultural population had characterized Hungarian society from the beginning of the 1980s.[54]

This was a noticeable change in a state claiming to be a workers' state with the equal allocation and distribution of resources. The labor force also was negatively affected by demographic factors. The baby-boom children born in the early 1950s (commonly referred as the "Ratkó children" because of the name of the Minister of Health who propagated Stalinist pronatalist policies) were maturing, and they represented a major force in the country's artistic and intellectual life. As we will see in the next chapter, many of these people came from rural backgrounds but became connected to urban centers and lifestyles because of their work. The great number of children born in the late 1960s and early 1970s was mainly the result of the introduction of health care, paid maternity leave, and benefits to expectant mothers. By the mid-1980s, it was clear that the educational system and the organization of the labor market would have to conform to the growing demands of this generational shift.[55]

This generational restructuring of Hungarian society (which was discussed further in Chapter 4) forced the government to combat critical social and economic issues and to implement a host of new policies of liberalization and democratization of the economy and production. A second economy, aspects of which were often called "illegal" or "black" up to the early 1980s, became the norm rather than the exception for Hungarians by the mid-1980s.[56] Private businesses increased manifold, industrial complexes became decentralized and liberalized, and joint Hungarian and Western ventures were slowly but surely introduced. Plant closures also were introduced for the first time for enterprises that were not profitable. Slowly, unemployment and increasingly visible poverty followed. Meeting the demands of intellectual opposition and pressing international human rights charters, free travel also was legalized by implementing a new passport law allowing citizens with foreign currency to visit Western countries. In the words of Hungarian sociologist Zsuzsa Ferge, a new society was in the making[57] but not, I add, necessarily the one that the government envisioned.

What is clear from the above is that in the wake of all of these socio-economical and political transformations, serious alterations in the cultural and artistic spheres of the country also were made. Because of the liberalization of cultural and artistic life, disenchanted intellectuals, critics of the policies, and alienated youth were allowed to express their opinions to a certain extent. While the Kádár regime was not, to be sure, hospitable to internal critics, the early 1980s saw a proliferation of independent organizations, cultural circles, intellectual forums, *samizdat* (illegal publications), and the creation of oppositional groups. Youth clubs had proliferated, many with extremist ideals. Hungary saw for the first time the appearance of Western-style punk fashion. Punk rock groups, often with xenophobic and nationalist messages, openly denied the power of the state with their lyrics opposing officials, politicians, and police. If Hungary received a negative rating by the punks, Romania was singled out as the worst. In one of the songs of Hungary's most extremist punk bands, ETA, Romania and the Ceaușescus were given a mandate. It also was suggested that its collapse was imminent, caused partly by the mistreatment of the Hungarians in Transylvania.[58]

In this climate, well underway in the early 1980s, the opposition movement in Hungary was an influential force in pressuring the Hungarian government to act to ensure the rights of millions of ethnic Hungarians outside of Hungary. For example, the 1985 Budapest Cultural Forum's weaknesses were subsequently addressed by an alternative forum, organized by Hungarian opposition and Western human rights groups. Here, concerned participants openly discussed and debated problems of Hungarian minorities living outside of the borders of Hungary. It is important to note here that this alternative forum preceded the governmental statement in 1986. The largely illegal, or *samizdat*, as it was called then, publication by the democratic opposition, "A Program for Democratic Renewal," urged the Hungarian government

> to assume protection of Hungarian minorities living in neighboring countries. It should bring their situation and concerns to the attention of public opinion at home and abroad. It should take initiatives with respect to the governments concerned in Bucharest and Prague in the first place and, if necessary, it should raise the issue of remedying grievances of the minorities at international forums.[59]

By 1987, the opposition forces gained an important, new momentum when more and more individuals joined these intellectual dissident organizations. Mostly formed by populist writers, filmmakers, poets, university teachers, and artists, the Democratic Forum was organized with the central goal of helping the Transylvanian cause. This involved consciousness-raising, both at home and in the West, an issue framed still somewhat cautiously as a human rights and democracy agenda, and not strictly as the "Trianon trauma," as claimed by the Romanian regime. Among their paramount activities, for instance, was the organization of a successful demonstration on February 1, 1988, at the Romanian consulates in Budapest, Prague, Warsaw, and a few Western capitals. Open confrontation with state bureaucrats was the order of the day, and not only with reference to the long-banned 1956 revolution. In March, meetings were held in the Jurta Theater in Budapest on the question of Transylvanian refugees. In specific, the resettlement of the refugees and the Romanian government's stand on human rights issues were discussed. This meeting was well attended by opposition groups, including Romanian human rights activists living in Hungary. For the first time, other intellectuals from East

Bloc countries and the West also were invited to Budapest. In this softer political climate, the Democratic Forum organized many public debates voicing the problems of Hungarian refugees from Romania, while it condemned the Romanian state's mistreatment of ethnic Hungarians living there.[60] By June of the same year, several demonstrations took place in front of Romanian consulates at major European cities, as well as in Washington, D.C., organized by Hungarian opposition and émigrés. The largest was organized in Budapest. During this march, tens of thousands carried signs inscribed with the names of Hungarian villages and towns objecting against the "bulldozer politics of Ceauşescu" attempting to erase thousands of Hungarian, German, and Romanian villages.

The Romanian government's response was immediate and firm. Seen strictly as nationalist agitation, a few days later the Hungarian consul in the western city of Cluj in Romania was given forty-eight hours to close and leave immediately. It should be noted, nevertheless, that for the first time in Eastern European history, a political movement unifying Hungarian, Romanian, Czechoslovakian and Polish dissidents had been launched with a primary agenda of human rights and ethnic politics. By 1988, the opposition uniting over the Transylvanian issue was so strong, internationalized, and well equipped in human rights forums that any move by the Romanian regime was seen as open provocation. It was, moreover, condemned not only in Brussels but at the United Nations (UN) headquarters and in Washington, D.C. How was this transnational union really achieved? Below I describe the more essential agent bringing about this change: the role the Hungarian émigré community in the West played as a catalyst of this transformation.

TRANSYLVANIA AND THE HUNGARIAN ÉMIGRÉ COMMUNITY

As seen above, transnational connections and a renewed sense of diasporan identities were firmly established by the mid-1980s in Hungary, Romania, and elsewhere in the world. What really contributed to the formation of a new Hungarian and a Hungarian-Transylvanian identity affecting Hungarian-Romanian and in fact Romanian-American relations were two émigré organizations that operated in the United States. The American-Transylvanian Federation and the Hungarian Human Rights Committee were the two key players in shaping the state of affairs in East-Central Europe as well as in the West with regard to the topic under investigation here.

Émigré groups are always important to the home country in rekindling national identities and sentiments. Transcending immediate kinship concerns, they bring back know-how, technology, and financial capital, and they often manage to reinvigorate local economic performance. Already, after World War I, when borders were redrawn and Hungarians from Transylvania were leaving first to Hungary and then to the West, a great number of them found their way to America and Canada. Whereas prior to the First World War poor agricultural laborers, cottars, and serfs constituted most of the immigrants, after the war the Hungarian aristocracy in Romania found itself decimated by hundreds of emigrants. From the 1930s to the 1960s, the American Transylvanian Federation (*Amerikai Erdélyi Szövetség*) and other groups of royalist political persuasion united politically active individuals, who served in "combating unjust" treatment of Hungarians living in post–Trianon Romania and Czechoslovakia.[61] Most of their activities, modest and rarely leaving the confines of the local émigré diaspora, however, were important in creating a hegemonic Hungarian nationalist ideology prevalent during those years.[62]

During much of the interwar period, the North American Hungarian society had always been a colorful mixture of different interests. This diversity was reflected in its variety of activities. Some individuals raised their voices in various institutionalized Hungarian forums, such as the World Federation of Hungarians (*Magyarok Világszövetsége*), an elitist organization manipulated by the various governments of interwar Hungary. Most Hungarians, apart from the Left, openly identified with the ideology of the Horthy regime, and the "No, No, Never" slogans decorated most of the clubs and church halls. A few aristocrats, such as István Bethlen, cousin of the Bethlen mentioned earlier, in conjunction with the suppression of the Bolshevik Council of Republic of Béla Kun in 1919, expressed an eccentric view concerning the Transylvanian controversy and the altered state borders. In a candid interview before his death, István Bethlen stated: "I would like to kick generations of Hungarian aristocrats in the rear for bringing Romanians from Wallachia into Transylvania. Our greatest, most unforgivable sin against the Hungarian nation was to have allowed the Romanians to settle in Transylvania over the course of history."[63] As marginal as it may seem today, this view nevertheless expresses a repentant attitude held by some members of the Hungarian nobility who have blamed their own class for the origin of the multiethnic situation in Transylvania and the presence of the Romanian majority there. More important is the fact that such community leaders managed to convey this sense of loss and trauma to the lay membership within émigré organizations. The diaspora elites, then, fashioned a coherent set of concepts, based on Transylvanianness, to complement the hated enemy, the royalist, and then the communist Romanian other.

The émigré society in North America, along with the rightist Hungarian governments, rejoiced when the latter received Nazi support in regaining Transylvania in 1940. They celebrated the territorial reorganization following the Vienna Decision as a real victory for the Hungarian nation and the possibility of a recreation of Saint Stephen's thousand-year-old realm. At the end of World War II, however, the nationalists' spirits turned sour. For them, the socialist border shifts meant that Transylvania was lost again, and they found themselves facing a new common enemy in fighting against communist Romania. The rank-and-file membership of the émigré society gained new support after World War II by the many thousands of newcomers both from Hungary and Romania, especially Transylvania.[64] The tens of thousands who fled after the revolution of 1956 also boosted membership in these organizations. From the late 1960s and early 1970s, when the 1956 generation matured and gained a strong foothold in North American professional life, nationalists turned their attention against Romania. They have tried, and they have succeeded, in gaining support against the "bloody terror" of Ceauşescu from American and Western governments. These efforts were long in the making but proved to be futile issues at first.

By the mid-1970s, and perhaps not wholly without the influence of the emerging populist movement at that time underway in Hungary, there appeared on the scene a new group of radical émigrés whose role proved decisive in the creation of a new Hungarianism. This organization was the Committee for Human Rights in Romania (CHRR), founded in 1976 with the aim of "fighting for the cultural, religious, and linguistic rights of the Hungarian minority in Romania, and for the defense and reinstatement of such rights."[65] The CHRR was different, both in its composition and in its generational spirit, from its conservative, gentry-aristocratic-oriented Transylvanian Federation. Those involved with the CHRR were younger, more agile, and better educated. They realized that U.S. foreign policy had many weaknesses and, in particular, that there were specific ways to enter the inner core of Washington beltway politics. Unlike with the old-timer Transylvanian Federation, remaining largely within the confines of the émigré society, the CHRR utilized the Washington lobby networks and the power of the American and international media.

The first such media attack occurred when, in May 1976, an advertisement was printed in the pages of the prestigious *New York Times*, attacking the alleged "cultural genocide" of the Hungarian minority by the Romanian state. Both the Romanians in Bucharest as well as the Hungarian politicians in Budapest were left gasping for air, for no one had dared to speak like this before, certainly not in one of the most prestigious

Western dailies. In the ensuing two years, the CHHR organized major demonstrations, one of which was timed cleverly during the U.S. visit of Nicolae Ceaușescu. (Visits to Washington, D.C., by foreign dignitaries are always imbued with all of the trappings of state symbolism and a flair for international importance.) Tens of thousand of Hungarians participated from various American and Canadian communities, carrying banners and signs depicting Hungarian city names in Transylvania and describing Ceaușescu as the "bloodthirsty dictator." The CHRR leadership knew well the Hollywood mythology concerning Transylvania and the power of popular culture: one of the inscriptions read "Dracula Lives." This was a clear reference that the Romanian regime was solely responsible for what was taking place in Romania with regard to the minority question. During this demonstration, the audience sang the Hungarian as well as the so-called Transylvanian (Szekler) anthems.[66]

Unabated, the CHRR lobbied successfully and organized several fund-raising events. It often managed to gain the sympathy of illustrious figures such as the mayor of New York City, Edward Koch, who identified with the Hungarian (trans)national cause. The money raised was for food supplies and medical packages for distribution in Hungarian communities in Romania. Such high politicking worked well, in that it managed to bring the remote region of Transylvania closer to the center of local and international political discourse. A relief fund was also established, and the Hungarian diaspora media carried articles describing the worsening conditions of Hungarians living in Romania. In 1984, the organization's name was changed to the Hungarian Human Rights Foundation (HHRF), an alteration reflecting the organization's new attitude and cooperation with dissidents in the West and in Hungary. This name change also has underscored the shift of attention to Hungarians not only in Romania but in neighboring states.

The HHRF, along with Hungarian opposition circles, was instrumental in coordinating the alternative Cultural Forum in 1985 in Budapest, where its members distributed leaflets and literature explaining the new political credo of Hungarianness to an international audience. As a consequence of this shift from nationalism to transnationalism in focus and methods, the problem of Hungarian minority and religious rights in Romania slowly became a concern for Western politicians and the media associating themselves with Hungarian and émigré circles. For a decade, however, the efforts of the CHRR were met with silence from the U.S. government. The principle of my enemy's enemy is my friend worked well for awhile in the case of U.S. diplomacy with regard to the Soviet Bloc, especially Romania. The United States viewed Ceaușescu as an independent East Bloc leader who was able to stand up against Moscow and provide secret information to Washington. During much of this time, Romania's status as a maverick among the East Bloc countries was continually strengthened throughout the 1970s and early 1980s because of its extravagant stance.

Hungarian diaspora politics, however, did not stop there. Citing flagrant human rights abuses and Romanian state terror in silencing Hungarian leaders in Transylvania, by 1986 they managed to procure enough material to gain the attention of some of the influential members of the U.S. Congress. With the backing of the Congressional Human Rights Caucuses, led by John Porter and Tom Lantos (of Hungarian origin), several hearings on this topic were held in the Senate. These new meetings did not replicate those of 1978, which terminated without bringing an immediate result for the HHRF.[67] But the ten-year struggle of the Hungarian national lobbying groups was not futile. In October 1987, the Subcommittee on International Trade of the U.S. Senate voted to suspend Romania's most-favored nation status, recognizing the flagrant human rights violations perpetrated by the Romanian government. In August 1988, no doubt influenced by the largest anti–Romanian demonstration in Budapest on June 27, 1988, the Senate voted unanimously (93–0) to stop all economic and trade privileges allocated to Romania because of religious persecutions and human rights violations in Transylvania.[68]

These adamant activities of the American Transylvanian Federation, the HHRF, and lesser-known organizations such as the Hungarian Action Committee in New York and the Hungarian Freedom Fighters' Association were indispensable in raising popular consciousness and pressuring the Hungarian government to take a firm stance against Romania. Especially pressing was the issue of silencing human rights and religious activists in Romania, an area that Western churches also took up.[69] The interaction between these units of opposition fostered a new international climate encouraging the emergence of a unique political agenda fostered by this transnational alliance. It was based on Hungarianism and Hungarian nationalism with Transylvania and the Hungarian Transylvanians at its core.

Indicating perhaps the dawning of the global age, the consolidation of agendas by these émigré and opposition groups obviously had been extremely successful. The dynamic interplay of these powerful forces continued to contribute simultaneously to the recreation and reemergence of a new Hungarian identity. At the same time, these transnational processes managed to progressively weaken both the very status of the Romanian state responsible for the oppression of its minorities and, interestingly, the Hungarian socialist state's status quo as well. The success of Hungarian human rights organizations reinforces Chen's argument concerning the present. For Chen, it "is indeed the era of transnationalism, but transnationalism in fact reinforces nationalism, just as nationalism reproduces transnationalism."[70] Even at the beginning of 2000, when both Hungary and Romania followed a parallel trajectory of democratic developments, Western émigré groups continued to mount pressure politics for Hungarian minority rights in Romania. In particular, they dared to speak for the reinstatement of the Hungarian university in Cluj, and even the possibility of full-scale autonomy for Hungarians in Romania.[71] Thus it is certain that the transnational connections developed by minority leaders and concerned human rights activists about Transylvania were precursors to the global changes that dismantled the party state and the East Bloc and precipitated the new border realignments of not only Eastern Europe but all of Europe.

CONCLUSION: SOCIALISM, POST–SOCIALISM, AND DIASPORA POLITICS

The astounding frenzy of reform that seized Eastern Europe in the late 1980s took everyone by surprise. Yet this type of "return to Europe" was enacted in a variety of guises. The notions of *patria and natio* rarely seemed to enjoy such a close allegiance as during the emergence of political crisis and the cultural reawakening that characterized, in Benedict Anderson's phrase, the "imagined communities" of Eastern Europe. In this sense, the twentieth century may be called the shortest one that began with World War I and, in its aftermath, with the emergence of totalitarian regimes and cultural practices, ended with the anti-communist revolutions of 1989, an *annus mirabilis*. Yet the 1989 changes in Hungary and Romania, as we have seen above, could not emerge without the social ferment of the 1970s and especially of the 1980s. It certainly could not have happened without the common efforts of dissident elites in Hungary, Romania, and the concerned émigré circles in the West. As Ella Shohat, in another context, remarks, the viability of any social movement against assimilation and disintegration has to do with the memory of its shared (invented) past and identity.[72] For the Western diaspora elites, the Transylvanian issue was just that—a rekindling of national memory in a new climate in which national identity was successfully fused with post–communism.

The issues I have reviewed in this chapter are important, not only because they reinforce ideas about nationalist movements and the negotiation of ethnonational identities, both from within and without the immediate confinement of nation-state politics, but because they remind us that the Transylvanian conflict has been elevated by concerned elites into a collective national ideology in order to help unify Hungarians at the mercy of communism. This remaking of national identity and refashioning of the Transylvanian controversy could not have taken place without the emergence of a new generation of émigré youth that utilized the language of the time. By not speaking about the actual restoration of the Trianon borders, as their interwar predecessors had done, but by creating a new discourse that combined human and minority rights of European standards, these words were close at home in Washington, D.C., Helsinki, and Brussels. Thus the historic and present contestation over Transylvania has resurfaced in a language capable of convincing both the Hungarian state and the Western powers of their responsibilities to step up pressures against state nationalism. At the same time, it has provided a new momentum for the awakening sense of national identity, both at home and outside the borders of Hungary. This movement found a common voice with the Transylvanian Hungarians and the populist intellectuals in Hungary, a topic that will be analyzed in detail in the following chapter.

Chapter 6

Youth and Political Action: The Dance-House Movement and Transylvania

In the previous chapter I argued that powerful political and literary undercurrents were working in the creation of the Hungarian nation with Transylvanian Hungarians at the core of this nationalism. None of these actions, however, could have been successful if they had taken place in isolation from the rest of the sociocultural ferment in Hungarian society. Issues of national identity and solidarity, visiting relatives in Romania, and the former status of Transylvania were repressed by the socialist governments and existed outside of the official media and consciousness. The first public occasion when such concerns were allowed to surface was in the mid-1970s, when an important youth movement emerged, called the dance-house movement (*táncház mozgalom* in Hungarian), a reference to a communal, recreational place where village dances were held in Transylvanian communities.[1]

This chapter details the development of how youth, in the words of Susan Gal, "turned to folk music and, quite independently of official cultural policy, created the Dance House Movement in the 1970s."[2] The dance-house movement signifies a fundamental societal process through which literary populism, peasantism, and Transylvanism were fused into a coherent set of ideas offering a sense of national unity and identity to Hungarians. This movement was an important precursor to the national revival of the 1990s as well as a catalyst for the contestation of nationality issues between Hungary and Romania in the last decades of the twentieth century. In fact, in terms of its development in the 1970s and early 1980s, it can best be characterized as a unique ethnonational process that helped shape Hungary's post–communist national self. Aside from its nationalist qualities—which it certainly acquired by the mid-1980s—this movement could be easily classified as populist regionalism because of its identification with specific territorial and peasant cultural values. In opposition to former literary peasantism, shown in the previous chapter as an important elitist cultural orientation in the making of Hungarianness, this new form of populism was covertly political. This covert overtone had focused on Hungarians living outside of Hungary, mostly in Slovakia and in the Transylvanian part of Romania. In this chapter, the primary goal is to link this youth movement to the ideas of the populist recreation of national identity. To analyze that, I first briefly describe its history by introducing its scope and content. Next I demonstrate that the altered structure of the East European political economy in general and of Hungary in particular is fundamental in understanding its development and vitality. I examine the nature of neopopulist ideology and the ways in which it achieved political national unity by attracting tens of thousands under the banner of national identification and the solidarity of Hungarians all over Eastern Europe. As a result of this success, this national movement managed to rearrange the troubled relationship between the Hungarian and Romanian states concerning Transylvania. Finally, I explore how this dance movement relied on historical, ethnographic, and literary precursors in its attempts to recreate the imaginary national territory of Transylvania.

IN THE BEGINNING . . .

The dance-house movement originated as a seemingly innocent folkloristic revival. Its primary aim was to teach youth folk dances, folk music, songs, and peasant traditions, especially from Transylvanian Hungarian communities. Thousands of young fans who otherwise would have been obsessed with Western popular culture suddenly found themselves instead in a peasant milieu.[3] By visiting special folk dance clubs, they sang folk songs and wore Transylvanian blouses, skirts, and shirts to express their identity with Hungarians across the borders. Increasing numbers decided to travel to the remote villages of Romania to look for authentic patterns of their newly discovered Hungarian heritage.[4] In retrospect, it is clear that this movement was more than a passing, fashionable folkloristic revival movement of the sort that frequently took place in Eastern European countries in the 1930s and 1950s, for artistic, cinematic, and literary representations emphasizing populist themes proliferated, many of them reminiscent of the populist "Pearly Bouquet" (*Gyöngyösbokréta*) revival movement of the 1930s and 1940s, a topic that I discussed previously.

This youth movement "officially" began in 1972, when the first dance house opened to the public in the Hungarian capital. A group of enthusiasts, dancers, choreographers, singers, and musicians modestly advertised the teaching of dances and authentic music from Transylvania. Later that year, several other urban dance houses were opened. In a short time, these dance clubs mushroomed throughout the entire country, appearing not only in the cities but also in regional centers and villages. Claiming Hungarianness and praising traditional peasant values, these clubs and their leaders concerned themselves with the diminishing lifeway and folk art giving way to mass culture. They claimed that village practitioners of traditional arts and crafts were not being adequately recognized by the state and that, subsequently, Hungarian peasant traditions faced rapid extinction. They saw the dance club as a possibility to save them.

It is safe to assert that, despite all of the political propaganda of the Kádár government (internationalism, socialist youth culture, etc.), Hungarian popular culture and the official youth movement promulgated by the Communist Youth League (KISZ) had stagnated since the late 1960s. Clearly these were times of economic and political pressure—the years following 1956, the personality cult, and the economic reorganization known as the New Economic Mechanism of 1968. As is clear from a speech by György Aczél, Hungary's leading political figure in 1968, the Hungarian regime was well aware of the needs of a viable socialist youth culture:

> The new economic reforms raise the need for up-to-date culture in every sphere of life more and more urgently. At the same time the wise and sober use of the opportunities offered by the reform can help a great deal in the dissemination of real culture, of truly valuable art, and thereby help to develop in the right direction and at the correct pace of tastes and capacity for artistic judgment of the broad masses.[5]

For Aczél and others in the Hungarian Socialist Workers Party (HSWP) central committee, real art and real tastes meant only to keep youth within the confinements of the country's political organization, the young Komsomol, the Hungarian KISZ. Youth culture in this context was meant to be socialist, internationalist, and in line with the central directives of the party. Aczél's speech at the political academy of the HSWP clarified this as follows:

> It is the essence of our cultural policy that in Hungary we should establish and continue to build new forms of socialist

culture, of national culture . . . (and in this) . . . we have left the West behind us as far as the humanist richness of education, of culture, and above all its democracy are concerned . . . we have surpassed the West in establishing relations between art and the broad masses.[6]

However, the formal and state-supported youth culture—mass sports, international communist youth meetings (the VIT in Hungarian), and socialist popular or workers' song contests (cultural competitions, as they were called)—was meaningless to a large number of youth.[7] In opposition to these party-directed mass recreational activities,[8] many sought freedom from the state elsewhere. Important in this process of rejection was the rediscovery of religion. Many returned to the churches and began to participate in religious activities within the confines of local parishes. Reflecting on these years, one observer saw positive gestures toward the churches on the part of the state. In his words, "Government representatives praise the churches for their positive influence on people's morality and for their role in the preservation of the national heritage through their continuing interest in and support of art, literature, music, folklore, and customs."[9] For example, in the "socialist city" of Csepel, where I conducted fieldwork in the early 1990s, both the Catholic and Protestant churches devoted considerable efforts to the fate of Hungarian religious communities in Slovakia, Yugoslavia, and, in particular, the largest of them all, Transylvania. As I have indicated in Chapter 3, they raised concerns over the preservation of Hungarian culture and identity there and supported meetings and rallies for the cause of Hungarians in those countries.

In this social milieu, a youth movement identifying similar issues was increasingly supported as a welcome addition. The first folk dance club (*táncház*) was organized in Budapest on May 6, 1972, as a single occasion marked by several folk dance groups and their dancers, musicians, and artistic directors. One key figure involved was Ferenc Novák, whose family traces its origin to Transylvania and the mixed Hungarian and Armenian community there. Novák wrote his ethnographic master's thesis on the dance traditions of a single village, Szék (Sic in Romanian), in middle Transylvania. He developed the idea that some of the local dances of this community should be taught to dancers, teachers, and interested youth. Little did Novák and his colleagues know that they were about to open a cultural can of worms. Perhaps one event facilitated this clever return-to-the roots movement more than any other, the III National Folk Music Congress in 1969, organized under the tutelage of Hungary's respected folk music researcher, composer and pedagogue, Zoltán Kodály. This event, which was legitimate and respected by the state, was followed by several important folk singing events that seemed innocent at first. Following Kodály's instructions, one basic idea gained more and more ground: to rediscover the real, authentic, and unspoiled remnants of the true peasant folklore and culture. As Kodály expressed it, the pure well-spring (*tiszta forrás*, in his words) of the peasant past must be located, preserved, and transmitted. The Hungarian television was the first to follow up on this idea by initiating a whole series of folk music competitions, aptly titled after a folk song collected by Kodály, "Fly Peacock" (*Röpülj páva*). Watched by millions, this show-competition was so successful that within months hundreds of "fly peacock" clubs, choirs, and performing ensembles mushroomed all over the country.

Given the historical contexts within which this emerged, it is easy to see why such a folkloristic revival was united by some Hungarian elites with socialist internationalism and patriotism.[10] Agricultural cooperatives, trade unions, and workers' brigades were urged to compete in this new culture in local-, regional-, and national-level competitions. What gives credence to this national mythmaking is the making of the instrumental ensembles called the "zither circles." In a sense, such experimentation was a far cry from the authentic peasant singing and musical practices, for such groups did not really exist in the peasant communities of former times.[11] For one, Hungarian peasant communities—aside from some occasions of work gatherings, funerals, and dances—generally did not sing in a choir arrangement (ethnomusicologists are ready to point out that this singing style is characteristic of Slavic folk cultures). Second, the zither rarely if ever was used as part of an instrumental band, preserved for small gatherings and rarely in tandem with other instruments.

For the nascent revival movement, however, this did not matter, as the party-controlled media quickly responded to popular demand. Through state sponsorship, millions watched folk singing competitions, dance festivals, and zither groups on television. During such a nationally televised folklore program, a young singer, Laura Faragó, was discovered. She then gained international respect when she competed and won a prize in England at a folk music festival. In fact, this was a rather surprising development in a country whose schools, although they required music appreciation classes as part of their curricula, still favored "international" and socialist songs. But the state-controlled media helped pave the way by introducing two other young performers, Ferenc Sebő and Béla Halmos. By playing guitars and singing folk songs, they popularized this style of music and their artistic arrangements. By arranging folk songs to poems, they soon were invited to practice their skills in a professional setting when the director of Hungary's "25th Theater" invited them to celebrate the work of Attila József, Hungary's tragic working-class poet, who committed suicide in 1937.[12] The lone singer with a guitar, a populist theme in American country and European pop music, was new for Hungarians, and Sebő and Halmos were placed in the limelight when they appeared in several films in the mid-1970s. By this time, the two young university students were coerced into playing as an instrumental band emanating the feeling of village (Gypsy) bands. Known from this point on as the "Sebő Ensemble," they accompanied one of Hungary's best-known amateur folk dance ensembles named after ethnomusicologist and composer Béla Bartók.

With the names of Bartók and Kodály, the folkloristic movement was on a seemingly solid ideological ground: both composers were highly respected figures appropriated by the communists of the 1970s. As this distilled "folk" and "peasant" culture emerged, more ideas were introduced. In 1971, for instance, the first "Camp of Young Folk Artists" was organized. Interested urban youth participated, learning how to weave, make pottery, and craft leather and other trades long associated with the traditional peasant lifeway. In the following year, the 6th Chamber Dance Festival was held in the southern city of Zalaegerszeg. The grand prize went to the "Béla Bartók" folk dance group, led by the agile Sándor Timár, himself of rural origin. In judging this group, the jury made special mention of the choreography for its authenticity and artistic quality—the musical group accompanying the dancers was the duo, "Sebő Ensemble." They were now able to utilize a book fresh off the press by Hungary's foremost folk dance researcher, György Martin, a publication that detailed folk dances in the Carpathian Basin in a functionalist fashion.[13] Instantly this scholarly book became a bible of folk dance and folk music enthusiasts, for it dealt with dances regardless of political boundaries by providing examples from Transylvania, Slovakia, and northern Yugoslavia, locations where Hungarian ethnic minorities have lived.

THE DANCE CLUBS TAKE CENTRAL PLACE

Riding on the wave of their national fame, the Sebő-Halmos music band was successful in establishing a club of its own. All of this, however, was confined within the accepted socialist cultural milieu, for the Budapest club was named after Lajos Kassák (1885–1967), Hungary's leftist painter and writer credited with transplanting Russian constructivism and activism to Hungarian soil. Interestingly, the Kassák name, just like the Bartók and Kodály names, was acceptable for both the regime and neopopulists—the former for their leftist ideas, the latter for their avant-garde roles in music and their concern for national matters. The Kassák Club thus was slowly transformed into the first officially sanctioned urban dance-house center in Budapest, or in Hungary for that matter. The club promoted dance and music instruction to interested children and youth one night a week with the accompaniment of live music. Every dance house was generally started with a "children's dance," an idea taken directly from the children's dance practiced in the community of Szék. In its traditional rural setting, children were socialized into the adult world of courting and recreation in their own dance event (referred to as the *aprók tánca*, dance of the small ones). The dance events at the Kassák Club were imitating this Transylvanian setting. The Szék community was discovered during the troubled years following the Vienna Dictate, when large portions of Transylvania were awarded to Hungary. Actually it was ethnomusicologist László Lajtha who in 1940 collected songs and instrumental music here, a collection hailing the rediscovery of long-lost Hungarian folk music in Transylvania.[14] At the Kassák Club, the musical band was set up as a three-man band (violin, viola, and double bass), and the dances followed the Szék community's dance repertoire. Often songs and stories were taught to the audience beforehand. After the children's dance, the adults would take over and sing and dance until midnight. Choreographers, ethnographers, and dance instructors would take care of the proper steps and styles; those needing lessons would be able to learn and practice on the side, while those who already new the steps could dance just as they wished. Thus, the structure of the urban dance-house was created by the patterns introduced at the Kassák club.[15]

With the first dance club inviting more and more youth, and of course intellectuals, the movement had a snowball effect. In the picturesque wine region of Tokaj in northeastern Hungary, the first experimental Folk Artist Colony was founded, not unlike some of the hippie communes in the late 1960s in America. Similar to dance and folk music, folk crafts also had to be centrally controlled by the state. This task was entrusted to the Institute of Culture, which initiated an award system for Masters of Folk Art and Young Masters of Folk Art. Craftsmen and artists were credited for their talent in preserving and disseminating traditional occupations as well as folklore. As the populist movement gained more and more momentum, a small and primitively printed, but tremendously important, magazine appeared on the newsstands called "With Drum and Fife" (*Sippal Dobbal*) to inform dance club fans. At the same time, another publication, *Mozgó Világ* (Moving World), appeared under the guidance of the Communist Youth League. In their own ways, both publications were important at that time, the first for printing songs, dances, and information about traditional folk arts and the latter as an avenue of what the elite thought about the movement and the new "socialist" culture in general.[16]

By this time, the term *folk* (*népi*) became an accepted adverb and adjective in Hungary. During the winter of 1973–1974, folk fashions were introduced for popular consumption:

> It was interesting to see the new fur fashion as it tried to incorporate many folk elements in its design; Romanian, Polish, and Transylvanian Saxon folk motives could be seen in the streets of Budapest. One can even detect traditional Hungarian furrier designs.[17]

In the summer of 1975, a large group of university students, organized by the Studio of Young Folk Artists and the Institute of Culture, spent two weeks in a small village in western Hungary surveying traditional crafts and buildings. Professional help came from no less of an intellectual than the director of the Ethnographic Museum. During the day surveys were conducted, while the evenings were spent dancing and singing. Often invited professionals provided authentication for the material that was heard, practiced, and learned.[18]

It slowly became obvious that the state and the popular cultural spheres were beginning to compete for the attention of youth. There were two choices, both of which subsequently became implemented. In 1975, the Hungarian Young Pioneers' Organization celebrated its thirtieth anniversary. For this occasion, a large camp was organized by the communist elite, but with one difference: this camp was not organized according to the usual communist slogans and ideology, instead it was named simply a "Folk Art Camp." Children between the ages of eight and fourteen from all over the country were taught to sing peasant songs, to dance folk dances, and to learn small crafts including weaving, carving, egg decorating, and bread baking.[19] One cannot help but draw an immediate parallel between this "communist" youth camp and those organized in the 1930s and early 1940s for scouts under a conservative extreme-rightist political banner. This time, however, this was all explained as a reinvented aspect of socialist culture. Legitimated by major publications and institutions, other studios and folk art workshops followed in rapid succession. For instance, in Kecskemét, the Ceramic Pottery Studio of Kecskemét was founded in 1975; the spinning and weaving house at Etyek in 1976; the wood-carving workshop at Velem in 1979; the folk artist colony at Magyarlukafa in 1979; the basketry workshop of Balatonszepezd in 1980; and the nomadic tent building project at the Kiskunság National Park in 1980—all the products of this period.[20]

By 1977, the dance-house movement achieved a momentum that was unstoppable. The state-controlled media could not help but feature selections of music and songs as well as reports of dance-house activities all over the country. In this spirit, in 1977, a television series was initiated, the "Children's Dance" (Aprók Tánca). The Sebő-Halmos ensemble provided live music, and the instructor, Sándor Timár, was noted as Hungary's foremost "alternative choreographer." It also is telling that in the footsteps of the Sebő-Halmos duo, new musical bands began to appear, creating their own niche as well as opening new dance houses.[21] Two additional names deserve special mention here: Márta Sebestyén, a vocalist discovered in the Kassák dance club, and the musical group, the *Muzsikás* (the Musicians). Both contributed to popularizing dance club style music and singing from the late 1970s on. Márta Sebestyén and the Musicians both achieved international fame and received in 1999 Hungary's foremost artistic award, the Kossuth Prize.[22]

With all of these new activities and groups appearing, new institutional structures also were created. Singing societies were organized into a trade union-type national association (KÓTA), a move that was followed by a similar association for folk dancers (ANOT). The members of the populist elites knew, however, that legitimation for the urban dance clubs had to come from an authentic village. More and more village performing ensembles were created and introduced at various regional and national festivals. Minority groups living in Hungary also were given a chance to follow this pattern set by the dance houses. In a few years, Romanians, Slovaks, Serbs, Croats, and Germans created their own dance clubs, institutions that produced meager successes. The only minority dance houses that survived the last years of communist collapse were the so-called "south Slavic," or Balkan, and Gypsy. In 1980, the first Gypsy festival was organized, to which more than ten "traditional" Gypsy performing ensembles were staged. When there were none, intellectuals, especially eager folklorists and ethnographers, made sure that they would be created. In fact, before 1972, there was only one Gypsy performing ensemble in Hungary, and by 1980, more than a dozen performed "authentic" Gypsy music and dances. With the new spirit in the making, urban youth performed idealized dances of an idealized image of the country's rural past. The ethnic diversity in the dance clubs, especially the performances of Romanian and Gypsy folk music and dance, actually reinforced the dance club movement's legitimacy. The dance club downplayed its nationalistic overtones and at the same time highlighted its seemingly internationalist stance. Moreover, it provided a model for neighboring Romania for the positive discrimination with which the Hungarian state treated its minorities.

But this form of neopopulist art did not remain within the confines of urban folk dance clubs. Its elevation into the film industry also is telling, for some of the early 1970s' films distributed touched an innocent historical cord: mythical and literary figures made it to the silver screen. Films such as *Palkó Csínom, The Turkish Lance, Petőfi '73,* and *Marci Kakuk* are truly folkloristic cinematic versions of popular literature. Yet, as they were at the time, they were not under the neopopulist swing. More serious were those experiments that identified Transylvanian Hungarian concerns. In specific, the Gulyás brothers and Pál Schiffer embarked upon creating a new documentary style that focused on the peasantry. One of the Gulyás brothers' films, for instance, was shot in the Transylvanian community of Szék, adding to its already mythologized status. In other movies, these filmmakers followed villagers in their daily routines. The Gulyás brothers created a moving tribute to a Hungarian "proper peasant," Alfonz Medve. Schiffer made the film *Earthly Paradise,* a cinematographic portrayal of Hungarian peasant workers struggling against all odds. However, the films of the Gulyás brothers and later the filmmaker Szomjas-Schiffer radically foregrounded Hungarian neopopulist themes[23] and at the same time began to show the peasant lifeway and Hungarian minorities in neighboring states to millions of viewers.

DANCE CLUBS, MINORITIES, AND NEOPOPULISM

The grassroots neopopulist movement of the late 1970s succeeded, ironically, in achieving precisely what socialist education failed to accomplish since the 1950s—to teach Hungarian youth folk music and folk dance, as Zoltán Kodály had so ardently advocated. By the early 1980s, the movement gathered such momentum that it was able to develop into a powerful cultural and political force for Hungarian national identity.

These were the years when the plight of Hungarian minorities living in neighboring countries was becoming central for the emerging national consciousness. This was witnessed openly first in the discussions of the 1970 World Congress of Hungarians, held in Budapest. This event was followed by a publication of an article by Kálmán Janics about Hungarians living in Slovakia.[24] Although this publication made only faint references to the distorted political issues of ethnic and minority relations within the "fraternal socialist states," Janics was instantly blacklisted, thus any mention of minority issues was taboo at that time. Yet Janics' idea, summarized in his book title as the "years of homelessness"—referring to the notion that Hungarians in the successor states were second-class citizens, which fostered their nostalgia and feeling of Hungarianness even more—was a fundamental beginning for Hungary and its neighbors. It was this swing in the political mood that created Pan-Hungarian institutions such as the International Hungarian Philological Society (in 1977) and its close associate, the International Congress of Hungarology (in 1981).[25] In fact, a pseudoscience at first, Hungarian studies (Hungarology) was a discipline that began during these years.

Thus, based on distilled folkloristic elements borrowed from the Transylvanian peasant tradition, the dance clubs turned into a forceful, dynamic anti-governmental and anti-communist movement. Although cautious at first, under the pressure of dance-house populist intellectuals, writers, artists, and public figures, the Hungarian government eventually had to make some concessions by changing its policy toward the Romania regime of Nicolae Ceauşescu. It also is clear that by doing so, the government of Hungary was able to silence a good portion of the opposition, which was outspoken about the system itself. However, the dance-house movement was more important as a cultural-political force: it paved the way for the development of the populist Hungarian Democratic Forum, a political embryo formed at first by a loosely structured group of intellectuals that won the first free elections in 1990.

Despite the efforts of the populists during the 1960s, the fate of the Hungarian minorities in the neighboring states was still largely unknown by the populace. It was a taboo subject in the eyes of the communist state, ironically dedicated to internationalism. After 1968, several important events took place that were to determine the direction of East-Central European literary and artistic life for the next decades. First, in Czechoslovakia, Prague Spring awakened the memory of 1956 in many Hungarians, especially the elites, who paid a heavy price for participation in the "counter-revolution." Their reemergence on the literary scene was predicated upon conditions of silence about sensitive subjects. The second event was the appointment of Ceauşescu as the Party Secretary in Romania and his subsequent state policies that aimed at creating a "unified Romanian state with all citizens' equal participation in building socialism." This last resulted in outright violations of nationality rights, including the closing of Hungarian language schools, the limitation of native language publications, and the elimination of the administrative Hungarian Maros Autonomous Region in Transylvania, topics discussed in previous chapters.

What were the societal changes in Hungary that encouraged neo-populism? First and foremost were the changes in social structure, a topic to be dealt with in detail below. Hungary experienced its only baby boom between 1950 and 1954, after the Stalinist pronatalist policies of Anna Ratkó, the Minister of Health and Education. As the "Ratkó kids," as they were then called, matured and finished their secondary education, they entered the labor force or higher-education institutes. However, the lack of space at universities, access to the labor market, and their—mostly rural—background created a gap between what was available and what they desired.

The maturing of this age group, known as the "nomadic generation," after the phrase coined by populist writer Sándor Csoóri, also coincided with the general failure of the Kádárist New Economic Mechanism and the inability of the government to cushion the side effects of the world oil crisis. As more relaxed policies were put into effect, by the mid-1970s Hungary was on its way to becoming the most liberal Soviet Bloc country, earning the label of "goulash communism." In retrospect, however, it is clear that the more liberal policies concerning artistic freedom, publication, travel, and "Westernization" were executed under the shadow of a general social malaise, which reached its height during the early-to-mid-1980s, with growing foreign debt, inefficiency of the state socialist industry and redistributive mechanisms, and a political crisis ending finally in the illegitimacy of the Kádár government and with it the state socialist system altogether.

In the first few years, a limited number of dance clubs were opened mostly in Budapest and in rural cities. But as more youngsters visited them, their followers grew on a daily basis, and the dance club became an institution, the success story of a generation of the present whose roots were in the past. Singing peasant songs, dancing regional dance forms, and eating *zsiroskenyér* (a larded slice of bread associated with the poorest social strata of Hungary), attending these clubs was seen as quite an apolitical, harmless activity. However, the fact was, the songs, music, and dances were predominantly from the Hungarian-speaking regions of Transylvania—first from the fashionable regions and, as the movement's momentum grew and its practitioners became more and more sophisticated, from increasingly distant archaic areas. While few of this movement's adherents had known something of Hungary's "pristine" peasant past, even fewer had any idea where Transylvania was or who lived there. To them, the dance club life brought with it a wave of fads and fashions among Hungary's youth. By the late 1970s, embroidered tablecloths, old-fashioned potteries, and wood carvings from Transylvania were sought-after commodities, and singing Transylvanian folk songs—as opposed to revolutionary or Soviet socialist "artistic songs"—was considered a symbolic protest against state education and ideology.[26]

The folkloristic movement, for that is how the dance house was recognized at first, slowly was transformed into something more serious as time went by, as inquiring minds began to question the origin of these dances and songs, especially the people who created them, their provenance, and their function in their native environment. This was the crucial turning point of the late 1970s, when the movement shifted into a revivalist, more politically oriented youth culture. No longer did clubs feature only excellent dancers, singers, and musicians: the evening's program was augmented to include guest artists such as poets, writers, and Transylvanian Hungarians themselves. The former were found among the neopopulists, the latter among those Transylvanian refugees who resettled to Hungary either during or after World War II (especially the Szeklers from Bukovina and the Csángós from Moldavia). Two performers should be mentioned in this context: Zsigmond Karsai, an excellent dancer and singer and a former citizen of Romania who opted for Hungarian citizenship instead of returning to Romania after World War II,[27] and Zoltán Kallós, a well-known collector of Hungarian folklore in Romania, who—facing the consequences of jail, fines, and intimidation—decided to collect and document Hungarian folklore in Romania. In their ways, both represented Transylvanian culture for Hungarian youth from the early 1970s—the former with his songs, dances, and idyllic paintings of the Transylvanian countryside, using his memory of his youth while living in the Transylvanian commune Lőrincréve (Laorint in Romanian), and the latter, whose celebrity status can be ascertained easily by visiting any dance club in Budapest where he is a featured singer, storyteller, and guest of honor, by sending to Budapest volumes of manuscripts of Hungarian songs and ballads to be published.[28]

As the movement gained more acceptance by the state and more dance clubs were created, performers and artists were brought directly from Transylvania to meet the growing demands of avid fans (the "*táncházasok*," an expression that epitomized this generation and its quests, the "dance housers"). Now Transylvanians—from the rediscovered "remote villages" of Szék, Méra, and Válaszút, and the Csángó groups from Gyimes, especially those of Moldavian stock—were featured guests in Budapest clubs to show the "archaic" and true folk art of Hungarian Transylvania.[29]

However, as I was able to tell during my research in urban dance clubs of the 1980s, the presence of Transylvanians in Hungary was a double-edged sword. In reality, they showed their ambiguous Hungarianness: by singing folk songs and performing their dances, they claimed not only their "proper" Hungarian identity but, at the same time, openly expressed their ability to maintain this identity as a diaspora in spite of the repression in Romania. Aside from their nationality, however, these unsuspecting villagers suddenly found themselves in the midst of another new identity: that of members of "performing ensembles." Often, while many members of these groups sang songs and danced local dances at various clubs at night, during the day they sold their wares and goods on the streets of Budapest and other major cities to tourists and Hungarians alike. At the same time, Transylvanian men were trying to find an easy way to make money in Hungary's thriving second economy as illegal laborers. The dance house was slowly transformed into what Marc Augé has termed *non-places*. Aside from the few Transylvanians, the urban dance clubs in Hungary were truly non-places. For Augé, a non-place "is others' space without the others in it, space constituted in spectacle, a spectacle itself already hammed in by the words and stereotypes that comment upon it in advance in the conventional language of folklore, the picturesque, or erudition."[30]

But this was not one-way traffic, for Hungarian peasant youth no longer possessed living and "authentic" dances and songs. These were to be found only in the archives of folkloristic and ethnographic collections, and they only existed to a certain extent in the memory of the elders. The solution was to visit neighboring countries where Hungarian minorities lived. From Budapest and other regional cities, the movement—not unlike the earlier scouts (especially those of the "*regőscserkészet*," folklore groups with a nationalistic taint) in Hungary, the "Sarlós" youth movement in Slovakia, or the Völkisch German youth brigades before World War II—descended upon the "remote villages" throughout Transylvania. By the start of the 1980s, youth from Hungary flocked to Transylvanian villages in increasing numbers. This form of cultural pilgrimage was watched with growing suspicion by Romanian border guards and the Romanian secret police. Initiated by the lessons at the dance houses, the youngsters' major aim was to witness and collect songs, to learn dance steps, to gather old pieces of embroidery, and to spend a few days observing "colorful" rituals, weddings, and folklore. In this search of the national self, "real" peasants were rediscovered by a new generation, which learned only about "socialist" peasant workers in collective farms. To them, Transylvania was the place to see real and proper Hungarian peasants. In this way, the lost territory, Transylvania, and the Magyars there were once again found, reconquered, and reintegrated into the Hungarian imagination as its own.

POLITICAL ECONOMIC CHANGES IN HUNGARY

It is safe to suggest that the emergence of the neopopulist dance-house movement had been initiated by the altered structures of the Hungarian political economy of the late 1960s and early 1970s, combined with the maturing of the post–war baby boomers. The fundamental changes implemented as the result of the New Economic Mechanism in

1968 affected not only the Hungarian industry but the agricultural sector
as well. These political economic changes went hand in hand with the
emergence of the new elite in Hungary. This group was heterogeneous in
its composition, but it was, for the most part, an elite slowly developing
an oppositional stance with regard to the Hungarian state and communism. Many of these intellectuals were from the Left, others came from
the disillusioned educated middle class, but all were influenced by the
artistic elite milieu led by Hungary's populists reemerging after the silencing of the 1950s and 1960s.

The end of the 1960s and the first half of the 1970s were crucial years
for the implementation of various economic, educational, and cultural
policies.[31] One reason was the reentry of Hungary, along with other socialist bloc countries, into the global technological and financial world economy after several decades of isolation.[32] These policies then affected agricultural policies, social stratification, and education. Naturally there were
repercussions in lifestyle, social mobility, and lifeway as well.[33] For instance,
in the mid-1960s, a full 50 percent of Hungary's rural population was still
engaged in agriculture, while the rest found employment in industry. The
1970s, however, reveal quite another picture. By this year, only 26 percent
worked in agriculture, 43 percent in industry, 15 percent in commerce and
transportation, and 15 percent in other sectors.[34] It is instructive to follow,
then, how these figures in social mobility parallel those of collective and
family farming during the same period. The following table demonstrates
the drastic alteration that transformed Hungary's rural production.

Number of Farms and Household Plots[35]

Farm Types	1969	1972
State Farms	271	176
Agricultural Producers' Co-ops	4,204	2,314
Cooperative Groups	319	226
Simple Cooperative Farms	1,605	—
Individual Farms	150,000	120,000

It is clear from these simplified statistics that following the forced collectivization of the 1950s, and during the period of 1962–1967, the number of peasant cooperatives stabilized, with most of the arable land
included in the agricultural productive sector. From 1968 on, further
concentration occurred as the number of state farms and cooperatives was
reduced through mergers and abolishment, and, at the same time, complementary farms—in the style of household plots, both for individual
families and for those in the agricultural producers' cooperatives—grew to
over 1 million.[36]

These figures, however, do not reveal that an increasing number of industrial workers and even intellectuals owned family plots, usually one hectare of land. What many contemporary observers witnessed in Eastern Europe, more specifically the development of the "second economy," or as in the case of Romania, the "second shift," was true in Hungary.[37] For Hungary's working class, the second economy meant the "hobby garden," a phrase that referred to the notion that Hungarians worked on family plots as a hobby. The changes in the second economy increased income and social mobility and allowed for the general well-being of the Hungarian countryside. The well-worn phrases of "window socialism" or "goulash communism" were in fact created to describe the visibility of this upward swing. But behind this facade, there were real problems. By early 1970,

> the total per capita income of cooperative members exceeded that of industrial workers by 0.1 percent, while cash income was 4 percent greater. Between 1970 and 1972, real peasant incomes continued to rise at a more rapid rate than those in the industrial sector, despite the floods of 1970 and the imposition of restrictions on ancillary activities by the state.[38]

Seeing all of these changes, the sociologist Hegedűs noted:

> The separation of administrative (teleological) and directly productive (executive) work in agriculture, or, in another respect, that of intellectual and manual work, is an extraordinarily significant process, and a necessary consequence of socialist reorganization, though not the one desired or put forward as an objective.[39]

Indeed, as it was during the early 1970s, the management social stratum grew at a rapid pace as a result of the new educational policies. In 1966, there were "1,300 [people who] obtained diplomas at universities and academies, 2,100 at higher grade agricultural colleges, and 4,600 at middle-level agricultural technical colleges."[40] Just how a new agricultural elite emerged by the late 1960s and early 1970s is obvious if we analyze briefly the nature of educational policy during the height of state socialism.

Noteworthy in this respect is the fact that Hungary stood alone in the Soviet Bloc in admitting more and more youth into higher-education institutions than any other state, save Poland. A brief comparison is revealing: in 1963—45 youth per 10,000 population entered higher education in Hungary. By 1973, this number jumped to 94.[41] Most of these students entered technical colleges and social sciences, a telling trend in elite development. Both elites, the managerial and the traditional cultural, were on the increase.[42] The social and cultural background of these students provides details about which cultural values they may have inherited from their family, peers, and regional backgrounds. What is even more striking is that students with rural and working-class backgrounds were admitted in increasing numbers.[43] This had been one of the major ideological justifications of the Communist Party's proper political socialization that ensured the adequate number of the socialist labor force and committed cadres for the socialist state. In a 1970 speech, György Aczél, the party's main ideologue, boasted:

> One-quarter of the persons at present engaged in intellectual pursuits were originally workers or peasants. If we take into account those who were not themselves manual workers, but whose parents were (or are today), then some 75 percent of the intellectual workers stemmed from the working class or the peasantry.[44]

What these figures tell us is that in Hungary the early 1970s was the period when the gap between the peasantry and the industrial working class widened and, especially, that a new strata of intellectuals were in the making. A survey, published in the Party's main newspaper, *Népszabadság* (People's Liberty), called attention to this fact: "The prevalent opinion of the workers would seem to be that Hungarian society is rapidly moving in the direction of greater income differentiation and that this process is not viewed favorably by most of those employed in physical labor."[45]

These contrasts had an immeasurable impact on the values and aspirations of Hungarians, on both the elite and the workers. Manual workers, while keenly aware of their second-class situation—because they lived in a "workers' state"[46]—were unable to counter their marginalization in the informal spheres of the economy. With the new intelligentsia in the making, mostly those in the managerial, technical, and agricultural sectors, the foundation of a new political ideology and discourse was laid. This ideology favored socialist peasantry, especially when this social layer was of the accepted, state-supported kind, even if in the form of the peasant worker.[47] It seemed that by the mid-1970s, the socialist state achieved its aim: to successfully eliminate the former "bourgeois peasantry" (or the much-hated category of the *kulak* class) and in its place to create a new, conscious socialist "rural worker" or "peasant worker" class.[48] This euphemistic category actually was more fitting for the ideology of the state, which prided itself as the true, existing peasant worker government (*munkás paraszt kormány*).

ACROSS THE BORDERS:
REPOLITICIZATION OF IDENTITIES

The story might end here, except for one small detail. The planners were simply wrong about one thing. The newly created intellectual class was neither homogeneous nor wholly supportive of the regime, for there were considerable regional differences among them. In specific, there was a deep intellectual cleavage between their national ideas and their orientation toward the socialist state. They were certainly not committed card-carrying members of the Communist Party, blindly adhering to its Marxist-Leninist ideology. Many in this new intellectual class celebrated their parents' former values and rural traditions, even though little was carried into their daily life. At the same time, they noticed the shocking discrepancies between what peasant life was in the interwar period and what the populist intellectuals were all about. Moreover, what they especially noted was what the everyday realities within the collective state farms really revealed. Becoming more conscious of their heritage and past, what they noticed in particular was that the peasantry not only was forced to lose its (former) identity but, on the contrary, their traditional rural existence was completely eradicated. Ferenc Erdei, Hungary's populist ideologue and Minister of Agriculture, referred to this "victory" with the statement, "The peasantry is not a class but an era."[49] For him, and for the state as a whole, the peasantry was a historically formed class and, as a natural consequence, would wither away as the state truly became the workers' state. Needless to say, the socialist state was quite keen to create a picture of the progressive socialist "peasant worker," which had nothing to do with values believed to be true, pristine, and untainted with Marxist-Leninist ideology. Thus when the dance houses and neopopulist youth appeared on the scene, most of the new intelligentsia celebrated this as living proof of their ideology.[50] There was another aspect of this cultural rejuvenation: since peasantry in Hungary was "losing its culture" at a rapid pace, Hungarian rural communities outside of the Hungarian state seemed to present a viable alternative. They were remote, conscious of their identities, and remained truer to their folk traditions than peasant workers in Hungary. Thus for the intellectuals, peasantism and Transylvanism seemed natural ingredients in the anti-state contestation of the new Hungarian identity.

Hungary's celebrated populist writer (second only to Gyula Illyés of the *People of the Puszta* fame, whom I dealt with in the previous chapter) Sándor Csoóri legitimized the dance-house movement and its concerns with the peasant past and identity. Responding to criticism, he wrote:

Those who take this idea [i.e., the criticism against the revival of peasant traditions] seriously or historically, confuse two basic phenomena: value and timelessness. Simply because the lifestyle of the peasantry, who perpetuated our folk culture until the last possible minute, has changed, why should have the value of folk culture changed?[51]

Thus, prime movers of this neopopulism were able to coherently summarize this new ideology needed for the justification and legitimation of the dance-house movement and the importance of Hungarian ethnic minorities living in Romania.[52]

Finding adequate and vocal support from the elites, and as more Hungarian youth crossed the state borders and entered the Transylvanian part of Romania, the more the Romanian regime grew agitated. In fact, many of these cultural pilgrims did not visit Romania per se: in their words, they did not have Romanian friends, did not visit Romanian cultural sites, and certainly did not speak a word of the Romanian language. They crossed the borders to Transylvania and went to visit Hungarians in Romania. As argued earlier, a certain amount of cultural paranoia had always been at the borders there, not only for Nicolae Ceauşescu but for his predecessors as well, who looked upon their Hungarian neighbor with intimidation and who increasingly viewed visitors from Hungary with

FIGURE 6.1   The death and rebirth of peasantism and Transylvanianism: The funeral process of Károly Kós in Cluj, Romania in 1977. (Author's collection.)

suspicion.[53] As the Romanian officialdom became more and more engulfed in what Katherine Verdery termed "contests for cultural representativeness"—specifying and proving the historic, archaic, and mystical Geto-Dacian national philosophical wisdom of the Romanians—Hungarians in Transylvania enjoyed the attention given to them by these youthful, cultural travelers from Hungary.[54] As these cultural tourists oscillated between Hungary and Romania, they did not fit in well with Ceauşescu's plans. Ceauşescu, in the minds of Hungarian elites, was intent on destroying not only the culture of the Magyars but of the German-Saxon, Schwab, Serbian, Gypsy, Jewish, and even Romanian peasant communities to create a unified, communist, fully Romanianized nation-state.[55] In order to bring this about, in 1980, the Romanian regime implemented a host of new laws to curb the visit and movements of "foreigners." This went hand in hand with the policies to limit the expressions of nationality identity and religion and to stop the flow of information between the two countries,[56] and all of this occurred just when Romania was plunged into its worst peacetime economic crisis.

Actually, the advocates of neopopulism benefited greatly from these official, extreme measures. Suddenly the new slogan was to save the remnants of Hungarian culture in Romania, especially to save the Magyar

FIGURE 6.2   Proper Magyars through ethnic tourism: Hungarian villagers selling their crafts along a major highway in the Kalotaszeg region, Transylvania, Romania in the late 1990s. (Author's collection.)

populations from extinction and the ruthless tyranny of Ceauşescu. One result of this massive cultural migration between Hungary and Transylvania was an increase in the production and sale of folk objects. The main road between Huedin and Cluj, the highway of Kalotaszeg, as informants asserted, is lined on both sides with small, homemade shelters and stands. For Hungarian villagers, especially women, selling their embroidery and old clothes to tourists has become big business. While the Kádár government reacted with caution to mounting popular pressure from below and wanted to halt solidarity meetings and cultural affairs concerning Transylvania, the movement gained important momentum that was not to be silenced. One might even suggest, as J. F. Brown has, that the inability of the Kádár government to control the neopopulist movement and to take a firm stance concerning the management of the affairs of Hungarian minorities outside of Hungary led to its eventual illegitimization and demise.[57]

The rediscovery of Transylvania and its various cultural and political forms of representation in literature, television, cinema, theater, and popular culture led in a sense to the development of a new spirit of Magyarness. This was both against the Hungarian state's willingness to engage in interethnic strife and the Romanian regime's attempt to implement its ethnocide plans. The slogan, a "multilaterally developed society," was empty and meaningless in Romania, not only for Hungarians living there but for the Romanian majority as well.

Equally troublesome was the situation of the peasants of Hungary, who had lost their means of subsistence under Stalinism and thus could no longer bear the burden of being the trustees of "real" Magyar culture as they had been originally assigned to do during the interwar period. But Hungarian intellectuals could not do much to change this. Transylvanian Hungarians, however, isolated from Hungary for decades and living under extremely unfavorable economic and political conditions, suddenly became ideal candidates for replacements. With this rediscovery of new Magyarness and national unity, the neopopulist movement also called for "truth" and "justice" from the governments—the former for all of the lies and evasion since Stalinism, the latter for the misdeeds and injustices incurred since. In this renewed sense of national mythology, to the question, "Who is a proper Magyar?" the answer was simple and easy: the Transylvanians (*Erdélyiek*). The appalling conditions under which they lived made them immune to questions regarding the validity and ideological underpinnings of this proposition.[58]

In this ideological essentialization of the peasantry, Hungarian elites were not alone. The Romanian villages of the Maramures district in northwestern Transylvania have been told by the Romanian elites to be "the cradle of Romanian civilization." They, as Gail Kligman has asserted, "function for the national cultural heritage as spatial-temporal symbols of the nation's lineage."[59] Similarly, in Poland, peasant farmers also have been stereotyped by the populist elites as representing the non-communist new Poles—traditional, independent, and "not producing to the dictates of the state and the Party."[60]

By the mid-1980s, Hungary's populist intellectuals—many of whom had acquired deep sympathies for the Transylvanian cause in the folk dance clubs—could act in unison as a serious political popular force.[61] When Ceaușescu embarked upon his monstrous course of village razing and rural reorganization (*planificare*) and systematization (*sistematizare*), the neopopulists immediately felt assured that time was on their side to make a move. They successfully organized mass rallies in front of the Romanian embassy, not only in Budapest but by establishing international networks in capitals all over Europe. It serves us well to remember that the very first major mass demonstration in Budapest was not against the Soviets or the aging János Kádár, and not about dismantling the Council for Mutual Economic Assistance or even the military organization of the Warsaw Pact—it was a solidarity demonstration for the plight of the Transylvanian Hungarians at a moment when a new nation celebrated, for the first time in an open forum since the revolution of 1956, its Magyarness, history, and unity.

The best illustration of the way in which the dance-house movement transformed Hungarian identity and the relationship between Hungarians in Transylvania and those in Hungary took place in 1988. This story concerns an elderly Csángó lady who came with one of the performing village groups to Hungary. She fell gravely ill and suddenly died. Her last wish was to be buried in the "mother country," not in Romania. By the early 1990s, her gravesite had been transferred to a pilgrimage center for both Hungarian dance-house fans and those Hungarians from Romania visiting Hungary. If Katherine Verdery is correct in suggesting that repatriating dead bodies means binding "people to their national territories in an orderly universe,"[62] then by burying a Transylvanian in Hungary, Hungarian intellectuals managed to do just exactly that: to successfully unite nation and territory.

Through such symbolic actions, the neopopulist movement was so successful that by the 1980s and 1990s, the former amateur dance-house enthusiasts had joined the ranks of Hungary's celebrated professionals. Today, films, theaters, dance concerts, radio programs, CD recordings, and book publishing exist to cater to the tastes of those of neopopulist leanings. Now the genre "dance-house" music is as accepted in Hungary as it is in Romania and elsewhere in Europe, as are the genres of classical, popular, and Gypsy music. International dance camps are held in Hungary and Transylvania every summer as well as throughout the Western world, with thousands of young fans eager to learn the Hungarian "authentic," "ancestral ways," phrases utilized by many leaders to advertise their craft.[63] Key members of the once-amateur clubs, bands, and dance groups were, by the early 1990s, transformed into professional artists, managers, and producers. This shift eventually facilitated the elevation of the dance-house movement into an accepted art form of modest commercial success.[64] Today, there is no movement, but professional foundations and organizations (*Tánchází Kamara*) that produce newsletters (for instance, *FolkMagazin*), publish books, videos, and CDs, and organize monster dance-house festivals.

Two names in specific signal the rise of this art form into the professional, international world of popular music. The ensemble the "Muzsikás" and the vocalist Márta Sebestyén are now part of the global music industry, participating in the production of the world beat and world music genre.[65] The latter in particular has managed to internationalize Hungarian folk music and mystify Transylvania by adding her singing to the 1995 Grammy-winning CD *Boheme*, produced by two well-known artists of the world beat genre, "Deep Forest." The following is how Deep Forest advertised the singer and, by so doing, managed to globalize remote Transylvania: "The enchanting timbre of a strange woman's voice unmistakably marked Transylvania as our new destination in that stationary journey which gives our music meaning. Echoes of deep forests, ancient legends, and buried tales still resounded there."[66] With this fundamental transformation, however, the unique dance-house movement of the 1970s and 1980s transferred its critical edge and subcultural style into mainstream popular art, and with that it ceased to be what it once was. Thus Transylvania, the enchanted land beyond the forest, was elevated into the remote corners of cyberspace.

PEASANT RADICALISM, DANCE HOUSE, AND NATIONAL IDENTITY

Following in the footsteps of the literary populist movement described earlier, in the 1970s and the 1980s came a new social movement that sought to rediscover the peasantry and embrace the new elite, which spoke for the peasantry. As shown in Chapter 4, populist sentiments mystified the peasants, as Theodor Shanin has suggested. This mystification created its own niche for that in a "remote" and an inaccessible, archaic Transylvania. In light of what I described above, it serves us well to remember how cross-cultural examples illustrate the reactions of peasants and intellectuals of peasant backgrounds to fundamental political and socioeconomic changes. Views on the actions of peasantry have been provided by anthropologists who study rural-based rebellions or radicalism, especially victimization and marginalization.[67] Barrington Moore, writing from the perspective of the history of peasant radicalism, for instance, argues that:

> The process of modernization begins with peasant revolutions that fail. It culminates during the twentieth century with peasant revolutions that succeed. No longer is it possible to take seriously the view that the peasant is an "object of history," a form of social life over which historical changes pass but which contributes nothing to the impetus of these changes.[68]

In a similar vein, Eric Wolf recognizes that the political economic shifts in peasant culture have serious repercussions that may lead to pressure, tension, and eventually radical actions:

> The changeover from peasant to farmer, however, is not merely a change in psychological orientation; it involves a major shift in the institutional context within which men make their choice. Perhaps it is precisely when the peasant can no longer rely on his accustomed institutional context to reduce his risks, but when alternative institutions are either too chaotic or too restrictive to guarantee a viable commitment to new ways, that the psychological, economic, social, and political tensions all mount toward peasant rebellion and involvement in revolution.[69]

Historian George D. Jackson agrees with the above when he states firmly that, "The first victim of industrialization is the peasant."[70] What these three perspectives have in common is the fact that in the wake of fundamental economic and industrial change, peasants—and their leading intellectuals—react in various ways: for Moore and Wolf, radicalism naturally follows. Yet it is clear, as Skocpol argues, that economic change not only affects people but "states and organized politics" as well.[71] Reactions of the population at large do not have to be displayed as an uprising but, as has been the case with the Transylvanian dispute and its 1980s' intellectual movement, the dance-house, culturally effervescent "ethnic processes," or "ethnic movements" as well.[72] In contraposition of communist nationalism in Romania, Czechoslovakia, and Yugoslavia, the combination of peasantism and Transylvanism characterized the Hungarian neopopulist movement. In this milieu, as Peter Sugar has aptly suggested, the rise of a "defensive nationalism" was both an imminent as well as a consequential resurgent social movement.[73]

As we have seen in this chapter, during the period 1969–1971, the rural populations in Hungary benefited somewhat from the state restructuring of agriculture. This process started with the disastrous nationalization and collectivization of agriculture all over the Soviet Bloc. Industrial workers were hard hit, but they were compensated by the state: they were allowed to enter the second economy as well as the informal sector of industrial production, a move actually only started on a massive scale in the early 1980s with the implementation of second-economy work units. As it was, in the period 1970–1971, Hungarian peasants and workers of agricultural second shifts earned more than industrial workers. This meant that rural populations were better off for the first time since World War II and had more money to spend. With more affluence came more educational possibilities for children, more leisurely activities, and, as a natural consequence, more recognition from the state regarding peasant values.

Interestingly, this recognition was first understood by policy makers to be a sign of the real success of socialist peasant consciousness and the victorious result of socialist agricultural planning. Rural workers and their children were supportive of the state in its efforts, economy, and ideology, however, their expressions were twofold: for one, they participated in the economic reorganization, worked more, earned more, and consequently spent more. Second, agricultural workers participated in the reorganized cultural milieu by identifying themselves as the "real peasants." They acted their best to convince both themselves and the state that they were well off, satisfied, and cultured. Industrial workers themselves were coerced into this process, since they were reduced to semi-peasants through agricultural second shifts. These new peasants, for the state the "socialist peasants," brought their songs and dances and showed off their Sunday best on the stage and during state holidays on the streets and in the media. In fact, if there had been free elections at that time in Hungary, this part of the population would have voted 100 percent for the existing government! This large swing vote of the rural population works extremely well, as was obvious during the 1990 and 1994 elections in Hungary. These free elections revealed that in 1990 they voted the communists out because of their dissatisfaction with the system. No doubt a large percentage of the rural vote was facilitated by the disgust with state socialism and at the same time the stringent policies of the later 1980s, which affected voters adversely. In the 1994 elections, they continued to make their voices heard by voting the nationalist center-right government out of office and giving the former socialists a vote of confidence by voting for them en masse. What is clear for the story of the dance-house neopopulist movement is that it was a rural-based contestation of Hungarian identity, developing first as a subculture and then, directed from above, developing later as a large-scale social movement with its own sense of direction and dynamism.

The story of remaking Hungarian national identity by coalescing peasantism and Transylvanism gives credence to historian Eric Hobsbawm, who, paraphrasing Gramsci, has suggested that peasants in the modern world "are in a perpetual ferment but, as a mass, incapable of providing a centralized expression for their aspirations and their needs."[74] The fundamental connection between the intellectuals, who actually formulate this expression, and the peasants is provided by Gramsci himself. In his *Selections from the Prison Notebooks*, he sees this particular symbiotic relationship as follows:

> One can understand nothing of the collective life of the peasantry and of the germs and ferments of development which exist within it, if one does not take into consideration and examine concretely and in depth this effective subordination to the intellectuals. Every organic development of the peasant masses, up to a certain point, is linked to and depends on movements among the intellectuals.[75]

It is clear then that in the nations placed within the orbit of the Soviet Union, social upheavals led by intellectuals were one answer to communism. The best illustrations for this are the 1956 revolution in Hungary, the 1968 and 1977 events in Czechoslovakia, the 1977 and 1980 strikes in Romania, and the 1980 Polish Solidarity. These were, however, mostly intellectually created and monitored industrial working-class movements from below. True populist, that is, rural and peasant, upheavals were not in the making for a long time, for large masses of agriculturalists depended on the state and enjoyed its social and cultural benefits. The only exception to this rule, however, was, in the words of Susan Gal, the "discourse battles."[76] These battles were between Hungarian elites creating and then leading the dance-house movement that successfully blended peasantism and regionalism by identifying with the plight of Hungarians in Transylvania. It incorporated nationalistic sentiments, folkloristic revival, and rural radicalism and combined them with international human and minority rights concerns. In this, the age-based neopopulism was radical and anti-state as well as progressive, a feature similar to some aspects of the literal populism and Pearly Bouquet movement of the inter-war period described in the previous chapter.

By the late 1970s and early 1980s, things had changed considerably, and the original plan of the regime had backfired. Since agricultural pro-duction declined and more and more workers left the rural sectors for commerce and service jobs, peasant values and traditions were even more removed from the people who were supposed to have them.[77] The elites who manipulated this cultural ferment were at a loss over trying to bridge the gap of this serious dilemma. If the peasantry was no more (as state planners argued), what happened to the archaic Hungarian past and the residues of Magyarness that were entrusted with the peasants? While elite discourse reflected on the loss of peasant values, tradition, and lifeway under existing state socialism, a new, more powerful, more "European" discourse made its way.[78] Nationalists discovered that the Hungarians of neighboring Romania were affected adversely by the megalomaniac rule of the Romanian government, as they remained more isolated from the forces of international political economy. The neopopulists realized that the "untainted" and "pristine" rural culture of Transylvania—existing on the periphery of Eastern Europe—offered a timely solution.

In conclusion, what the dance-house movement really achieved was a genuine contribution to create a transnational political discourse. For dance-house fans and neopopulists, state borders suddenly were seen as no borders at all. They identified Transylvanian Hungarian culture as remote and archaic and, moreover, that the borders between Hungary and Romania were not insurmountble. No matter how many miles apart they lived, for them, Transylvanians became the "real" or "proper Magyars" who were part of the Hungarian nation. Their non-communist and non-Romanian identities were seen as a testimony to their unwavering national identity—and this construct helped in fact to reconfigure new social relations both in Hungary as well as between Hungary and Roma-nia. For this reason, the dance-house movement became a dangerous, offensive subculture to both the Hungarian and Romanian states as soon as elites openly identified themselves with the plight of the minority and diaspora populations in Transylvania. Now the state borders of Hungary suddenly were transcended and the borders of the nation reopened. On June 27, 1988, Hungarians in Hungary were able to mount the largest anti-state demonstration since the 1956 revolution in Budapest's Heroes' Square to express their unity with Hungarians in Romania.[79] The remote regions of Transylvania, all interethnic to be sure but for the dance-house followers primarily Hungarian, represented the new borders, within which remnants of the national culture could be found. This stance was directly anti-state, for it smacked on the face internationalist and fraternal socialist interstate relations. On the one hand, it accused Romania of grave human and minority rights violations, a politically sharpened discourse often recalling the Tragedy of Trianon cloaked in peasant traditionalism, isolation, and an archaic mode of life. On the other hand, it criticized the Hungarian state for its non-committed stance and non-interference into the so-called "internal matters" of Romania. When in 1988 the democratic opposition organized a mass rally in Budapest, in particular in front of the Romanian embassy in Budapest and in Heroes' Square, tens of thousands marched willingly. Numerous among them were the dance-house youth, who carried proudly the banners of Hungary and Transylvania. Surely this was not the peasant radicalism of the 1930s but a new, wholly self-generated ideology that aimed at recreating Hungarian nationhood and national identity. What followed in 1989 and after was open confrontation and violence between Hungarians and Romanians, and an acceleration of tension between the two states.

Chapter 7

Transylvania Reimagined: Democracy, Regionalism, and Post–Communist Identity

The social undercurrents, described in previous chapters, signaled change in Hungary and Romania. However important, influential, and widespread this change was, neither politicians or scholars were able to predict the rapid collapse of state socialism. Even after the 1989 revolutions, the new power elite was poking about in the dark regarding what was coming. Vaclav Hável, the first president of the Czechoslovak and then the Czech Republic, for instance, had questioned the American president and the joint session of the U.S. Congress about to help the newly liberated East European states. In his presidential address, Hável stated: "You can help us most of all if you help the Soviet Union on its irreversible, but immensely complicated road to democracy."[1] The "we" implied in that historic statement was, of course, the Czechoslovak Republic. But neither the Soviet Union nor the communist Czechoslovak state survived the tumultuous year that followed. Even though many observers of the Soviet system in the 1980s sensed that such a totalitarian system could not continue much longer, no one was ready for the fundamental sweeping change that took East-Central Europe by surprise.

In analyzing the year 1989, American political scientist Charles Gati summarized the causes for the collapse of Hungarian socialism, emphasizing the importance the Transylvanian conflict played.[2] This was the moment at which, as E. P. Thompson noted sarcastically, "The lumpenintelligentsia of Washington think-tanks are rabbiting on about 'the end of history.'"[3] Yet during 1989 and 1990, more and more utterances were heard about the former East Bloc countries being part of the European

Union and their willingness to return to Europe. France's President, Fran-
cois Mitterand, said that Europe "is returning in its history and geography like one who is returning home."⁴ Jacques Attali, advisor to President
Mitterand and president of the European Bank of Reconstruction and
Development, wrote in similar euphoric tones: "Dictatorships are col-
lapsing throughout the world . . . traditional notions of national sovereignty are increasingly irrelevant."⁵ With the collapse of the East Bloc, a
new notion of Central Europe emerged in the minds of many. As
espoused by the former mayor of Vienna, Central Europe literally means
Europe—not the German idea of "Mitteleuropa"—which, when the project is completed, would differ from the Eastern antecedent in that it will
not have nationalist and nation-state ideologies.⁶

Following 1989, the so-called *annus mirabilis* experts testified about
the need for the historical collapse of totalitarianism and the building of
a civil society and celebrated the moment for the implementation of a free
market. Yet as the East disintegrated, the West integrated. E. P. Thompson wrote whimsically:

> In the winter of 1989–90 much of the Western media was
> obsessed with the ludicrous notion that the whole of Eastern
> and Central Europe was intent upon hurling itself helter-skel-
> ter into a "market economy," the institution of capitalism in a
> Thatcherite or Milton Freedmanite form. Certainly the absur-
> dities and absolute failures of the Communist command
> economies made many heads turn in that direction, and these
> were often the heads that spoke English and could talk with
> Roger Scroutin, Timothy Garton Ash, and the endless flow of
> American, British, and German funders, advisers, political
> and academic voyeurs, business agents, and others flooding
> through Prague, East Berlin, Warsaw, and Budapest.⁷

Since 1990, when Thompson viewed this Western rush for capitalist
investments, some states—the "wayward children of Europe," to borrow
Vaclav Hável's phrase—did in fact become members of the Council of
Europe. Moreover, many managed to shed their former Soviet heritage
and applied for—in the case of Hungary, Poland, and the Czech Republic—and later received—membership in the North Atlantic Treaty Organization (NATO). All of these states, however, now eagerly await their
admission into the European Union.

With all of these abrupt changes, one would expect that the relationship between the non-communist states of Romania and Hungary would
improve and that the whole issue of the Hungarian minority in Romania

and the historical controversy over Transylvania could be solved instanta-neously. Moreover, hopes were expressed by both countries' elites that ter-ritorial disputes would wither away as a necessary consequence of the dis-mantling of the Communist Party-State, a system wholeheartedly supporting, as we have seen in the preceding chapters, policies of non-interference and, at times, outright nationalistic hostility. Developments between the two states and nations in the 1990s, however, proved both sides wrong. As this chapter will argue, nationalistic controversies, while follow the international fluctuation of capital and geopolitics, tend to develop their own momentum and progress quite independently, though not separately, from larger political economic transformations. For despite of, or perhaps on account of, the joyous months of 1989 and 1990, real-ities turned sour for Hungarians and Romanians alike as negative aspects of this rapid transformation were voiced in both Romania and Hungary.[8]

REVOLUTION, PEACE, AND TRANSYLVANIANNESS

The demise of the Ceaușescu clan riveted international spectators as Romanians, Hungarians, Gypsies, workers, villagers, and students took to the streets of Romanian cities during the Christmas season of 1989.[9] Dur-ing that still-disputed December battle, Hungarian volunteers and their Western counterparts assisted the "revolutionaries": convoys of trucks car-ried food, medical supplies, and clothing into riot-torn Romania. Mili-tary reconnaissance was provided for the coordinates of Romanian "secu-ritate" planes and bases to anti-democracy loyalist interventions that contributed to a short-lived revival of fraternal relations between Hungary and Romania. In fact, the early months of 1990 were interpreted by the Hungarian oppositional intelligentsia as testimony of revitalized Hungar-ian goodwill. But shortly after the waning of "revolutionary" fervor, Hun-garians and Romanians found ample opportunity to escalate hostilities against one another. The ways in which these gestures were enacted bear striking resemblance to earlier patterns of hostile relations, discernible in the specifics of international developments and the ways in which the embattled countries appropriated them to their own respective purposes. What was new, however, was the struggle of Ceaușescu loyalists, in the popular phrase of the time, to steal the revolution from the peoples.

In the months subsequent to the "December events," and now recon-figured under their respective banners of unity, ethnic groups reemerged from the shadows of a prior communist existence. Now Lippovans, Czech, Slovaks, Ukrainians, Romanies (Gypsies), and ethnic Hungarians began in earnest to find their non-communist selves. Hungarian and

Romanian national identities, especially, coalesced in great vehemence, as discernible in the rhetoric of the new political parties. Vocal among them were the majority Democratic Forum in Hungary, the National Salvation Front in Romania, and the ultra-nationalist Romanian cultural association, *Vatra Romanesca* (Romanian Hearth). In Hungary, there also were extremists such as the Christian fundamentalist organizations, centered around the weekly newspaper *Holy Crown*, and the "Hungarian Way" movement and its later offshoot, the Hungarian Justice and Life Party, led by dramatist and writer István Csurka. A new departure was to be found in a repoliticized Hungarian ethnic consciousness and a concomitant intensification of the Hungaro-Romanian conflict, manifested among other ways in the formation of an official Hungarian political party, the Romanian Hungarian Democratic Association, the RMDSZ (or UDMR, as it is known in Romanian).[10]

The Hungarian ethnic party, although scarcely a homogeneous body representing the interests of all Hungarian diasporas in Romania, during the 1990 elections secured over 1 million votes, by far the largest oppositional votes cast for any party, save for the ruling National Salvation Front.[11] Touching sensitive chords with its slogans for "unity" and "the common fate of Hungarians," the organization successfully united three major Hungarian parties fighting for power: the Romanian-Hungarian Christian Democratic Party, the Independent Party, and the Smallholders' Party. At the time, however, this fusion was not taken to represent deep-seated conflicts between and within the membership and its leaders, for in terms of Hungarian and Romanian conflict, the Hungarian Transylvanian population has continued to be fairly homogeneous.

Several points relevant to the question of nationalist conflict highlight the rising tensions. Only two parties apart from the RMDSZ earned enough votes based primarily on ethnic alliances: the "Democratic Gypsy Union" (also referred to as the Romanian Gypsy Party) and the German Democratic Forum. Although the Ukrainian and Serbian Unions and the Lippovans' Community each gained less than 0.1 percent of the vote, only the Germans and Gypsies were able to send one deputy each to the Chamber of Deputies. It is interesting to note that among Transylvanian Romanians, radicalization also took a political form. They united in the Alliance of Unity of Romanians in Transylvania (AUR) and contested the elections in an ethnic appeal that was far more reactionary and nationalistic than the *Vatra*. The AUR finally managed to gain a total of eleven seats in the Senate and in the Chamber of Deputies.

With 7.2 percent of the total votes cast, the RMDSZ was allowed to send forty-one deputies to both houses, making it the second largest opposition party in the Romanian parliament, an election that fundamentally repoliticized Hungarian identity in Transylvania. The regional voting behavior is equally interesting, especially in light of the long-contested geographical distribution of ethnic Hungarians. The four counties in which RMDSZ candidates received the most votes were Harghita (85%), Covasna (77%), Mureş (42%), and Satu Mare (39%). The first two are traditional Szekler counties, an area where Hungarianism and regionalism always have been tied together.[12] These percentages also indicate the number of Hungarians in Romania, that figure itself having long been a subject of dispute between the two countries. A similar distribution can be noted in electoral behavior in the results of votes cast for the three major presidential contenders: in Covasna, 65 percent of the electorate cast their votes for Radu Campeanu of the National Liberal Party and only 32 percent for Iliescu. In Harghita county, these figures were 76 percent and 19 percent, respectively, undoubtedly suggesting that Hungarians supported the opposition's more democratic candidate, Campeanu, and not the former communist, I. Iliescu.[13]

By the time of the Second Congress of the RMDSZ, during the summer of 1991, the reelection of the party's officials followed divisions among leading candidates, among whom Géza Szőcs, Géza Domokos, and László Tőkés represented three distinct political directions, some compatible and others less so. Géza Szőcs, a dissident writer who had lived in the West for several years after his expulsion from Romania in 1987, represented perhaps the most visible radical program within the RMDSZ. Since the beginning of 1990, its proposal has been critical of the Iliescu government and of the extreme form of Romanian majority nationalism emanating from official parties seeking to create a federative system. Equally radical and perhaps even more powerful and dominant has been the Christian faction of the RMDSZ, led by László Tőkés. A pastor of the Protestant Reformed Church, and since the spring of 1990 a bishop, he announced from the beginning that he did not seek any form of compromise with the ruling powers. At the same time, the Protestant bishop argued for territorial integrity and regionalist policy within Romania and a unified voice for Hungarians and other minorities, recalling the Transylvanism school of the 1930s.[14]

During 1990, the most conservative but most influential party group in high political circles was the faction led by Domokos. As suggested in many policy statements, he contended that only by remaining in unison with Romanians at large would Hungarians find political and legal frameworks to survive as a recognized, legal minority opposition. Solidarity in place of regionalism and factioning was an important strategy in his followers' program to preserve the image of a strong group identity and cohesiveness. In those early months, dissenting voices were discouraged and silenced by Domokos. This was especially true with regard to the question of the autonomous status for Transylvania. Domokos' faction argued that the image of a split party politics would only serve the Romanian agenda, which was too willing to capitalize on such divisions by perpetuating historical—yet potent—negative stereotypes about Hungarian political unreliability and anti-state agitation.[15] However, time was not on the side of either Szőcs or Domokos. In a few years, both were ousted from the Hungarian party. Throughout the rest of the 1990s, the RMDSZ's new president, Béla Markó—a poet and writer from Transylvania—was able to unite the Hungarian party which, despite internal fighting, seemed to move in unison. In a sense, Domokos' nonconfrontational stance remained central to the official Hungarian party program throughout the decade.

MARCH 19–20, 1990—TIRGU MUREŞ

The chaotic election propaganda in early 1990, along with diverse debates concerning independent Hungarian language schools and different (nationalist) interpretations concerning the March 15 commemoration of the 1848 Hungarian War of Independence, generated profoundly altered national expectations and resentments on both sides. Romanian pamphlets, whose xenophobic, fascist content accused Hungarians of irredentism and separatist tendencies aimed at border realignment by severing Transylvania from Romania, circulated in several cities, including Tirgu Mureş.[16] Such anti-minority agitation took place at a time when the Romanian economy had reached an all-time low: shelves were again emptied, and the black market was once more accepted as the only way of life for many, turning citizens against one another in an incessant, futile struggle to make ends meet. The following brief chronicle is intended to illustrate and recapitulate the escalation of tensions between Hungarians and Romanians that eventually led to the bloody clashes of March 1990.

Only two months after the less than glorious revolution, from February 8–10, 1990, a demonstration in Tirgu Mureş took place. Romanians protested the status of Hungarian language schools and their legalization turned, in a matter of hours, into an anti-Hungarian march as thousands of villagers appeared under the aegis of the Vatra Romaneasca. As a countervailing effort, a peaceful Hungarian counter-demonstration was organized by the RMDSZ that deflected anticipated charges of chauvinism and separatism and urged the reinstatement of the Bolyai Hungarian University in Cluj. Beginning on March 6, a sit-in strike was held by Hungarian students of the Medical School, demanding Hungarian-language classes and the reinstatement of a balanced admission quota that would allow ethnic Hungarian co-nationals to be admitted in greater numbers. March 11 saw the birth of the Timişoara (Temesvár) Declaration, a document drafted to protest chauvinism, the continuation of communist tactics employed by the Iliescu government, and the slow pace of change in the country.[17] The event that heightened sentiment toward the Hungarian diaspora in Transylvania took place on March 15, when nationwide celebrations of the 1848 Hungarian War of Independence were held in major towns throughout Romania. In Arad and Cluj, for example, peaceful commemorative festivities were organized by the local RMDSZ. Since the Arad commemoration was visited by dignitaries from Hungary, anti-Hungarian sentiments were ignited. In Satu Mare, furthermore, a mood of pogrom was created as Romanians attacked demonstrators carrying Hungarian flags and singing the patriotic songs of the 1848 revolution.

On March 16, in the Tudor district of the Transylvanian city of Tirgu Mureş, a few hundred Romanians caused disturbances and, in an allegedly spontaneous eruption, several drunken men assaulted Hungarian stores. It was purported that Hungarian language signs displayed in the window and exclusive patronage by Hungarian clients caused this rage. The following day, during a demonstration organized by the Romanian University Student League, anti-Hungarian slogans were voiced; Romanians entered a Hungarian Protestant church, roughing up worshipers and vandalizing church property.

On Monday and Tuesday, March 19 and 20, 1990, demonstrations and strikes turned suddenly into bloody riots and street skirmishes as thousands gathered around Opera Square and in front of the RMDSZ headquarters. According to largely unsubstantiated accounts, most villagers were said to have been transported by buses and trucks from hamlets around the Gurghiu valley: Hungarian eyewitnesses insisted that many appeared to be in a drunken state, their participation bought and supported by Romanian Orthodox priests. According to these eyewitnesses, Romanian peasants from Hodac, Iobanesti, and other nearby villages were heard screaming such epithets and slogans as "Out with the Huns!" "We are prepared to die defending Transylvania," and "Bozgor (Hungarian), don't forget, this is not your homeland." All of these added an eerie dimension, recalling the fascist World War II pogroms, to the escalating tension and violence. On March 20, large groups of Gypsies (by all accounts, "Hungarian Gypsies," meaning those speaking Hungarian and sympathizing with Hungarians) joined the struggle and participated in creating a war-zone demarcated by unclaimed corpses and rampages throughout the city. A small group of Hungarians arrived from the nearby villages of Niraj Sardu (Nyárádszereda) and Sovata, but the Romanian Molotov cocktails had already achieved their aim: the RMDSZ headquarters were gutted, those inside were attacked, and Hungarian signs and plaques were burned or knocked down.

The angry mob, seemingly fueled by the ideology of Vatra Romaneasca, demanded the immediate dismissal of all Hungarian leaders and the disbandment of Hungarian ethnic organizations. In retrospect, in instigating this anti-Hungarian riot, the state and the government may be implicated, for the police and army took no action against the vandalism which, despite repeated attempts by Hungarians to call in reinforcements from Bucharest, left six dead and over 300 wounded. Clearly the Timişoara Declaration was utterly ineffectual during this nationalist riot in Tirgu Mureş. At the end of the riot, thirteen Gypsy males were arrested and tried, many receiving jail sentences as a consequence of their involvement. Aside from a few jailed Hungarians, other sentences were not passed by the Romanian courts.[18]

The irony of this interethnic violence lies in the fact that during the same weekend, Romanian and Hungarian intellectuals were engaged in day-long discussions in Hungary on the feasibility of decreasing hostilities between the two nations. Following the events of March 19–20, the RMDSZ led solidarity actions throughout Transylvanian cities in Romania. In Mircurea Ciuc, for example, thousands demanded human and nationality rights, thorough investigations into the violence, and the outlawing of anti-minority and nationalistic propaganda emanating from the media.

The casual attitude of the Iliescu government in persecuting those involved in instigating the violence led Géza Jeszenszky, Hungary's Minister of Foreign Affairs, to declare on August 8, 1990, that he was not "optimistic about Hungary's future relations with Romania." This upheaval was followed by a brief "thaw" on October 18, 1990, when Hungarian and Romanian defense ministers met in what was described by both parties as a "very positive" step, but without tangible results.

The Early 1990s: The Accusations Continue

In attempting to analyze these often terrifying, hostile events, we would do well to remember that the years that followed were not exceptional. The demonstrations and the miners' rampage in Bucharest, not unexpectedly, turned citizens' attention away from other developing interethnic conflicts, in particular, the educational question that raged through the media, as thousands of families eagerly waited the opening of

Hungarian language classes and the repossession of their schools. A substantial backlash took place following the Tirgu Mureş events covered by the international media. Hungarian officials deployed rhetorical flourishes based on these issues to propagandistic ends to the effect that, "Well, we warned you about those Romanians." For its part, the Iliescu government resorted to earlier accusations. The state's discourse was undeniably racist, portraying Hungarians as "a bunch of savages, Huns, and an overzealous, restless people," fascist sympathizers, who are prone to violence and secession and should be held responsible for the deteriorating state of affairs.[19]

Linked to this Romanian accusation was perhaps a still more questionable expression of the political imagination. It was claimed that the Hungarian government attempted to influence the military outcome of the December 1989 events and the March 1990 violence in Tirgu Mureş. It would be difficult to wholly dismiss these charges, despite the Hungarian government's official proclamations of democracy, the inviolability of borders, and non-interference into internal affairs. At the same time, the popular media and extremists in Hungary continued to present not the official government's position but their own sense of nationalism, and in so doing they influenced private and public opinion by fostering the emergence of a transnational culture of "Magyarness," and the need for creating a unified "Magyar" culture across the borders. It is possible to account for the ways in which overt nationalistic propaganda emanated from Hungarian elite circles at least since late 1989, pouring oil on the eternally and viciously burning fire of hostilities between the two countries. Even the government kept sending contradictory messages. One of the most misunderstood statements was uttered by Hungary's Prime Minister, József Antall, in 1990. In his words, he managed to unite state and nation, for he wished to be "in spirit and feeling, the Prime Minister of 15 million Hungarians." This was an obvious reference to Hungarians outside of the state of Hungary.[20]

While the Hungarian government (along with the leaders of the RMDSZ) raised its voice against the perpetuation of the anti-Hungarian policies of the Romanian government, nationalist Romanians accused the Hungarian government of certain fascist and "irredentist" slogans. The immediacy of such accusations also was illustrated during the visit to Hungary of Pope John Paul II for the national celebrations of August 20, 1991. This historic trip was seen by Romanian nationalists as an attempt on the part of Catholic clergy (a majority of Hungarians in Transylvania are Catholics, with a minor Romanian population also adhering to Roman Catholicism, the rest being Orthodox) to disempower the majority of Romanian Orthodox believers. Such enmity was encouraged by the

Pope's unmitigated acceptance of Hungary's claim that Catholic Hungarians in Romania, especially the *Csángós* of Moldavia, faced severe prejudice and anti-Catholic assaults by the Romanian state.[21] It is also true, nevertheless, that the tens of thousands of Catholic pilgrims traveling from Romania to Hungary in August to hear the Pope met disinterested Romanian border guards who, despite the objections of Hungary's Minister of Foreign Affairs, were indifferent to facilitating newly relaxed border crossing and visa controls. As reported by many Transylvanians, spending fifteen to twenty hours in waiting lines was not uncommon during that time.[22]

Undoubtedly the most controversial occurrence took place in October, when the Romanian parliament was in flames on the heels of a proposal of Hungarians with plans to organize a political rally in Agyagfalva (Lutita) on October 19, 1991. This proposal was instigated by an article published on October 12 by the Alliance for the Unity of Romanians in Transylvania, which petitioned the government to ban the RMDSZ because of acts of separatism and disloyalty. Although far from an innocent cultural gathering (originally intended to commemorate the 1848 events on the exact spot the Szeklers had joined the Hungarian War of Independence), this planned rally wreaked havoc among Romanian politicians, who saw this march as the beginning of a full-scale separatist movement of Hungarians living in the Szekler region of Transylvania.

In retrospect, the origin of this meeting is still unclear, shrouded in mystery and suspicion. Rumors circulated to the effect that the Mures-Magyar Autonomous Region, abolished by Ceaușescu in 1968, was to be revived or, as some believed, that a separatist province would be established in its place. The instigators of this meeting were the so-called Forum of Young Szeklers (*Székely Fiatalok Fóruma*), founded during the summer of 1991 in Székelyudvarhely, and the Alliance of Szekler Lands (*Székelyföldi Egyeztető Csoport*). Both of these groups sprang from the RMDSZ, which publicly announced its intention to form a separate Szekler Democratic Party.[23] However, this separation from the RMDSZ was met with immediate resistance and objection by the national leadership. For instance, even the former president, Géza Domokos, called it "an irresponsible and unfortunate act."[24]

Arguments and rebuttals were resuscitated, many of a historical nature, about whether such separatist and regionalist factioning was useful or even necessary. Arguments were rekindled that since the Szeklers, roughly one-third of the Hungarians living in Romania, were indeed a different nationality they deserved a separate party outside of the RMDSZ. The underlying agenda of the Szeklers' movement against the RMDSZ was that the elected leadership failed to represent the interests of the Szekler nation which, because of historical circumstances, lived in a homogeneous bloc in the counties of Harghita and Covasna, demanding special treatment.

Particularly remarkable in this development was the survival of the idea that separate Magyar and Szekler nations lived side by side in Transylvania. As mentioned in previous chapters, during a substantial portion of the Ceauşescu era, political propaganda represented the Szeklers as a separate nationality (the 1977 census, in fact, lists 1,500 who declared themselves to be of Szekler nationality in Romania). This nationalistic ideology formed the core of the revitalized media deception of the early 1990s in ultra-nationalist newspapers such as the *Vatra Romanesca* and the *Romania Mare*. What was different between the 1970s and the 1990s, however, was that such claims for separate nationality emerged among the high-ranking Szekler politicians themselves. Flabbergasted at first, the RMDSZ leadership rejected this separatist mentality, arguing that any political attempts of "divide and conquer" only served the cause of greater Romanian chauvinism and ran counter to effective Hungarian participation in national Romanian political life. The RMDSZ leadership devised its own status quo by claiming the legitimacy of Szekler cultural specificities, but it has adamantly argued for unity. In fact, the nineteenth-century terms "Szekler-magyar" or "Csángó-magyar"[25] have not been uncommon in this debate.

This alleged "Szekler conspiracy," while certainly radicalizing Hungarian national identity in Romania, led in interesting ways to yet another friction in Romanian national politics concerning borders, nations, and citizenship. The newly formed government of Theodor Stolojan, replacing that of Petre Roman, ousted during the miners' demonstration in September 1991, offered three important positions—including that of Finance Minister—to be filled by individuals of the RMDSZ's own choice. This new offer, obviously meant to bring majority and minority platforms closer, was immediately and flatly rejected by the Hungarian party. The basic argument was that, until a Ministry of Minority Affairs was established, it wanted nothing to do with the new government. Such a ministry, although close to the hearts of other nationalities as well, was not at all popular among Romanian parties. The only exception was the National Peasant Party, which favored the establishment of such a ministry but only on the condition that it must include under its aegis Romanians outside of Romanian borders. After taking such a radical stance, all other parties rejected any cooperation with the Hungarian party in Transylvania. Especially ferocious was the reaction of the extremist circles. With the formation of the party *Romania Mare* in June 1991, the anti-Hungarian platform became a legitimate political agenda within the

Romanian parliament. The Great Romania Party constituted the legit-imization of xenophobic and chauvinistic themes that appeared earlier in a newspaper under the same name.[26]

The raging civil war in Yugoslavia—referred to by the euphemism "ethnic cleansing," though in English "ethnic purification" would serve better—provided yet another source of conflict between the two states. The significance of state borders suddenly became magnified, receiving more power as both arbiters and dividers between states and nations. Arti-cles appeared in the Romanian press accusing the Hungarian state of involvement with the Serbo–Croatian civil war in the former Yugoslavia, an assertion based on an appeal by a member of the Hungarian parlia-ment who criticized the Antall government for selling surplus Russian-made weapons to Croatia. In addition, as reported by Hungarian jour-nals, the Hungarian government opened its southern border by offering asylum to over 35,000 refugees from neighboring Yugoslavia, an action that earned Hungary $3 million in aid from the United Nations. With this gesture, however, Hungary's image in Romania was cast as that of an "agitator" acting as a counter-force against democratic processes in East-ern Europe.

By the first week of October 1991, the Hungarian government resorted to closing off its borders, turning away those who lacked ade-quate sums of hard currency, papers, or the documents and visas required for foreign travel. According to a statement made by a spokesman for the border guards, between October 4 and October 8, 1991, while 700,000 foreigners were allowed to cross into Hungary, 66,000 were denied entry, many of them Romanian citizens.[27] What is not generally acknowledged, however, is that with the demolishment of the Iron Curtain in 1989, the Romanian anti-Gypsy pogroms forced various Gypsy populations to make their way toward the West—just like in the late 1990s, when Czech and Slovak Roma tried to emigrate, in search of security, peace, and employment opportunities. As a result, many caught at the borders were Gypsies who then were forcibly repatriated to Romania (in November 1990, the German foreign minister announced his plan to send back tens of thousands of Romanian Gypsies, to the bafflement of the international community).[28]

This allegedly retrograde image of the Hungarian government, replacing that of communist Moscow, was clearly refashioned by Roman-ian leaders and nationalists. They viewed the Antall and later the Boross governments with suspicion, seeking to remake Hungary's international image to wield their influence in politics, more properly the domain of strictly internal matters. Romanians felt that the threat arose from the potential for civil war in Romania in the wake of murderous battles in

Serbia, Bosnia, and Croatia. This potential was exploited in its own interest by the Hungarian government (to divide Romania and establish Hungarian control over this contested terrain), according to some Romanians.

THE MID-1990S: CONFLICTING HOPES

The mid-1990s brought no détente in policies between the two countries, despite an official rhetoric of democratization and privatization and the emergence of more moderate political factions, such as the Civic Alliance and the Coalition for Democracy in Romania.[29] Cabinet-level shuffles (Petre Roman was dismissed in Romania, the beginning of the Vacariou government, and high-level ministerial changes followed in Hungary as well) did little to influence the reciprocally retrograde image through which the neighboring states and existing parties contemplated one another. Local elections in Transylvanian towns brought some easing of tensions: while Tirgu Mureş elected a Hungarian mayor, Cluj, on the contrary, brought to power a xenophobic Romanian mayor, G. Funar, a painful thorn in the eyes of the local Hungarian population. All the while the relationship of the two countries was far from improved. Since the spring of 1992, other high-level ministerial talks were initiated, and the Hungarian and Romanian "cultural houses" in Bucharest and Budapest, respectively, were opened, only to culminate in superficial cultural exchanges without serious attention to the smoldering interethnic conflict plaguing them. Not to be discussed in particular was the question of the closed Hungarian embassy in Cluj, shut down during the final months of Ceauşescu's rule; the relationship of the Hungarian diaspora to Hungary; the legitimacy of extremist nationalist parties; and the reestablishment of Hungarian higher-education institutions in Romania.

This last point was dismissed simply as a "technical and administrative problem" by Traian Chebeleu, a spokesman for the Presidential Office of Iliescu.[30] Moreover, the question of autonomy—personal, collective, territorial, or cultural—seemed to be a "non-question" in the eyes of the leaders of the government of Ion Iliescu, an area that was becoming more and more of a consensus of the RMDSZ's radical wing.[31] A bilateral agreement between the two countries was continually put off by extremist circles, and the Romanian government played a hide-and-seek game both with Hungary and the Hungarian minority in Transylvania. This was the reason Bishop Tőkés—using the language of the time— referred to the Hungarian-Romanian stalemate in Transylvania in the mid-1990s as a "special form of ethnic cleansing."[32]

Clearly by this time the question of Transylvania had been elevated into the language of political discourse. This symbolic conflict ignited more serious actions: for example, the Hungarian government made a serious blunder when it decided not to support Romania's admittance into the Council of Europe, which in turn outraged Romanian politicians.[33] The setting up of the Council of National Minorities, by order of the Bucharest government on March 24, 1993, was viewed, on the contrary, by many Hungarians as a smoke screen for the troubles but not a fitting, democratic solution to the problems of the Hungarian minority in Romania.[34]

With the conservative Antall–Boros government in power between 1990 and 1994, populistic language and politics were at the core of national and international attempts to create a viable Hungarian political platform. This extremism, however, worked against them, as conservatism had become a discredited political force by the elites in Hungary,[35] which contributed considerably to the general elections in 1994, when the victory of the socialist–liberal coalition drastically altered the political tapestry of the country and the ways in which the socialist-led government of Gyula Horn began to consider taking generous steps toward Hungary's neighbors. A meeting between Horn and Slovak President Vladimir Meciar in late 1994 signaled a willing step on the part of both states to reconcile over least some of their differences. Although actual positive results were not at hand, especially concerning liberal and democratic minority policies concerning Hungarians in Slovakia and the international legal quagmire concerning the building of the Danube Dam, this meeting laid the foundation for later rapprochement between the two states. Following this lead, similar steps were taken in the winter of 1994 to bring about high-level governmental talks between Hungary and Romania. Success was minimal, yet it seemed for the moment that the two governments were at least willing to discuss democracy and membership in NATO and the European Union *only* with Western leaders and less so between themselves.

Despite the moderately democratic climate, the tension between the Romanian government and the Hungarian minority in Romania continues to remain acute, with a constant fluctuation of accusations and counter-accusations between factions representing the two sides. One figure under consistent attack by Romanian politicians has remained the honorary president of the RMDSZ, László Tőkés.[36] How the position of Tőkés as a radical champion of Hungarian rights was created is easy to see: after his elevation to national and in fact international fame, he had easy access to media and high-political and international circles. Acting as safety valves, many of Tőkés' ideas have been more radical as well as more cautious than the rest of the RMDSZ's leadership. There were few signs on the horizon that the Hungarian and Romanian governments—no doubt under pressure by the West—were adamant in signing a basic, two-states agreement. Its creation reveals the serious influence the West could exert when it so desired. In February 1995, the New York-based Project on Ethnic Relations (PER) and the Carter Center of Atlanta set up a roundtable dialogue between RMDSZ leaders and the Romanian government.[37] Whether such outside intervention may be needed in the future to bring together the two parties to discuss Transylvanian autonomy cannot be ascertained. Yet it is true that up until that meeting, no such talks were initiated; even more significant is that only accusations and counteraccusations against Bishop Tőkés were made.

Even though there were signs for the making of a "East-Central European Peace Accord," Hungarian leaders in Transylvania proposed that a high-level governmental talk could not, and should not leave out Romania's Hungarian minority. In fact, Bishop Tőkés sent a letter to President Göncz of Hungary and to President Iliescu of Romania, suggesting that the two countries' agreement should be preceded by a similar peace accord between the Hungarians in Romania and the Romanian state. Tőkés argued forcefully that any other kind of settlements between the two countries would be insufficient, for such an agreement "must involve the two [Hungarian and Romanian] nations, since the source of the problems is the disorderly state of affairs concerning the Hungarian minority in Transylvania."[38] While this statement is a clear indication for the cleavage between state and nation in the development and negotiation of East-Central European identities during the 1990s, it also points to the important repoliticization of nationality and regionality in the Transylvanian conflict.

The success of such a controversial climate in the two countries' stance toward each other was that both Budapest and Bucharest had to realize that they could not overstep the quintessential supranational forces and institutions that emerged. Outside pressures notwithstanding, there were (both in Hungary and in Romania) initiators to bring the two countries to the bargaining tables. Two factors signify that such a wish was not falling on deaf ears: one was the local elections in Romania in the fall of 1996 and the other was the signing of the bilateral treaty between the two countries. The national and local elections resulted in no substantial change. The RMDSZ was able to ascertain a few more municipal positions, yet conflicts between the myopic mayor of Cluj, Georghe Funar, and the Hungarian citizens of that city have remained incessantly acute. One such local conflict was ignited by the archaeological excavation commissioned in the center of the town around the Catholic church. Hungarian nationals felt,

and rightfully so, given the controversial history concerning ethnic institutions, that such an act was a direct attack on one of their most sacred historical symbols. A Romanian counter-argument claimed that under the
medieval Hungarian remains, older (namely archaic Romanian and
Dacian) artifacts needed to be unearthed. Since history and archaeology
are both nationalized sciences, as I have shown in previous chapters, these
arguments created an even more hostile existence in the city of Cluj. Surely
enough, the excavations yielded both medieval and earlier discoveries!

Without any doubt, however, the most significant development of
1996 was the signing of the bilateral treaty between the two countries and
the ensuing controversies that it generated. A special session of the Hungarian parliament was called to decide whether such a treaty should be
signed at all. The socialist-ruled parliament, not giving in to the claims of
the opposition—arguing that this would be tantamount to abandoning
Hungarians in Transylvania—passed the bill with a resounding yes. What
seems strange in this fiery debate is the fact that the original bilateral
treaty was suggested first by the Antall government in 1992. However,
opposition parties and nationalist leaders in both Romania and Hungary
argued that this treaty was of no use. Hungary's peasant party even suggested that Bill Clinton and Ion Iliescu would only benefit from the
treaty, since both were running for reelection. Yet it should be mentioned
in this context that well over 70 percent of Hungarians in Romania saw
the treaty as a positive step between the two countries.[39]

The text of the agreement, printed in all of the Hungarian and
Romanian newspapers, entails several important points concerning the
rights of Hungarians living in Romania. Most important is the use of
native language in education, schools, the media, and local affairs. The
treaty does not address, however, one of the most sensitive points in the
eyes of Hungarian leaders in Transylvania, namely, the question of the
restitution of nationalized ethnic and church properties. Seeing the
oncoming reignited debates, the Romanian government promised that a
separate agreement would be drafted to deal with this special issue, a
promise still in the making. The RMDSZ's radical wing, led by Bishop
Tőkés, was still not satisfied. Tőkés claimed that despite its progressive
outlook, the treaty did not entail the supervisory mechanism for the
promises. In an open letter to Prime Minister Gyula Horn, the determined bishop argued: "In Romania there is a missing political will to
implement the stated changes. The past seventy-five years of anti-minority policies reveal that, even with the treaty signed, there will be no significant improvement for the Hungarians in Romania."[40]

Despite all of the rhetoric and attacks, on September 16, 1996, in the
historic and often troubled city of Timisoara, the bilateral agreement

between the Hungarian and Romanian governments was signed. Horn and his Romanian counterpart, Prime Minister Vacariou, gave their blessings to the document that will be in effect until 2006, and an additional five years if neither country objects to its existence. The controversial nature of this symbolic political cease-fire is easily ascertained from the fact that leaders of Hungary's liberal Free Democratic Party—most notably Minister of Culture, Bálint Magyar, Minister of Internal Affairs, Gábor Kuncze, and Hungarian President, Árpád Göncz—were missing from the signing ceremony. Equally noticeable was the lack of presence of the entire RMDSZ leadership.

This oppositional stance of leading political figures illustrates that Hungarian intellectuals were cautious throughout the 1990s about the Transylvanian conflict and the fate of Hungarians living there. The ink hardly dried on the treaty when the national elections in Romania were held, with disastrous results to the ruling Romanian socialists. Learning from the government's nonchalant attitude, the RMDSZ decided not to support Ion Iliescu but instead had its own candidate for president, Gy. Frunda, even though it was obvious that Democrat Emil Constantinescu would be a sure winner. However, it also was clear that Romania could not accept a Hungarian as president. The elections turned out to be marginal between the ruling party and the democratic opposition, but the runoff election ended with the defeat of President Iliescu. Constantinescu's victory was facilitated by the massive participation of the Hungarian Transylvanians casting their votes for him.[41] With this, a new era of political culture and discourse started in the life of the Hungarian party in specific and for Hungarians in Romania in general.

Thus with the new president and new parliament in office, the year 1997 brought fundamental changes in Romania and for Romanian citizens: an increase in the price of consumer goods, escalating inflation, empty store shelves (yet again), and general economic malaise. Such privations notwithstanding, the relations between the new Romanian government and the Hungarian socialist regime started off on a new ground. State-level meetings ensued in rapid succession. The new Romanian government offered several ministerial and state secretarial positions to the Hungarian party, an offer gladly accepted by the RMDSZ, and both the Ministry of Tourism and the Ministry of Minority and Nationality Affairs were given to Hungarian candidates of the RMDSZ's own choice. In addition, two county prefectures and several state secretarial positions were filled by Hungarians. Yet some of the skeptics argued that now, with this symbolic coercion of Hungarians into Romanian state apparatuses, the age-old dream of national autonomy and international support for minority agendas would not be forthcoming.[42] Nationalists offered several doomsday scenarios, claiming further poverty for minorities in Romania and a continuation of Hungarian emigration to Hungary. Such warnings were not wholly unreasonable though. According to a figure released by the Hungarian Ministry of Interior Affairs, in 1996 a total of 11,977 people applied for naturalization: out of this number, 6,794 people were former citizens of Romanian, and only 1,273 were from war-torn Yugoslavia (the rest were from the former Soviet Union).[43] It serves us well to remember that this roughly corresponds to the number of Hungarians who emigrated during the height of the Ceaușescu era, discussed earlier. This unabated flow of émigrés signals that, democratic developments aside, Hungarians from Romania continued to emigrate to the "motherland" in the early-to-mid-1990s, and at a steady rate. As reported by the Hungarian daily, *Népszabadság*, in 1998, 3,224, and in 1999 5,266 individuals requested naturalization permits, most of these were Hungarians from Romania (September 16, 2000, p. 26).

Such a doubtful prognosis notwithstanding, however, it is necessary to realize that with these changes Hungarians in Transylvania found themselves at the doorstep of a new era, signaling perhaps the dawn of the new millennium. The way in which the relations between the two nations progressed since the late 1990s showed signs of a healthy development between the two states. It revealed that the testing ground for democracy stood up extremely well, and that the Hungarian party in Romania was able to create a viable political platform to contest Romanian majority and state policies.[44]

The developments in 1997 and 1999 illustrate that both regimes were serious about democratic principles and, moreover, that both became weary of Western monitoring of their policies. As a goodwill gesture, the Romanian government reinstated the Hungarian consulate in the Transylvanian city of Cluj, a step immediately followed by the establishment of a Romanian consulate in the southern Hungarian city of Szeged.[45] Nevertheless, it must be emphasized that such a high-level international political struggle goes hand in hand with more troublesome and controversial local political strife. Among the contending Hungarian parties, criticism of Hungary's foreign policy has emerged. In specific, opposition parties voiced their opinion that Hungary has been involved with a mild form of political "window dressing," but that a solution to Transylvanian minority problems has not been offered.[46] Bishop László Tőkés, as well as the radical core formed around him within the RMDSZ, also has continued his open attack on both governments, although the center-right government of Viktor Orbán, in power since 1998, has been close to Tőkés. Particularly, he has raised concern over the slow agreement on the restitution of formerly nationalized Hungarian church properties and the reinstatement of the Hungarian Bolyai University in Cluj.[47] No sooner did the clicking of the champagne glasses subside at the Romanian consulate opening in Budapest and Bucharest, but an immediate nationalist backlash followed among Romania's extremists. In an act of open defiance of the Romanian constitution, the xenophobic prefect of Cluj county ordered local police to remove Hungarian names and road signs. In his eyes, such ethnic signs recalled the interwar Horthyist administrative redrawing of Transylvania's political map.[48] Even the Hungarian flag at the Hungarian embassy in Cluj was a thorn in his eyes.

The mid-1998 events brought further polarization in majority and minority relations in Romania and in interstate relations between the two countries. In particular, the victory of the center-right Young Democrats' Party (FIDESZ) in the Hungarian national elections resulted in the creation of a new national program of the government of Viktor Orbán. The new Romanian government of Radu Vasile, from April 15, 1998, until December 1999, continued the soft minority policy of the previous government (with the maintenance of two Hungarian ministers in the Romanian cabinet) but with no serious concessions regarding the creation of the Hungarian university in Romania. One event in particular stands out. This concerns the dismissal of the RMDSZ's own minister of health, who was asked to resign by the Romanian regime leaders for his alleged involvement with the country's dreaded secret police in the 1960s.[49] As far as the reinstatement of the Hungarian university in Cluj is concerned, Bishop Tőkés' radical policy was uncompromising. Seeing the Romanian government back off from supporting this claim, he called for transnational support in creating a private university in Romania. His call did not fall on deaf ears. In September 1999, the Hungarian–Partium Protestant University in the city of Oradea (Nagyvárad) opened its doors to Hungarian students. What caused an outcry among Romanian nationalists was not that it was private or a religious, ethnic-based academic institution but that the Hungarian government decided to support it with 2 billion forints.

CONCLUSIONS

What is certain from the above is that the controversy between the Romanian and Hungarian governments, as well as the Romanian state and Hungarian minority in Romania, has continued, despite the enormous political and economic transformations since 1990. The nature of the political discourse changed throughout the decade, starting as a violent confrontation and continuing as a heated debate about ethnic schools, language use, and regional autonomy. Michael Walzer has suggested that a "new tribalism" has emerged out of the ashes of communist legacies, creating a whole new way of life, a culture of enmity, in fact, for citizens in both states.[50] It is my assertion that the reason is not due to some sort of longevity of nationalistic feelings, although some of those no doubt have survived state socialist governments; what was fundamental in the rejuvenation of this historic controversy was that the global transformation of world polity, economy, and population transfers retriggered identity crises on a massive scale. The remaking of local and ethnic identities in both Hungary and Romania, in particular the Transylvanian controversy, has followed national crises, changes in governments, and the international shuffling of political alliances. As a natural consequence, they too underwent alterations, as leaders, institutions, and cultural workers questioned their status quo and legitimacy.[51]

The reemergence of contestable nationalist discourses and transnational identities in East-Central Europe has further implications for theoretical discourses of diaspora and border communities. William Safran defines a diaspora as any exiled group dispersed from a specific historic homeland that collectively develops ethnic consciousness and solidarity both among its members and toward that "mythical" land.[52] He states: "The Magyars of Transylvania cannot be regarded as living in a diaspora. Despite the fact that (under the dictatorship of Ceauşescu) they did not enjoy full cultural autonomy, the Magyars of Romania were not dispersed; rather, their communities were politically detached from the motherland."[53] However encompassing and flexible it might be when applied to groups as diverse as Jews, Armenians abroad, Corsicans in France, and Chinese and Latinos in the United States, this definition nevertheless falls short of accounting for the cultural variations such as the Transylvanian case to which he refers. For in the historical and ethnographic case study presented above, I have suggested that Hungarians and Romanians alike view each other with resentment, suspicion, and an aggrieved sense of historical mistreatment, both as a peripherialized community in this realigned global ethnoscape. Exactly who constitutes the host society and the indigene, on the one hand, and who belongs to the settler or migrant group, on the other hands, depends upon the nationalist view of the political subject whose perspective the author represents. The question of point of view, then, cannot be elided. Transylvanian Hungarians are members of that nation's ethnic diaspora, both because of what happened after World War I with the borders and because of the forceful dispersion of Hungarians under Ceauşescu.

Citing Gabriel Sheffer's work, Safran expands his discussion of the meaning of diaspora by claiming a "triangular relationship" among the entities of a diaspora group, homeland, and host society, a model closely resembling Rogers Brubaker's "triadic nexus" characterization.[54] For Hungarians in Romania, this relationship is reconfigured in multiple form, transgressing such functionalist categorization. As seen before, many different Hungarian-speaking groups live in Romania—the Csángós of Moldavia, for instance, who are considered a "remote" diaspora group *within* the Hungarian national community in Romania—and their intergroup and intragroup relations reveal complex constellations of purpose and political interest. Various definitions and rebuttals have been offered for questions of who constitutes a diaspora, what is a national territory, and what rights do nationalities have. As this chapter has shown, despite regional diversity, Hungarians in Romania continued to view themselves throughout the 1990s as a unit in contrast to the Romanian majority (the host society). They continue to manifest differing attitudes and degrees of closeness toward the Hungarian government and Hungarians in Hungary *as well as* toward those abroad. As the Hungarian-Romanian controversy over Transylvania, its definition and population, demonstrates, any definition of diaspora—its minority and majority implications—must be solidly anchored within a specific cultural and historical framework.

The Transylvanian conflict is surely a pressing one, to be solved according to established and accepted legal, political, and cultural understandings. With the privatization of former industrial state enterprises and agricultural lands largely completed, the influx of western joint ventures and a surmounting monetary and trade shortage are looming large. Times are now difficult for both countries. The future of interethnic controversy between Hungarians and Romanians in Transylvania remains uncertain. In both states, as Larry Watts has pointed out, "The adversarial atmosphere also greatly inhibits ethnic minority approaches to majority governments. The zero-sum thinking on both sides leaves minorities with almost no options except to deliver ultimatums or accept defeats."[55]

It remains to be seen whether this duality in thinking and reality, the policies of Hungary's government, and the reinterpretations of the bilateral treaty will bring fruition and solutions to the two states' enduring problems in the third millennium. As negotiations continue between the governments, both states view this ethnic problem as a potential source of friction and as an embarrassment in the face of the international community, as both are at the moment hoping to become EU members.[56] Yet as the past decade's controversy and this treaty's overheated debates revealed, there may be serious cracks in the system for quite some time to come.

Chapter 8

Conclusion:
New Nations, Identities,
and Regionalism in the New Europe

The previous chapters revealed the importance and seriousness of the inner and outer workings of nationalist projects and contested imaginations between Hungarian and Romanian elites. In the Hungarian and Romanian states' negotiation of their own as well as each others' histories and identities, Transylvania was elevated to the status of a remote region. My focus has been on Hungarians' perspectives of Transylvania, as they are residents in both states.[1] Historical, literary, ethnographic, and social negotiations have illustrated that throughout the twentieth century, Transylvania continued to produce its own national dilemmas and contradictions. These contradictions, I argued, will continue well into the third millennium.[2] By calling attention to both the premises and perhaps limitations of this political geo-mandering, however, the intent is not to offer ready-made solutions and not even to raise all of the points, but rather to stimulate analysis and discussion. This analysis has been directed specifically toward the contests both in Hungary and Romania and to an anthropological understanding of the ways in which elites have negotiated over Transylvania. Moreover, by uniting Transylvania as both a remote and a border region, a broader view of the developments in other regions and disciplines was offered, which could reinvigorate anthropological studies on regions, borders, and states in the newly configured Europe.[3]

The notion of the remote area has been borrowed from anthropologist Edwin Ardener, who has provided a model that best captures the conflict between, what Anthony D. Smith refers to as the "modernist" and "post-modernist" debates on nationalism. Smith argues that the modernists—

FIGURE 8.1 Monuments to the nations: Dracula poster in the window of a travel agency, Cluj, Romania. (Author's collection.)

among them K. Deutsch, H. Kohn, E. Kedourie, E.Gellner, T. Nair, H. Seton-Watson, and C. Tilly—"all assumed that nations, once formed, were real communities of culture and power: circumscribed, but potent, unifying, energizing, constraining."[4] In contrast, for the postmodernists (E. Hobsbawm and B. Anderson), "the nation is like the artificial nightingale . . . a piece of social engineering . . . a composite artifact, cobbled together from a rich variety of cultural sources."[5] While Smith does not deny the imagined quality of a national community and the fictive nature of unifying myths as cultural and ideological artifacts, he argues that:

> These artifacts have created an image of the nation for compatriots and outsiders alike, and in doing so have forged the nation itself. Signifier and signified have been fused. Image and reality have become identical; ultimately, the nation has no existence outside its imagery and its representations.[6]

In a similar vein, Wilson and Donnan argue that: "Post-modern political analyses often fail to query the degree to which the state sustains its historically dominant role as an arbiter of control, violence, order, and organization for those whose identities are being transformed by world forces."[7] This is why Ardener's "remote areas" is a useful model, for it both connects and transcends what Smith, Wilson, and Donnan have presented. Ardener argues that "the age of discovery showed us that the 'remote' was actually compounded of 'imaginary' as well as 'real' places" . . . [and] "it is obviously necessary that 'remoteness' has a position in topographical space, but it is defined within a topological space whose features are expressed in a cultural vocabulary."[8] Transylvania, both as a real terrain of the modernists and as an imaginary national homeland of the postmodernists, is a remote "land beyond the forest" where Dracula emerged and where children of the German city of Hamelin went to become the Saxon settlers of Transylvania.[9] As this example illustrates, cultural vocabularies form powerful myths and historical narratives connecting Transylvania to majority and minority populations living there. This book has argued that Transylvania has been viewed by nationalists through specific cultural vocabularies told and retold by Hungarian and Romanian elites. These narratives have always concerned how to create, define, and negotiate their perspectives in a meaningful and powerful way over others.

Materials of this nature have considerable potential for the analysis of national movements and the ways in which post–communist nationalism continues to negotiate its contestable geopolitical projects in the new Europe. However, as scholars, we must learn how elements and ideas in such territorialized negotiations and conflicts emanate from the borders and peripheries before we can be of more than limited use, not only in anthropology but in areas labeled variously as cultural, nationality, ethnic, or border studies.

In this analysis of nationalist controversy between two states, Transylvania serves as an object lesson. It reminds us that unless we are mindful of the important implications of space, territories, and borders—and especially their function in nationalistic state myths—we are likely to create analyses whose theoretical values are limited because our understanding of these cultural terrains remains biased, inconclusive, and incomplete. Therefore, a revitalization of studies on nationalism, nationalist conflicts, and territorial issues that will be at the cutting edge of anthropological thought and development is needed. This is becoming increasingly important as Western globalization integrates more and more parts of Eastern and Southern Europe and indeed the whole world. As this terrain contracts, expands, and shakes itself from time to time, our world is becoming increasingly connected. Yet, at the same time, it seems to grow farther apart. Therefore, we cannot disregard the important repercussions of territorial identities, ethnoregional movements, and local initiatives contributing to the formation of our globe well beyond the third millennium. Only in this way is it possible to understand the recently published program of the Hungarian writers' union, "to restore the spiritual and cultural unity of Hungarians by maintaining national identity both within and without the borders of Hungary,"[10] This is indeed a transnational negotiation aiming at cultural preservation and maintenance, which Gloria Anzaldúa analyzes as characteristic "new consciousness," emblematic of borderlands."[11]

The remaking of Hungarian and Romanian national selves, however, is not an isolated instance of nationalism going berserk in the region recently liberated from Soviet domination. Since 1990, to be sure, scholars have noted that the rediscovery of Europe as "new" and the reimagination of a non-communist Eastern Europe go hand in hand. The adjective "new" celebrates not only the postmodernist debate about interculturalism, globalization and the transnationalization of various parts of the world but, equally important, the post–totalitarian sense or reawakened fragmented and regional identities as well. Clearly this adjective has become the adverb, noun, and verb that closed the 1990s.[12] No nation or state can now be theorized or written about in the same way or without comparative theoretical hindsight about what the 1990s entailed, starting with the opening of the Berlin Wall and Iron Curtain.[13] This may be more true perhaps for the eastern parts of Europe, especially, the war-torn regions of the Balkan peninsula,[14] than for most of the western or

FIGURE 8.2 Monumental statue to the Romanian peasant rebel Avram Iancu, Cluj, Romania. (Author's collection.)

FIGURE 8.3   Erected in the mid-1910s, the romantic statue of King Matthias on the main square in Cluj is claimed by both the Hungarians and the Romanians. The romanian language quote from Nicolae Iorga reads: "Victorious in battles only losing to his own nation, in Baia, when he wanted to conquer unconquerable Moldavia." (Author's collection.)

northern parts, regions that had earlier undergone a similar fundamental transformation. At the beginning of the third millennium, the new transnational policies of the EU, NATO, International Monetary Fund (IMF), and Poland and Hungary: Aid for Economic Restructuring (PHARE) make it certain that Europe is not what it was before. The rapid but often confusing and painful incorporation of Eastern European states will certainly continue to reverberate throughout the entire system for some time to come.

The Transylvanian case analyzed here is only one case study suggesting how population dislocations, emergent transnational identities, and diaspora nationalism assisted in the creation of new national movements and concomitant identities at the end of the twentieth century. This process entailed an unprecedented degree of reinforcements of older selves, invention of new ones and, in addition, an increase in territorial disputes with the emergence of regional identities. The replacement of the socialist "humpty-dumpty states" with new nation-states and the conflict over Macedonia are some visible examples.[15] Eric Hobsbawm was correct in pointing out that Western Europe could be held responsible for some of these changes, including the unnecessary violent confrontations, for much of the 1990s interethnic hostilities and nationalistic violence was the direct result of the disastrous Wilsonian formula creating new states, borders, and homogenous ethnolinguistic nations following the First World War.[16]

Territorial disputes were not novel to Eastern Europe or central to the state myths of the European twentieth century alone, nor will they disappear in the third millennium. There are too many regionalist movements to discard them as being anything but serious. States are made and created; the international geopolitics and national contestations involved must be understood and studied. The fight for an independent Kurdistan, Kashmir, Eritrea, Tamil Sri Lanka, East Timor, Palestine, or Baluchistan are all well-known, non-European movements involving both irredentist as well as secessionist claims. All are, however, connected somehow to the legacies of the European colonialist past. In Europe itself, not only the eastern parts can be credited with such sentiments, for the persistence of ethnoterritorial political movements has been familiar to the Western world for ages.[17] Wales' self-determination, Northern Ireland's special status, the continuation of much-publicized Basque or Corsican terrorism, and the question of Gibraltar or Cyprus have been surfacing from time to time, even though many of these regionally based political movements may be an embarrassment to the states in question.

Since the beginning of the 1990s, there has been serious discussion in Europe about the emergence of the continent's political renaissance. Even those states without the immediate experiences of the Berlin Wall's collapse, such as France, Great Britain, Spain, and the countries of Scandinavia, also are in the process of reinventing themselves, and no one doubts that they should not, since globalization and (Western) Europeanization—in the minds of many, one and the same—not only refer to the economic and technological unification of states and nations but a recreation of groups that is integral to them. It is a truism by now that the parallel political and cultural processes involve the recreation of identities and a collective sense of belonging. These processes, often cloaked in preposterous and dangerous myths of invented unity and national homogeneity—through the banal forms of nationalism, as Michael Billig suggests—are equally intertwined. Since identities are recreated and renegotiated both internally and externally, they metastasize, warning us that no states or nations are immune to such powerful political and cultural restructuring.

It is clear that instead of arguing about national consciousness and ethnolinguistic categories, there is increasingly a new notion of territoriality and regionalism observable in Europe. This new discourse is embedded in questions concerning state borders, nationality, and minorities issues.[18] The European Parliament, European Union, Council of Europe, and European Commission all now recognize the existence of the Committee of the Regions (of the European Union), included in the Maastricht Treaty, as one of the most important organizational principles. Since 1990, this emphasis on regionality instead of simply ethnicity and nationality has no doubt provided a different structure and means for European integration. Moreover, it should decrease extreme nationalism and promote cross-border and interregional cooperation as well as provide for a policy for economic and technological planning.[19] This idea has spread so rapidly that by the beginning of the 1990s, various Euroregions were set up, often in historic border zones between Eastern and Western European states.[20] Such Euroregions were established between Hungary and its neighbors—Alpine-Adriatic, Carpathian, and Maros-Duna Euroregions being the most notable ones.[21] The question on everyone's mind now is, will this new territorial policy, emanating from the Eurocentric core, assist in the creation of new identities by surpassing (or suppressing) older ones while managing to alter controversial historic animosities over regions and border zones? Or, to put it another way, will the making of new borders result in an eventual conflict—border skirmishes? territorial resettlements? regional hierarchy?—as a heightened sense of nation making affects some and overrides others. As a Polish political geographer puts it: "In present-day Western Europe, which has a long experience in the formation of nation-states, there collide the conceptions of *Europe of fatherlands* and *Europe of regions*, while in the countries of Central-East Europe, aspiring to join the European Union, there seems to be complete unpreparedness for the latter conception."[22] Perhaps the long contestable project over Transylvania prompts more pessimism than is warranted. When Hungarian sociologist Zsuzsa Ferge writes of "refeudalization"[23] of Hungarian society in the 1990s, and Katherine Verdery stresses the transition from "socialism to feudalism" in contemporary Romania,[24] it just might be that intellectuals continue to create and define more remote regions in the East than there actually are. These are areas, then, where "un-European" events are always possible.[25]

However, as argued in this book, intellectuals are just as suspect in creating borders than are politicians and statesmen. Based on what we have just learned from the Transylvanian case, it must be stressed that transformations in national identities and borders have been among the most important phenomena in the creation of the new, post–communist Europe.[26] Yet, and this also has been stressed with specific reference to the contestation of Transylvania by Hungarian and Romanian elites, none of the present borders, or the previous ones for that matter, are self-evident and easily definable. "Demarcation of the boundary between east and west in Europe in the late twentieth century is no straightforward task. It evidently depends on the boundaries of Europe itself, but these have never been unambiguous," writes Chris Hann. He argues that Europe's boundaries have to do with a sense of moral geography in addition to the ambiguity of state borders.[27] This book has prompted a series of questions about such ambiguous links between nation, state, and territory.

As Chapters 2 and 4 illustrate, Eastern Europe certainly existed for centuries as various parts of the multiethnic Ottoman, Habsburg, and Romanov empires. Many aspects of this region had, to be sure, been invented by the West, while others were created by the local elites themselves.[28] In Chapters 5 and 6, it was argued that Transylvania and Transylvanian Hungarians were situated to refashion a new image of Hungarianness, an identity taken away by the state and the Marxist–Leninist ideology. This form of literary and neopopulist sentiment was directly related to the inherent weaknesses of the political system in which it emerged, Stalinism and its aftermath, and Kádárist state socialism. Neopopulist writers imagined their Transylvania as a remote place at the heart of the national body. No other character illustrates this position better than Áron Tamási's figure Ábel, the true trickster who, faithful to his vocation of being a transnational migrant, returns home from America. Ábel is the quintessential border vice, "an opportunist, a chameleon, and a survivor."[29] With help from the populist literature, Hungarian youth also have invented their own Tranylvania by transcending state borders. Through the dance-house youth subculture, Hungarian elites relied on the exportation of a new image, the Hungarian rural culture of Transylvania, to remake the non-communist Hungarian nation.

Yet no matter how neopopulism refashioned Hungarianness, strong foundations of a concomitant territorial hierarchy and boundedness have been firmly cemented as well, and this is one of the major points to argue for an investigation of the contestable mechanisms involved with the Transylvanian conflict. For with territorialization, a new characteristic culture has been added in which "borderlands may appear on the surface as locations of equal cultural exchange, but they are products of historical inequalities, and their historical legacy continues to haunt them."[30] These are the politically sensitive and often troubled terrains, what Maria Todorova ingeniously but perhaps too kindly calls "contact zones."[31] The border zone, then, has become remote and contested at once. Here, in the words of Ang, "fixed and unitary identities are hybridized, sharp demarcations between self and other are unsettled, singular and absolute truths are ruptured."[32] Both Romanian and Hungarian elites have located their cultural vocabularies within the remote area of Transylvania. Through its controversial history, populations, and regions they attempted to unsettle each other's identities by proving its absolute truths to be a mere figment of imagination. In this contestation, the questioning of its borders is a constant trope, "creating persistent waves of sympathies and antagonism transcending borders."[33]

Whether a single European United States will become a reality in the third millennium is an exciting question. Surely there are plenty of signs for the confluence of the local and the global through the transnational flow of commodities within Europe as a whole.[34] But given the realities of the end of the millennium, there also may be a troubling answer that we do not wish to hear, for increasing Europeanization entails the economic, political, and military homogenization of various parts with supranational organizations (NATO, Community of Twelve, the Rome-Maastricht-Schengen Treaties, and European Free Trade Agreement [EFTA] and Central European Free Trade Agreement [CEFTA]). However, it also should be imminently clear to proponents of the new Euroregionalism that new border cultures bring new problems. They, just like some nation-states, may wish to celebrate their local difference and alterity as they face integration into these larger polities. The integration of the various states of Eastern Europe in the larger European framework, as I have shown in this book with regard to Transylvania, will not progress rapidly. Given the troubling political and economic legacies of the 1990s, there is no reason to accept why this should be a welcome form of artificial acceleration. Nor will this process be a smooth and easy ride for everyone. Aside from Transylvania, analyses have already pointed to the fundamental incongruence of economical and technological as well as military aid on local communities and regional cultures.[35] As one member of the German Bundestag, Peter Glotz, argues, differences in the way in which states respond must be taken into account: "Romania, Bulgaria, Serbia, Albania, and Macedonia make up a completely different world from Bohemia, Lithuania, Hungary, and Poland. Anyone who lumps these countries together in an 'Eastern bloc without communism' is bound to fail, for they are anything but a 'bloc.'"[36] But Glotz, in addition to his willingness to help, falls into the general Western intellectual trap when he qualifies his statement. He argues for the integration of these states into the "European structures" by developing a healthy, working "Europe of regions." This is clearly one of the primary motivations of many statesmen and politicians of the third millennial kind, for "how else are the radical conflicts of Hungarians in Slovakia, Hungarians in Transylvania, Serbs in Croatia, Kurds in Turkey, Irish in Britain, [and] Basques in Spain and France, to be resolved, if not through a combination of federalist and supranationalist structures?"[37]

In a strange way, but in light of what we have learned above, not wholly unexpectedly, the shadows of the past continue to play important

FIGURE 8.4   A column in front of the archaeological excavation on the main square of Cluj reads: "The authentic copy of the column of Traianus will be erected here. December 1, 1998, office of the mayor of Cluj." (Author's collection.)

roles in post–communist Europe.[38] The remote region of Transylvania is very close to the contemporary politics of intellectual production determining the reshaping of Europe for the third millennium. The contestation over its past, its identity and peoples, has not subsided, despite the increasing push for Europeanization in international politics and intradisciplinarity in scholarly pursuits. Intellectual contests both inside and outside this terrain continue regarding the very image they want to create or demolish so dearly.

Transnational contestations continue in various forms. Columbia University historian István Deák, when reviewing the *The Romanians, 1774–1866,* a book by Keith Hitchins, challenges the author by rekindling this historical debate. Deák blatantly accuses his American colleague of ethnocentrism, actually of *déformation professionelle*, when the latter discusses Transylvania and its historic borders:

> Witness, for instance, the map on page 8, which covers the period 1775–1811 and gives the distinct impression that Transylvania was one of several Romanian principalities, separated by a clearly marked political border from the Habsburg monarchy. Yet, Transylvania was very much part of the Habsburg monarchy at that time, and constitutionally it belonged to Hungary, a fact that is barely if at all mentioned in the text.[39]

Does it seem odd that at the turn of the third millennium, Transylvania's borders continue to ignite such a heated argument between two American scholars, neither of whom would call themselves populists or nationalists? Yet, and this is what the Transylvanian imagination has revealed in this book, the study of borders sometimes knows no boundaries. To nationalists and politicians, just as to scholars, such a *déformation professionelle* seems to be a continual occupational hazard. How can we not, then, take seriously those who are involved with such a contestation on a day-to-day basis? Hungary, Romania, and Transylvania are at a major intersection at the beginning of the third millennium. All three will, to quote Larry Wolff, "continue to occupy an ambiguous space between inclusion and exclusion."[40] But as Misha Glenny so cogently summarized earlier, for the Hungarian elites, the choice has always been clear:

> The road south-east towards Transylvania looks the most treacherous; nonetheless it must be negotiated. Even in the face of extreme provocation by Romanian nationalists, Hun-

gary must remain level-headed. It must represent the interests of the Hungarian minority abroad without upsetting the *status quo*. If Hungarian democracy wants to win the respect of its newly found colleagues, it has to resist the temptation of demanding a revision of the post-war borders, as the Romanians would interpret this as nothing less than a declaration of war.[41]

For anthropologists who at this post–communist and postmodernist moment theorize about the nature of relationships between territories, nations, and power, the choice should be clear. It just may be to "insist that these phenomena must be recognized as particular, historicized materializations of transnational movements that penetrate specifically constructed localities and that demand particular scrutiny of unruly and as yet undisciplined practices."[42]

Notes

NOTES TO CHAPTER I

1. A. Triandafylliou, M. Calloni, and A. Mikrakis, "New Greek Nationalism," *Sociological Research On-line* 2, no. 1 (1997): 1.

2. While the literature on this is vast, I call attention to two pioneering volumes that aided me throughout this work: S. Rokkan and D. W. Urwin, eds., *The Politics of Territorial Identity: Studies in European Regionalism* (London: Sage, 1982); and E. A. Tiryakian and R. Rogowski, eds., *New Nationalisms of the Developed West* (London: Allen and Unwin, 1985).

3. Macedonia has been for some time in the limelight of scholarly debates. For some of the anthropological highlights, see P. Mackridge and E. Yannakakis, eds., *Ourselves and Others: The Development of a Greek Macedonian Cultural Identity Since 1912* (Oxford: Berg, 1997); L. Danforth, *The Macedonian Conflict: Ethnic Nationlism in a Transnational World* (Princeton: Princeton University Press, 1995); D. E. Sutton, "Local Names, Foreign Claims: Family Inheritance and National Heritage on a Greek Island," *American Ethnologist* 24, no. 2 (1997): 415–37; J. Schwartz, "Listening for Macedonian Identity: Reflections from Sveti Naum," in *Beyond Borders*, eds. L. Kürti and J. Langman (Boulder, CO: Westview Press, 1997): 95–110; C. P. Danopoulos and K. G. Messas, eds., *Crises in the Balkans: Views from the Participants* (Boulder: Westview, 1997); A. Karakasidou, *Fields of Wheat, Hills of Blood: Passages to Nationhood in Greek Macedonia, 1870–1990* (Chicago: University of Chicago Press, 1997).

4. M. Herzfeld, "Theorizing Europe: Persuasive Paradoxes," *American Anthropologist* 99, no. 4 (1997): 715.

5. See T. Mangot, "Project 'Democracy, Human Rights, Minorities: Educational and Cultural Aspects," Council for Cultural Cooperation, *Council of Europe* (Strasbourg: European Center for Research and Action on Racism and Antisemitism, 1997): 24–27;

and K. Benda-Beckman and M. Verkuyten, eds., *Nationalism, Ethnicity, and Cultural Identity in Europe* (Utrecth: Utrecht University, 1995).

6. The scholarly literature on extremism, xenophobia, and racism is large and continues to grow: for a few examples, see J. Cole, *The New Racism in Europe* (Cambridge: Cambridge University Press, 1997); J. Y. Camus, ed., *Extremism in Europe* (Paris: CERA, 1997).

7. Some of the recent studies on border cultures and border contestations include P. Sahlins, *Boundaries: The Making of France and Spain in the Pyrenees* (Berkeley: University of California Press, 1989); E. W. Soja, *Postmodern Geographies: The Reassertion of Space in Critical Social Theory* (London: Verso, 1989); P. Vereni, "Boundaries, Frontiers, Persons, Individuals: Questioning 'Identity' at National Borders," *Europae* 2 (1996): 1–9; T. M. Wilson and H. Donnan, eds., *Border Approaches: Anthropological Perspectives on Frontiers*, (Lanham Md.: University Press of America, 1994); L. O'Dowd and T. M. Wilson, eds., *Borders, Nations and States: Frontiers of Sovereignty in the New Europe* (Aldershot: Avebury, 1996); T. Bjorgo and R. Witte, eds., *Racist Violence in Europe* (London: Macmillan, 1993); P. Werber and T. Modood, eds., *Debating Cultural Hibridity: Multicultural Identities and the Politics of Anti-Racism* (London: Zed Books, 1997); V. Tishkov, *Ethnicity, Nationalism, and Conflict in and after the Soviet Union: The Mind Aflame* (Oslo: International Peace Research Institute, 1997).

8. Stalin's views were publicized in most major European languages: for the English version, see J. Stalin, *Marxism and the National Question: Selected Writing and Speeches* (New York: International Publishers, 1942). Later critics, both from the right and left, utilized and revised this definition considerably. Perhaps the most important criticism in this regard is H. Kohn's classic book *Nationalism in the Soviet Union* (New York: AMS Press, 1966). Later critical reflections I have utilized are H. B. Davis, *Toward a Marxist Theory of Nationalism* (New York: Monthly Review Press, 1978) and R. Munck, *The Difficult Dialogue: Marxism and Nationalism* (London: Zed Books, 1986).

9. See Munck, ibid., ch. 7, pp. 126–43. Other sources on this are numerous. I only mention here those that I have been relying on for an understanding of the ways in which state socialism worked with regard to this topic: P. Shoup, *Communism and the Yugoslav National Question* (New York: Columbia University Press, 1968); P. F. Sugar, ed., *Ethnic Diversity and Conflict in Eastern Europe* (Santa Barbara, Calif.: ABXC Clio, 1980); R. Karlins, *Ethnic Relations in the USSR: The Perspective from Below* (London: Allen & Unwin, 1986); R. Szporluk, *Communism and Nationalism: Karl Marx versus Friedrich List* (New York: Oxford University Press, 1988); A. J. Motyl, ed., *Thinking Theoretically about Soviet Nationalities* (New York: Columbia University Press, 1992).

10. Munck, ibid., p. 152.

11. See "Introduction," in Frederik Barth, *Ethnic Groups and Boundaries: The Social Organization of Cultural Difference* (Oslo-London: George Allen & Unwin, 1970).

12. See A. B. Smith, *The Ethnic Origins of Nations* (London: Basil Blackwell, 1987).

13. In fact, one socialist attempt to redefine the nature of ethnicity and non-Barthian discussion was the notion of "ethnos," developed by Soviet ethnographer Y. Bromley. On this, see the debate between Western and Soviet anthropologists in E. Gellner, ed., *Soviet and Western Anthropology* (New York: Columbia University Press, 1980).

14. Ibid., p. 28.

15. Ibid.

16. For some highlights, see the works of B. Kapferer, *Legends of People, Myths of State: Violence, Intolerance, and Political Culture in Sri Lanka and Australia* (Washington and London: Smithsonian Press, 1988); M. Herzfeld, *Anthropology through the Looking-Glass: Critical Ethnography in the Margins of Europe* (Cambridge: Cambridge University Press, 1989); J. Boissevain, ed., *Revitalizing European rituals* (London: Routledge, 1992).

17. J. C. Heesterman, "Two Types of Spatial Boundaries," in *Comparative Social Dynamics*, eds. E. Cohen, M. Lissak, and U. Almagor (Boulder: Westview Press, 1985), 69.

18. Ibid. For an earlier discussion on territorialization and conflict over space, see E. W. Soja, *The Political Organization of Space* (Washington D.C.: Association of American Geographers, 1971).

19. Renato Rosaldo, *Culture and Truth* (Boston: Beacon 1989), 217.

20. See S. Eisenstadt, "Reflections on Center-Periphery Relations in Small European States," in *European Civilization in a Comparative Perspective: A Study in the Relations between Culture and Social Structure*, ed. S. Eisenstad (Oslo: Norwegian University Press, 1987), 68–69.

21. Ibid., p. 69.

22. J. Coakley, "Introduction: The Territorial Management of Ethnic Conflict," *Regional Politics and Policy* 3, no. 1 (1993): 1–22.

23. Ibid., p. 2.

24. The notion of "mini-Europe" has been borrowed from B. Thomassen, "Border Studies in Europe: Symbolic and Political Boundaries, Anthropological Perspectives," *Europae* 2 (1996): 2.

25. Quoted in Heesterman, p. 59.

26. Sahlins, *Boundaries.*

27. Ibid., p. 8.

28. B. Anderson, *Imagined Communities: Reflections on the Origin and Spread of Nationalism* (London: Verso, 1983), 15.

29. F. Znaniecki, *Modern Nationalities* (Urbana: The University of Illinois Press, 1952), 93.

30. Ibid., p. 96.

31. E. Kedurie, *Nationalism* (New York: Praeger, 1967), 69–70.

32. Ibid., p. 125.

33. J. Mayall, *Nationalism and International Society* (Cambridge: Cambridge University Press, 1990), 80.

34. Kedurie, *Nationalism*, 125.

35. See J. Anderson, "On Theories of Nationalism and the Size of States," *Antipode* 18, no. 2 (1986): 218.

36. Similar points are also made by J. Mayall, *Nationalism*, 82–83.

37. K. Coates, "Boundaries and the Pacific Northwest: The Historical and Contemporary Significance of Borders in Western North America," in *The Dividing Line: Borders and National Peripheries*, eds. L. Landgren and M. Hayrynen (Helsinki: Renvall Institute, 1997), 166.

38. Ibid., pp. 166–67.

39. See note 7; see also the contributions to *Border Identities*, eds. T. Wilson and H. Donnan (Cambridge: Cambridge University Press, 1998).

40. Loring Danforth, *The Macedonian Conflict.*

41. See also the discussion by J. Schwartz, "Listening for Macedonian Identity," 95–110.

42. Larry Wolf, *Inventing Eastern Europe: The Map of Civilization on the Mind of the Enlightenment* (Stanford: Stanford University Press, 1994); see especially ch. 4.

43. This definition is provided by P. R. Magocsi in his *Historical Atlas of East Central Europe* (Seattle: University of Washington Press, 1993), xi.

44. H. G. Wanklyn, *The Eastern Marchlands of Europe* (London: Macmillan Co., n.d.), 3.

45. R. Donald, *The Tragedy of Trianon: Hungary's Appeal to Humanity* (London: Thornton Butterworth LTD, 1928), 12.

46. See Berend, Juan T. Ivan, *The Crisis Zone of Europe: An Interpretation of East-Central European History in the First Half of the Twentieth Century* (New York: Columbia University Press, 1986).

47. All of these concepts, of course, have their origin in the politicohistorical framework in which they were born. Clearly, John Cole's "ethnic shatter zone" owes a great deal to the discussions on European regional development of the early 1980s, the "internal colonialism" of Michael Hechter, the core-periphery model of the Wallersteinian world-system theory, and the economic regional development model, as espoused by Derek Urwin and Stein Rokkan and Dudley Seers. See J. W. Cole, "Culture and Economy in Peripheral Europe," *Ethnologia Europaea* XV (1985): 14–15.

48. See my article "Globalization and the Discourse of Otherness in the New East and Central Europe," in *The Politics of Multiculturalism in the New Europe*, eds. T. Modood and P. Werbner (London: Zed Books, 1997), 29–53.

49. See D. Seers, "The Periphery of Europe," in *Underdeveloped Europe: Studies in Core-Periphery Relations*, eds. D. Seers, B. Schaffer, and M-L. Kiljunen (Atlantic Highlands, N.J.: Humanities Press, 1979), 20.

50. Jenő Szűcs (1928–1988) was an excellent student of medieval Hungarian history who published extensively on the foundation of the Hungarian kingdom, its state formation, and its early centuries. It was, however, his 1981 article "A Sketch on the Three Historic Regions of Europe," published originally in Hungarian in the historical periodical *Történelmi Szemle*, which, despite his description of it as a sketch, elevated Szűcs from being a medievalist to being a "theoretician" of European development. This article later appeared in German and English ("The Three Historical Regions of Europe: An Outline," *Acta Historica* 29 (1983): 131–84) and as a Hungarian language book the same year. The latest English version is J. Szűcs', "The Historical Regions of Europe," in *Civil Society and the State*, ed. J. Keane (London: Verso, 1988), 291–332. The Hungarian political scientist, István Bibó, also contributed to this idea with his classic 1946 essay "A kelet európai kisállamok nyomorúsága" (Misery of the small east European states), republished in *Bibó István összegyűjtött munkái* I, eds. I. Kemény and M. Sárközy (Bern: Európai Protestáns Magyar Szabadegyetem, 1981), 202–51.

51. In Bibó's view, the main difference was the development of the modern state in the west and north and the linguistic nationalism of the East European monarchies; ibid, p. 207.

52. See L. Makkai, "Hungary Before the Hungarian Conquest," in *A History of Hungary*, eds. P. F. Sugar, P. Hanák, and T. Frank (Bloomington: Indiana University Press, 1990), 8.

53. I do not intend here to analyze in detail the complete history of the region but only to illustrate, in broad strokes, the political background for the region's history. My understanding of its early medieval history, while admittedly highly selective and personal, is based on the following readings: D. Austin and L. Alcock, eds., *From the Baltic to the Black Sea: Studies in Medieval Archeology* (London: Unwin Hyman, 1990); K. Randsborg, *The First Millennium A.D. in Europe and the Mediterranean: An Archeologial essay* (Cambridge: Cambridge University Press, 1991); J. J. Yiannias, ed., *The Byzantine Tradition after the Fall of Constantinople* (Charlottesville: University Press of Virginia, 1991). I must admit that I view these scholarly references as more "neutral" than the ones I use in later chapters to discuss the scholarly contestation of Transylvania.

54. See C. A. MacCartney, *Hungary: A Short History* (Chicago: Aldine, 1962), 1.

55. See, for example, what Krekovicova writes about Slovakness and the shepherd tradition: "Similarly as in the nations of northern Europe (mainly Danes and Finns), the relationship to nature and natural scenery belongs to the national picture and the self-portrait. . . . In Slovakia, it is village culture that has become the basis of such a picture. In the process of ethnic and national identification, it was sheepherding that was highlighted as the element of many-sided and internally differentiated folk culture in a village. All of this has been despite the fact that traditional Slovak folk culture has been in principle of "peasant's" and not of shepherd's character. E. Krekovicova, "From the Shepherdic Image in Slovak Folklore to That of National Identification," *Human Affairs* 5 (1995): 94. Interestingly, opposed to such an internally generated nationalist self-image, Hungarians harbored the wandering Slovak merchants and wire makers as an "external" image of the Slovaks living in the northern part of the Austro-Hungarian Monarchy; see the analysis by V. Ferko, *Volt egyszer egy mesterség: A drótosok története* [Once there was a profession: History of the Slovak wire makers] (Budapest: Európa Kiadó, 1985). See also F. Gross, *Ethnics in a Borderland: An Inquiry into the Nature of Ethnicity and Reduction of Ethnic Tension in a One-Time Genocide Area* (Westport, Conn.: Greenwood Press, 1978).

56. See L. Witkowski, "The Paradox of Borders: Ambivalence at Home," *Common Knowledge* (1995), 101.

57. S. Hall, "Cultural Identity and Diaspora," in *Identity, Community, Culture, Difference*, ed. J. Rutheford (London: Lawrence & Wishart, 1990).

58. M. Taussig, *Mimesis and Alterity: A Particular History of the Senses* (London: Routledge, 1993), 249.

59. See E. Ardener, "Remote Areas: Some Theoretical Considerations," in *Anthropology at Home*, ed. A. Jackson (London: Tavistock, 1987), 38–54.

60. Much to my surprise and amusement, I have found that aside from Ardener the British traveler Patrick Leigh Fermor also has used the epithet "remote" for Transylvania in his fascinating interwar travelogue *Between the Woods and the Water* (New York: Viking, 1986). Read, for instance, the description of feudal relationships that "gave a strange, almost a disembodied feeling of remoteness to this Transylvanian life" (p. 96); and later,

"But Transylvania had been a familiar name as long as I could remember. It was the very essence and symbol of remote, leafy, half-mythical strangeness; and, on the spot, it seemed remoter still, and more fraught with charms" (p. 146).

61. Ibid., p. 38.

62. Ibid., p. 41.

63. Ibid., p. 49.

64. See P. Howe, "Neorealism Revisited: The Neorealist Landscape Surveyed through Nationalist Spectacles," *International Journal* 66 (1991): 340.

65. G. Orwell, "Notes on Nationalism," in *Decline of the English Murder and Other Essays* (Harmondsworth: Penguin, 1965), 166.

66. Ibid., pp. 161–65.

67. See T. Forsberg, ed., *Contested Territory: Border Disputes at the Edge of the Former Soviet Empire* (Aldershot: Edward Elgar, 1995).

68. Marc Augé, *A Sense of the Other: The Timeliness and Relevance of Anthropology* (Stanford: Stanford University Press, 1998), 122.

69. D. K. Flynn, "We Are the Border: Identity, Exchange, and the State Along the Bénin-Nigeria Border," *American Ethnologist* 24, no. 2 (1997): 327.

70. And justifiably so. Anthropologist Renato Rosaldo argues for a sound analysis of the culture of borderlands. He continues: "More often than we usually care to think, our everyday lives are crisscrossed by border zones, pockets, and eruptions of all kinds. Social borders frequently become salient around such lines as sexual orientation, gender, class, race, ethnicity, nationality, age, politics, dress, food, or taste. Along with 'our' supposedly transparent cultural selves, such borderlands should be regarded not as analytically empty transitional zones but as sites of creative cultural production that require investigation." See *Texts and Pretexts: An Anthology with Commentaries* (London: Cholte and Windus, 1992), 50.

71. A recent analysis of the Dracula myth's relation to Transylvania is M. Lőrinczi, "Transylvania and the Balkans as Multiethnic Regions in the Works of Bram Stoker," *Europae* 2 (1996): 1–13.

72. I must warn the reader here, even if cursorily, that my study is not postmodern in the sense that I do not describe that there are no borders and, more than that, that we are all living on and in the margins. In other words, I do not believe in the notion that there is no center, that is, everything is fragmented into smaller centers of equal value, arguments well known to postmodern and globalization theorists. In this analysis, I read cultural space as a potential battleground—a "nearly distant," continuous, vast border region—which is more often populated than not, and which when analyzed with an interdisciplinary view of nationalism, provides populations with a terrain within which they may define, contest, and remake their own and others' identities and relations.

73. Similar ideas also surround Japanese village tourism and the cult of the mountains; see J. Knight, "Tourist As Stranger? Explaining Tourism in Rural Japan," *Social Anthropology* 3, no. 3 (1994): 219–34; I. Hori, *Folk Religion in Japan: Continuity and Change* (Chicago and London: The University of Chicago Press, 1969), see especially 141–79.

74. See C. C. Giurescu, *The Making of the Romanian People and Language* (Bucharest: Meridiane, 1972), 11.

75. I. A. Pop, *Romanians and Hungarians from the Ninth to the Fourteenth Century: The Genesis of the Transylvanian Medieval State* (Cluj-Napoca: Fundatia Culturala Romana, 1996), 210.

76. For Tamási's works see G. Féja, ed., *Tamási Áron válogatott müvei* I–II [Collected works of Áron Tamási] (Budapest: Szépirodalmi Könyvkiadó, 1974).

77. Tamási, *Abel Amerikában*, 639.

78. On Transylvanian literature and its history and relevance to national identity, see H. Mózes, *Sajtó, kritika, irodalom* [Press, criticism, literature] (Bukarest: Kriterion, 1983) and É. Cs. Gyimesi, *Gyöngy és homok* [Pearl and sand] (Bukarest: Kriterion, 1992). Romanian perspectives on the same topic are many: for an English-language example see I. Chinezu, *Aspects of Transylvanian Hungarian Literature, 1919–1929* (Cluj-Napoca: Fundatia Culturala Romana, 1997). The relationship between Saxons and Hungarians in Saxon literature is discussed by A. F. András, *Az erdélyi szász irodalom magyarságképe* [Hungarian images in the Transylvanian Saxon literature] (Budapest: Litera Nova, 1996). The characters of the aristocratic and classist Transylvania also had their own portrayal in the novels of interwar Hungarian Transylvanian novelists such as Wass, Bánffy, and Berde.

NOTES TO CHAPTER 2

1. During the 1960s and 1970s, some of the standard references on East European nationalism were found in R. R. King, *Minorities under Communism: Nationalities As a Source of Tension among Balkan Communist States* (Cambridge: Harvard University Press, 1973); W. Connor, *The National Question in Marxist–Leninist Theory and Strategy* (Princeton: Princeton University Press,1984); H. Seton-Watson, *Nations and States: An Inquiry into the Origins of Nations and Politics of Nationalism* (London: Methuen, 1977); J. F. Brown, *Eastern Europe and Communist Rule* (Durham, N.C.: Duke University Press, 1988), 415–44; E. Gellner, *Culture, Identity and Politics* (Cambridge: Cambridge University Press, 1987), especially pp.123–33; R. Sussex and J. C. Eade, eds., *Culture and Nationalism in Nineteenth-Century Eastern Europe* (Columbus: Slavica, 1985); P. Sugar, *The Problems of Nationalism in Eastern Europe. Past and Present*, Occasional Paper No.13 (Washington, D.C.: The Wilson Center, 1988); P. Sugar, ed., *Ethnic Diversity and Conflict in Eastern Europe* (Santa Barbara, Calif.: ABC Clio, 1980); A. S. Markovits and F. E. Sysyn, eds., *Nationbuilding and the Politics of Nationalism: Essays on Austrian Galicia* (Cambridge: Harvard University Press, 1982).

2. For anthropological analyses of nationalism of the 1970s in Eastern Europe, see, for example, S. Beck and J. W. Cole, eds., *Ethnicity and Nationalism in Southeastern Europe* (Amsterdam: Universiteit van Amsterdam, 1981); Y. Bromley, *Ethnography and Ethnic Processes* (Moscow: USSR Academy of Sciences, 1978); J. W. Cole, "Reflections in the Political Economy of Ethnicity: South Tyrol and Transylvania," in *The Ethnic Challenge: The Politics of Ethnicity in Europe*, eds. H. Vermeulen and J. Boissevain (Gottingen: Herodot, 1984), 84–99; "Culture and Economy in Peripheral Europe," *Ethnologia Europaea* XV (1985): 3–26; A. Lass, "Romantic Documents and Political Monuments: The Meaning-Fulfillment of History in 19th-Century Czech Nationalism," *American Ethnologist* 15 (1988): 456–71; W. G. Lockwood, *European Moslems: Ethnicity and Economy in Eastern*

Bosnia (New York: Academic Press, 1975); Z. Salzmann, *Two Contributions to the Study of Czechs and Slovaks in Romania,* Occasional Paper No. 9 (Amherst: University of Massachusetts, 1983); K. Verdery, *Transylvanian Villagers: Three Centuries of Political and Ethnic Change* (Berkeley: University of California Press, 1983); I. P. Winner and R. Susel, eds., *The Dynamics of East European Ethnicity Outside of Eastern Europe* (Cambridge: Schenkman, 1984).

3. Katherine Verdery, *National Ideology under Socialism. Identity and Cultural Politics in Ceaușescu's Romania* (Berkeley: University of California Press, 1992), 220.

4. This period of East European and economic history is well researched, due to the thorough analyses of Hungarian economists I. T. Berend and Gy. Ránki; see, for example, *Economic Development in East-Central Europe in the 19th and 20th centuries* (New York: Columbia University Press, 1974); *Underdevelopment in Europe in the Context of East-West Relations in the 19th and 20th Centuries* (Budapest: Akadémiai, 1980); *The European Periphery and Industrialization, 1780–1914* (Cambridge: Cambridge University Press, 1981); D. Berindei, "Economic Prerequisites for the Establishment of Independent Romania," *East European Quarterly* 22 (1988): 23–35.

5. See I. Popescu-Petru et al., eds., *Documente privind marea rascoala a taranilor din 1907,* vol. I [Documents of the Great Peasant Revolt of 1907] (Bucuresti: Editura Academiei, 1977); L. Vajda, *Erdélyi Bányák, Kohók, Emberek, Századok. Gazdaság-Társadalom és Munkásmozgalom a XVIII. Század Második Felétől 1918–ig* [Peoples, Centuries, Mines, Foundries in Transylvania—Social, Economic, and Working-Class History from the Second Half of the Eighteenth Century up to 1918] (Bukarest: Politikai Könyvkiadó, 1981).

6. A. C. Janos, *The Politics of Backwardness 1825–1945* (Princeton, N.J.: Princeton University Press, 1982).

7. This line of reasoning can be best supported by the "Wild Rose" (*Vadrózsa*) case, the first and most publicized folkloristic controversy between Hungarians and Romanians in the late nineteenth century. The "Wild-Rose Case" ignited a heated debate in which the folkloristic content became secondary after the political controversy. Hungarian folklorist J. Kriza was accused by Romanian folklore collectors, who claimed that the folk ballads published in Kriza's collection were plagiarized Hungarian versions of the original Romanian folk ballads. Since this case, the two sides are more than eager to clarify the "origin" of the folklore complexes and to separate the "ethno-specific characteristics." This case is analyzed by Gy. Ortutay, "János Kriza," in *Halhatatlan népköltészet* [Immortal folklore] (Budapest: Magvető, 1966), 54–60. Hungarians and Romanians both found "archaic regions" in Transylvania; Maramureş and Oaş for Romanians, Gyimes and Mezőség for Hungarians. Romanian folklore and ethnographic collections are filled with "facts" and "proof" of the Geto-Dacian continuity; see R. Vulcanescu and P. Simionescu, "Some Special Aspects of Rumanian Ethnology," *Rumanian Studies* 2 (1973): 195–215. For a recent example in which the author tries to argue for the direct connection between neolithic pottery designs and present-day forms of Romanian ritual cakes, see G. Sulițeanu, "Elemente de continuitate ethnologică ale culturi neolitice Cucuteni-Băiceni la poporul roman," *Revista de Etnografie și Folclor* 33 (1988): 17–38. The history of Hungarian ethnography and folklore is discussed in English by M. Sozan, *The History of Hungarian Ethnography* (Washington, D.C.: University Press of America, 1978) and more recently in C. Hann, "The Politics of Anthropology in Socialist Eastern Europe," in *Anthropology at Home,* ed. A. Jackson (London: Tavistock, 1987), 139–53.

8. See M. Contantinescu and S. Pascu, *Unification of the Romanian National State: The Union of Transylvania with Old Romania* (Bucharest: Romanian Academy of Sciences,

1971), especially chs. II–V; E. Niederhauser, *A Nemzeti Megújulási Mozgalmak Kelet-Európában* (Budapest: Akadémiai Kiadó, 1977).

9. See S. Tóth, *Rólunk van szó* (It concerns us) (Bukarest: Kriterion, 1982); I. Mikó, *Változatok egy témára* [Variations of a theme] (Bukarest: Kriterion, 1981). See also the reassessment of nineteenth-century politician Lajos Mocsáry's role in attempting to create a healthy interethnic atmosphere in the Austro-Hungarian Monarchy by G. Denke, "Mocsáry Lajos és a nemzetiségek," *Magyar Fórum* (June 1994): 70–75.

10. G. Moldován, *A Románság* [The Romanians] (Nagybecskerek: Pleitz, 1895), 9.

11. Ibid.

12. Quoted in Mikó, *Változatok*, 134.

13. O. Jászi, *The Dissolution of the Habsburg Monarchy* (Chicago: The University of Chicago Press, 1958). For Saguna's ideas, see K. Hitchens, *Orthodoxy and Nationality: Andrieu Şaguna and the Rumanians of Transylvania, 1846–1878* (Cambridge: Harvard University Press, 1977).

14. The origin of the Partium dates to the 1570 peace settlement between Hungarian, Habsburg, and Ottoman leaders to give certain territorial rights in eastern Hungary to the Transylvanian princely house of Szapolya; these "parts" then identitified the political dividing border between Transylvania and Hungary, and in fact the extent of Habsburg, Hungarian, Ottoman, and Transylvanian polities. This geographical division may be best viewed in the 1809 map of János Lipszky, reissued in J. Herner, ed., *Erdély és a Részek térképe és helységnévtára. Készült Lipszky János 1806-ban megjelent műve alapján* [Map of Tranyslvania and the Partium according to the 1806 map of János Lipszky] (Szeged: Franklin Nyomda, 1987).

15. See S. P. Ramet, *Whose Democracy? Nationalism, Religion, and the Doctrine of Collective Rights in post–1989 Eastern Europe* (Lanham: Rowman & Littlefield, 1997), 67.

16. C. C. Giurescu, *The Making of the Romanian People and Language* (Bucharest: Meridiane, 1972), 253.

17. Ibid., p. 255. For interesting accounts, see the memoirs of the U.S. envoy to Romania, C. J. Vopicka, *Secrets of the Balkans: Seven Years of a Diplomatist's Life in the Storm Centre of Europe* (Chicago: Rand McNally, 1921), concerning the political strifes and intrigues that led to the decisions at Trianon.

18. H. L. Roberts, *Romania: Political Problems of an Agrarian State* (New Haven, Conn.: Archon Books, 1951), 117, 250.

19. K. Hitchins, "The Rumanian Socialists and the Hungarian Republic," in *Revolution in Perspective: Essay on the Hungarian Soviet Republic of 1919*, eds. A. C. Janos and W. B. Slottman (Berkeley: University of California Press, 1971), 109–44.

20. See R. Brubaker, *Nationalism Reframed: Nationhood and the National Question in the New Europe* (Cambridge: Cambridge University Press, 1996), 159. See also A. Komjathy and R. Stockwell, *German Minorities and the Third Reich: Ethnic Germans of East Central Europe between the Wars* (New York: Holmes and Meier, 1980), 106. It was the Karlsburg Declaration, on December 1, 1918, signed by Saxons and Schwabians, which announced the separation of Transylvania and the Banat from Hungary and their annexation to Romania. For the socially constructed form of Romanians' idea of "Greater Romania," see Irina Livezeanu, *Cultural Politics in Greater Romania: Regionalism, Nation Building, and Ethnic Struggle, 1918–1930* (Ithaca, N.Y.: Cornell University Press, 1995).

21. Roberts, *Romania* (1951): 85–88.

22. Ibid., p. 81.

23. I. T. Berend and Gy. Ranki (1974): 123–24.

24. Ibid.; and see A. C. Janos, *The Politics* (1982): 24–32.

25. I. Racz, ed., *The Politics*, 177–78; and R. Joó, ed., *Jelentés a romániai magyar kisebbség helyzetéről* [Report on the situation of the Hungarian minority in Romania] (Budapest: Magyar Demokrata Forum, 1988), 101–2; R. Joó, *Nemzeti és nemzetközi önrendelkezés, önkormányzat, egyenjogúság* [National and nationality autonomy, government, and equality] (Budapest: Kossuth, 1984), 98. For a comparable dispute, see the analysis by E. Chaszar, "The Ethnic Principle and National Boundaries. A Case Study of the Czechoslovak-Hungarian Border Dispute of 1938," *Documentation sur L'Europe Centrale* 15, no. 4, (1977): 267–77.

26. See Veritas, *A magyarországi Románok egyházi, iskolai, közművelődési, közgazdasági intézményei és mozgalmainak ismertetése* [Information concerning the religious, educational, cultural, and economic institutions and social processes of Romanians in Hungary] (Budapest: Urania, 1908); Zs. Szasz, *The Minorities in Romanian Transylvania* (London: The Richards Press, 1927).

27. M. Móricz, *Az erdélyi föld sorsa. Az 1921. évi Román földreform* [The fate of Transylvania and the Romanian land-reform of 1921] (Budapest: Erdélyi Férfiak Egyesülete, 1932), 151. Móricz argued that while Hungarian aristocrats owned the large estates in Transylvania, the smaller land holdings belonged to Romanians. According to his statistics, 77 percent of the 100 cadastral holds and above belonged to Hungarians and those between five and 100 holds to Romanians. Thus, while 55.4 percent of the Romanian population owned land, only 11 percent of the Germans and 33.6 percent of the Hungarians were land owners in pre-Trianon Transylvania. As argued by C. A. Macartney, *Hungary and Her Successors* (London: Oxford University Press, 1937), 316, "No exact figures are or ever have been available for the land distribution in 1919 in the total area annexed by Romania." Cf. also Roberts, *Romania*, p. 37, who agrees that the Hungarian claims for land holdings "may have been extreme."

28. See P. Binder, *Tanulmányok az erdélyi nemzetiségek történetéből* [Studies about the history of Transylvanian nationalities] (Bukarest: Kriterion, 1982); K. Verdery, "Social Differentation in the Transylvanian Countryside between the Two World Wars," *Rumanian Studies* 5 (1986): 84–104.

29. L. Vajda, *Erdélyi Bányák*, 383–83.

30. See A. Komjathy and R. Stockwell, *German Minorities and the Third Reich*, pp. 160–65; A. Heinen, *op. cit.*, 1986; N. Nagy-Talavera, *The Green Shirts and the Others. A History of Fascism in Hungary and Rumania* (Stanford: Hoover Institution Press, 1970); A. Heinen, *Die Legion 'Erzengel Michael' in Rumanien Soziale Bewegung und Politische Organisation.* Sudosteuropaische Arbeiten, Band 83 (Munchen: R. Oldenburg Verlag, 1986).

31. See D. B. Lungu, *Romania and the Great Powers, 1933–1940* (Durham, N.C.: Duke University Press, 1989), 233. As a result of the Vienna treaty, Romania not only lost 40 percent of Transylvania to Hungary but also the Southern Dobrudja region to Bulgaria.

32. R. Joó, ed., *Jelentés*, 101–2. The usage of terminology is important here. Hungarian sources generally use the phrase "Second Vienna Award," but Romanian sources refer to it as "Fascist Dictate of Vienna," and Western sources simply call it "Dictate of Vienna."

33. Joó, *Nemzeti*, 98.

34. The number of Romanian publications ceased almost completely: one daily, one weekly, one monthly, and two irregularly published religious papers appeared legally during the four-year Hungarian rule in Transylvania. Similarly, under Romanian rule in southern Transylvania, only two Hungarian publications were allowed to be printed; see M. Korom, "A második bécsi döntéstől a fegyverszünetig," in *Tanulmányok Erdély történetéről*, ed. I. Rácz (Debrecen: Csokonai, 1988), 178.

35. Between March and October 1944, Governor Horthy had formed three governments led by Sztójay, Lakatos, and, finally, Arrow Cross leader Ferenc Szálasi. Detailed studies on these months with regard to the Hungarian army and gendarmerie' involvement in Transylvania are still few and far between. Some information may be found in the émigré scholar P. Gosztonyi's work, *A magyar honvédség a második világháborúban* [The Hungarian army in World War II] (Budapest: Európa, 1992), 170–76; in the history of the Hungarian gendarmerie, published by Canadian-Hungarian émigrés, in K. Kövendy, ed., *Magyar királyi csendőrség* [The Hungarian royal gendarmerie] (Toronto: Sovereign Press, 1973); and in the analysis of the Bánffyhunyad (Huedin) massacre by J. Varga, "Levente és értelmezője nyomán" [Following Levente and his interpreter], in Rácz, ed., *Tanulmányok*, 212–25. Sztójay and Szálasi were executed as war criminals in 1945. Other high-ranking government ministers during World War II, namely Imrédy, Bárdossy, Jaross, and Beregfy, also had met similar fates. Hungary's ruler from 1919 to 1944, Admiral Miklós Horthy, was never charged as a war criminal.

36. See M. Fătu and M. Mușat, eds., *Horthyist-Fascist Terror in Northwestern Romania, September 1940–October 1944* (Bucharest: Meridiane, 1986), 100.

37. Even G. Gheorgiu Dej, who visited some of these camps, was appalled by the cruel treatment of Hungarian prisoners; see S. Balogh, "A Groza-kormány nemzetiségi politikájának történetéből (1945–1946)" [History of the nationality policy of the Groza government], in Rácz, *Tanulmányok*, 183. General I. Antonescu and his foreign minister brother, M. Antonescu, were both executed as war criminals on June 1, 1946.

38. M. Fatu and M. Musat, ibid., pp. 260–76; *Remember, 40 de ani de la masacrare evreilor din Ardealul de nord sub ocupatia horthysta* [Remember, 40 years since the massacre of the Jews in Northern Transylvania under Horthyist Occupation] (Bucharest: Federation of Jewish Communities in Romania, 1985), 59; compare, for example, the ideas of M. Lehre, *Transylvania: History and Reality* (Silver Spring, Md.: Bartley Press, 1986).

39. One of the characteristic flare-ups during Ceaușescu's time was a controversy between writers dealing with the same time period. I would call this the "Ion Lancrajan case," after the highly personalized views of I. Lancrajan, *Cuvint despre Transilvania* [Verbs about Transylvania] (Bucuresti: Editura Sport-Turistica, 1982) and *Vocatia constructiva* [Constructive profession] (Bucuresti: Cartea Romanesca, 1983), discussing the history of Transylvania from a nationalist point of view books that have been followed by many others both in Hungary and Romania. One of the first Hungarian responses, causing quite an uproar in political circles, came from prominent literary figures and was published in the prestigious official literary weekly of the Hungarian Writer's Union and the social science monthly *Valóság*; see "Kísértetek ellen" [Against ghosts], *Élet és Irodalom*, May 13, 1983, p. 3; Gy. Száraz, "Egy különös könyvről" [About a strange book], *Valóság* 10 (1982): 98.

40. P. Groza's speech is quoted in M. Fülöp, "A Sebestyén-misszió. Petru Groza és a magyar-román határkérdés" [The Sebestyén mission. Petru Groza and the Romanian-Hungarian border dispute], in Rácz, ed., *Tanulmányok*, 202.

41. See F. Feher, "Eastern Europe's Long Revolution Against Yalta," *Eastern European Politics and Societies* 2 (1988): 1–35. The post–war settlements and negotiations are discussed in detail in S. D. Kertész, *Between Russia and the West: Hungary and the Illusions of Peacemaking, 1945–1947* (Notre Dame: University of Notre Dame Press, 1984), and *The Last European Peace Conference: Paris, 1946* (Lanham, Md.: University Press of America, 1985).

42. W. King, *Minorities Under Communism*, 113–15.

43. The Transylvanian Saxons, the Schwabians of Hungary, and the Hungarians in Slovakia all shared similar fates directly after World War II; imprisonment, mass evacuations, forced labor, revoked citizenship, and deportation. For the Hungarian situation in Czechoslovakia, see K. Janics, *A hontalanság évei—a szlovákiai magyar kisebbség a második világháború után 1945–1948* [Years of homelessness—The Hungarian minority of Slovakia after World War II] (Bern: Európai Protestáns Magyar Szabadegyetem, 1979); the Schwabian situation is discussed in A. Komjathy and R. Stockwell, *German Minorities and the Third Reich* and in G. Wildmann, ed., *Entwicklung und Erbe des donauschwabisches Volkstammes*, Donauschwabisches Archiv. Band 10 (München: Donauschwabischer Kulturstiftung, 1982); for the Transylvanian Saxon situation, see the two anthropological monographs, M. McArthur, *The Politics of Identity. Transylvanian Saxons in Socialist Romania* (unpublished Ph.D. dissertation, University of Massachusetts, Amherst, 1981), and K. Verdery, *Translyvanian Villagers*, especially ch. 5. The West German slogan after World War II—for the possible return of the lost territories and unification of all Germany— "Deutschaland geteilt? Niemals" [Germany divided? Never!] is extremely close to the Hungarian irredentist slogan of "No, No, Never" of the 1920s.

44. See R. A. Helin, "The Volatile Adminsitrative Map of Rumania," *Annals of the Association of American Geographers* 57, no. 3 (1967): 496–97.

45. Ibid., p. 499.

46. Documentations are now available: See V. Szereda and A. Sztikalin, eds., *Hiányzó lapok 1956 történetéből* [Missing pages from the 1956 revolution] (Budapest: Zenit, 1993); Gy. Litván, ed., *Az 1956–os magyar forradalom* [The Hungarian revolution of 1956] (Budapest: Tankönyvkiadó, 1991); and more recently the articles by Romanian historian M. Grigoriu, "Titkos iratok a román levéltárokból 1956–57" [Secret documents from Romanian archives], *Magyar Nemzet*, June 13, 1998, p. 16.

47. See Hugh Seton-Watson, *Nations and States : An Enquiry into the Origins of Nations and the Politics of Nationalism* (Boulder: Westview, 1977), 148. On invented traditions and nationalism, see the classic work by E. J. Hobsbawm and T. Ranger, eds., *The Invention of Tradition* (Cambridge: Cambridge University Press, 1983); E. J. Hobsbawm, *Nations and Nationalism since 1780: Programme, Myth, Reality* (Cambridge: Cambridge University Press, 1990), esp. ch. 2.

48. Quoted in S. Newens, ed., *Nicolae Ceauşescu: Speeches and Writings* (Nottingham: Spokesman, 1978), 176.

49. In *The Economist Intelligence Unit* (London), it was printed that West Germany paid roughy 10 million DM a month to Romania per 1,000 German émigrés leaving Romania; see p. 13. The situation of Saxons in Ceauşescu's Romania and their dilemma is described in detail by the German scholars G. and R. Weber, *Zendersch. Eine Sibenbürgische Geimende im Wendel* (München: Delp, 1985).

50. Political scientists and international specialists noted the worsening of conditions in the early 1980s in Romania: see M. Shafir, *Romania: Politics, Economics and Society:*

Political Stagnation and Simulated Change (London: Frances Pinter, 1985); L. D. Tyson, *Economic Adjustment in Eastern Europe* (Santa Monica: The Rand Corporation, 1984).

51. See V. Cucu, *Sistematizarea teritoriala și localitatilor din Romania* (Bucuresti: Editura Științifica și Enciclopedică, 1977); S. Sampson, *The Planners and the Peasants: An Anthropological Study of Urban Development in Romania* (Esbjerg: University Center of South Jutland, East-West Studies, 1982).

52. E. Traistaru, *Mobilitatea Socioprofesionala A Populatiei Active* [Socioprofessional Mobility of the Active Romanian Population] (București: Editura Scrisul Romanesc, 1975); for a more thorough and objective analysis, see D. Turnock, *The Romanian Economy in the Twentieth Century* (London: Croom Helm, 1986).

53. The plight of Romania's Jewish population during Ceaușescu's time is detailed in L. Mertens, "Die Lage des rumanischen Judentums," *Südosteuropa* 37 (1988): 1–7.

54. For the Romanian justification of these, see M. Nicolae, ed., *Invătămîntul în Limbile Naționalităților Conlocuitoare din Romania* (București: Editura Didactică și pedagogică, 1982). Since many of the official socialist statistics concerning ethnic schools and the education of minority children were either unreliable or gross extrapolations, other information should be consulted. While statistics in nationalist controversies are suspect from all sides, I only suggest for comparison the following examples: E. Illyés, *National Minorities in Romania: Change in Transylvania* (Boulder-New York: Columbia University Press, 1982); M. Ratner, *Educational and Occupational Selection in Contemporary Romania: An Anthropological Account* (unpublished Ph.D. dissertation, American University, 1980).

55. Literature on the situation of Hungarians in Romania during the 1980s ranged from highly questionable observations to ambiguous reports. Yet human and minority rights agencies did their best to provide reliable information on such matters: in English, see the American Transylvanian Federation and Committee for Human Rights in Rumania, eds., *Witnesses to Cultural Genocide. Firsthand Reports on Rumania's Minority Policies Today* (New York: ATF and CHRR, 1979); Amnesty International, *Romania: Forced Labor, Psychiatric Repression of Dissent, Persecution of Religious Believers, Ethnic Discrimination and Persecution, Law and Suppression of Human Rights in Romania* (New York: AIUSA, 1978); Committee for Human Rights in Romania, *Statement by the Committee for Human Rights in Romania before the Subcommittee on International Trade of the Committee on Finance of the United States Senate* (New York: CHRR, 1978); B. C. Funnemark, ed., *S. O. S. Transylvania: A Report for the International Helsinki Federation for Human Rights* (Vienna: IHFHR, 1988). For more detailed analyses, see J. F. Cadzow, A. Ludanyi, and L. Elteto, eds., *Transylvania: The Roots of Ethnic Conflict* (Kent, Ohio: Kent State University Press, 1983); G. Schopflin, *The Hungarians in Rumania* (London: Minority Rights Group, 1978).

56. See D. Ghermani, "Die historische Legitimierung der rumanischen Nationalpolitiken," *Südosteuropa* 35 (1986): 340–54.

57. M. Sozan was a Hungarian émigré who never researched the issue of Transylvania, nor did he conduct fieldwork in Romania. Yet his connections to the Hungarian émigré circles and to Hungarian scholars in Hungary were extensive. From these sources he was able to create an image which he then publicized; see "Ethnocide in Rumania," *Current Anthropology* 18 (1977): 781–82; "A Reply," *Current Anthropology* 20 (1979): 140–46; "More on Romanian Cities," *Newsletter of the East European Anthropology Group* 6 (1986–1987): .7–8; Romanian Research Group, "On Transylvanian Ethnicity," *Current Anthropology* 20 (1979): 135–40.

58. For historical antecedents, see S. Fischer-Galati, "Smokescreen and Iron Curtain: A Reassessment of Territorial Revisionism Vis-à-Vis Romania Since World War I," *East European Quarterly* 22 (1988): 37–53; D. Mitrany, *Greater Rumania: A Study of National Ideas* (London-New York: Hodder and Stoughton, n.d.), 20.

59. John Campbell, *French Influence and the Rise of Rumanian Nationalism* (New York: Arno Press, 1971 [1940]), 18.

60. Romanian socialist state myths are analyzed by R. Anty, "Language and Nationality in East-Central Europe 1750–1950," *Oxford Slavonic Papers* 12 (1979): 76; S. Fischer-Galati, "Myths in Romanian History," *East European Quarterly* 15 (1981): 329; A. Ludanyi, *Hungarians in Rumania and Yugoslavia: A Comparative Study of Communist Nationality Politics* (unpublished Ph.D. dissertation, Louisiana State University, 1971), 61–62.

61. Such ideas were sanctioned in the Romanian historical studies of the time. See M. Musat and G. Zaharia, "Romania," in *A független és egységes nemzeti államok kialakulása Közép és Délkelet-Európában 1821–1923* [Development of independent and unified nation-states in Central and Southeastern Europe], eds. V. Moisuc and I. Calafeteanu (Bukarest: Kriterion, 1984).

62. These myths are published in A. Otetea, ed., *The History of the Rumanian People* (New York: Twayne Publishers, 1970); S. Pascu, *A History of Transylvania* (Detroit: Wayne State University Press, 1982); A. MacKenzie and A. Otetea, eds., *A Concise History of Romania* (London: Robert Hale, 1985).

63. M. Constantinescu, ed., *Relations between the Autochthonous Populations and the Migratory Populations on the Territory of Romania* (Bucuresti: Editura Academieu, 1975).

64. I. Ceaușescu, *Transilvania Străvechi Pămint Românesc* (București: Editura Militara, 1984).

65. Ibid., p. 18.

66. Ibid., p. 329.

67. According to the official Romanian historiography: "1213—First documentary mention of the Szekler population in Transylvania. The Szeklers, a population originating from the fusion by assimilation of several Turkic tribes, were met in northwestern Transylvania by the Magyars (who were moving towards Pannonia at the end of the ninth century). Later, the Szeklers were employed as frontier guards. During the thirteenth century they were removed to the territory they have been inhabiting down to the present day." See H. Matei et al., eds., *Chronological History of Romania*, 54–55.

68. Ibid., p. 120; C. C. Giurescu, *The Making of the Romanian People and Language* (Bucharest: Meridiane, 1972), 47. Nevertheless, Romanian historiography also relies on the early medieval Byzantine chronicles. See, for example, H. Matei, ed., *Chronological History of Romania* (Bucharest: Editura Enciclopedica Romana, 1972), 48–50; S. Brezeanu, "Les 'Vlaques' dans les sources Byzantines concernant les debuts de l'etat des Asenides. Terminologie ethnique et ideologie Politique. II," *Revue des Sud-Est Europeennes* 25 (1987): 315–27.

69. See Rene Ristelhueber, *A History of the Balkan Peoples* (New York: Twayne, 1970 [1950]), 47–49.

70. One of the best English language explanations of this Hungarian political myth may be found in J. Winternitz, "The 'Turanian' Hypothesis and Magyar Nationalism in

the Nineteenth Century," in *Culture and Nationalism in Nineteenth Century Eastern Europe*, eds. R. Sussex and J. C. Eade (Columbus, OH: Slavica, 1985), 143–58. Early explanations and criticism of this political myth may be found in Gy. Avar, "Miért veszedelmes a turanizmus?" *Vigilia* 1 (1935): 178–86; L. Zrinszky, "A turanizmus fajvallásról," *Világosság* (1961): 38–41.

71. Gail Kligman, *The Wedding of the Dead: Ritual, Poetics, and Popular Culture in Transylvania* (Berkeley, Calif.: University of California Press, 1988), 9.

72. B. Köpeczi, ed., *Erdély Története I-III* [*History of Transylvania*] (Budapest: Akadémiai, 1986).

73. English language Romanian responses may be found in S. Pascu, M. Musat, and M. Constantinu, "A Conscious Forgery under the Aegis of the Hungarian Academy of Sciences," *Romanian Review* 4 (1987): 3–21; T. Popovici, "Deliberate Falsification of History: Method and Style," *Romanian Review* 5 (1987): 86–102.

74. See Committee for Human Rights in Rumania, "Will the United States Endorse Cultural Genocide in Rumania," *New York Times*, May 7, 1976.

75. The political reverberations were so serious that a "more scholarly" and "objective" Hungarian follow-up volume was published. See I. Rácz, ed., *Tanulmányok Erdély Történetéről* [Studies about the History of Transylvania] (Debrecen: Csokonai, 1987).

76. See R. Vulpe, "The Geto-Daciens," in ed. A. Otetea, *The History of the Rumanian People*, 49–90. A more neutral archaeological research that addresses this topic is R. F. Hoddinott, *The Thracians* (London: Thames and Hudson, 1981).

77. Hungarian history and the archaeology of Transylvania is discussed by Gy. Györffy, *István király és műve* [King Stephen and his work] (Budapest: Gondolat, 1977); Gy. László, *A honfoglaló magyarok művészete Erdélyben* [Hungarian art in Transylvania from the period of conquest) (Kolozsvár: Minerva, 1943); L. Rásonyi, *Hidak a Dunán. Régi török népek a Dunánál* [Ancient Turkic peoples at the Danube] (Budapest: Magvető, 1981).

78. See D. Prodan, *Supplex Libellus Valachorum or The Political Struggle of the Romanians in Transylvania during the Eighteenth Century* (Bucharest: Romanian Academy of Sciences, 1971).

79. These are to be found in Ceauşescu, *Transilvania Stravechi Pamint Romanesc*, 20; St. Olteanu, *Les Pays Roumains al'Epoquee de Michael Le Brave (L'Union de 1600)* (Bucuresti: Editura Academiei, 1975).

80. See D. Prodan, *Iobagia in Transilvania in Secolul al XVI-lea* I-II [Serfdom in Transylvania in the Sixteenth Century] (Bucureşti: Editura Academiei, 1968); D. Chirot, *Social Change in a Peripheral Society: The Creation of a Balkan Colony* (New York: Academic Press, 1974); H. Stahl, *Traditional Romanian Village Communities* (Cambridge: Cambridge University Press, 1980). In Hungarian, one of the most useful sources is Á. Egyed, *Falu, város, civilizáció* [Village, town, civilization] (Bukarest: Kriterion, 1981).

81. See V. Georgescu, *Ideile Politice si Iluminismul in Principatele Romane 1750–1831* [Political ideas and the enlightenment in the Romanian principalities] (Bucuresti: Editura Academiei, 1972).

82. Marx and Engels expressed a bias during the 1848 revolutions when they believed that only the Germans, Magyars, and Poles were "revolutionary" and all of the other nationalities (the "historyless Slavs," for example) were "counter-revolutionary." See

Cummins, "Marx, Engels, and the Springtime of the Peoples," in *Culture and Nationalism*, eds. Sussex and Eade, *Culture and Nationalism*, 33.

83. J. H. Jensen, quoted in Sussex and Eade, eds., *Culture and Nationalism*, 74, "Nationalism and Cultural Revivals: The Romanian and Serbian Experience, 1780s–1870s," p. 74.

84. See I. Deak, *The Lawful Revolution. Louis Kossuth and the Hungarians, 1848–1849* (New York: Columbia University Press, 1979), 119–29.

85. One short story in particular comes to mind: it is the 1850 "The Bárdy family" by Mór Jókai, Hungary's celebrated romantic writer. Jókai describes the bloody murder of the whole Bárdy family by Romanian irregulars (the Moti) in the Apuseni Mountains. The Romanian leader of the unit tries to save the lives of one young couple, but they are killed by the blood-thirsty peasants, an act revenged by the leader by killing all of his men. The story was taken from a newspaper report that criticized Jókai for his cruelty. This story provided the Romanian phrase "Tine minte" (Remember, don't forget), which became a slogan for Hungarian irredentists after World War I. See M. Györffy, ed., *Jókai Mór Elbeszélések 2/A* (Budapest: Akadémiai, 1989), 246.

86. See I. Coman et al., eds., *Romania in Razboiul de Independenta 1877–1878* (Bucuresti: Editura Militara, 1977); E. Niederhauser, *A nemzeti megújulási mozgalmak Kelet-Európában* [National revival movements in Eastern Europe] (Budapest: Akadémiai, 1977); M. Contantinescu and S. Pascu, eds., *Unification of the Romanian National State: The Union of Transylvania with Old Romania* (Bucharest: Romanian Academy of Sciences, 1971); K. Hitchins, *Orthodoxy and Nationality: Andrei Saguna and the Rumanians in Transylvania, 1846–1878* (Cambridge: Harvard University Press, 1977).

87. Stephen Fischer-Galati, "Smokescreen and Iron Curtain," 51.

88. I have in mind two books, both published in the United States. One represents the Romanian view, an English translation of Romanian history by V. Georgescu, *The Romanians: A History* (Columbus: Ohio State University Press, 1991), see esp. pp. 12–15; and see P. F. Sugar, P. Hanak, and T. Frank, eds., *A History of Hungary* (Bloomington: Indiana University Press, 1990), esp. chs. 2 and 3 by L. Makkai.

NOTES TO CHAPTER 3

1. See the studies by P. Atkinson, *The Ethnographic Imagination: Textual Constructions of Reality* (London: Routledge, 1990) and H. F. Wolcott, *The Art of Fieldwork.* (London: Sage, 1995).

2. Some of this literature includes M. Buchowski, "The Shifting Meanings of Civil and Civic Society in Poland," in *Civil Society: Challenging Western Models*, eds. C. Hann and E. Dunn (London: Routledge, 1996), 79–98; L. Kürti, "Homecoming: Affairs of Anthropologists in and of Eastern Europe," *Anthropology Today* 12, no. 3 (1996): 11–15; L. Kürti and J. Langman, eds., *Beyond Borders: Remaking Cultural Identities in the New East and Central Europe* (Boulder: Westview, 1997); M. Lampland, *The Object of Labor: Commodification in Socialist Hungary* (Chicago: University of Chicago Press, 1995); S. Sampson, "The Social Life of Projects: Imparting Civil Society to Albania," in *Civil Society: Challenging Western Models*, eds. C. Hann and E. Dunn (London: Routledge, 1996), 121–42; K. Verdery, *What Was Socialism, and What Comes Next?* (Princeton: Princeton University Press, 1996).

3. See E. E. Evans-Pritchard, "Some Reflections on Fieldwork in the Twenties," *Anthropological Quarterly* 46, no. 4 (1973): 235–42; P. Rabinow, *Reflections on Fieldwork in Morocco* (Berkeley: University of California Press, 1977).

4. Evans-Pritchard, "Some Reflections," 235.

5. See E. R. Leach, *Rethinking Anthropology* (London: Athlone Press, 1971), 1.

6. See K. Hastrup, "Writing Ethnography: State of the Art," in *Anthropology and Autobiography*, ASA Monographs No. 29, eds. J. Okely and H. Callaway (London: Routledge, 1992), 117.

7. In fact, the few publications about fieldwork experiences in the former East Bloc are S. Sampson's and D. Kideckel's "Anthropologists Going into the Cold," in *Anthropology of War and Peace*, eds. P. Turner and D. Pitt (Hadley: Bergin and Garvey, 1989), 160–73. Moreover, British anthropologist Chris Hann has written about his experiences in Hungary. See "The Politics of Anthropology in Socialist Eastern Europe," in *Anthropology at Home*, ed. A. Jackson (London: Tavistock, 1987), 139–53; "After Communism: Reflections on East European Anthropology and the 'Transition,'" *Social Anthropology* 2, no. 3 (1994): 229–50.

8. See R. Williams, *Keywords: A Vocabulary of Culture and Society* (New York: Oxford University Press, 1983), 87–93.

9. See Martha Lampland's excellent book on how this relates to Hungarian rural workers; M. Lampland, *The Object of Labor: Commodification in Socialist Hungary* (Chicago: University of Chicago Press, 1995), esp. chs. 1 and 5.

10. Two edited anthropological collections offer excellent examples for the relevance of the socialist experience in Eastern Europe to anthropological theory: see C. Hann, ed., *Socialism: Ideals, Ideologies, and Local Practice* (London: Routledge, 1993), and R. S. Watson, ed., *Memory, History, and Opposition Under State Socialism* (Santa Fe: School of American Research Press, 1994).

11. The parochial nature of East European anthropology is easily discernible if we realize that the view from the village was, it seems to continue to remain, a focus for most anthropologists. As a natural consequence, then, large segments of society, as well as important aspects of societal processes, were left out of anthropological inquiry. Eccentricities, while including a good dosage of sensible research and interpretation, never really made headlines in anthropological circles From Dracula's castles to blood feuds and from ritual mid-winter dances to Gypsy traders, the list is long; yet some of these analyses, their seriousness and importance notwithstanding, could have helped the anthropology of the East to be even more marginalized. See, for example, C. Boehm, *Blood Revenge: The Enactment and Management of Conflict in Montenegro and Other Tribal Societies* (Philadelphia: University of Pennsylvania Press, 1987); T. Bringa, *Being Muslim in the Bosnian Way: Identity and Community in a Central Bosnian Village* (Princeton: Princeton University Press, 1995).

12. See Gail Kligman, *The Wedding of the Dead: Ritual, Politics, and Popular Culture in Transylvania* (Berkeley: University of California Press, 1988), 3.

13. Chris Hann makes an apt point concerning this when he discusses American anthropologists studying Romanian society in the 1980s, in "After Communism," 241. Katherine Verdery's pioneering study, *Transylvanian Villagers: Three Centuries of Political, Economic, and Ethnic Change* (Los Angeles: University of California Press, 1983), deals largely with the historical advancement of the national ideology and less so with the realities of Ceaușescu's Romania, an idea she discusses in detail in her later studies.

14. See, for example, the debate between anthropologists concerning the study of Iceland, K. Hastrup's, "The Native Voice and the Anthropological Vision," *Social Anthropology* 1, no. 1 (1993): 73–86; "Anthropological Theory as Practice," *Social Anthropology* 4, no. 1 (1996): 75–82; S. D. Kristmundsdóttir, "Reply to Kirsten Hastrup," *Social Anthropology* 4, no. 2 (1996): 187–88.

15. See T. Hofer, "Anthropologists and Native Ethnographers in Central European Villages: Comparative Notes on the Professional Personality of Two Disciplines," *Current Anthropology* 9, no. 4 (1968): 311–15.

16. See R. Rosaldo, *Culture and Truth: The Remaking of Social Analysis* (Boston: Beacon Press, 1993), 245.

17. See C. Lévi-Strauss, *Tristes tropiques* (New York: Criterion Books, 1961), 58. Such gender bias notwithstanding, we can add amputated women too; for the gender-specific aspects of fieldwork, see H. Callaway, "Ethnography and Experience: Participatory Experience and Embodied Knowledge," in *Anthropology and Autobiography*, ASA Monographs No. 29, eds. J. Okely and H. Callaway (London: Routledge, 1992), 29–49; D. Kulick and M. Wilson, eds., *Taboo: Sex, Identity and Erotic Subjectivity in Anthropological Fieldwork* (London: Routledge, 1995).

18. British anthropologist Hann analyzes some of these points in greater detail in "The Politics of Anthropology in Socialist Eastern Europe," 139–53.

19. Although "fieldwork" has long been a hallmark of anthropological endeavor, as postmodern cross-disciplinary fertilization took place throughout the 1980s, practitioners from other disciplines appropriated the term to signify other concepts and practices; see R. Fox, ed., *Recapturing Anthropology: Working in the Present* (Santa Fe: School of American Research Press, 1991). For the defense of traditional fieldwork practices, see E. F. Moran, "Introduction: Norms for Ethnographic Reporting," in *The Comparative Analysis of Human Societies. Toward Common Standards for Data Collection and Reporting*, ed. E. Moran (Boulder: Lynne Rienner, 1995), 1–20.

20. See L. Abu-Lughod, "Writing against Culture," in *Recapturing Anthropology*, ed. R. Fox (Santa Fe: School of American Research Press, 1991), 139.

21. See S. Lavie and T. Swedenburg, "Between and Among the Boundaries of Culture: Bridging Text and Lived Experience in the Third Timespace," *Cultural Studies* 10, no. 1 (1996): 154–79.

22. H. Bhaba, "The Third Space: Interview," in *Identity: Community, Culture, Difference*, ed. J. Rutherford (London: Lawrence & Wishart, 1990), 207–21; and T. T. Minh-ha, *When the Moon Waxes Red* (New York: Routledge, 1991).

23. Leach, *Rethinking Anthropology*, 3.

24. For some of the recent anthropological works on the Mediterranean and Western Europe, see V. Goddard, J. Llobera, and C. Shore, eds., *The Anthropology of Europe: Identity and Boundaries in Conflict* (Oxford: Berg, 1994); S. McDonald, ed., *Inside European Identities* (Oslo: Berg, 1993); T. Wilson and M. E. Smith, eds., *Cultural Change and the New Europe* (Boulder: Westview, 1993).

25. This has been the rule rather than the exception from the Americans Eva Huseby-Darvas, Susan Gal, Michael Sozan, and Martha Lampland to the British Chris Hann and Ildikó Vásáry. Sozan and Vásáry had already passed away. Two other American anthropologists (Lajos Vincze and Béla Máday), both immigrants from Hungary after World War II, also published on Hungarian topics.

26. It was the sign of the 1990s, and perhaps the result of the postmodernist turn in anthropology, that since the mid-1990s there were more detailed explanations to that effect; see Lampland, *The Object of Labor*, 357–59.

27. For a comparison, see Gail Kligman's work about conducting research in Romania in the mid-1970s, *Calus: Symbolic Transformation in Romanian Ritual* (Chicago: University of Chicago Press, 1981), xiv–xv.

28. H. M. Enzensberger, *Europe, Europe: Forays into a Continent* (New York: Pantheon Books, 1989), 104–05.

29. In fact, upon my return, several requested copies of my publications. Knowing English somewhat, they immediately began arguing with me, pointing out some of the issues which, in their minds, were not discussed in full detail.

30. In European anthropology, it was David I. Kertzer who, in his book *Comrades and Christians: Religion and Political Struggle in Communist Italy* (Cambridge: Cambridge University Press, 1980), documented well this contradictory nature of the working-class existence.

31. Rosaldo, *Culture and Truth*, 7.

32. I have described Csepel and its workers in my articles; see "Red Csepel: Working Youth in a Socialist Firm," *East European Quarterly* 23 (1989): 445–68 and "Hierarchy and Workers' Power in a Csepel Factory," *The Journal of Communist Studies* 6, no. 2 (1990): 61–84. More detailed explanations can be found in my doctoral dissertation, *Youth and the State: An Anthropological Analysis of Work and Political Socialization* (unpublished doctoral dissertation, University of Massachusetts, 1989).

33. G. Zanetti, "Rekviem a 'vörös Csepelért'" [A Requiem for Red Csepel] *Heti Magyarország*, January 3, 1992, 14–15.

34. See Catherine Wanner, *Burden of Dreams. History and Identity in Post–Soviet Ukraine* (University Park: Pennsylvania State University Press, 1998).

35. This was a one-page published interview with the director of the hostel describing the refugees' plight (see *Csepel*, June 22, 1988, p. 6).

36. See Mart Bax, "Religious Regimes and State-Formation: Toward a Research Perspective," in *Religious Regimes and State-Formation. Perspectives from European Ethnology*, ed. E. R. Wolf (Albany: State University of New York Press, 1991), 7–28.

37. I have described this in more detail elsewhere. See "People vs. the State: Political Rituals in Contemporary Hungary," *Anthropology Today* 6, no. 2 (1990): 5–9; "The Wingless Eros of Socialism: Nationalism and Sexuality in Hungary," *Anthropological Quarterly* 64, no. 2 (1991): 55–67.

38. See K. Verdery, *National Ideology under Socialism: Identity and Cultural Politics in Ceaușescu's Romania* (Berkeley: University of California Press, 1991), 433.

39. Western anthropologists first called attention to the situation of Hungarian Gypsies in C. Hann, *Tázlár: A Village in Hungary* (Cambridge: Cambridge University Press, 1980) and D. P. Bell, *Peasants in Socialist Transition* (Berkeley: University of California Press, 1983). A full anthropological monograph on Hungarian Gypsies is M. Stewart's, *The Time of the Gypsies* (Boulder: Westview, 1997).

40. No other punk rockers carried this xenophobic and racist message as far as *Mosoi*, a group whose members were banned from public performances and faced court trials

for their anti-state and racist propaganda. The song popular in Hungary in the mid-1980s among unskilled workers is indicative:

> The flame-thrower is the only weapon I need to win,
> All Gypsy adults and children we'll exterminate,
> But we can kill all of them at once in unison,
> When it's done we can advertise: Gypsy-free zone.

Another slogan I heard in Csepel, a clear signal of anti-Gypsy sentiments as a result of the reemergence of Gypsy political organizations and parties, was the juvenile "skin-head" proffering: "Sárkányoknak, sárkányfû; Cigányoknak bõrfejû" [Dragons with dragon-weed; Gypsies with skin-heads]. I have discussed the anti-Gypsy sentiments in Hungary in "Rocking the State: Youth and Rock Music Culture in Hungary, 1976–1990," *East European Politics and Societies* 5, no. 3 (1991): 483–513.

41. This refers to the article by the Hungarian émigré anthropologist Michael Sozan, which was rebutted by the Romanian Research Group's essay, also published in "Ethnocide in Rumania," *Current Anthropology* 18 (1977): 781–82; see ch. 2.

42. Americans had to pay thirty dollars for a visa for thirty days and ten dollars for each day of stay in Romania. In addition, gasoline tickets had to be purchased with dollars and, as the law required, foreigners had to be housed at a hotel that charged separate prices for foreigners and native guests. However, times are changing in a strange way: in the summer of 1995, when I left Romania, I was forced to pay a gasoline tax, a spurious amount of money, the validity of which I was not able to check in any official documents, even though most border guards refered to a 1990 law. The gasoline tax was in effect until the summer of 1998 as a regular custom procedure at the Romanian border.

43. Film and notebooks were taken away from me on numerous occasions, just as I had to pay fines for embroideries and pottery considered by Romanian border guards to be invaluable "art objects" of the national treasury that had to stay in Romania.

44. See Kligman, *The Wedding of the Dead*, 19.

45. See László Kürti, "Juhmérés és henderikázás Magyarlónán" [Sheepherding and ritual in a Hungarian community in Transylvania], *Ethnographia* 98, nos. 2–4 (1987): 385–93; "Transylvania, Land Beyond Reason: An Anthropological Analysis of a Contested Terrain," *Dialectical Anthropology* 14 (1990): 21–52.

46. For historical studies on Cluj and its Hungarian aspects, see A. Kiss, *Források és értelmezések* [Sources and interpretations] (Bukarest: Kriterion, 1994).

47. See Irina Livezeanu, *Cultural Politics in Greater Romania* (Ithaca, N.Y.: Cornell University Press, 1995), 154.

48. See Kligman, *Calus*, 170.

49. The population census for the county of Cluj reveals a growth of 580,344 in 1956 to 725,110 in 1978. See *Annuarul statistic al republicii socialiste România 1979* (Bucureşti: Direcţia Centrala de Statistică, 1979), 46. Hungarian studies, however, stress that the town's ethnic makeup had been altered considerably by forceful expulsion and governmental policies: in 1930, there were 47,689 Hungarians in Cluj (roughly 47 percent of the total population), in 1956, 74,155 (47 percent), in 1966, 76,000 (41 percent), in 1977, 85,400 (32 percent), and in 1992, 74,483 (22 percent). See S. Vogel, "A magyar kisebbség Romániában" [Hungarian minority in Romania], Hungarian Institute of International Affairs, Report No. 8, Budapest, p. 6; R. Joó and A. Ludanyi, eds., *The Hungar-*

ian Minority's Situation in Ceauşescu's Romania (Boulder: Social Science Monographs, 1994), 69. I. Semlyén does document the influx of Moldavians to Cluj in search of better jobs: see *Hétmilliárd lélek* [Seven-billion souls] (Bukarest: Kriterion, 1980), 197.

50. Semlyén, *Hétmilliárd,* 185. From this study, it is clear that as a result of Ceauşescu's forced pronatalist policies, Romania's population grew from 19 million to 22 million from 1966 to 1979. However, the Hungarian areas were not the regions where the birthrate dropped significantly, as Hungarian nationalists claim. The birthrate remained the lowest in the southwest corner of Timis, Arad, and Caras-Severin, counties bordering Hungary and Yugoslavia (186). Ceauşescu's pronatalist policies are discussed in more detail by G. Kligman, *The Politics of Duplicity: Controlling Reproduction in Ceauşescu's Romania* (Berkeley: University of California Press, 1998). For the underestimation of Hungarian population in Transylvania, see G. D. Satmarescu, "The Changing Demographic Structure of the Population of Transylvania," *East European Quarterly* 8, no. 4 (1975): 425–52.

51. For the educational situation in Transylvania in the late 1970s, see Z. M. Szaz, "Contemporary Educational Policies in Transylvania," *East European Quarterly* 11, no. 4 (1977): 493–501.

52. S. Csoóri writes about one such story concerning Hungarian and Romanian soldiers. Somewhere in a Romanian army barracks, youth are watching the Hungarian–Romanian soccer game. When the Hungarian team scores a goal, a young recruit jumps up happily, thereby revealing his Hungarianness; one of his outraged Romanian mates shoots him in the head. The family of the deceased received only a short official notice of the son's death. See S. Csoóri, "Kapaszkodás a megmaradásért" [Hanging on for survival], in *Kutyaszorító* [A trap], ed. M. Duray (New York: Püski, 1983), 10.

53. See "Resolution on Romanian Resettlement" (offered by Martha Lampland, M. Carole Nagengast, Eva Huseby-Darvas, and David Kideckel), which reads:

> Whereas it is widely and publicly known that the government of Romania is planning to embark upon a new settlement policy; and Whereas this new policy entails reducing the current number of 13,000 villages by approximately 7,000–8,000, thereby forcibly resettling many thousands of citizens of Romania; and Whereas Articles 12 and 27 of the Political and Civil Covenant of the Universal Declaration of Human Rights guarantee freedom of internal movement; and Whereas the government of Romania is a signatory to this treaty; and therefore, Be it resolved that the American Anthropological Association call upon the government of Romania in a written communication to fulfill its treaty obligations to guarantee and protect the human and civil rights of all its citizens by abandoning its new settlement plan. (American Anthropological Association, resolutions at the 1988 annual business meeting in Phoenix, Arizona)

This resolution—with the AIDS and Tasaday resolutions—was presented for the general membership for vote on February 15, 1989.

54. Indeed, this is what has been suggested by American anthropologist Steven Sampson, who was conducting research in Romania in the mid-1980s; see "Rumors in Socialist Romania," *Survey* 28 (1984): 142–64.

55. Professor Aluas—a younger colleague of Henri H. Stahl (1901–1991)—was a kind and an extremely knowledgeable man. He was of the old rural sociology school, following in the footsteps of D. Gusti (1880–1955), who wanted to understand the Hungarian–Romanian conflict. Aluas was instrumental in bringing Hungarians to the

Department of Sociology at Cluj, one of the most important being perhaps József Venczel (1913–1972), a Hungarian scholar from the D. Gusti school who spent years in jail on trumped-up charges. I. Aluas was an important figure who was instrumental in reforming sociology at the University of Cluj, including bringing cultural anthropology into the curriculum and developing a center for studying interethnic conflict in Transylvania. For the Cluj sociological traditions, see I. Aluas, and T. Rotariu, "L'enseignement sociologique de Cluj. Présent et perspectives," in *Rencontre internationale sur L'enseignement de la Sociologie. Actes*, eds. I. Aluas and G. Gosselin (Cluj-Paris: Université Babes-Bolyai, 1992), 67–82; J. Venczel, *A falumunka útján. Válogatott írások* [On the road to village research. Selected writings]. (Székelyudvarhely-Budapest: Orbán Balázs Közművelődési Egyesület, 1993).

56. I treasure this letter very much. It is written, of course, in Romanian; it has three official signatures and stamps on it. It also "allowed" me to move more freely in parts of Romania. Aluas asked me one morning: "And where would you like to travel?" "Mostly in Transylvania," I answered, with bafflement. "No," he said, "I mean *where* in Romania?" So he ended up putting down Transylvania *as well as* Moldavia as the main research site of my fieldwork! After all, a Hungarian–American anthropologist could not just conduct fieldwork in Transylvania about Romanian–Hungarian interethnic relations, not in 1993.

57. On secrecy, see, for example, R. G. Mitchell, *Secrecy and Fieldwork* (Newbury Park-London: Sage, 1993).

58. Having a laptop computer when crossing into Romania was no easy adventure either. Twice I was asked to fill out papers declaring it, along with the video camera, and both serial numbers made it onto my visa papers. I guess that much of this is simply following the law and trying to counter the illegal transport of these high-priced products, yet knowing the country's totalitarian past somewhat, one cannot help but wonder how far the state can go in keeping both citizens and travelers in a state of constant surveillance by limiting their use of technology.

59. See, "Rights of the Persons Belonging to the National Minorities: Human Rights in Romania," The Romanian Institute for Human Rights, Bucuresti, 1993.

60. Ibid., 79.

61. S. P. Ramet, *Whose Democracy?* (Lanham: Rowman & Littlefield, 1997), 58.

62. See, for example, the recent works by M. McDonald, "Unity in Diversity: Some Tensions in the Construction of Europe," *Social Anthropology* 4, no. 1 (1996): 47–60; D. Kideckel, ed., *East-Central European Communities: The Struggle for Balance in Turbulent Times* (Boulder: Westview, 1995).

63. No doubt, under the influence of state ideology, most of the Hungarian language ethnographies were either largely silent about interethnic conflict or tried to foster an image of peaceful coexistence on the local level, arguing that Hungarian and Romanian villagers have always lived in peaceful harmony with each other.

64. V. Crapanzano, *Hermes' Dilemma and Hamlet's Desire: On the Epistemology of Interpretation* (Cambridge: Harvard University Press, 1992), 139.

65. See K. Verdery, "The Elasticity of Land: Problems of Property Restitution in Transylvania," *Slavic Review* 53, no. 4 (1994): 1071–1109; see also D. Kideckel, "Two Incidents on the Plains of Southern Transylvania: Pitfalls of Privatization in a Romanian Community," in *East European Communities: The Struggle for Balance in Turbulent Times*, ed. D. Kideckel (Boulder: Westview, 1995), 47–64. For a comparison, see G. Creed's

study on Bulgaria, *Domesticating Revolution: From Socialist Reform to Ambivalent Transition in a Bulgarian Village* (University Park: Pennsylvania State University Press, 1998).

66. Some of these are described in A. Biró, "What Others Can Do," *World Policy Journal* 12 (1995): 97–101; L. Watts, "Romania and the Balkan Imbroglio," in *Crises in the Balkans: Views from the Participants*, eds. C. P. Danopoulos and K. G. Messas (Boulder: Westview, 1997), 233.

67. For example, this is how the RMDSZ frames its argument:

> The DAHR estimates that the forms of autonomy and self-government which appear in Recommendation No. 1201 of the Council of Europe, applied successfully by countries with democratic traditions, would assure a convenient frame for the Hungarian minority from Romania to cultivate its national identity. Hereby this large national community could decide itself in questions related to its survival. (The Democratic Alliance of Hungarians in Romania, *Documents* 1, Cluj: DAHR, 1994, 25)

68. Another aspect of national identity has to do with Hungarian food, spices, and drugs, all of which are major commodities traded and exchanged by Hungarian villagers and visitors from Hungary. Villagers constantly complain about the quality of Romanian foodstuff, and the extent to which they try to obtain "quality products" from Hungary sometimes borders on the ridiculous. While I have not seriously considered the notion of nationalist taste and consumerism, the way in which Hungarian villagers return with large packages of food when they visit Hungary illustrates that food can be a powerful stimulant of national identity and belonging.

69. For the German case, see J. Bornman, *Belonging in the Two Berlins: Kin, State, Nation* (Cambridge: Cambridge University Press, 1992); the emergence of Czech and Slovak nations is well documented by L. Holy, *The Little Czech and the Great Czech Nation* (Cambridge: Cambridge University Press, 1996); the Yugoslav state's collapse and the remaking of Croatian and Serbian nations in the wake of the four-year-long Balkan War is documented by C. Giordani, "Affiliation, Exclusion, and the National State: Ethnic Discourses and Minorities in East Central Europe," in *Rethinking Nationalism and Ethnicity: The Struggle for Meaning and Order in Europe*, ed. H.R. Wicker (Oxford: Berg, 1997), 175–92; and J. R. Kirin and M. Povrzanovic, eds., *War, Exile, Everyday Life: Cultural Perspectives* (Zagreb: Institute of Ethnology and Folklore Research, 1996). See also W. Kokot and D. Dracklé, eds., *Ethnologie Europas: Grenzen-Konlikte-Identitaten* (Berlin: Reimer, 1996).

NOTES TO CHAPTER 4

1. H. K. Bhabha, "Introduction: Narrating the Nation," in *Nation and Narration* (London: Routlege, 1990), 4.

2. How French peasants, for instance, were turned into Frenchmen is discussed by the classic historical work of E. Weber, *Peasants into Frenchmen: The Modernization of Rural France, 1870–1914* (Stanford: Stanford University Press, 1976).

3. The following is how the authors describe Hungarian peasants depicted as "proper": "A proper peasant could only be a man who 'was born into it,' who was brought up in this way of life as a child. . . . The land he cultivated was inherited from his ancestors;

to keep and work it with care and responsibility was his moral duty to his precursors and successors, and also to the fatherland and God. . . . In addition to the land and the ancestral house lot, a proper peasant inherits a populous crowd of kinsmen from his ancestors. . . . Thus he not only lives in a village where everyone knows and greets each other, but also he has personal connections with a large proportion of the population"; see E. Fél and T. Hofer, *Proper Peasants. Traditional Life in a Hungarian Village* (Chicago: Aldine, 1969), 380.

4. For some of the theoretical arguments on race and racial purity, see M. Banton, *Racial Theories* (Cambridge: Cambridge University Press, 1989); S. J. Gould, *The Mismeasure of Man* (New York: W. W. Norton, 1981); for a more contemporary debate about racism and multicultural identities, see P. Werbner and T. Modood, eds., *Debating Cultural Hibridity: Multicultural Identities and the Politics of Anti-Racism* (London: Zed, 1997).

5. A classic definition and treatment of Hungarian populism is found in Gy. Borbándi, *A magyar népi mozgalom* [Hungarian populism] (New York: Püski, 1983). For populist political ideology in contemporary American politics, see W. S. Maddox and S. A. Lilie, *Beyond Liberal and Conservative: Reassessing the Political Spectrum* (Washington, D.C.: Cato Institute, 1984); J. F. Zimmerman, *Participatory Democracy: Populism Revived* (New York: Praeger, 1986).

6. Since its inception in the mid-nineteenth century, Russian populism, *narodnikism*, was more anarchist, radical, and socialist; see R. Szporluk, *Communism and Nationalism: Karl Marx Versus Friedrich List* (New York: Oxford University Press, 1988). The Ukrainian populist movement is discussed in I. Rudnytsky, "The Ukrainians in Galicia under Austrian Rule," in *Nationbuilding and the Politics of Nationalism: Essays on Austrian Galicia*, eds. A. Markovits and F. Sysyn (Cambridge: Harvard University Press, 1982), 23–67. In Russian, *narod* means both "people" and "nation." In Hungarian, the same concept is described by two terms: *nép* and *nemzet.*

7. See Anthony Smith, *Nationalism in the Twentieth Century* (New York: New York University Press, 1979), 11.

8. This important point is discussed by J. Rezler, "Economic and Social Differentiation and Ethnicity: The Case of Eastern Europe," in *Ethnic diversity and conflict in Eastern Europe*, ed. P. F. Sugar (Santa Barbara: ABC-Clio, 1980), 307–10.

9. See T. Shanin, *Defining Peasants* (Oxford: Basil Blackwell, 1990), 50–52.

10. See E. Gellner, *Nations and Nationalism* (Ithaca, N.Y.: Cornell University Press, 1983), 57. Cf. also Smith, *Nationalism*, esp. pp. 69–70.

11. At the Council of Constance, in 1416, there were four historic nations: Spain, Italy, Germany, and France; England was chosen as the fifth nation instead of Hungary, as the Holy Roman Emperor requested; see L. R. Loomis, J. H. Mundy, and K. M. Woody, eds., *The Council of Constance: The Unification of the Church* (New York: Columbia University Press, 1961), esp. pp. 84–85, 449. This form of "nation"-thinking also was similar in medieval education: when Charles IV founded the University of Prague in 1348, the student body was divided into Polish, Saxon, Czech, and Bavarian "nationes," all of them faithfull subjects of the German nation.

12. Hungary's seventeenth-century warring count, Miklós Zrinyi, demonstrated beautifully the separate ethnic and class/national identities prevalent among aristocrats since the seventeenth century when he wrote: "I am not a worthless Croat, and I am also a Zrinyi"; see "Letter to Rucsics, 1658," in *Zrínyi Miklós levelei*, ed. Á. Makó (Budapest: Akadémiai

Kiadó, 1950), 71; a slightly different translation of this letter also has been in S. Bene and G. Hausner, eds., *Zrínyi Miklós válogatott levelei* (Budapest: Balassi, 1997), 110.

13. See A. J. Patterson, *The Magyars: Their Country and Institutions* 2 (London: Smith, Elder and Co., 1869), 24–25.

14. P. S. Fichtner, *The Habsburg Empire: From Dynasticism to Multinationalism* (Malabar: Krieger, 1997), 66–67.

15. Quoted in L. Czigány, *The Oxford History of Hungarian Literature: From the Earliest Times to the Present* (Oxford: Clarendon Press, 1984), 84.

16. See M. Herzfeld, *Anthropology through the Looking-Glass: Critical Ethnography in the Margins of Europe* (Cambridge: Cambridge University Press, 1989), 9.

17. Ibid., 199.

18. In this respect, the historical analyses of the pioneer of nationalism studies, Hans Kohn, deserve a special mention. See *The Idea of Nationalism: A Study of Its Origins and Background* (New York: Macmillan, 1944) and *Nationalism: Its Meaning and History* (New York: D. Van Nostrand, 1955). On the Polish notion of defending Christianity, the *antemurale christanitatis*, see J. Tazbir, "Poland and the Concept of Europe in the Sixteenth–Eighteenth Centuries," *European Studies Review* 7 (1977): 29–45.

19. Bene and Hauser, *Zrínyi Miklós*, 82–83.

20. Ibid., 107.

21. D. M. Jones, *Five Hungarian Writers* (Oxford: Clarendon Press, 1966), 63–65.

22. The Englishman Patterson notes a favored Hungarian saying of the time, "The Hungarian is fond of trappings" (sallangos a magyar); see *The Magyars*, 37.

23. Also translated as:

> What do you mean to me, region of the grim Carpathians,
> Wildly romantic with pine forest?
> I may admire you, but I do not love you,
> And my thoughts do not range over your hills and valleys.

See D. M. Jones, *Five Hungarian Writers* (Oxford: Clarendon Press, 1966), 239.

24. J. Paget, *Hungary and Transylvania with Remarks on Their Conditions Social, Political and Economical* (London: John Murray, 1850), vol. I, pp. 519–20.

25. I only cite here the opening verse:

Egy szegény nő, Isten látja,	A poor woman, God sees her,
Nincs a földön egy barátja,	Without a friend on this earth,
Agg, szegény és gyámoltalan,	Aged, poor and helpless,
Ül magán, a csendes lakban.	In her quiet abode, sits in solitude.
Dolga nincs, hogy volna dolga?	She is not busy, how could she be?
Kis ebédhez nem kell szolga,	For meager lunch, no servant needs,
S az ebédnél nincs vendége,	At meals she has no guest,
Csak a múlt idők emléke.	Only her memory of time past.

26. See I. Békés, *Magyar ponyva pitaval* [Hungarian pulp fiction] (Budapest: Minerva, 1966).

27. The figure of the outlaw in ethnography and folklore has been detailed in many studies, among them: I. Küllős, *Betyárok könyve* [Book of outlaws] (Budapest:

Mezőgazdasági, 1988); K. Sinkó, "Az Alföld és az alföldi pásztorok felfedezése külföldi és hazai képzőmûvészetben" [Discovery of the Alföld herdsman in Hungarian and foreign fine arts], *Ethnographia* 100, nos. 1–4, (1992): 121–54.

28. Eötvös's literary work is analyzed in detail by Jones, *Five Hungarian Writers*, 160–228, and his statesmanship by R. A. Kann, *The Multinational Empire: Nationalism and National Reform in the Habsburg Monarchy, 1848–1918* (New York: Columbia University Press, 1964), 93–99.

29. Two poems in particular deserve attention: *The Noble (A nemes,)* of 1844, and *The Magyar Noble (A magyar nemes),* written a year later. Here the adjective "Magyar" adds to the sarcasm with which Petőfi denigrates the nobility, and not without the anti-aristocratic spirit that one detects in most European literature of that time. The second and final two verses are telling:

> My life has no need of work.
> In idleness I truly live.
> Work is for the peasant.
> *I* am of a noble descent!
> What do I care for my homeland?
> With its endless troubles?
> For *they* will soon disappear,
> But *I* will remain a Hungarian noble!
> I smoked away my patrimony like ashes in
> a pipe:
> In the end, angels take me up to Heaven.
> *I* am a Hungarian nobleman!

30. For the interethnic mixture of Hungarian nobility and the assimilation of the Jewish middle classes, see the fine study of W. O. McCagg, *Jewish Nobles and Geniuses in Modern Hungary* (New York: Columbia University Press, 1972) and "The Jewish Position in Interwar Central Europe: A Structural Study of Jewry at Vienna, Budapest, and Prague," in *A Social and Economic History of Central European Jewry*, eds. Y. Don and V. Karady (New Brunswick, N.J.: Transaction Press, 1990), 47–82.

31. See I. Deak, *Beyond Nationalism: A Social and Political History of the Habsburg Officer Corps, 1848–1918* (New York: Oxford University Press, 1990).

32. For the assimilation of Jewish middle classes, see, for example, A. Handler, ed., *The Holocaust in Hungary: An Anthology of Jewish Response* (Alabama: University of Alabama Press, 1982), 5.

33. Positive or overemphasized self-concepts and self-stereotypes exist as part of most ethnic identities; see M. Horowitz, *Ethnic Groups in Conflict* (Berkeley: University of California Press, 1985), esp. ch. 4.

34. Indeed, the Englishman Patterson refers to the notion of "denationalization"; see vol. II, p. 24.

35. One such example is the grade-school geographical description of Transylvania, with its ethnographic regions representing the "best," "most noble," and historically "important communities"; see J. Gáspár, ed., *Olvasókönyv a Népskolák V. és VI. osztálya számára* [Reader for V. and VI. grades of elementary schools] (Budapest: M. Kir. Tudományegyetemi Nyomda, 1910), 185–91.

36. See, especially, L. Németh, *Magyarság és Európa* [Hungary and Europe] (Budapest: Franklin Társulat, 1935), 35–61.

37. During my fieldwork stay in the Kalotaszeg region, I was told many times about the pride of members of the community of Kalotaszentkiraly (Sincrai in Romanian) concerning an old mulberry tree under which the poet Ady supposedly wrote this poem, hence its name *Ady's Tree*. This clearly represents one aspect of popular sentiment as ideologized among Hungarians, yet this is just one of the examples of the way in which the past and literature form a rationalized explanation in patriotic outbursts, for example, the letter published in the local Hungarian journal. See "Ady emlékmû a Kalotaszeg partján?" [Ady memorial on the Kalota riverbank], *Kalotaszeg* (March 1–15, 1991: 3.

38. See E. Ady, *Jóslások Magyarországról* [*Prophesyzing about Hungary*] (Budapest: Atheneum, 1936), 306–08. I should mention that this edition of Ady's collected essays was prepared by Géza Féja, Hungary's populist writer of the 1930s. Although Ady died before populism became a social and political movement, his writings and poetry were elevated to the ideology of populism of the 1930s.

39. Quoted in T. Spira, "Aspects of the Magyar Linguistic and Literary Renaissance During the *Vormärz*," *East European Quarterly* 7, no. 2 (1972): 110.

40. T. Eagleton, "Nationalism: Irony and Commitment," in *Nationalism, Colonialism, and Literature*, eds. T. Eagleton, F. Jameson, and E. W. Said (Minneapolis: University of Minnesota Press, 1990), 28.

41. Several studies paint a vivid picture of this feverish, nineteenth-century process: B. Borsi-Kálmán, *Illúziókergtés vagy ismétléskényszer* [Illusions or Repetitions] (Budapest: Balassa-Kriterion, 1995); B. Köpeczi, *Nemzetképkutatás és a XIX. századi román irodalom magyarságképe* [Image of the Hungarians in the 19th century Romanian literature] (Budapest: Akadémiai Kiadó, 1995); A. Miskolczy, "A román folklórszemlélet és a romantika" [Romanian folklore ideology and the romantic period], *Aetas* 2, no. 2 (1994): 134–69.

42. E. Szemkeõ, "Bevezetés," in *Jankó János A Milleneumi falu* [János Jankó and the Millennial village], ed. E. Szemkeõ (Budapest: Néprajzi Múzeum, 1989), 8.

43. The Hunyadi family of Transylvania gave a governor and a king to Hungary and Transylvania: the former is immortalized in Romanian nationalist historiography as Iancu de Hunedoara, or János Hunyadi in Hungarian; the latter is King Mathias Corvinus.

44. See Zs. Gyarmathy, *Tarka képek a kalotaszegi varrottas világából* [Colorful pictures of the Kalotaszeg embroidery] (Budapest: Franklin, 1896), 43.

45. Mrs. Gyarmathy, a daughter of a Protestant minister in Kalotaszeg, wrote popular novels and stories, but her literary talent was overshadowed by her ethnographic desriptions of the region and her love for embroideries that she helped exhibit all over Europe. K. Kós was a novelist and an architect. It should be mentioned that Bey Szeffedin Szefket was born in Cluj, of a Turkish father and a Hungarian mother. He wrote perhaps one of the most characteristic populist novels *The Madonna of Kalotaszeg* (*Kalotaszegi madonna*, 1942), a book that was an instant hit, immortalizing the region of Kalotaszeg. His book was made into a popular 1942 film as well. For his nationalistic views, Szeffedin was forced to leave Romania after World War II, eventually moving to Egypt.

46. See McCagg, *Jewish Nobles*, 98–102.

47. This is a quote from the writer Zsigmond Justh, quoted in V. Finn, "Zsigmond Justh: In Search of a New Nobility," in *Intellectuals and the Future in the Habsburg Monarchy 1890–1914*, eds. L. Peter and R. B. Pynsent (New York: St. Martin's Press, 1988), 148.

48. See McCagg, *Jewish Nobles,* 79.

49. See Finn, "Zsigmond Justh," 127–51.

50. See Finn, "Zsigmond Justh," 134–35.

51. The book by Bey Szeffedin Szefket, *The Kalotaszeg Madonna* has a similar (unfulfilled) love theme: a prosperous Budapest industrialist falls in love with a Transylvanian woman, but she, despite a few years of marriage, decides to leave him and marry a famous but poor painter.

52. See Horowitz, *Ethnic Groups in Conflict,* 176–78.

53. M. Ormos, *Nácizmus—fasizmus* [Nazism and fascism] (Budapest: Magvető, 1987), 149–57.

54. The most important, exclusivist paramilitary organization was the "Etelköz Association" (*Etelközi Szövetség,* or EX), a group including extremist military high officers. See Ormos, *Nácizmus,* 257.

55. L. Pasvolsky, *Economic Nationalism of the Danubian States* (New York: Macmillan, 1928), 545.

56. Gale Stokes makes a similar point about the Serbian radicals of the late nineteenth century, proposing that in their program, "The nation (narod) is sovereign and to it belong all political rights, including the right to organize the land economically"; see *The Politics as Development: The Emergence of Political Parties in Nineteenth-Century Serbia* (Durham, N.C.: Duke University Press, 1990), 98.

57. See Czigány, *The Oxford History,* 103, 323–25.

58. No other works summarize this idea better than the book by historian I. Dékány, *A magyarság lelki arca* [The face of the Hungarian soul] (Budapest: Athenaeum, 1942) and ethnographer G. Lükő's, *A magyar lélek formái* [Forms of the Hungarian soul] (Budapest: Exodus, 1942). Both recall the American culture and personality and national character studies of the 1940s.

59. Transylvania as an ethnographic curiosity as well as an obsession is embedded in the fact that after 1918, Transylvania became a part of Romania and thus emerged not only as different but as politically isolated, in the phrase of Ardener, "remote." Instead of listing all of the ethnographic monographs, I only call attention to larger corpora summarizing the research results up until the end of World War II. See L. Bartucz, ed., *A magyar nép* [The Hungarian people] (Budapest: Singer & Wolfner, 1943; L. Bartucz, *A magyar ember: A magyarság antropológiája* (Budapest: Királyi Magyar Egyetemi Nyomda, 1938); and the four-volume work of the ethnography of the Hungarians, *A magyarság néprajza I-IV* (Budapest: Királyi Magyar Egyetem Nyomda, 1933–1937).

60. The Szeklers, or Székelys in Hungarian, were living in the four historic counties of Marosszék, Udvarhely, Csik, and Háromszék; see Gy. Bözödi, *Székely Bánja* [The Szekler Chroniclers] (Budapest: Magyar Élet, 1943).

61. One of the best sources for the fictionalization of the Transylvanian count is the annotated Dracula by L. Wolf, ed., *The Annotated Dracula; Dracula by Bram Stoker* (New York: Clarkson N. Potter, 1975). For historical analyses of the Romanian Dracula myth, the following works should suffice: K. W. Treptow, ed., *Dracula: Essays on the Life and Times of Vlad Tepes* (New York: Columbia University Press, 1991). Interestingly, it was the American scholar of Romanian origin, Radu Florescu, who spent his scholarly life analyzing the historical Dracula, his life and his deeds: see R. T. McNally and R. Florescu, *In*

Search of Dracula: A True History of Dracula and Vampire Legends (New York: Galahad Books, 1972); R. Florescu, *Dracula, the Prince of Many Faces: His Life and His Times* (Boston: Little, Brown, 1989); *Dracula, a Biography of Vlad the Impaler, 1431–1476* (New York: Hawthorn Books, 1979). The literary representation of the Dracula myth is analyzed by M. M. Carlson, "What Stoker Saw: An Introduction to the History of the Literary Vampire," *Folklore Forum* 10, no. 2 (1977): 26–32, and by M. Lõrinczi, "Transylvania and the Balkans as Multiethnic Regions in the Works of Bram Stoker," *Europae* 2 (1996): 1–13.

62. Lõrinczi, "Transylvania," 2.

63. The tests were conducted by L. Csík and E. Kállay, *Vércsoportvizsgálatok Kalotaszegi községekben* [Blood serological tests in Kalotaszeg villages] (Kolozsvár: Minerva, 1942).

64. Ibid., 15–17, 23.

65. The new science of Hungarology and its aims and research agenda is described by linguist L. Ligeti, ed., *A Magyarságtudományi Intézet Évkönyve 1941–42* [Yearbook of the Hungarology Institute] (Budapest: A Kir. M. Pázmány Péter Tudományegyetem Magyarságtudományi Intézetének Kiadása, 1942).

66. See Rezler, "Economic and Social Differentiation," 307–11.

67. While, for example, János Kodolányi (1899–1969) and László Németh (1901–1975) were of middle-class background, and Dezsõ Szabó (1879–1945) was the son of a Transylvanian Calvinist pastor, those of working-class origin are impressive, including Pál Szabó (1893–1970), Péter Veres (1897–1970), József Darvas (1912–1973), Zoltán Szabó (1912–1986), Imre Kovács (1913–1980), Géza Féja (1900–1978), and Gyula Illyés (1902–1983).

68. Czigány, *The Oxford History*, 392.

69. D. Némedi has summarized this literary venture in *A népi szociográfia 1930–1938* [The populist sociography] (Budapest: Gondolat, 1985). See also P. Benkõ, *A magyar népi mozgalom almanachja* [Almanac of the Hungarian populist movement] (Budapest: Deák, 1996).

70. To my mind, one of the best summaries of the populist movement is Gyula Borbándi's study published, not in Hungary, where the subject was still off limits, as I will show later, but in émigré circles in the United States; see *A magyar népi mozgalom* (New York: Püski, 1983).

71. Némedi, *A népi szociográfia*, 114–27.

72. See, G. Illyés, *People of the Puszta* (Budapest: Corvina, 1967), 11.

73. Szabó's rise to national fame is attributed to his two books: *Tardi helyzet* [The situation at Tard] (Budapest: Cserépfalvi, 1936), a village monograph, and *Cifra nyomorúság* [The fancy of poverty] (Budapest: Cserépfalvi, 1937), a description of poverty connected to the extraordinary spending of peasant families. In all fairness, however, there were rural sociologists at that time who already warned about the populist narratives, their content and ideological slant; see B. Reizer, *Válogatott Irásai* [Selected Writings], vols. I–II, (Budapest: Országos Közművelõdési Központ, 1986).

74. G. Bözödi, *Székely Bánja*, 118–38.

75. The Pearly Bouquet movement received its name from the pearly ornaments that unmarried young males placed in their hats. Because of its nationalistic overtones, the

Pearly Bouquet movement was not discussed during socialism in Hungary. Only one analysis exists on this movement by dance folklorist Cs. Pálfi, "A Gyöngyösbokréta története" [History of the Pearly Bouquet], *Tánctudományi Tanulmányok* 1969–1970 (Budapest: Magyar Táncművészek Szövetsége, 1970), 115–63

76. B. Paulini, ed., *The Pearly Bouquet* (London: Simpkin Marshall, 1937), 3–5. It should be mentioned that after the post–World War II reorganization of Hungary's cultural life, the Pearly Bouquet movement was made illegal and was disbanded; its founder/organizer, Paulini, committed suicide.

77. Analyses of the revisionist terrorist acts are analyzed in T. Cseres, *Vérbosszú Bácskában* [Bloody terror in Bácska] (Budapest: Magvető, 1991) and P. Gosztonyi, *A kormányzó Horthy Miklós és az emigráció* [Governor Miklós Horthy and the Emigres] (Budapest: Százszorszép, 1991).

78. The Hungarian Office of Tourism, with help from both the Ministry of Public Education and the Ministry of Commerce and Communication, was able to advertise internationally through its offices in Western cities, including one in New York City.

79. For an analysis of Jancsó's films, see P. Józsa, *Adalékok az ideológia és a jelentés elméletéhez* [Studies on ideology and theory of semiotics] (Budapest: Népművelési Propaganda Iroda, 1979), esp. part II.

80. Romanian film history of the period is best represented in I. Cantacuzino and M. Gheorghiu, eds., *Cinematograful Romanesc Contemporan, 1949–1975* [Contemporary Românian Cinematography] (București: Meridiane, 1976). This book, like many of the others published in the "Era of Ceasusescu," begins with a quote from Ceaușescu, who extolls the virtues of cinema in creating the socialist values and person.

81. The emergence of this generation is described in Y. Blumenfeld, *Seesaw: Cultural Life in Eastern Europe* (New York: Harcourt, Brace and World Inc., 1968), 145.

82. Quoted in ibid., 152.

83. In A. Tezla, ed., *Ocean at the Window: Hungarian Prose and Poetry Since 1945* (Minneapolis: University of Minnesota Press, 1980), 189.

84. See Y. Blumenfeld, *Seesaw*, 150.

85. He writes: ". . . both alike proclaim the iniquity of 'partition,' regardless of the presence in Transylvania and Ulster, respectively, of large majorities in favour of such partition. In both, the irredentist minority have committed acts of aggression against the majority; in both, the servants of the Government have been guilty of hasty and ill-advised actions in restoring order and administering the law"; see C. J. C. Street, *Hungary and Democracy* (London: T. Fisher Unwin LTD, 1923), 157. The similarity between Transylvania and Ireland was already raised by Arthur J. Patterson who wrote: "At present Transylvania is a Hungarian Ireland, presenting many similar difficulties of pacification"; see *The Magyars: Their Country and Institutions* 2 (London: Smith, Elder and Co., 1869), 335.

NOTES TO CHAPTER 5

1. After the death of Petru Groza, Romania's first post–war party secretary (actually president of the Presidium of the Grand National Assembly), Gheorghe Gheorghiu-Dej,

held the highest post in Romania until his death in 1965. On March 22, 1965, Nicolae Ceauşescu was elected as the first secretary of the Central Committee of the Romanian Communist Party; the Ninth Congress of that party then elected him as General Secretary in July of the same year.

2. Quoted in "On to the Horizons of the Third Millennium," *Romanian Review* 1 (1989): 4.

3. For the history of stereotypical images, see László Makkai, "Az erdélyi románok a középkori magyar oklevelekben" [Romanians in Transylvania in medieval Hungarian manuscripts], *Erdélyi Múzeum* 48, nos. 1–4 (1943): 17–45; Lajos Kántor, "Magyarok a román népköltészetben" [Hungarians in Romanian folklore], *Erdélyi Múzeum* 38, nos. 1–3 (1933): 46–64. Hungarian stereotypes in Transylvanian-Saxon literature are discussed in A. F. Balogh, *Az erdélyi szász irodalom magyarságképe* (Budapest: Littera Nova, 1996). Romanian stereotypes of Hungarians in Romanian newspapers are discussed (anonymously!) in E. K. "Magyarság-kép a mai román lapokban" [Images of Hungarians in Romanian newspapers], *Korunk* 2 (1995): 119–26. The vicious sense of humor in Hungarian, especially the jokes of the Szekler population, has been a popular weapon for the national alliance, cohesion, and stereotyping of Romanians. These jokes also have reinforced existing racist ethnic bias, myopia, and ethnocentrism. For example, "What's the difference between a Hungarian in Romania and a pig? It is illegal to kill a pig."

4. In Chapter 5, I discuss the literary origin of this Romanian expression. See also my article "Hungary and Her Neighbors: Stereotypes and Realities," *Acta Ethnographica* 42, nos. 1–2 (1997): 103–18.

5. See K. Verdery, *National Ideology under Socialism: Identity and Cultural Politics in Ceauşescu's Romania* (Berkeley: University of California, 1991), 303.

6. See Y. Blumenfeld, *Seesaw: Cultural life in Eastern Europe* (New York: Harcourt, Brace and World, 1968), 165.

7. Géza Szőcs, a prominent member of the Hungarian party in Romania, describes his own and his comrades' ordeal during these times in *Az uniformis látogatása* [Visits by the uniforms] (New York: Hungarian Human Rights Foundation, 1987).

8. The Szeklers from Bukovina, their history and culture, have been studied extensively by Hungarian ethnographers and folklorists. For a few noted studies, see B. Andrásfalvy, "A Bukovinai Székelyek kultúrájáról" [Culture of the Szekelys from Bukovina], *Népi Kultúra-Népi Társadalom* 7 (1973): 7–22; T. Csupor, *Mikor Csikból elindultam: A Bukovinai Székelyek élettörténete* [When I left Csik County: Life history of the Szeklers from Bukovina] (Budapest: Szépirodalmi, 1987); A. S. Gáspár, *Az én szülőföldem a bukovinai Istensegits* [I am from the village of Istensegits from Bukovina] (Budapest: Akadémiai Kiadó, 1986).

9. A fair number of repatriated Hungarians settled through an "arranged" marriage contract. The cost of such "fixed marriages" in 1987 was between 20,000 to 30,000 forints, but 50,000 was common. While the people were waiting for their final papers, they visited each other, mostly Hungarians traveling to Romania, a situation that accounted for the existence of "love trains" taking singles across the border. A program aired on Hungarian television on July 25, 1988, titled "Mikor Csikbol elindultam" [When I left Csik County], dealt with this question openly. See also I. Varga, "Fogadás és befogadás, Beszélgetés áttelepültekkel" [Reception and assimilation, Interviews with refugees], *Kortárs* 9 (1988): 98–108.

10. The situation of the Hungarian refugees in the mid-1980s from Romania is discussed in the following works: Z. Ács, ed., *Tíz kérdés az erdélyi menekültekről* [Ten questions about the Transylvanian refugees] (Budapest: Népszava, 1988); T. Franka, *Most jöttem Erdélyből* [I just arrived from Transylvania] (Budapest: Lang, 1988); P. Kende, *Erdélyből jöttek* [They came from Transylvania] (Budapest: Ifjúsági Lap-és Könyvkiadó, 1988); I. Nemeskürthy, *Édes Erdély* [Sweet Transylvania] (Budapest: Szabadtéri, 1988); A. Végh, *De mi lesz a harangokkal* [What will happen to the bells] (Budapest: MN Mûvészeti Alap, 1988).

11. See Ghermani, "Die historische Legitimierung der rumanischen Nationalpolitiken," *Südosteuropa* 35 (1986): 352–54. The Hungarian claim for the Hungarian origin of the Csángós is presented by P. P. Domokos, *A moldvai magyarság* [Hungarians in Moldavia] (Budapest: Magvetõ, 1987); L. Mikecs, *Csángók* (Budapest: Optimum, 1989); G. Csoma, *Moldvai Csángó Magyarok* [Hungarian Csangos in Moldavia] (Budapest: Corvina, 1988). The Romanian argument is presented by D. Mãrtinaş, *Originea ceangăilor din Moldava* [Origin of the Moldavian Csángó] (Bucureşti: Editura Ştiinţifică si Enciclopedică, 1985).

12. For the Hungarian ethnographic representation of the Csángós of Moldova, see K. Kós, J. Szentimrei, and J. Nagy, *Moldvai Csángó népmûvészet* [Csángó folk art from Moldavia] (Bukarest: Kriterion, 1981); see also the special issue of *Néprajzi Látóhatár* 3, nos. 1–2 (1994) for Moldavian Csángó folklore and ethnography.

13. For recent analyses of Szekler early medieval history, see E. Benkõ, "A székelyföldi régészeti kutatások eredményei" [Archaeological results of the Szekler region], *Aetas* 3 (1993): 5–20 and Zoltán Kordé, "A székely eredetkérdés" [Origin of the Szeklers], *Aetas* 3 (1993): 21–39. The Romanian official view concerning the Romanian origin of the Szeklers and how to de-Hungarianize them is discussed by I. Livezeanu, *Cultural Politics in Greater Romania* (Ithaca, N.Y.: Cornell University Press, 1995), esp. pp. 139–40, 179–80.

14. See I. Chinezu, *Aspects of Transylvanian Hungarian Literature, 1919–1929* (Cluj-Napoca: Fundatia Culturala Romana, 1997), 104. Similarly, Romanian historian Ioan-Aurel Pop argues: "The Szeklers could be the remainders of the khabaro-khazar tribes that had preceded the Hungarian conquest of the Pannonian Plains"; see *Romanians and Hungarians from the 9th to the 14th Century* (Cluj-Napoca: Fundaţia Culturala Româna, 1996), 162. Hungarian romantic sentiments have contributed to this Asiatic theory as well. The Szekler traveler, Sándor Kõrösi Csoma (1784–1842), actually went to Tibet to find the long-lost ancestors of the Szeklers. Although he was not successful in that endeavor, he did indeed become a skilled linguist credited with the writing of the first English–Tibetan dictionary. He is buried in Darjeeling, and his gravesite has become the pride of Szekler–Hungarian determination and survival. On this, see S. Szõke, "Székely hegyekbõl messze Ázsiába" [From the Szekler mountains to faraway Asia], *Erdélyi Magyarság* 3, no. 11 (1992): 15.

15. See Illyés, *National Minorities in Romania: Change in Transylvania* (Boulder-New York: Columbia University Press, 1982), 32–33; R. Joó, *Nemzeti és nemzetközi önrendelkezés, önkormányzat, egyenjogúság* [National and nationality autonomy, government and equality] (Budapest: Kossuth, 1984), 101; I. Semlyén, *Hétmilliárd lélek* [Seven billion souls] (Bukarest: Kriterion, 1980), 215.

16. Hungarian Transylvanian museologist Péter Veress has rekindled arguments for the unique Szekler identity by using folk culture architecture; see P. Veress, "Az identitás jelképei" [Symbols of identity], *Aetas* 3 (1993): 163–75. As Gail Kligman has shown, the

northern Transylvanian region of Maramures also is held in high esteem by Romanian ethnographers for its carved wooden gates expressing "an ongoing reconstruction of value and identity, within both local and national contexts"; see *The Wedding of the Dead: Ritual, Politics, and Popular Culture in Transylvania* (Berkeley: University of California Press, 1988), 30.

17. This event has been recently reevaluated in I. Imreh, ed.,*Látom az életem nem igen gyönyörű—a madéfalvi veszedelem tanúkihallgatási jegyzőkönyve 1764* [I see my life turns ugly . . . Court hearings of witnesses to the Madéfalva battle in 1764] (Bukarest: Kriterion, 1994).

18. The elevation of Csikszentdomokos into the ethnographic limelight owes a great deal to author-ethnographer Lajos Balázs, who was born there: see L. Balázs, *Az én első tisztességes napom: Párválasztás és lakodalom Csikszentdomokoson* [My first honorable day. Mate selection and wedding in Csikszentdomokos] (Bukarest: Kriterion, 1994) and *Menj ki én lelkem a testből: Elmúlás és temetkezés Csikszentdomokoson* [Leave my soul this body: Passing away and funeral customs in Csikszereda] (Csikszereda: Pallas-Akadémia, 1995).

19. For descriptions of some of these local identities in the 1980s, see P. Egyed, ed., *Változó valóság, Városkutatás, Szociológiai kutatások* [Changing realities, urban research, and sociological research] (Bukarest: Kriterion, 1984); I. Imreh, ed., *Változó valóság, szociográfiai tanulmányok* [Changing realities, sociographic works] (Bukarest: Kriterion, 1978); G. Herédi, ed., *Korunk évkönyv* [Korunk Yearbook] (Kolozsvár: Korunk, 1982). The historical-ethnographic literature of this region is vast. A few recent illustrative examples include D. Garda, *Gyergyó a történelmi idő vonzásában* [The region of Gyergyó in history] (Székelyudvarhely: Infopress, 1992); I. Imreh and J. Pataki, *Kászonszéki krónika 1650–1750* [Chronicles of Kászonszék, 1650–1750] (Budapest: Európa-Kriterion, 1992); M. Tarisznyás, *Gyergyó történeti néprajza* [Historical ethnography of Gyergyó] (Budapest: Akadémia, 1994); M. Endes, *Csík-Gyergyó-, Kászon-székek (Csík megye) földjének és népének története 1918–ig* [History of the peoples of Csík, Gyergyó, and Kászon counties] (Budapest: Akadémiai, 1994).

20. See A. Z. Bíró and J. Bodó, "A 'hargitaiság' egy régió kultúraépítési gyakorlatáról" (The Hargita-image: A region's cultural significance), *KAM Átmenetek* 2 (1991): 87.

21. Orbán's six-volume 1871 work was republished by E. Illyés, a Transylvanian émigré writer living in Germany. See B. Orbán, *A Székelyföld leírása* I-VI, ed. E. Illyés (München: Bibliofilo, 1981).

22. See B. Bíró, "Modell vagy rögeszme?" [Model or obsession], *Valóság* 1 (1997): 89.

23. See E. Illyés, "Orbán Balázs hagyatéka" [The legacy of Balázs Orbán], in *A székelyföld leírása* I–VI, ed. E. Illyés (München: Bibliofilo, 1981).

24. See J. Zepeczaner, "Orbán Balázs temetései" [Burials of Balázs Orbán], *Aetas* 3 (1993): 57–75. For a critical reevaluation of Orbán's life and work, see Gy. Ortutay, "Balázs Orbán," in *Halhatatlan népköltészet. Néprajzi vázlatok* [The immortal folklore: Ethnographic sketches] (Budapest: Magvető, 1966), 83–103. The literary interpretation may be found in A. Sütő, *Az idő markában: Esszék, naplójegyzetek* [In the hold of time: Essays, diaries] (Budapest: Szépirodalmi, 1984), 34–38.

25. See Sütő, *Az idő markában*, 44.

26. See K. Verdery, *The Political Lives of Dead Bodies: Reburial in Postsocialist Change* (New York: Columbia University Press, 1999), 41.

27. See Semlyén, *Hétmilliárd lélek*, 209.

28. Some of these patterns are documented in Z. Biró, J. Gagyi, and J. Péntek, eds., *Néphagyományok új környezetben* [Folk Traditions in New Environment] (Bukarest: Kriterion, 1987) and L. Pillich, *Városom évgyűrűi* [Years of my hometown] (Bukarest: Kriterion, 1985).

29. See V. Tismaneau, "Byzantine Rites, Stalinist Follies: The Twilight of Dynastic Socialism in Romania," *Orbis* 30 (1986): 65–90. The socialist state's version has been printed in several propagandistic works, among them, Zs. Szabó, ed., *Ember és föld Riportok az agrárforradalom hétköznapjaiból* [Man and earth: Reports of the daily life of the agrarian revolution] (Bukarest: Kriterion, 1987) and F. Hatházy, ed., *Jövőépítők: Munkatelepek Krónikája* [Future builders: Chronicles of workers' towns] (Bukarest: Kriterion, 1987).

30. The region east of the city of Cluj, Kalotaszeg (or Calata in Romanian), also has been known as *cifravidék*, or "fancy country." This native description is well suited for an area that exhibits vital signs of wealth and prosperity compared to other Hungarian settlements facing poverty, depopulation, and an aging labor force; see A. Salamon and S. Vasas, *Kalotaszegi ünnepek* [Holidays in Kalotaszeg] (Budapest: Gondolat, 1986).

31. This was the creation of the "social mobility" ideology of most socialist states; see Zs. Lengyel, *Mezőgazdaság, szövetkezete, parasztság a hetvenes években* [Agriculture, state farms, peasantry in the 1970s] (Budapest: Kossuth, 1982), 127–35.

32. A pioneering anthropological analysis of this phenomenon is J. W. Cole's, "Family, Farm, and Factory: Rural Workers in Contemporary Romania," in *Romania in the 1980s*, ed. D. N. Nelson (Boulder: Westview, 1981), 71–116.

33. This is described in G. Hunya, "Feszültségi pontok a román mezőgazdaság szervezeti és irányítási rendszerében" [Tensions in the structural and organizational system of Romanian agriculture], *Medvetánc* 4 (1986–1987): 45–62.

34. Romania's economic performance is analyzed in D. N. Nelson, ed., *Romania in the 1980s* (Boulder: Westview, 1981), esp. chs. 6 and 9.

35. This propagandistic text is printed in R. Zaharia, ed., *Hungarians and Germans in Romania Today* (Bucharest: Meridiane, 1978), 104–05. Similar publications were numerous from the late 1970s.

36. There was a high-level meeting between Hungarian and Romanian party officials in the beginning of 1957, when Imre Nagy, Hungary's prime minister during the 1956 revolution, and his colleagues were held hostage in Romania. This meeting is not, however, listed in the official Romanian historical chronology of the time. See H. C. Matei et al., eds., *Chronological History of Romania* (Bucharest: Editure Enciclopedica Romana, 1972).

37. Romania recognized South Vietnam already in 1968, when the South Vietnamese embassy was opened in Bucharest on June 13. Richard Nixon visited Bucharest on August 2–3 of the same year.

38. Daniel Chirot analyzes the 1970s with regard to Romania's rise to international stardom: see "Social Change in Communist Romania," *Social Forces* 57, no. 2 (1978): 457–98. See also T. Gilberg, *Nationalism and Communism in Romania: The Rise and Fall of Ceauşescu's Personal Dictatorship* (Boulder: Westview, 1990), esp. ch. 10. Kenneth Jowitt has referred to this as a "theoretical innovation." See "Political Innovation in Rumania," *Survey* 20, no. 4 (1974): 132–51.

39. See J. Broun, "The Catholic Church in Romania," in *Catholicism and Politics in Communist Societies*, ed. P. Ramet (Durham, N.C.: Duke University Press, 1990), 222.

40. Hungarian women from the Kalotaszeg region were visiting Budapest regularly selling their embroideries. As most admitted, they smuggled these objects under their clothes.

41. See R. Joó, ed., *Jelentés a romániai magyar kisebbség helyzetéről* [Report on the situation of the Hungarian minority in Romania] (Budapest: Magyar Demokrata Forum, 1988), 102 and B. C. Funnemark, ed., *S. O. S. Transylvania: A Report for the International Helsinki Federation for Human Rights* (Vienna: IHFHR, 1988), 12–22.

42. Hungarian filmmakers, nevertheless, often referred to Transylvanian Hungarians or utilized Transylvanian themes during the 1980s. The populist S. Sándor's 1988 trilogy, "The Road Before Me Weeps" [*Sir az út előttem*], dealing with the past and present situation of the Bukovinian Szeklers, was one of the additions to this cinematic endeavor revolutionizing Hungarian cinema in the late 1980s. After 1990, Sára was supported by the nationalist elites and the center-right government to obtain the prestigious presidency of the Duna television station.

43. See Közponli Statisztikai Hivatal, *Magyar Statisztikai Zsebkönyv* [Hungarian Statistical Pocketbook, 1986] (Budapest: KSH, 1987), 191. Hungarian complaints about shoddy products were frequent in the mid-1980s' media. Popular wit also caricatured the Dacia, the Romanian-made passenger car, as follows: "When can the Dacia reach the speed of 100 kilometers per hour? Answer: When it goes down the slope of Mt. Everest."

44. See B. Köpeczi, "Meditations on the Budapest Cultural Forum," *New Hungarian Quarterly* 27 (1986): 87.

45. Printed in the Socialist Party Daily *Népszabadság*, April 4, 1986, p. 1.

46. See L. Demus, "National Minorities in Hungary and in East-Central Europe," *New Hungarian Quarterly* 28 (1987): 129.

47. See A. B. Székely, "Access to Culture for National Minorities," *New Hungarian Quarterly* 28, (1987): 115.

48. *New York Times*, May 29, 1988, p. 15.

49. Objections have been voiced not only by the Hungarian government but by other governments and organizations as well; the Yugoslav *Vetsernie Novosty* (July 24, 1988), the West German *Siebenbürgische Zeitung* (August 1988), the *New York Times* (July 2, 1988), *The Times* (London, June 30, 1988), *The Economist* (July 2–3, 1988), and other magazines also carried stories about the "bulldozer politics." In fact, in June and July 1988, the International Rural Sociological Association, the International Architects Association, and the International Congress of Anthropological and Ethnological Sciences all signed a memorandum condemning the Romanian action.

50. Ceauşescu's speech was printed in full in Hungarian in the Hungarian Transylvanian periodical *Új Élet* [Tirgu Mureş] 13 (1988): 4, 7.

51. Ibid.

52. See L. Tőkés, "Sermons of Liberation," in *An Eastern European Liberation Theology*, ed. J. Pungur (Calgary: Angelus, 1994), 190–202. László Tőkés's father, himself also a Protestant pastor, has written a valuable summary of the liberationist stance of the Hungarian Protestant Church in Romania; see István Tőkés, "The Churches and Revolution in Romania," ibid., 203–22.

53. See L. D. Tyson, *Economic Adjustment in Eastern Europe* (Santa Monica: The Rand Corporation, 1984), 32–72.

54. Descriptions vary about the exact nature of socialist peasantry in 1980. For descriptions, see I. Szelenyi, *Socialist Entrepreneurs: Embourgeoisement in Rural Hungary* (Oxford: Polity Press, 1987) and M. Hollos and B. Maday, eds., *New Hungarian Peasants: An East-Central European Experience with Collectivization* (New York: Brooklyn College Press, 1983).

55. See F. Gazsó, ed., *Társadalmi Folyamatok az Ifjúság Körében* [Social processes among youth] (Budapest: MSZMP Társadalomtudományi Intézet, 1987). I also have analyzed some of these social undercurrents in Hungary in the 1980s in my article "The Wingless Eros of Socialism: Nationalism and Sexuality in Hungary," *Anthropological Quarterly* 64, no. 2 (1991): 55–67.

56. See J. Kenedi, *Do It Yourself: Hungary's Hidden Economy* (London: Pluto Press, 1981) and P. Galasi and Gy. Sziráczky, eds., *Labour Market and Second Economy in Hungary* (Frankfurt: Campus Verlag, 1985).

57. See Zs. Ferge, *Hungary: A Society in the Making* (New York: M. E. Sharpe, 1981).

58. I have detailed this in "How Can I Be a Human Being? Culture, Youth, and Musical Opposition in Hungary," in *Rocking the State: Rock Music and Politics in Eastern Europe and Russia*, ed. S. P. Ramet (Boulder: Westview, 1994), 73–102.

59. Programme of Democratic Renewal, "A Draft Proposal," *East European Quarterly* 2 (1986): 7.

60. The populist program has been printed as the Lakitelek's meeting proceedings: see S. Agócs and E. Medvigy, eds., *Lakitelek 1987: A Magyarság Esélyei* [The Lakitelek meeting in 1987: Chances of the Hungarians] (Budapest: Antológia-Püski, 1991).

61. The American Transylvanian Federation published a quarterly news bulletin reporting on the situation of Hungarians in Romania; see *Transylvania: Erdélyi Tájékoztató* (New York: Quarterly of the American Transylvanian Federation, 1986).

62. J. Puskás has analyzed the Hungarian immigrant society in North America in *Kivándorló Magyarok Észak-Amerikában* [Emigrant Hungarians in North America] (Budapest: Akadémiai Kiadó, 1983).

63. See A. Dunai, *Magyar főnemesek az emigrációban* [Hungarian aristocrats in emigration] (Youngstown: Katholikus Magyarok Vasárnapja, 1983), 133–35.

64. Ideas concerning the Transylvanian question propagated by émigré circles can be found in A. F. Sannborn and G. C. Wass, eds., *Transylvania and the Hungarian–Rumanian Problem* (Astor Park: Danubian Press, 1979); F. S. Wagner, ed., *Toward a New Central Europe: A Symposium on the Problem of the Danubian Nation* (Astor Park: Danubian Press, 1970); E. Bakó, ed., *Emlékkönyv az Amerikai Magyar Szövetség 80. Évfordulójára* (Washington, D.C.: AMSZ, 1988).

65. See Hungarian Human Rights Foundation, *Felhívás és beszámoló* [Call and Report] (New York: HHRF, 1988), 1.

66. The defected Romanian high official, M. Pacepa, the former chief of the Romanian secret service, discusses these Hungarian actions in his *Red Horizons: Chronicles of a Communist Spy Chief* (Washington, D.C.: Regnery Gateway, 1987), 327–29. Pacepa reaffirms that Ceauşescu even wanted to hire professionals to kill the Hungarian organizers of the demonstration. On Ceauşescu and the Romanian *nomenklatura*, see also M. E. Fischer,

Nicolae Ceauşescu and the Romanian Political Leadership: Nationalism and Personalization of Power, The Edwin M. Moseley Faculty Research Lecture, Skidmore College.

67. Committee for Human Rights in Rumania, *Witnesses to Cultural Genocide: First-Hand Reports on Rumania's Minority Policies Today* (New York: American Transylvanian Federation and Committee for Human Rights in Rumania, 1979). For a detailed analysis of the Committee for Human Rights in Romania, see Andrew Ludanyi, "Hungarian Lobbying Efforts for the Human Rights of Minorities in Rumania: The CHRR/HHRF As a Case Study," *Hungarian Studies* 6, no. 1 (1990): 77–90.

68. "Senate Adopts Lautenberg Resolution (93–0) Condemning Rumania for Its Human Rights Abuses, Particularly Its Plan to Raze Agricultural Villages in Traditionally Hungarian Areas," *Congressional Record,* Proceedings and Debates of the 100th Congress, Second Session Transcript of Floor Debate and Recorded Vote (August 5, 1988); "Expressing Support for H.Res.505, House Members Condemn Rumania's Planned Destruction of 8,000 Villages and Its Persecution of Ethnic Minorities," *Congressional Record,* Proceedings and Debates of the 100th Congress, Second Session (August 3, 1988). See also Ludanyi, "Hungarian Lobbying Efforts," 84–85.

69. See the analyses of the Hungarian Protestant Church in Romania and its role in standing up for nationality issues in Pungur, "The Contribution of the Reformed Churches to the Fall of Communism in Hungary and Romania," in *An Eastern European Liberation Theology,* ed. J. Pungur (Calgary: Angelus, 1994), 168–88. See also J. Harrington, "American-Romanian Relations, 1953–1998," *Romania, Culture, and Nationalism: A Tribute to Radu Florescu,* A. R. DeLuca and P. D. Quinlan, eds., East European Monographs, No. DXIX (New York: Columbia University Press, 1998), 107–26.

70. See Kuan-Hsing Chen, "Not Yet the Postcolonial Era: The (Super) Nation-State and Transnationalism of Cultural Studies," *Cultural Studies* 10, no. 1 (1996): 59.

71. See, for example, the articles "Csonka csatlakozás" [Truncated European parts] and "Ne adjuk fel a Bolyait" [Let's not give up the Hungarian University], printed in the Canadian–Hungarian weekly *Nyugati Magyarság* 15, nos. 1–2 (January–February 1998): 4, 9; "Erdélyi egyetem csak jövőre," *Népszabadság,* October 2, 2000, 3.

72. See E. Shohat, "Notes on the 'Post-colonial,'" *Social Text* 32, no. 33, (1992): 99–113.

NOTES TO CHAPTER 6

1. The most important historical documentations on the dance-house movement are: F. Bodor and J. Albert, eds., *Nomád nemzedék* [Nomadic Generation] (Budapest:Népművelési Propaganda Iroda, 1981) and L. Sükösd, *Táncház* [The dance-house] (Budapest: Zeneműkiadó, 1977).

2. See S. Gal, "Bartók's Funeral: Representations of Europe in Hungarian Political Rhetoric," *American Ethnologist* 18, no. 3 (1991): 446.

3. For the 1920s' and 1930s' youth movements, the scouts and the "sarló" in particular, concerning peasant traditions, see D. S. Cornelius, "In Search of the Nation: Hungarian Minority Youth in the New Czechoslovak Republic," *Nationalities Papers* 24, no. 2 (1996): 709–20.

4. The questions raised by D. Kramer, "Who Benefits from Folklore?" in J. R. Dow and H. Lixfeld, eds., *German Volkskunde: A Decade of Theoretical Confrontation, Debate, and Reorientation (1967–1977)* (Bloomington: Indiana University Press, 1986), 41–53, should also concern critical social scientists in dealing with the use of folklore in modern urban society. I have touched upon this in my article on Hungarian youth culture in the 1980s, "Rocking the State: Youth Culture and Popular Music in Hungary in the 1980s," *East European Politics and Societies* 5, no. 3 (1991): 145–64.

5. See G. Aczél, *Culture and Socialist Democracy* (London: Lawrence & Wishart, 1975), 75.

6. Ibid., 77.

7. On the reasons for their collapse, see Á. Losonczi, *Zene-ifjúság-mozgalom* [Music-youth-movement] (Budapest: Zeneműkiadó, 1974), 210–12, and J. Maróthy, *Ember és zene* (Budapest: Zeneműkiadó, 1980), 290–301. On the socialist official song contests and song styles, see A. Tokaji, *Mozgalom és hivatal: Tömegdal Magyarországon 1945–1956* [Movement and the office: Mass songs in Hungary 1948–1956] (Budapest: Zeneműkiadó, 1983).

8. It is worthwile to recall Hungary's minister of culture, populist Péter Veres, who argued, "We have to teach everyone how to learn the language of music, songs, and dancing; we have to teach everyone how to sing and dance beautifully, so he or she can develop aesthetics and be able to learn what is beautiful. . . . Only good schools, good radio stations, and a healthy artistic mass movement are needed, and Hungarian folk art will be rejuvenated as socialist folk art." Later, when addressing the question of how to do all of this in a socialist state, he argued, "We have to start this in those permanent communities where the same people work and where they could also entertain themselves. Every human community becomes a real community only when people work together and, after work, they are able to enjoy each others's company in entertainment too." See "A szórakozás és a népi kultúra" [Entertainment and folk culture], in *Művészet és szórakozás*, ed. Népművészeti Intézet (Budapest: Művelt Nép Könyvkiadó, 1954), 5, 7.

9. See L. Laszlo, "Religion and Nationality in Hungary," in *Religion and Nationalism in Soviet and East European Politics*, ed. P. Ramet (Durham, N.C.: Duke University Press, 1984), 146.

10. See Gy. Báron, "Városi népzene—közösségi zene," in *Vélemények, viták Zenekultúránkról* [Arguments, discussions about our musical culture], ed. I. Balázs (Budapest: Kossuth, 1982), 260–274. Originally this article was published in 1977 in *Mozgó Világ*, a literary and an ideological monthly.

11. For the best summaries on Hungarian instrumental folk music, see B. Sárosi, *Zenei anyanyelvünk* [Hungarian folk music] (Budapest: Gondolat, 1973) and *Cigányzene* (Budapest: Gondolat, 1971); I. Pávai, *Az erdélyi és moldvai magyarság népi tánczenéje* [Folk dance music of Hungarians in Transylvania and Moldavia] (Budapest: Teleki László Alapítvány, 1993).

12. See L. Sükösd, *Táncház*, 23.

13. See Gy. Martin, *Magyar Tánctipusok és Táncdialektusok* [Hungarian folk dance types and dance dialects] (Budapest: Népművelési Propaganda Iroda, 1970–1972).

14. See L. Lajtha, "Újra megtalált magyar nédaltípus" [The rediscovered Hungarian folk song], in *Emlékkönyv Kodály Zoltán hatvanadik születésnapjára*, ed. B. Gunda (Budapest: Magyar Néprajzi Társaság, 1943), 219–34, and *Széki gyûjtés* [The Szék collection] (Budapest: Zeneműkiadó, 1954).

15. On how the dance clubs multiplied, see Gy. Martin, "A széki hagyományok felfedezése és szerepe a magyarországi folklorizmusban" [The discovery of Szék traditions and their role in the folkloristic movement in Hungary], *Ethnographia* XCIII (1982): 73–83.

16. See note 10, and the articles reprinted in Balázs, ibid.

17. Quoted in Siklós, *Táncház*, 161.

18. It is quite a revelation to read the diary of a young university student when she describes enthusiastically her meeting with real peasants; see Siklós, *Táncház*, 212–17.

19. See Bodor and Albert, 105–13.

20. All of these are described in detail in F. Bodor and Zs. Albert, *Nomád Nemzedék*, 102–36.

21. The names are telling: Vizöntő, Muzsikás, Vujicsics, Kaláka, Délibáb, Kolinda, Gereben, Mákvirág, Téka, Boróka, Fanyűvő, Jánosi, Tekergő, Forrás, Makám, Szirtosz, Zsarátnok, Kormorán, and many other of lesser fame. Not all however were, strictly speaking, Hungarian music bands, for the latter three played music termed Balkan, or South Slavic. While many of these pioneer bands disappeared or regrouped in the late 1970s and early 1980s, there are dozens today in Hungary and Romania continuing this tradition. Timár's contribution to the folkloristic movement gained even more recognition during the celebrations of his seventieth birthday, see "Elismerte a világ," *Népszabadság*, October 2, 2000, 10.

22. See A. Bankó, *Muzsikás évtizedek* [Musicians' Decades] (Budapest: Kós Károly Alapítvány, 1994).

23. Two of the Gulyás brothers' films *There Are Changes* [*Vannak változások*], (1978) and *Alfonz Medve* (1978–1979), follow in recalling the investigative writing style known as the sociography of the 1930s. They are referred to as "film sociographies."

24. Janics' ideas were first published in the Hungarian literary magazine *Reality* [*Valóság* 1 (1971)] and only later in a book in Germany; see K. Janics, *A hontalanság évei* [Years of homelessness] (München: Európai Protestáns Magyar Szabadegyetem, 1979).

25. The term *Hungarology*, which exists in Hungarian and is utilized extensively, is just another way to say "Hungarian Studies," as I pointed out in the previous chapter. Yet since the 1960s, this new discipline, while not taught in Hungary per se, has been offered as a special area of study outside of Hungary.

26. Here I illustrate how this growing sense of Transylvanism was inscribed in symbolic forms intended to avoid the wrath of censors by describing a film sequence. It is from Fabri's film, entitled not without some obvious meaning *Magyarok* (Hungarians), a story describing the plight of a small group of peasants from northeast Hungary. The group, at the beginning of World War II, takes up work in Germany and, being lonely and far away from home, one of the young protagonists experiences a nightmarish dream. The dream sequence from the film shows the hero's feverish search for the lost "Magyarok." An old man of the woods frightens him into believing that he is the only Magyar left. But what is extraordinary is that the old man is dressed in the characteristic clothes of the Szeklers, a Hungarian group in Transylvania, but only for the dream sequence, when he argues that there are no more Magyars left.

27. Two books in particular illustrate well the cult of Transylvanianness in Hungary and the legacy of the Transylvanian Zsigmond Karsai in Hungary: Zs. Karsai and Gy. Martin, eds., *Lőrincréve táncélete és táncai* [Dance tradition and dances from Lőrincréve]

(Budapest: Zenetudományi Intézet, 1989) and L. Kiss, ed., *Lőrincréve népzenéje: Karsai Zsigmond dalai* [The folk music of Lőrincréve, the songs of Zsigmond Karsai] (Budapest: Zeneműkiadó, 1982).

28. Zoltán Kallós, though not a professionally trained folklorist, has an impressive list of publications to his credit. The folklore collection that elevated him into the neopopulist limelight was *Balladák könyve: Élő hazai magyar népballadák* [The book of ballads: Living national Hungarian folk ballads] (Bukarest: Kriterion, 1971), an instant classic that was reprinted in a new edition in Hungary as *Balladák könyve: Élő erdélyi és moldvai magyar népballadák* [The book of ballads: Living Transylvanian and Moldavian Hungarian ballads] (Budapest: Magvető, 1973). The slight difference in the subtitle speaks for itself. Kallós's philosophy about Hungarianness is included in the interview "Ha minden magyar elmenne, én a legutolsó volnék" ("If all Hungarians will leave, I will be the last one"), *Magyar Nemzet*, December 20, 1997, p. 19. Kallós, who created a cultural foundation to promote his movement, was given back his family estate in Válaszút (Rascruci), Transylvania, where he organized international dance houses. Cf. also note 29.

29. The publishing of ethnographic and folkloristic works has risen astronomically as the result of the dance-house movement. Most books on Transylvanian Hungarian folk culture, for instance, have been reissued as the result of increasing demands. This process has, since the early 1990s, resulted in the creation of independent publishing houses focusing on ethnographic and minority literature. From the publishing revival, a few illustrative examples are: M. Domokos, ed., *Tegnap a Gyimesben jártam: Kallós Zoltán és Marton György gyűjtése* [Yesterday I was in Gyimes: Folk music collection of Zoltán Kallós and György Martin] (Budapest: Európa 1989); I. Szenik, *Erdélyi és moldvai magyar siratók, siratóparódiák és halottas énekek* [Transylvanian and Moldavian laments, lamenting parodies and wake songs] (Kolozsvár-Bukarest: Kriterion, 1996); Z. Kallós *Ez az utazólevelem: Balladák új könyve* [This is my passport: New book of ballads] (Budapest: Akadémiai Kiadó, 1996); Pávai, *Az erdélyi és moldvai magyarság népi tánczenéje* (Budapest: Teleki László Alapítvány, 1993).

30. See M. Augé, *A Sense of the Other: The Timeliness and Relevance of Anthropology* (Stanford: Stanford University Press, 1998), 106.

31. See Aczél, *Culture and Socialist Democracy*, 200, and A. Hegedűs, *The Structure of Socialist Society* (New York: St. Martin's Press, 1977).

32. For a discussion of the economic integration, see A. Abonyi, "Eastern Europe's Reintegration," in *Socialist States in the World System*, ed. C. Chase-Dunn (London: SAGE, 1982), 181–202; G. Kozma, "The Role of the Exchange Rate in Hungary's Foreign Trade, 1968–1979," in *Hungary: A Decade of Economic Reform*, eds. P. G. Hare, H. K. Radice, and N. Swain (London: George Allen & Unwin, 1981), 205–24; P. Marer, "The Mechanism and Performance of Hungary's Foreign Trade," in *Hungary: A Decade of Economic Reform*, eds. P. G. Hare, H. K. Radice, and N. Swain (London: George Allen & Unwin, 1981), 161–204.

33. Some of these are discussed in English in F. E. Dohrs, "Nature versus Ideology in Hungarian Agriculture: Problems of Intensification," in *Eastern Europe: Essays in Geographical Problems*, ed. G. W. Hoffman (New York: Praeger, 1971), 271–95; see also A. Gyenes, "Some Aspects of Stratification in Hungarian Co-operative Farms," *Sociologia Ruralis* 16 (1976): 161–74.

34. Calculations are based on the analysis by I. Völgyes, "Modernization, Stratification, and Elite Development in Hungary," *Social Forces* 57 (1978): 500–21.

35. See the figures in B. Csendes and B. Pálovics, "The Principal Questions on the Progress and Further Development of Hungarian Agriculture," in *Economic Policy and Planning in Hungary*, ed. F. Kiss (Budapest: Corvina, 1978), 171–223.

36. See Csendes and Pálovics, "The Principal Questions," 176–77.

37. See the analysis of J. W. Cole, "Family, Farm, and Factory: Rural Workers in Contemporary Romania," in *Romania in the 1980s*, ed. D. N. Nelson (Boulder: Westview Press, 1981).

38. See W. F. Robinson, "Paying the Hungarian Cooperative Farmer," *Studies in Comparative Communism* 9 (1976): 270–74.

39. See Hegedûs, *The Structure of Socialist Society*, 95.

40. Ibid., 96.

41. See J. R. Fiszman, "Education and Equality of Opportunity in Eastern Europe, with Special Focus on Poland," *Politics and Society* 3 (1977): 297–329.

42. Ibid., 304.

43. See the calculations in W. D. Connor, *Socialism, Politics, and Equality: Hierarchy and Change in Eastern Europe and the USSR* (New York: Columbia University Press, 1979), 135–38.

44. See Aczél, *Culture and Socialist Democracy*, 209.

45. See Völgyes, "Modernization, Stratification, and Elite Development in Hungary," 513.

46. For the best writings of the time, readers should consult: M. Haraszti, *A Worker in a Worker's State* (New York: Universe Books, 1978); I. Szelényi, "The Position of the Intelligentsia in the Class Structure of State Socialist Societies," *Critique* 10–11 (1978–1979): 51–76; M. Burawoy, *The Politics of Production* (London: Verso, 1985).

47. On socialist peasantry, see the anthropological monographs by C. M. Hann, *Tázlár: A Village in Hungary* (Cambridge: Cambridge University Press, 1980); C. Humphrey, *Karl Marx Collective* (Cambridge: Cambridge University Press, 1983); P. D. Bell, *Peasants in Socialist Transition: Life in a Collectivized Hungarian Village* (Berkeley: University of California Press, 1984); I. Vásáry, *Beyond the Plan: Social Change in a Hungarian Village* (Boulder: Westview, 1987); G. Kligman, *The Wedding of the Dead: Ritual, Poetics, and Popular Culture in Transylvania* (Berkeley: University of California Press, 1988); C. Nagengast, *Reluctant Socialists, Rural Entrepreneurs: Class, Culture, and the Polish State* (Boulder: Westview, 1991); M. Lampland, *The Object of Labor: Commodification in Socialist Hungary* (Chicago: University of Chicago Press, 1995).

48. See Hegedûs, *The Structure of Socialist Society*, 90–96, 119–28; J. W. Cole, "Family, Farm, and Factory," 88–89.

49. C. M. Hann aptly summarized Erdei's contribution to the making of Hungarian socialist peasantry; see "Subverting Strong States: The Dialectics of Social Engineering in Hungary and Turkey," *Daedalus* (spring 1995), esp. 138–40.

50. The neopopulist writer Erzsébet Galgóczy has written elegantly about this in her *A törvény szövedéke* [The texture of the law] (Budapest: Szépirodalmi, 1988), 25–29.

51. Quoted in Bodor and Albert, *Nomadic Generation*, 76. Although the book has its own English translation of Hungarian texts, I use my own translation here.

52. For this description, see the sociological treatment in M. Andrássy and I. Vitányi, *Ifjúság és kultúra* [Youth and culture] (Budapest: Kossuth, 1979).

53. One of the most detailed analyses of the Ceauşescu cult is M. E. Fischer, *Nicolae Ceauşescu: A Study in Political Leadership* (Boulder: Lynne Rienner, 1989). G. Kligman makes this point also with regard to the research possibilities in Ceauşescu's Romania from the early 1980s on; see Kligman, *The Wedding of the Dead,* 18.

54. See K. Verdery, "Romanian Identity and Cultural Politics under Ceauşescu: An Example from Philosophy," Occasional Paper No. 17 (Washington, D.C.: The Wilson Center, 1990), 4, 9; and, for more detail, *National Ideology under Socialism: Identity and Cultural Politics in Ceauşescu's Romania* (Berkeley: University of California Press, 1991).

55. Americans received shocking dosages of the monstrous plans of the Ceauşescu government, which was destroying historic buildings, districts, and villages shortly thereafter. See the compilation in "Romania's Reign of Terror," *Reader's Digest* (February 1989), 91–95, and G. Y. Dryansky, "Goodbye Romania," *Conde Nast Traveler* (April 1989), 136–41, 176–83. See also the Helsinki Watch Report, *Destroying Ethnic Identity: The Hungarians in Romania* (Vienna: International Helsinki Federation, 1989). All major Western newspapers from the *International Herald Tribune* to *The Wall Street Journal* and from *Time* to *The Economist* carried articles describing the situation in Romania in 1988 and 1989.

56. The plight of the Hungarian Protestant and Catholic churches in Ceauşescu's Romania is discussed by S. P. Ramet, *Nihil Obstat: Religion, Politics and Social Change in East-Central Europe and Russia* (Durham, N.C.: Duke University Press, 1997); see esp. chs. 4 and 7; and see J. Pungur, "The Contribution of the Reformed Churches to the Fall of Communism in Hungary and Romania," in *An Eastern European Liberation Theology,* ed. J. Pungur (Calgary: Angelus Publishers, 1994), 168–89.

57. In fact, the political scientist and East European specialist J. F. Brown paraphrases six interrelated factors according to which public disenchantment with the communist regime may be understood: economic (inflation, debt, economic insecurity); social (the chasm between rich and poor, decreasing wages, suicide, alcoholism, and drugs); generational (the coming of age of the post–1956 generation); oppositional (the emergence of dissident circles); Gorbachev's presence (the impact of his early "perestroika"); and the Romanian factor (the issue of the Hungarian minority in Transylvania). In particular, he has suggested that: "The majority of the workers everywhere had become so contemptuous of their regimes, and so disaffected from them, that they would do nothing to support them. This finally sealed communism's fate." See *Surge to Freedom: The End of Communist Rule in Eastern Europe* (Durham, N.C.: Duke University Press, 1991), 39.

58. Analyses of these conditions can be found in J. Bodó and S. Oláh, eds., *Így élünk: elszegényedési folyamatok a Székelyföldön* [This is how we live: poverty in Szeklerland] (Csikszereda: Kommunikációs Antropológiai Munkacsoport, 1997); and see J. Bodó, ed., *Elvándorlók? Vendégmunka és életforma a Székelyföldön* [Migrants? Guest workers and lifestyles in Szeklerland] (Csikszereda: Pro-Print, 1996).

59. See Kligman, *The Wedding of the Dead,* 260.

60. See Nagengast, *Reluctant Socialists,* 26.

61. I have in mind Judith Okely, who by analyzing the emerging transnational territorialized nationalism of European Gypsies, argues for various ways in which intellectuals may influence power politics; see "Some Political Consequencess of Theories of Gypsy Ethnicity: The Place of the Intellectual," in *After Writing Culture: Epistemology and Praxis*

in Contemporary Anthropology, eds. A. James, J. Hockey, and A. Dawson (London: Routledge, 1997), 224–43.

62. See K. Verdery, *The Political Lives of Dead Bodies: Reburial and Postsocialist Change* (New York: Columbia University Press, 1999), 49.

63. To illustrate the globalization of the dance house, it is worthwhile to call attention to the fact that in 1998 a Japanese dance club leader, Oka Josaki, was awarded the state prize "Pro Cultura Hungarica" by the Ministry of Culture for "the two decades of teaching Japanese dance groups Hungarian dances"; see *Népszabadság*, June 5, 1998, p. 13.

64. One of the members of the Sebő ensemble, Ferenc Sebő, now heads Hungary's state-supported National Folk Ballet; János Dévai, once a leading member of the Délibáb music group, is a producer at Hungary's number one radio station, Kossuth radio; and Béla Halmos produces his own folklore program for Hungarian television. Ferenc Novák is a respected artist involved with popular but highly commercialized productions on stage and in films and television.

65. The Internet address, All-Music Guide, at http://www. allmusic.com/, has all of the necessary information for music fans throughout the world about Hungarian and Transylvanian music.

66. See T. D. Taylor, *Global Pop: World Music, World Markets* (New York: Routledge, 1997), 12–13.

67. For some of the more recent anthropological analyses of European rural communities, see A. H. Galt, *Town and Country in Locorotondo* (Fort Worth: Harcourt Brace Jovanovich, 1992); W. Kavanagh, *Villagers of the Sierra de Gredos: Transhumant Cattle-Raisers in Central Spain* (Oxford: Berg, 1994); J. Pratt, *The Rationality of Rural Life. Economic and Cultural Change in Tuscany* (Chur: Harwood Academic, 1994); S. C. Rogers, *Shaping Modern Times in Rural France* (Princeton: Princeton University Press, 1991); M. C. Ward, *The Hidden Life of Tirol* (Prospect Heights: Waveland, 1993).

68. See B. Moore, *Social Origins of Dictatorship and Democracy: Lord and Peasant in the Making of the Modern World* (Boston: Beacon, 1967), 453.

69. See E. Wolf, *Peasant Wars of the Twentieth Century* (New York: Harper & Row, 1969), xv.

70. See G. D. Jackson, "Peasant Political Movements in Eastern Europe," in *Rural Protest: Peasant Movements and Social Change*, ed. H. A. Landsberger (New York: Barnes and Noble, 1973), 259.

71. See T. Skocpol, "What Makes Peasants Revolutionary; Review Article," *Comparative Politics* 14 (1982): 371.

72. In fact, this is the suggestion of John Cole, who looked at the various European ethnonational processes; see "Culture and Economy in Peripheral Europe," *Ethnologia Europaea* 15 (1985): 3–26.

73. See P. Sugar, "The Problems of Nationalism in Eastern Europe: Past and Present," Occasional Paper No. 13, The Wilson Center (Washington, D.C.: The Wilson Center, 1988), 15. Analyzing the role of the peasant or folk culture in its East-Central European setting, Czech ethnographer Vaclav Hubinger sees it as serving the "political purpose of their time and the communities of the day as they strove to explain the present as a process of fulfilling a purpose, as a developmental phase." See "The Present: A Bridge between the Past and the Future," in *Grasping the Changing World*, ed. V. Hubinger (London: Routledge, 1996), 26.

74. See E. Hobsbawm, *Primitive Rebels* (New York: W. W. Norton & Co., 1965), 10.

75. See Gramsci, *Selections from the Prison Notebooks* (New York: International Publishers, 1971), 14–15.

76. See S. Gal, *Bartók's Funeral*, 455.

77. Rural gender relations in socialist Hungary are detailed in E. Huseby-Darvas, "Elderly Women in a Hungarian Village: Childlessness, Generativity, and Social Control," *Journal of Cross Cultural Gerontology* 2 (1987): 15–42; "Migration and Gender: Perspectives for Rural Hungary," *East European Quarterly* 23, no. 4 (1990): 487–98; Lampland, *The Object of Labor*, 183–85.

78. As Susan Gal puts it with regard to the developments of the late 1980s: "For populists and urbanites alike, 'Europe' carried more moral meanings of liberal democracy and human rights, as well as market mechanism"; see Gal, "Bartók's Funeral," 454.

79. The way in which this demonstration was planned and actualized is described in Cs. Varga, ed., *Hősök tere '88. június 27* (Heroes' Square, June 27, 1988) (Budapest: Artunion, 1988).

NOTES TO CHAPTER 7

1. Vaclav Hável was indeed the first East European leader to visit Washington, D.C., to ask for support for the implementation of democracy. See "Address of the President of the Czechoslovak Republic to a Joint Session of the United States Congress," Washington, D.C., February 21, 1990, p. 8.

2. See "Reforming Communist Systems: Lessons from the Hungarian Experience," in *Central and Eastern Europe: The Opening Curtain?* ed. W. E. Griffith (Boulder: Westview, 1989), 218–41.

3. See E. P. Thompson, "Ends and Histories," in *Europe from Below: An East-West Dialogue*, ed. Mary Kaldor (London: Verso, 1991), 7.

4. Quoted in J. Derrida, *The Other Heading: Reflections on Today's Europe* (Bloomington: Indiana University Press, 1992), 8.

5. See J. Attali, *Millennium: Winners and Losers in the Coming World Order* (New York: Random House, 1991), 35.

6. See E. Busek, *Az elképzelt Közép-Európa* [The Imagined Eastern Europe] (Budapest: Századvég, 1992), 120–21. I have written a criticism on the making of Central Europe in my "Globalization and the Discourse of Otherness in the 'New' Eastern and Central Europe," in *The Politics of Multiculturalism in the New Europe*, eds. T. Modood and P. Werbner (London: Zed Books, 1997), 29–53.

7. See Thompson, "Ends and Histories," 15.

8. For English language sources for the early 1990s' developments in Romania, see D. N. Nelson, ed., *Romania after Tyranny* (Boulder: Westview, 1992) and T. Gallagher, *Romania after Ceauşescu* (Edingburgh: Edinburgh University Press, 1995). For Hungary, see R. Tőkés, *Hungary's Negotiated Revolution: Economic Reform, Social Change, and Political Succession* (Cambridge: Cambridge University Press, 1996).

9. Eyewitness accounts of the streetfights are detailed in many excellent studies: for a specific Hungarian perspective, see J. Gazda, *Megváltó karácsony* [Redeeming Christmas]

(Budapest: Aura, 1990). For an American anthropological interpretation, see S. Beck, "The Struggle for Space and the Development of Civil Society in Romania, June 1990," in *The Curtain Rises*, eds. H. DeSoto and D. Anderson (Atlantic Highlands, N.J.: The Humanities Press, 1993), 232–65; for a British perspective, see Gallagher, *Romania after Ceauşescu,* esp. ch. 3.

10. Throughout this chapter, I cite the abbreviation as it is used by Hungarians (RMDSZ) rather than by Romanians, UDMR.

11. The third largest party, the National Liberal Party (led by Radu Campeanu), drew 7 percent in the Senate and 6.4 percent in the Assembly of Deputies. Gallagher also discusses the election results in detail. See *Romania after Ceauşescu,* esp. ch. 4.

12. As a statistical curiosity, I mention the other counties: Bihor (28%), Sălaj (24%), Cluj (20%), Arad (12%), Maramureş (10%) and Braşov (9%). On the voting patterns, see also: F. Takács, "Helyhatósági választások Székelyföldön" [Local elections in the Szekler region], *Limes* 2, nos. 7–8 (1992): 14–16. These voting patterns also rekindled discussions about the distribution of Hungarians in Romania: see Z. Dávid, "Szlovákia és Románia vallási megoszlása az 1991. és 1992. évi népszámlálás szerint" [Ethnic and religious cleavage in Slovaki and Romania after the 1991 and 1992 elections], *Hitel* (February 1993): 88–93, and K. Kocsis, "A Kárpát-Balkán régió változó etnikai-vallási arculata" [The changing ethno-religious face of the Carpathian-Balkan region], *Földrajzi Közlemények* 39, nos. 3–4 (1991): 165–89.

13. Election figures are from *Elections in Central and Eastern Europe,* July 1990, Washington, D.C.; and *The May 1990 Elections in Romania,* International Delegation Report, 1991, published by the National Republican Institute of International Affairs and National Democratic Institute of International Affairs. Interestingly, the October 1992 elections did not change this political tapestry. The RMDSZ was able to continue as the largest opposition with the same number of seats, and President Iliescu was reelected, a "normalization" in the eyes of many who believed or continue to believe in the securities of the old system.

14. Populism is discussed in the previous chapters, but see also Tőkés, *Hungary's Negotiated Revolution,* 188–90. The negative and extremist populist tradition in Ceauşescu's Romania is discussed by T. Gilberg, *Nationalism and Communism in Romania* (Boulder: Westview, 1990), 49–50.

15. Political scientist Herbert Kitschelt observes in his analysis of the post–1989 election and subsequent party cleavages "that a strong anti-market and authoritarian sector and ethnic-particularist sentiments undercut the consolidation of democratic party systems in Rumania and Bulgaria." See "The Formation of Party Systems in East Central Europe," *Politics and Society* 20, no. 1 (1992): 40. The implication of this observation for the future of nationality issues and transnational politics is a cause for concern.

16. For a glaring example, let me quote the one published by Verdery: "[Our] sacred Romanian soil is defiled by the Asiatic feet of Hungarians, Gypsies, and other leftovers. Let's unite and throw them out of the country. Out with the Huns and Hunkies who are an embarrassment to our land! Don't hesitate to spill their filthy blood!"; see K. Verdery, "Comment: Hobsbawm in the East," *Anthropology Today* 18, no. 1 (1992): 9. An interwar tourist brochure published in Bucharest (of anonymous authorship) printed a similar xenophobic message: "How many an insurging this wave of invaders has galloped across our land flatting everything in its course like a summer hail strom. The Huns, Avars, Petchnegs, Hungarians, Cumans, and Turks have all trodden Dacia under their horses

hoofs, leaving behind them a wake of death and desolation"; see *Roumanian People* (Bucharest: n.d.), no pagination.

17. A product of mutual respect and interethnic cooperation, the Timisoara Declaration was signed by both Hungarians (the Timsec, the Democratic Union of Banat Hungarians, and the Romanian–Hungarian Friendship Association) and Romanians. One section reads: "Together with the Romanians, Hungarians, Germans, Serbs, and members of other ethnic groups that have for centuries peacefully and as good neighbors shared our city and sacrificed their lives for the victory of the revolution. Timisoara is a European city whose nationalities have refused and are still refusing to accept nationalism. We invite all the country's chauvinists—whether Romanian, Hungarian, or German—to come to Timisoara and take a course in tolerance and mutual respect, the only principles that will rule in the future European home." The entire text was published in "The Timisoara Declaration," March 11, 1990," *Radio Free Europe/Report on Eastern Europe* 1 (1990): 41–45.

18. Chronicles of the Tirgu Mureş events are on B. Marosi, et al., eds., *Fehér könyv* [The White Book] (Budapest: Püski, 1991); I. Judith. "Smaranda Enache: A Transylvanian Life," *Uncaptive Mind* 6, no. 2 (1991): 118–28; and Gallagher, *Romania after Ceauşescu*, ch. 3.

19. It should be noted that some Romanian intellectuals do not share these extreme ethnocentric views; see, for example, the democratic and somewhat pro-Hungarian essays in the special issue, "A gyűlölet életrajza" [Biography of Hatred], *Korunk* [Kolozsvár] 4 (1991). For a short history of peaceful interethnic existence, see N. Harsanyi, "A Case of Cultural Interference in Romania," *The European Studies Journal* VIII, no. 2 (1991): 1–11. Another Romanian scholar also expressed his optimism: see D. A. Lazarescu, "Une contribution precieuse a l'histoire des relations entre le peuple roumain et le peuple magyar," *Revue Romaine d'Etudes Internationales* (January–February 1990): 31–36.

20. This statement of Antall's has often been misquoted. It reads: "Törvényes értelemben, a magyar közjog alapján minden magyar állampolgárnak, ennek a tízmilliós országnak a kormányfőjeként—lélekben, érzésben tizenötmillió magyar miniszterelnöke kivánok lenni" [I wish to be, lawfully and according to legal understanding, the head of the government for all Hungarian citizens, for this country of ten millions, [but] in spirit and feeling, I wish to be the Prime Minister of 15 million Hungarians]. For an analysis of this and interrelated issues with regard to the center-right FIDESZ government, see K. Király, "Magyarok vagy románok. A nemzethez tartozást valljuk és vállaljuk" [Hungarians or Romanians. We belong to the Hungarian nation], *Népszabadság*, June 5, 1998, p. 12. Among the more extreme examples, a statement written by Hungary's extremist populist writer, Istvan Csurka, is instructive:

> If this government stays in power—even if its hands are tied—sooner or later it will gain strength and will be able to lead the country out of the crisis. That will mean the coming of the end of bolshevism, cosmopolitanism, the foreign-ruled nation-trampling parading in the rags of liberalism, and the leftist and communist power established here since the Soviet conquest in 1945. If that is true, then it will be obvious that a European Hungary will be established by the Christian centrist masses. And when that happens, Hungary will belong to the Magyars, and the borders will not be wide open to any sorts of new foreign exodus, and final disempowerment of the Magyars will never come. See "Helyszini közvetites" [Local report], *Magyar Fórum*, February 28, 1991, p. 1.

21. For a comprehensive Hungarian treatment on the *Csángós* of Moldavia, see D. Pál Péter, *A moldvai magyarság* [The Hungarians in Moldavia] (Budapest: Magvető, 1987) and L. Mikecs, *Csángók* (Budapest: Optimum, 1989).

22. The Hungarian government issued a proclamation demanding the urgent resolution that border-crossing disputes between the two states be resolved in a timely fashion; see *Népszabadság*, August 16, 1991, p. 1.

23. The motion was made by Ádám Katona, deputy president of the RMDSZ of Székelyudvarhely [Odorheiu Secuiesc]; see *Népszabadság*, October 14, 1991, p. 3.

24. See *Népszabadság*, October 14, 1991, p. 3, and *Magyar Nemzet*, October 10, 1991, p. 2.

25. See László Kürti, "Transylvania, Land Beyond Reason: An Anthropological Analysis of a Contested Terrain," *Dialectical Anthropology* 15 (Spring 1989): 21–52"; for the Romanian origin of the *Csángós*, see D. Mărtinaş, *Originea ceangăilor din Moldova* [On the origin of the Csángós of Moldavia] (Bucureşti: Editura Stiinfică şi Enciclopedică, 1985); cf. also Mikecs, *Csángók*. The RMDSZ's rhetoric, the sense of isolation, the small size of the Hungarian group in Romania (due to increasing emigration, a lower birthrate, etc.), and the importance of solidarity in countering the difficulties that lie ahead (Romanian nationalism) are, of course, familiar tropes dominant in nationalistic discourses since the eighteenth and nineteenth centuries. For the overtly Csángó-centric nationalistic perspective, see the articles upholding the view of this population's disappearance, see B. György, "Pusztuljon a 'beteg' csángó" [The sick Csángó should die], *Új Ember* (February 1, 1998): 6, and M. Sarusi, "Csángó sikoly" [Csángó cries], *Hitel* (February 1998): 16–22.

26. According to Romanian-Hungarian scholar Nicolae Harsanyi, funding for these programs comes from former Iron Guard member Iosif Constantin Dragan, residing in Italy, further reinforcing the idea that nationalist interest knows no national borders; see N. Harsanyi, "Old Conflicts in New Times," paper presented at the annual meeting of the American Association for the Advancement of Slavic Studies, 1991, p. 6.

27. These figures were quoted in the Hungarian daily *Magyar Nemzet*, October 10, 1991, p. 8.

28. It must be mentioned, however, that from January to November 1992, the Hungarian border patrol stopped 21,499 people who tried illegally to cross Hungary (*határsértés*), which is 17.7 percent less than the previous year's figure. Among the repatriated were: 13,000 Romanians and 2,612 Turks, 1,396 from the former Yugoslavia; see *Népszabadság*, November 11, 1992, p. 5.

29. Another liberal-democratic coalition is the Liga Pro Europa, with headquarters in Tirgu Mureş, which published the newspaper *GM—Gazeta de Mureş, Saptaminal Transilvan*. The impact of such intellectual circles remains to be seen.

30. See the letters by T. Chebleu and Balázs Sándor in *Szabadság*, May 26, 1993, pp. II–III.

31. From interviews with Hungarian and Romanian intellectuals, the actual understanding of autonomy, its meaning and implementation, is far from clear; see M. Schafir and A. A. Reisch, eds., "Roundtable: Transylvania's Past and Future," *RFE/RL Research Report* 2, no. 24 (1993): 26–34. A Hungarian collection is even more specific on the Transylvanian autonomy: see G. Bíró et al. eds., *Autonómia és integráció* [Autonomy and integration] (Budapest: Magyar Szemle Könyvek, 1993). The point of view of the RMDSZ

leadership was expressed by former Hungarian Minister of Nationalities György Tokay, "Interjú," *Népszabadság,* April 10, 1997, p. 7.

32. See "Egy kifejezés és ami mögötte van," *Korunk* 5 (1993): 73–79; for a slightly different point of view, see the interview with RMDSZ president B. Markó, "Románia számára nem távlat asszimilálni a magyarságot," *Magyar Nemzet,* April 6, 1993, p. 7.

33. For the hostile development between Hungarians and Romanians, see the events analyzed by D. Ionescu and A. Reisch, "Still No Breaktrough in Romanian-Hungarian Relations," *RFE/RL Research Reports* 2, no. 42 (October 22, 1993): 26–32. The negative press campaign against Hungarians in Transylvania has been documented by V. Tánczos, "Hungarofóbia a székelyföldi román sajtóban" [Hungaro-phobia in the Romanian press in the Szekler region], *Limes* 2, nos. 7–8 (1992): 17–20.

34. See M. Shafir, "Minorities Council Raises Questions," *RFE/RF Research Report* 2, no. 24 (June 1993): 35–40.

35 The following articles provide ample documentations for this intellectual contestation: see I. Vitányi, "A népi irók öröksége" [The legacy of the populist writers], *Magyar Nemzet,* November 21, 1992, p. 9; M. Laczkó, "A populizmus Európában és Magyarországon," [Populism in Europe and Hungary], *Magyar Nemzet,* February 6, 1993, p. 9; J. Antall, "Kisujszállás után, Szárszó előtt" [After Kisújszállás and before Szárszó], *Magyar Nemzet,* August 7, 1993, p. 5; E. Bilecz, "Szárszói kérdések" [Questions about Szárszó], *Népszabadság,* August 7, 1993, p. 17.

36. In the Bucharest newspaper *Tinerama* (December 27, 1994), editor Narcis Barbu published documents allegedly claiming that Tőkés was a securitate informer in the 1970s. It was alleged that Tőkés, while a student at the Cluj Protestant Theology, had been requested (forced) to sign several confessions, a case that could have been made with great probability of several Hungarian as well as Romanian oppositional figures of the 1970s.

37. Even this meeting was shrouded in mystery and conflict since its inception. This was, no doubt, facilitated by the fact that earlier the PER had already organized a "secret" meeting at Neptune in Romania, which was not officially recognized by the RMDSZ. The RMDSZ leadership almost declined the invitation to Atlanta, since it was brought to light that a delegate from a nationalist AUR party would also be present. Under tremendous popular and international pressure, the RMDSZ leadership finally consented to participate.

38 Quoted in the Hungarian daily *Magyar Nemzet,* January 15, 1995, p. 2.

39. Poll quoted in the Hungarian daily *Népszabadság,* September 14, 1996, p. 3.

40. The letter was pubished in *Magyar Nemzet,* September 13, 1996, p. 13. For a full analysis of the controversy surrounding the signing of the bilateral treaty, see G. Jeszenszky, "Viták a magyar-román szerződés körül" [Debates concerning the Hungarian-Romanian basic treaty], in *Magyarország politikai évkönyve 1996–ról,* eds. S. Kurtán, P. Sándor, and Vass L. (Budapest: Demokrácia Kutatások Magyar Központja Alapítvány, 1997), 220-27.

41. See G. Molnár, "Az erdélyi kérdés" [The Transylvanian Question], *Magyar Kisebbség* III, nos. 9–10 (1997): 208–32.

42. See I. Kreczinger, "Hogyan tovább erdélyi magyarság?" [Hungarians in Transylvania—How to Continue?], *Magyar Nemzet,* January 22, 1997, p. 6, and B. Borsi-Kálmán, "Román lehetőségkeret—Magyar külpolitika" [Hungarian foreign policy and possibilities for Romania], *Pro Minoritate* V, no. 3 (1996): 86–89. See also the report by

the Hungarian government's Office of Hungarians Abroad (HTMH), É. Ring, ed., *Jelentés a romániai magyarság helyzetéről* [Report on the situation of Hungarians in Romania] (Budapest: HTMH, 1998). For a balanced analysis of Romanian state-church relations with special reference to minority religious freedom, see E. A. Pope, "Ecumenims, Religious Freedom, and the National Church: Controversy in Romania," in *Romania, Culture, and Nationalism: A Tribute to Radu Florescu,* eds. A. R. DeLuca and P. D. Quinlan (New York: Columbia University Press, 1993), 158–80.

43. See "Tizenkétezer honosítás 1996–ban" [Twelve-thousand naturalization applications in 1996], *Magyar Nemzet,* January 22, 1997, p. 4. For analyses of the Transylvanian Hungarian refugees resettling in Hungary, see E. Sík, "Erdélyi menekültek Magyarországon" [Transylvanian refugees in Hungary], in *Társadalmi riport,* eds. R. Andorka, T. Kolosi, and Gy. Vukovich (Budapest: TÁRKI, 1990), 516–33; M. Szakáts, "Az Erdélyből áttelepült magyarok társadalmi integrációja" [Integration of Hungarians resettling in Hungary], *Társadalmi Szemle* 5 (1995): 69–79; Cs. Bartha, "Az erdélyi menekültek magyar nyelvi viszontagságai" [Linguistic problems of Transylvanian Hungarian refugees], *Regio* 1 (1991): 77–86.

44. M. Bakk has summarized the 1990s' Hungarian party politics in Transylvania in "Az RMDSZ mint a romániai magyarság politikai önmeghatározásának kisérlete 1989 után" [The RMDSZ as an attempt of self-definition of the Hungarian minority in Romania after 1989], *Pro Minoritate* v, no. 3 (1996): 11–30.

45. See the headlines "Román főkonzulátus nyílt Szegeden" [Romanian consulate opened in Szeged], *Népszabadság,* January 28, 1998, p. 1.

46. See the article by the Young Democrat's, Zs. Németh and Z. Rockenbauer, "A magyar külpolitika elmúlt négy éve" [Four years of Hungarian foreign policy], *Népszabadság,* February 14, 1998, p. 16.

47. For coherent, analytical perspectives on the situation of Hungarian higher education in Romania, see the special issue of the Transylvanian minority journal *Magyar Kisebbség* III, nos. 9–10 (1997). Gy. Tokay, one of the former Hungarian ministers in the Romanian government, however, expressed openly his conviction that eventually a Hungarian university would be created in Transylvania; see "Tokay a koalició közös érdek" [The coalition is a common cause], *Népszabadság,* April 10, 1997, p. 7. However, in contrast, Bishop Tőkés' anti-governmental reflection was printed in "Tőkés püspök árulással vádolja a magyar kormányt" [Bishop Tőkés charges the Hungarian government with treason], *Népszabadság,* February 11, 1998, p. 3.

48. See "Funárék csatája a helységnévtáblák ellen" [Funar's party against town signs], *Népszabadság,* February 14, 1998, p. 3.

49. Ferenc Bárány admitted that he was forced to cooperate with the Romanian secret police, but that he never reported anyone. László Tőkés immediately defended his compatriot, arguing that most Hungarians in managerial positions were forced to become secret informers to the state, but he admitted that that was a compromising situation and that all Hungarian leaders in the Hungarian party should undergo some sort of "security check." At the same time, he argued that this was another nationalistic campaign of the Romanian elites to delegitimize the Hungarian party, its purpose, and its membership; see "Tőkés László level Markó Bélához" [László Tőkés' letter to Béla Markó], *Magyar Nemzet,* June 20, 1998, p. 3.

50. See M. Walzer, "The New Tribalism," *Dissent* (spring 1992): 164.

51. I have described these in more detail in my articles concerning the specific form of "otherness" in Hungary and Romania, "A másság mindig a saját tükörképe," *Magyar Nemzet,* April 16, 1993, p. 6, and "Etnikai viszályok és a többszólamú azonosság: néhány antropológiai gondolat az identitásról," *Korunk* 1 (1993): 91–99. The emergence of right-wing extremism is discussed in my "The Emergence of Postcommunist Youth Identities in Eastern Europe: From Communist Youth, to Skinheads, to National Socialists and Beyond," in *Nation and Race: The Developing of Euro-American Racist Subculture,* eds. J. Kaplan and T. Bjorgo (Boston: Northeastern University Press, 1998), 175–201.

52. See W. Safran, "Diasporas in Modern Societies: Myths of Homeland and Return," *Diaspora* 1, no. 1 (1991): 83–99.

53. Ibid., 86.

54. Ibid., 92. I find it extremely curious that seeing the nationalistic developments of the early 1990s in Eurasia, some Western observers utilize "triadic" or "triangular" categories for describing the interplay of nationalistic forces. For Brubaker, nationalism is a dynamic interplay "linking national minorities, the newly nationalizing states, and the external national 'homelands'"; see R. Brubaker, *Nationalism Reframed: Nationhood and the National Question in the New Europe* (Cambridge: Cambridge University Press, 1996), 4.

55. See L. Watts, "Ethnic Tensions: How the West Can Help," *World Policy Journal* 12, no. 1 (spring 1995): 91.

56. See the special issue of the journal of the Political Sciences Association, *Politikatudományi Szemle* 7, no. 1 (1998): 93–154, for Hungarian intellectuals' ideas for joining NATO and the EU.

NOTES TO CHAPTER 8

1. For perspectives on Romanian nation formation and national movements in the twentieth century, see T. Gilberg, *Nationalism and Communism in Romania: The Rise and Fall of Ceaușescu's Personal Dictatorship* (Boulder: Westview, 1990); I. Livezeanu, *Cultural Politics in Greater Romania: Regionalism, Nation Building, and Ethnic Struggle, 1918–1930* (Ithaca, N.Y.:Cornell University Press, 1995); K. Hitchins, *Rumania, 1866–1947* (Oxford: Clarendon Press, 1994); K. Verdery, *National Ideology under Socialism* (Berkeley: University of California Press, 1993); L. Watts, *Romanian Cassandra: Ion Antonescu and the Struggle for Reform, 1916–1941* (Boulder: East European Monographs, 1993).

2. Writing at the beginning of the 1990s, Stephen Fischer-Galati argues in a similar vein suggesting, "Thus, resolution of the Hungarian nationality problem in Romania appears unlikely in the foreseeable future." See "National Minority Problems in Romania: Continuity or Change?" *Nationalities Papers* 22, no. 1 (1994): 78. Bennet Kovrig arrives at a similar conclusion. See "Partitioned Nation: Hungarian Minorities in Central Europe," in *The New European Diasporas: National Minorities and Conflict in Eastern Europe,* ed. Michael Mandelbaum (New York: Council on Foreign Relations Press, 2000), 76.

3. The focus on borders or borderlands has different and theoretically significant departures from regional studies: while the latter mostly focuses on the core, the former focuses on the periphery of a "small, local-scale dimension within an international context . . . and, at the same time, the concept creates a type of miniature but very readable

barometer of the changes in the relations between the states divided when studied in a temporal setting." See J. V. Minghi, "From Conflict to Harmony in Border Landscapes," in *The Geography of Border Landscapes*, eds. D. Rumley and J. V. Minghi (London: Routlege, 1991), 15.

4. See A. D. Smith, "Gastronomy or Geology? The Role of Nationalism in the Reconstruction of Nations," *Nations and Nationalism* 1, no. 1 (1995): 4.

5. Ibid., 4–5.

6. Ibid., 6.

7. See T. Wilson and H. Donnan,eds., *Border Identities: Nation and State at International Frontiers* (Cambridge: Cambridge University Press, 1998), 2.

8. Ardener, "Remote Areas: Some Theoretical Considerations," in *Anthropology at Home*, ed. A. Jackson (London: Tavistock, 1987), 40–41.

9. The story of the Pied Piper of Hamelin, a romantic poem by Robert Browning, has its roots in the folkloristic origin myth of Transylvanian Saxons. See C. L. Daniels and C. M. Stevens, eds., *Encyclopedia of Superstitions, Folklore, and the Occult Sciences of the World*, vol. II (Detroit: Gale Research Company, 1971 [1903]), 684. Today, the German town of Hamelin is filled with tourist objects reminding the visitors of the Pied Piper connection.

10. See "A Magyar Irószövetség tizenkét pontja" [The twelve point declaration of the Hungarian Writers' Association], *Magyar Nemzet*, March 7, 1998, p. 6.

11. See G. Anzaldúa, *Borderlands/La frontera: The New Mestiza* (San Francisco: Aunt Lute Books, 1987), 80.

12. I can only cite here a few works that have "new" in its title, celebrating the transformation of the 1990s: T. M. Wilson and M. E. Smith, eds., *Cultural Change and the New Europe* (Boulder: Westview, 1993); T. Modood and P. Werbner, eds., T*he Politics of Multiculturalism in the New Europe* (London: Zed, 1997); C. A. Kupchan, ed., *Nationalism and Nationalities in the New Europe* (Ithaca, N.Y.: Cornell University Press, 1995); R. Caplan and J. Feffer, eds., *Europe's New Nationalism: States and Minorities in Conflict* (New York: Oxford University Press, 1996); L. Kürti and J. Langman, eds., *Beyond Borders: Remaking Cultural Identities in the New East and Central Europe* (Boulder: Westview, 1997). I must mention here that the transformation of Western states into new—in between capitalist/socialist—polities has been noted earlier: see S. Chodak, *The New State: Etatization of Western Societies* (Boulder: Lynne Rienner, 1989).

13. I recall two studies in specific that suggest similar notions with regard to the subject at hand: P. James, *Nation Formation: Towards a Theory of Abstract Community* (London: Sage, 1996), and C. Applegate, *A Nation of Provincials: The German Idea of Heimat* (Berkeley: University of California Press, 1990).

14. Literature on the Yugoslav war, its meaning and aftermath, is huge and still growing. As indications, I cite only these: J. Mertus et al., eds., *The Suitcase: Refugee Voices from Bosnia and Croatia* (Berkeley: University of California Press, 1996); S. Ramet and L. S. Adamovic, eds., *Beyond Yugoslavia: Economics and Culture in a Shattered Community* (Boulder: Westview, 1995). For the voices of local scholars theorizing about the Yugoslav war, see R. Jambresic-Kirin and M. Povrzanovic, eds., *War, Exile and Everyday Life* (Zagreb: Institute of Ethnology and Folklore Research, 1996) and L. Cale-Feldman, I. Prica, and R. Senjkovic, eds., *Fear, Death and Resistance: An Ethnography of War, Croatia 1991–1992* (Zagreb: X-Press, 1993).

15. The characterization of Czechoslovakia, East Germany, Yugoslavia, and the Soviet Union as the "humpty-dumpty" states is taken from George Schöpflin, "Nationhood, Communism, and State Legitimation," *Nations and Nationalism* 1, no. 1 (1995): 84—85. The breakup of Czechoslovakia and the reemergence of the two independent Czech and Slovak states are anayzed by L. Holy, *The Little Czech and the Great Czech Nation: National Identity and the Post–Communist Social Transformation* (Cambridge: Cambridge University Press, 1996), and C. S. Leff, *The Czech and Slovak Republics: Nation versus State* (Boulder: Westview, 1997). The Macedonian conflict has received perhaps the most thorough scholarly attention. See L. M. Danforth, *The Macedonian Conflict: Ethnic Nationalism in a Transnational World* (Princeton: Princeton University Press, 1995); P. Mackridge and E. Yannakis, eds., *Ourselves and Others: The Development of a Greek Macedonian Cultural Identity since 1912* (Oxford: Berg, 1997); A. N. Karakasidou, *Field of Wheat, Hills of Blood: Passages to Nationhood in Greek Macedonia, 1870–1990* (Chicago: University of Chicago Press, 1997); J. M. Schwartz, *Pieces of Mosaic: An Essay on the Making of Makedonija* (Hojbjerg: Intervention Press, 1996).

16. See E. Hobsbawm, "Ethnicity, Migration, and the Validity of the Nation-State," in *Toward a Global Civil Society*, ed. Michael Walzer (Providence: Berghahn, 1998), 236.

17. I have in mind, for example, the following notable studies: H. Vermeulen and J. Boissevain, eds., *Ethnic Challenge: The Politics of Ethnicity in Europe* (Göttingen: Edition Herodot, 1984); J. R. Rudolph and R. J. Thompson, eds., *Ethnoterritorial Politics, Policy, and the Western World* (Boulder: Lynne Rienner, 1989); N. Chazan, ed., *Irredentism and International Politics* (Boulder: Lynne Rienner, 1990).

18. Political scientist Peter Preston, for instance, goes so far as to suggest a new political map of Europe. See P. W. Preston, *Political/Cultural Identity: Citizens and Nations in a Global Era* (London: Sage, 1997).

19. See B. Millan, "The Committee of the Regions: In at the Birth," *Regional and Federal Studies* 7, no. 1 (1997): 5–10.

20. See M. Anderson and E. Bort, eds., *Boundaries and Identities: The Eastern Frontier of the European Union* (Edinburgh: International Social Sciences Institute, 1996). See also the articles in the Polish journal *Region and Regionalism* 2 (1995), and R. G. Minnich's study on the three-border region between Austria, Slovenia, and Italy, "Prospects for Transnational Civil Society Following the Arrival of the European Union in a Contested Borderland," *Anthropology of East European Review* 16, no. 1 (1998): 51–57.

21. See J. Corrigan, I. Süli-Zakar, and Cs. Béres, "The Carpathian Euroregion. An Example of Cross-Border Cooperation," *European Spatial Research and Policy* 4, no. 1 (1997): 113–24.

22. See M. Koter, "Foreword," *Regions and Regionalism* 2 (1995): 5.

23. I have detailed this concept with reference to Hungary in the 1990s in L. Kürti, "The Political Anthropology of Regime Changes," in *Forward to the Past: Continuity and Change in Political Development in Hungary, Austria, and the Czech and Slovak Republics*, eds. L. B. Sorensen and L. B. Eliason (Aarhus: Aarhus University Press, 1997), 236–37.

24. See K. Verdery, *What Was Socialism, and What Comes Next?* (Princeton: Princeton University Press, 1996), 220–34.

25. Two Western political scientists, for instance, have argued that, "Anything is still possible in Eastern Europe." See S. Berglund and J. A. Dellenbrant, eds., "Prospects for the New Democracies in Eastern Europe," in *The New Democracies in Eastern Europe: Party Systems and Political Cleavages* (Aldershot: Edward Elgar, 1991), 222.

26. Although not every scholar of nationalism is as interested in borders or identities. See, for example, C. Calhoun, "Nationalism and Ethnicity," *Annual Review of Sociology* 19 (1993): 211–39. The multi-volume encyclopedia of anthropology, to provide another example, while it deals with border studies with specific reference to the U.S.-Mexican border, does not address identity per se; see D. Levinson and M. Ember, eds., *Encyclopedia of Cultural Anthropology*, vols. 1–4 (New York: Henry Holt and Company, 1996). Others have focused on the confluence in identities and borders. See T. M. Wilson and H. Donnan, eds., *Border Identities: Nation and State at International Frontiers* (Cambridge University Press, 1997), 1–30.

27. See C. Hann, "Boundaries and Histories," in *The Skeleton at the Feast: Contributions to East European Anthropology* (Canterbury: University of Kent, 1995), 1, 27.

28. For the invention of Eastern Europe, especially the Balkans, see the comprehensible studies by L. Wolff, *Inventing Eastern Europe: The Map of Civilization on the Mind of the Enlightenment* (Stanford: Stanford University Press, 1994), and M. Todorova, "The Balkans: From Discovery to Invention," *Slavic Review* 53, no. 2 (1994): 453–82, and *Imagining the Balkans* (New York: Oxford University Press, 1997). The invention theory owes a great deal to the Orientalist notion of E. Said and his followers, although as Maria Todorova argues, Orientalism and Balkanism are not the same. For an application of Orientalism to the Balkan region, see M. Bakic-Hayden and R. Hayden, "Orientalist Variations on the Theme 'Balkans': Symbolic Geography in Recent Yugoslav Cultural Politics," *Slavic Review* 51, no. 1 (1992): 1–15. For criticism of the East European "invention" theory, see Chris Hann, Skeleton at the Feast, 1–23.

29. See K. S. Bowman, "The Border as Locator and Innovator of Vice," *Journal of Borderland Studies* 9, no. 1 (1994): 51.

30. See A. Dirlik, *After the Revolution: Waking to Global Capitalism* (Hanover: Wesleyan University Press, 1994), 97.

31. For historian Todorova, not only Transylvania but Macedonia, Bosnia, Dobrudzha, Kosovo, Vojvodina, and Istanbul also belong to that category; see *Imagining the Balkans*, 176.

32. See I. Ang, "Doing Cultural Studies at the Crossroads: Local/Global Negotiations," *European Journal of Cultural Studies* 1, no.1 (1998): 14.

33. See D. Rapaport, "The Importance of Space in Violent Ethno-Religious Strife," *Nationalism and Ethnic Politics* 2, no. 2 (1996): 263. The RMDSZ, for instance, has declared several times that it does not seek the realignment of the present borders, statements that must be read in conjunction with other Hungarian convictions concerning autonomy and self-rule. For instance, its Council of Representatives declared in 1994: "The Hungarian community in Romania in accordance with its specific historical and territorial circumstances, will support agreements on the inviolability of borders with the condition that national and international guarantees are provided for personal autonomy, local self-government with special status, and regional autonomy. Such guarantees make possible the preservation and promotion of the Hungarian minority in Romania." See the "Position of the Democratic Alliance of Hungarians in Romania on Its Participation in the Conference on Stability in Europe," Tirgu Mureş, May 20, 1994.

34. On the globalization/localization question in anthropological literature, see J. Friedman, *Cultural Identity and Global Process* (London: Sage, 1994), 12; U. Hannerz, *Cultural Complexity: Studies in the Social Organization of Meaning* (New York: Columbia

University Press, 1992), 256; U. Hannerz, *Transnational Connections: Culture, People, Places* (London: Routledge, 1996), 4.

35. See, for example, R. Abrahams, ed., *After Socialism: Land Reform and Social Change in Eastern Europe* (London: Berghahn, 1996), and D. Kideckel, ed., *East European Communities: The Struggle for Balance in Turbulent Times* (Boulder: Westview, 1995).

36. See P. Glotz, "Eastern European Reform and West European Integration," in *Toward a Global Civil Society*, ed. M. Walzer (Providence: Berghahn, 1998), 216.

37. Ibid., 221.

38. See J. Elster, C. Offe, and U. K. Preuss, *Institutional Design in Post–Communist Societies* (Cambridge: Cambridge University Press, 1998), 61.

39. See the book review by I. Deák, "*The Romanians, 1774–1866*, by Keith Hitchins," *Slavic Review* 56, no. 3 (1997): 566. The seventy-fifth anniversary of the Treaty of Trianon was commemorated by a historical volume; see B. Király and L. Veszprémy, eds., *Trianon and East Central Europe: Antecedents and Repercussions* (Highland Lakes, N.J.: Atlantic Research, 1995).

40. See L. Wolff, *Inventing Eastern Europe: The Map of Civilization on the Mind of the Enlightenment* (Stanford: Stanford University Press 1994), 9.

41. See M. Glenny, *The Rebirth of History: Eastern Europe in the Age of Democracy* (London: Penguin, 1990), 95.

42. See D. Palumbo-Liu, "Introduction: Unhabituated Habituses," in *Streams of Cultural Capital*, eds. D. Palumbo-Liu and H. U. Gumbrecht (Stanford: Stanford University Press, 1997), 21.

Index